Media Arabic Vocabulary

Book 4

lingualism

ISBN: 978-1-962752-01-5

website: www.lingualism.com

email: contact@lingualism.com

Written by Ahmad Al-Masri and Matthew Aldrich
Edited by Hend Khaled and Matthew Aldrich
Cover design by Matthew Aldrich

Disclaimer:

This publication is designed exclusively as a language educational resource. The contents of this book, which include sentences and texts, typically do not reflect or comment on real situations, whether historical or contemporary. When real events, individuals, or organizations are referenced, the specifics may not always uphold factual accuracy.

Where certain names or trademarks may appear, they are used strictly for educational purposes. They do not imply any affiliation with or endorsement by the respective rights holders and should not be considered as infringement.

Opinions expressed in the content are ascribed to fictional characters and journalists and do not necessarily reflect the views of the book's contributors or publisher. These opinions are included solely to mimic realistic language use in media settings and do not intend to endorse, critique, or influence real-world ideologies.

By using this book, readers acknowledge that it is for language education, not a source of reliable real-world information. Any errors or inaccuracies are unintentional and do not detract from the book's purpose as a language-learning tool.

Table of Contents

Introduction

Media Arabic Vocabulary is a series specially designed to bridge the gap between **intermediate** learning and reading real-world Arabic news articles. These books are intended to make the often-daunting journey into Arabic media literacy not only accessible, but engaging and enjoyable.

In our experience, many learners find themselves stuck in a language learning plateau, where they can handle classroom scenarios but are left feeling overwhelmed by the complexity of authentic, native-speaker materials, such as news articles. That is exactly where this book series comes in. Each volume is structured to help you scale that seemingly daunting wall by presenting carefully selected vocabulary and controlled texts that emulate the style and complexity of real-world Arabic media.

In this fourth book of the series, we will navigate through three distinct units: Law, Media, and Accidents. Each unit is further broken down into manageable sections and subsections. Subsections introduce you to key vocabulary in context, helping you understand not only the meaning of the words but also their appropriate use. As an additional aid to word recognition and correct pronunciation, all Arabic content in the book contains **diacritics** (tashkeel). You will find **English translations** for all Arabic content, which allows for better comprehension and learning, plus **audio tracks** to help you get a firm grasp on pronunciation and listening comprehension.

This dynamic approach, combining the introduction of **topical vocabulary** with **example sentences** and end-of-section practice **texts**, ensures you are not just memorizing words, but actively learning to use them in context. Over time, this exposure will greatly increase your confidence and proficiency in reading actual media Arabic-style texts.

While the volumes are numbered, they are not incremental in learning level. They simply cover different topics. Feel free to pick any book from the series that aligns with your interest in a particular theme or topic. We hope you find this approach as empowering and rewarding as we do.

Acknowledgments

This series would not have been possible without the dedicated work of some exceptional individuals. I would like to express my deepest gratitude to Ahmad Al-Masri for his invaluable contributions in compiling the extensive vocabulary list and crafting the example sentences and texts. Ahmad's insights and expertise in the Arabic language have been fundamental in shaping this book.

Likewise, I would like to extend my heartfelt thanks to Hend Khaled for her meticulous editing and proofreading of our materials. Her thoughtful feedback and suggestions have significantly elevated the quality and usability of this series. Likewise, her diligence and dedication have been indispensable in shaping the final product.

–Matthew Aldrich

How to Use This Book

Media Arabic Vocabulary is a versatile, flexible tool that can adapt to your personal learning style, immediate needs, and specific interests. Here's how to make the most of it:

Follow Your Interests

The organization of the book allows you to chart your own learning path. Feel free to delve into any unit that piques your interest or aligns with your immediate learning needs. There is no strict order to follow; every path leads to enrichment.

Understand the Structure

Vocabulary Lists: Vocabulary lists serve as your first contact with the topic-specific words and phrases. Each vocabulary item appears on the right-hand side, while its English translation appears on the opposite side. Sometimes you will notice word forms between them, preceded by a large dot. These are irregular plurals of nouns or verbal nouns (masdars) of verbs. Following each vocabulary item, in a shaded box, is an example sentence to demonstrate its use in context. Dozens of note boxes appear throughout the book with lexical and grammatical notes, learning tips, and references to other vocabulary items.

End-of-Section Texts: Following the vocabulary lists, you'll encounter different kinds of texts, including mini-articles, news reports, interviews, and more. These texts aim to immerse you in a variety of real-world contexts, further reinforcing the vocabulary and enhancing your reading proficiency.

Engage in Self-Discovery

We've consciously decided not to include traditional exercises such as multiple-choice or true-false questions. Instead, we promote a self-discovery approach, empowering you to actively engage with the material.

To effectively analyze the texts, try to identify the vocabulary from the lists in the actual context. Notice how these words interact with each other, what collocations they form, and how they contribute to the overall meaning of the text. As you progress through the content, you may notice that the English translations for certain vocabulary items in the example sentences and texts sometimes differ from those presented in the vocabulary lists. Far from an oversight, this is an intentional aspect of the methodology. Our aim here is to encourage you to ponder more deeply on the meanings of words and the nuances in their usage.

Lingualism offers a series of notebooks designed for recording Arabic vocabulary, all with beautiful covers:

www.lingualism.com/vocabulary-notebooks

As for vocabulary organization, we encourage you to keep a dedicated notebook. Classify and group words according to logical categories that make sense to you – be it themes, synonyms, antonyms, or even roots for Arabic words. This personalized lexical resource will greatly aid your recall and application of vocabulary.

Utilize the Audio Tracks

The accompanying audio tracks can be used in conjunction with the text or separately for additional listening practice. You can listen before, during, or after reading the texts, depending on your individual preference. They are designed to help improve your listening comprehension and pronunciation. Each section in the book is preceded by its track number.

Visit www.lingualism.com/audio, where you can find the free accompanying audio to download or stream (at variable playback rates).

Expand Your Vocabulary

One of the key strengths of this book is the wealth of vocabulary embedded within its pages beyond the given lists. Each section is filled with relevant vocabulary items not explicitly listed as vocabulary items. These additional vocabulary treasures can be found within the example sentences and texts. We encourage you to be an active explorer, seeking them out and adding them to your notes. The more you interact with the texts, the more you will uncover additional topical vocabulary to bolster your Arabic language repertoire.

Happy Learning!

Remember, the journey of language learning is not a linear one. It's a process of exploration, discovery, and personal growth. We hope this book will serve as your faithful companion on this fascinating voyage into the vibrant world of Arabic media.

Unit 10
Law and Justice

The intricate world of Law and Justice is a cornerstone of any society, providing structure and maintaining order. This unit offers an in-depth exploration of the vocabulary used to discuss legal systems and judicial processes commonly found in Arabic media, equipping you with the language needed to navigate and understand this vital area.

We begin with **Criminal Justice and Law Enforcement**, where you will explore the foundational aspects of the criminal justice system. Starting with **Police Procedures and Investigations**, you will learn the terminology used to describe the roles, responsibilities, and processes of law enforcement agencies, including vocabulary related to crime scene investigations, evidence collection, and police protocols.

Moving forward, **Trial Procedures and Sentencing** introduces you to the language of courtroom dynamics, covering the stages of a trial, from arraignment to sentencing. You will become familiar with terms used by judges, lawyers, and other legal professionals during court proceedings. The focus then shifts to **Prisons and Corrections**, covering the terminology surrounding incarceration, rehabilitation, and correctional facilities.

Next, we explore **Legal Terminology and Court Procedures**, covering essential vocabulary related to different branches of law. **Civil and Criminal Law** introduces you to the distinctions and specific terms used in civil lawsuits and criminal cases. **International Law and Human Rights** broadens your scope to include the language used in global legal contexts, such as treaties, human rights conventions, and international courts. **Contracts and Business Law** offers insight into the terminology related to commercial transactions, agreements, and corporate law.

We then address the increasingly important area of **Intellectual Property and Copyright Law**. Starting with **Patents, Trademarks, and Copyrights**, you will learn the terms related to the protection of inventions, brand identities, and creative works. **Digital Rights and Privacy** explores the vocabulary associated with online privacy, data protection, and digital content rights.

Some vocabulary in this unit may overlap with Unit 2 (Crime) of Book 1. Referring to that unit can complement your understanding and enhance your vocabulary. Additionally, it's important to note that legal systems vary among Arab countries. The vocabulary covered here may pertain to legal systems in certain Arab countries but not others or even non-Arab countries, providing you with a diverse range of contexts. This breadth will enable you to understand and discuss legal news from both your own country and around the world.

10.1 Criminal Justice and Law Enforcement

10.1.1 Police Procedures and Investigations

Track **1**

to prove guilt • إِثْبَاتٌ   أَثْبَتَ جُرْمًا

نَجَحَتِ الشُّرْطَةُ في إِثْبَاتِ جُرْمِ المُتَّهَمِ بَعْدَ جَمْعِ الأَدِلَّةِ.

The police succeeded in proving the guilt of the accused after gathering evidence.

to secure • تَأْمِينٌ   أَمَّنَ

قَامَتْ قُوَّاتُ الأَمْنِ بِتَأْمِينِ المِنْطَقَةِ بَعْدَ الإِبْلَاغِ عَنْ تَهْدِيدٍ.

The security forces secured the area after a threat was reported.

public safety   أَمْنٌ عامٌّ

خِلَالَ مَهْرَجَانِ المَدِينَةِ الكَبِيرِ، تَمَّ تَعْزِيزُ الأَمْنِ العامِّ مِنْ خِلَالِ نَشْرِ دَوْرِيَّاتٍ إِضَافِيَّةٍ وَكامِيراتٍ مُراقَبَةٍ.

During the city's large festival, public safety was enhanced by deploying additional patrols and surveillance cameras.

police procedure   إِجْراءٌ شُرْطِيٌّ

شَمِلَ الإِجْراءُ الشُّرْطِيُّ تَفْتِيشَ السَّيَّارَةِ بَحْثًا عَنْ مَوادَّ مُخَدِّرَةٍ.

The police procedure included searching the car for narcotics.

bail release   إِفْراجٌ بِكَفالَةٍ

تَمَّ الإِفْراجُ عَنِ المُتَّهَمِ بِكَفالَةٍ في انْتِظارِ مُحاكَمَتِه.

The accused was released on bail pending his trial.

protest   اِحْتِجاجٌ

نَظَّمَتْ مَجْموعاتٌ حُقوقِيَّةٌ احْتِجاجًا ضِدَّ سِياساتِ الاِحْتِجازِ التَّعَسُّفِيِّ.

Human rights groups organized a protest against arbitrary detention policies.

arbitrary detention

اِحْتِجازٌ تَعَسُّفِيٌّ

وَقَعَ احْتِجازٌ تَعَسُّفِيٌّ لِمُدَّةِ 24 ساعَةً دونَ تُهْمَةٍ أَوْ مُحاكَمَةٍ.

There was arbitrary detention for 24 hours without charge or trial.

lawful detention

اِحْتِجازٌ قانونِيٌّ

تَمَّ الِاحْتِجازُ القانونِيُّ لِلْمُشْتَبَهِ بِهِ بِناءً عَلى أَمْرٍ قَضائِيٍّ صادِرٍ مِنَ المَحْكَمَةِ.

The suspect was legally detained based on a judicial order issued by the court.

> Note that the term above ('lawful detention') is a noun phrase but is translated as a passive structure ('was legally detained') in the example sentence, following the verb تَمَّ (to be carried out / completed). This demonstrates the flexibility allowed in crafting a natural translation. However, the meaning of the noun phrase is preserved, as the sentence could be more literally translated as 'a lawful detention was carried out...'. (→ Refer to the note on p. 34 of Book 1 for more on this structure.)

to detain

اِحْتِجازٌ • اِحْتَجَزَ

اِحْتَجَزَتِ الشُّرْطَةُ المُشْتَبَهَ بِهِ لِاسْتِجْوابِهِ حَوْلَ الجَريمَةِ.

The police detained the suspect for questioning about the crime.

interrogation

اِسْتِجْوابٌ

خَضَعَ المُشْتَبَهُ بِهِ لِاسْتِجْوابٍ مُكَثَّفٍ مِنْ قِبَلِ المُحَقِّقينَ لِكَشْفِ مُلابَساتِ الجَريمَةِ.

The suspect underwent intensive interrogation by the investigators to uncover the details of the crime.

to interrogate

اِسْتِجْوابٌ • اِسْتَجْوَبَ

اِسْتَجْوَبَ المُحَقِّقونَ عِدَّةَ أَشْخاصٍ لِلْحُصولِ عَلى تَفاصيلَ حَوْلَ الحادِثِ.

The investigators questioned several people to obtain details about the incident.

to recover

اِسْتِرْدادٌ • اِسْتَرَدَّ

نَجَحَتِ القُوّاتُ الخاصَّةُ في اسْتِرْدادِ المُمْتَلَكاتِ المَسْروقَةِ بَعْدَ عَمَلِيَّةِ بَحْثٍ واسِعَةِ النِّطاقِ.

The special forces successfully recovered the stolen property after an extensive search operation.

to consult an expert

اِسْتَعانَ بِخَبيرٍ • اِسْتِعانَةٌ

اِسْتَعانَتِ الشُّرْطَةُ بِخَبيرٍ في الأَدِلَّةِ الجِنائِيَّةِ لِفَحْصِ مَسْرَحِ الجَريمَةِ.

The police called upon a forensic expert to examine the crime scene.

to suspect

اِشْتَبَهَ • اِشْتِباهٌ

اِشْتَبَهَ المُحَقِّقونَ في شَخْصٍ كانَ مَوْجودًا بِالْقُرْبِ مِنْ مَوْقِعِ الحادِثِ.

The investigators suspected a person who was near the incident location.

arrest

اِعْتِقالٌ

أَصْدَرَ القاضي أَمْرَ اِعْتِقالٍ ضِدَّ المُتَّهَمِ بَعْدَ جَمْعِ الأَدِلَّةِ.

The judge issued an arrest warrant for the suspect after gathering evidence.

to arrest

اِعْتَقَلَ • اِعْتِقالٌ

اِعْتَقَلَتِ الشُّرْطَةُ اللِّصَّ بَعْدَ مُطارَدَةٍ في الشَّوارِعِ.

The police arrested the thief after a street chase.

to violate

اِنْتَهَكَ • اِنْتِهاكٌ

اِنْتَهَكَ المُجْرِمُ حَظْرَ التَّجَوُّلِ المَفْروضِ في المَدينَةِ.

The criminal violated the curfew imposed in the city.

innocent

بَريءٌ • أَبْرِياءُ

أَثْبَتَتِ الأَدِلَّةُ أَنَّ المُتَّهَمَ بَريءٌ مِنَ التُّهَمِ المُوَجَّهَةِ إِلَيْهِ.

The evidence proved that the accused was innocent of the charges against him.

legally

بِطَريقَةٍ قانونِيَّةٍ

تَمَّ اتِّخاذُ جَميعِ الإِجْراءاتِ بِطَريقَةٍ قانونِيَّةٍ لِضَمانِ حُقوقِ المُتَّهَمِ.

All procedures were carried out legally to ensure the accused's rights.

identification

تَحْدِيدُ هُوِيَّةٍ

تَمَّ تَحْدِيدُ هُوِيَّةِ الجاني بِفَضْلِ شَهاداتِ الشُّهودِ.

The identity of the perpetrator was established thanks to witness testimonies.

investigation, detective work

تَحَرٍّ

قامَ المُحَقِّقونَ بِالتَّحَرّي عَنِ الأَنْشِطَةِ الأَخيرَةِ لِلْمُشْتَبَهِ بِهِ.

The investigators conducted an inquiry into the suspect's recent activities.

to verify identity

تَحَقَّقَ مِنْ هُوِيَّةٍ • تَحَقَّقَ

تَحَقَّقَ الضّابِطُ مِنْ هُوِيَّةِ الرَّجُلِ عِنْدَ نُقْطَةِ التَّفْتيشِ.

The officer verified the man's identity at the checkpoint.

investigation

تَحْقيقٌ

بَدَأَتِ الشُّرْطَةُ تَحْقيقًا في سِلْسِلَةٍ مِنْ عَمَلِيّاتِ السَّطْوِ المُسَلَّحِ.

The police began an investigation into a series of armed robberies.

criminal investigation

تَحْقيقٌ جِنائِيٌّ

أَدارَ المُحَقِّقونَ تَحْقيقًا جِنائِيًّا لِكَشْفِ مُلابَساتِ جَريمَةِ القَتْلِ.

The investigators conducted a criminal investigation to uncover the circumstances of the murder.

fair investigation

تَحْقيقٌ نَزيهٌ

طالَبَ المُواطِنونَ بِإِجْراءِ تَحْقيقٍ نَزيهٍ لِضَمانِ العَدالَةِ لِلضَّحِيَّةِ.

The citizens demanded a fair investigation to ensure justice for the victim.

DNA testing

تَحْليلُ الحَمْضِ النَّوَوِيِّ

أَدّى تَحْليلُ الحَمْضِ النَّوَوِيِّ إلى رَبْطِ المُشْتَبَهِ بِهِ بِمَسْرَحِ الجَريمَةِ.

DNA analysis linked the suspect to the crime scene.

fingerprint analysis

تَحْليلُ بَصَماتٍ

ساعَدَ تَحْليلُ بَصَماتِ الأَصابِعِ في التَّعَرُّفِ عَلى اللِّصِّ.

Fingerprint analysis helped in identifying the thief.

rapid response

تَدَخُّلٌ سَريعٌ

تَمَّ اسْتِدْعاءُ وَحْدَةِ التَّدَخُّلِ السَّريعِ لِلتَّعامُلِ مَعَ الوَضْعِ الطّارِئِ.

The rapid response unit was called in to deal with the emergency situation.

to demonstrate

تَظاهَرَ • تَظاهُرٌ

تَظاهَرَ النّاسُ ضِدَّ العُنْفِ الشُّرْطِيِّ في العاصِمَةِ.

People demonstrated against police violence in the capital.

Keep in mind that words may have different meanings depending on the context. تَظاهَرَ is a good example of this, as it can mean 'to pretend' in other contexts.

demonstration

تَظاهُرَةٌ

تَحَوَّلَتِ التَّظاهُرَةُ إلى اشْتِباكاتٍ مَعَ قُوّاتِ الأَمْنِ.

The demonstration turned into clashes with security forces.

A synonym is مُظاهَرَةٌ.

international law enforcement cooperation

تَعاوُنٌ دَوْلِيٌّ في مَجالِ إنْفاذِ القانونِ

يُظْهِرُ التَّعاوُنُ الدَّوْلِيُّ في مَجالِ إنْفاذِ القانونِ القُدْرَةَ عَلى مُكافَحَةِ الجَريمَةِ المُنَظَّمَةِ.

International cooperation in law enforcement shows the capacity to combat organized crime.

to identify

تَعَرَّفَ عَلى • تَعَرُّفٌ

تَعَرَّفَ أَحَدُ الشُّهودِ عَلى الضَّحِيَّةِ في مَكانِ الحادِثِ.

A witness identified the victim at the scene of the incident.

تَعَقَّب • تَعَقُّبٌ

to track, tail

تَعَقَّبَ المُحَقِّقونَ المُشْتَبَهَ بِهِ لِأَيَّامٍ قَبْلَ القَبْضِ عَلَيْهِ في المَدينَةِ.

The investigators tracked the suspect for days before arresting him in the city.

تَفاوَض • تَفاوُضٌ

to negotiate

تَفاوَضَتِ الشُّرْطَةُ مَعَ الخاطِفينَ لِإِطْلاقِ سَراحِ الرَّهائِنِ.

The police negotiated with the kidnappers to release the hostages.

تَفْتيشٌ

search

أَجْرَتِ السُّلْطاتُ تَفْتيشًا دَقيقًا في مَنْزِلِ المُشْتَبَهِ بِهِ.

The authorities conducted a thorough search of the suspect's house.

تَفْتيشٌ is a synonym for بَحْثٌ. However, تَفْتيشٌ is more specifically related to the search of a place or a person, whereas بَحْثٌ refers to a search in general.

تَهْريبٌ

smuggling

ضُبِطَتْ شَبَكَةُ تَهْريبِ المُخَدِّراتِ بَعْدَ تَحَرٍّ اسْتَمَرَّ لِأَشْهُرٍ.

The drug smuggling network was busted after a months-long investigation.

جَريمَةٌ • جَرائِمُ

crime

تَناوَلَتِ الأَخْبارُ تَزايُدَ جَرائِمِ السَّطْوِ في المَناطِقِ التِّجارِيَّةِ.

The news covered the increase in robbery crimes in commercial areas.

جَريمَةُ شَرَفٍ

honor killing

أَثارَتْ جَريمَةُ شَرَفٍ في القَرْيَةِ الجَدَلَ حَوْلَ القَوانينِ وَالعاداتِ الاِجْتِماعِيَّةِ.

An honor killing in the village sparked debate about laws and social customs.

These are crimes committed against family members, usually women, who are perceived to have brought dishonor upon the family. In some communities, such as those in certain regions of the Middle East, this dishonor can stem from actions like refusing an arranged marriage, being a victim of sexual assault, or engaging in relationships disapproved by the family. These acts are seen as violations of social and cultural norms, and, tragically, some families believe that committing an honor killing will restore their reputation within the community. It is important to note that these practices are condemned by many within these communities and are not representative of the culture as a whole.

جَمَعَ أَدِلَّةً • جَمْعٌ

to collect evidence

قامَ المُحَقِّقونَ بِجَمْعِ الأَدِلَّةِ مِنْ مَوْقِعِ الجَريمَةِ لِتَحْليلِها.

The investigators collected evidence from the crime scene for analysis.

حَرَسَ • حِراسَةٌ

to guard

حَرَسَ الضُّبّاطُ المَبْنى طَوالَ اللَّيْلِ لِمَنْعِ أَيِّ تَسَلُّلٍ مُحْتَمَلٍ.

The officers guarded the building throughout the night to prevent any potential intrusion.

حَصَلَ عَلى إِذْنِ تَفْتيشٍ • حُصولٌ

to obtain a search warrant

حَصَلَتِ الشُّرْطَةُ عَلى إِذْنِ تَفْتيشٍ مِنَ المَحْكَمَةِ لِفَحْصِ المَنْزِلِ.

The police obtained a search warrant from the court to inspect the house.

حَقٌّ مَدَنِيٌّ • حُقوقٌ

civil right

يُعْتَبَرُ حَقُّ التَّجَمُّعِ السِّلْمِيِّ حَقًّا مَدَنِيًّا أَساسِيًّا في الدُّوَلِ الدّيمُقْراطِيَّةِ.

The right to peaceful assembly is considered a fundamental civil right in democracies.

حَقَّقَ في • تَحْقيقٌ

to investigate

حَقَّقَ الضّابِطُ في سِلْسِلَةٍ مِنَ السَّرِقاتِ في الحَيِّ.

The officer investigated a series of thefts in the neighborhood.

حَلَّلَ • تَحْليلٌ

to analyze

حَلَّلَ الخُبَراءُ الرَّسائِلَ الإِلِكْترونِيَّةَ كَجُزْءٍ مِنَ التَّحْقيقِ الجِنائِيِّ.

The experts analyzed the emails as part of the criminal investigation.

حِمايَةٌ

protection

تَضَمَّنَتِ الاِتِّفاقِياتُ الدَّوْلِيَّةُ بُنودًا لِحِمايَةِ الأَفْرادِ مِنَ التَّعْذيبِ.

International agreements included provisions for the protection of individuals from torture.

خُصوصِيَّةٌ

privacy

تُعَدُّ خُصوصِيَّةُ الأَفْرادِ حَقًّا مَحْمِيًّا يَجِبُ عَدَمُ انْتِهاكِهِ دونَ مُبَرِّرٍ قانونِيٍّ.

Individual privacy is a protected right that should not be violated without legal justification.

داهَمَ • مُداهَمَةٌ

to raid

داهَمَتِ القُوّاتُ الخاصَّةُ المَبْنى حَيْثُ كانَ يَخْتَبِئُ الأَشْخاصُ المَطْلوبونَ.

The special forces raided the building where the wanted individuals were hiding.

دَوْرِيَّةٌ شُرْطِيَّةٌ

police patrol

تَقومُ الدَّوْرِيَّةُ الشُّرْطِيَّةُ بِجَوْلاتٍ مُنْتَظِمَةٍ لِضَمانِ أَمانِ الحَيِّ.

The police patrol conducts regular rounds to ensure the neighborhood's safety.

رَصَدَ • رَصْدٌ

to track

اِسْتَخْدَمَتِ الشُّرْطَةُ التَّكْنولوجيا لِرَصْدِ هاتِفٍ مَحْمولٍ لِتَعَقُّبِ المُشْتَبَهِ بِهِ.

The police used technology to monitor a mobile phone to track the suspect.

سَجَّلَ • تَسْجيلٌ

to record, log

سَجَّلَ الضّابِطُ التَّفاصيلَ الكامِلَةَ لِلْحادِثِ في تَقْريرِهِ.

The officer recorded the full details of the incident in his report.

سِرِّيٌّ

secret, confidential

ظَلَّتِ المَعْلوماتُ المُتَعَلِّقَةُ بِالْقَضِيَّةِ سِرِّيَّةً لِحِمايَةِ التَّحْقيقِ.

The information related to the case remained confidential to protect the investigation.

witness

شاهِدٌ • شُهودٌ

اِسْتَجْوَبَتِ الشُّرْطَةُ الشُّهودَ الَّذينَ رَأَوْا الحادِثَ لِجَمْعِ مَعْلوماتٍ حَوْلَ الواقِعَةِ.

The police interviewed witnesses who saw the incident to gather information about what happened.

police

شُرْطَةٌ

تَعامَلَتِ الشُّرْطَةُ مَعَ الوَضْعِ بِمِهْنِيَّةٍ وَسُرْعَةٍ.

The police dealt with the situation professionally and swiftly.

religious police

شُرْطَةٌ دينِيَّةٌ

تَعْمَلُ الشُّرْطَةُ الدينِيَّةُ في بَعْضِ الدُّوَلِ لِمُراقَبَةِ الالْتِزامِ بِالْقَواعِدِ الدِّينِيَّةِ.

Religious police operate in some countries to monitor adherence to religious rules.

> In some Islamic countries, notably Saudi Arabia and Sudan, there are law enforcement bodies, generically referred to as 'religious police,' specifically tasked with enforcing Islamic codes of conduct. These organizations ensure adherence to religious laws and customs, which can include dress codes, public behavior, and other aspects of daily life.

transparency

شَفافِيَّةٌ

طالَبَ النّاسُ بِالشَّفافِيَّةِ في التَّحقيقاتِ لِزِيادَةِ الثِّقَةِ في النِّظامِ القَضائِيِّ.

People demanded transparency in the investigations to increase trust in the judicial system.

liaison officer

ضابِطُ اتِّصالٍ • ضُبّاطٌ

عُيِّنَ ضابِطُ اتِّصالٍ لِتَسْهيلِ التَّواصُلِ بَيْنَ الأَجْهِزَةِ المُخْتَلِفَةِ خِلالَ التَّحْقيقِ.

A liaison officer was appointed to facilitate communication between different agencies during the investigation.

to search

فَتَّشَ • تَفْتيشٌ

فَتَّشَ الضّابِطُ السَّيّارَةَ بَحْثًا عَنْ أَسْلِحَةٍ غَيْرِ مَشْروعَةٍ.

The officer searched the car for illegal weapons.

فَحَص • فَحَصَ

to inspect, examine

فَحَصَ الطَّبيبُ الشَّرْعِيُّ الجُثَّةَ لِتَحْديدِ سَبَبِ الوَفاةِ.

The forensic doctor examined the body to determine the cause of death.

قانونيٌّ

legal

تَصَرَّفَ الضّابِطُ وَفْقًا لِلْإِجْراءاتِ القانونيَّةِ المُعْتَمَدَةِ خِلالَ العَمَليَّةِ.

The officer acted according to the legal procedures adopted during the operation.

قَبَضَ عَلى • قَبْض

to arrest

قَبَضَتِ الشُّرْطَةُ عَلى المُشْتَبَهِ بِهِ بَعْدَ مُطارَدَةٍ طَويلَةٍ.

The police arrested the suspect after a long chase.

قِطاعُ الأَمْنِ العامِّ = جِهازُ الأَمْنِ العامِّ

public security agency

نَفَّذَ قِطاعُ الأَمْنِ العامِّ عَمَليَّةَ مُكافَحَةِ إِرْهابٍ واسِعَةَ النِّطاقِ.

The public security sector conducted a large-scale counter-terrorism operation.

> The division of the police has different names in different countries. For example, in Egypt, it is called الأَمْنُ المَرْكَزِيُّ. This term typically refers to a government agency or department responsible for maintaining public order, enforcing laws, ensuring national security, and handling various administrative and security-related tasks within a country. The specific responsibilities and scope of authority may vary depending on the country and its legal and political structure.

قُوَّةٌ أَمْنيَّةٌ

security force

دَعَمَتْ قُوَّةٌ أَمْنيَّةٌ الجُهودَ المَحَليَّةِ لِلْحِفاظِ عَلى النِّظامِ.

A security force supported local efforts to maintain order.

قُوَّةُ مُكافَحَةِ شَغَبٍ

riot control force

اِسْتَدْعَتِ السُّلُطاتُ قُوَّةَ مُكافَحَةِ الشَّغَبِ لِلتَّعامُلِ مَعَ الاِضْطِراباتِ.

The authorities called in the riot control force to deal with the disturbances.

to struggle

كافَحَ • مُكافَحَةٌ

كافَحَ رِجالُ الشُّرْطَةِ لِلسَّيْطَرَةِ عَلى الوَضْعِ خِلالَ الاحْتِجاجاتِ.

The police struggled to control the situation during the protests.

security camera

كاميرا مُراقَبَةٍ

ساهَمَتْ كاميرا المُراقَبَةِ في تَحْديدِ هُوِيَّةِ اللِّصِّ.

The surveillance camera helped identify the thief.

criminal

مُجْرِمٌ

حُكِمَ عَلى الشَّخْصِ بِأَنَّهُ مُجْرِمٌ بَعْدَ إِثْباتِ تَوَرُّطِهِ في السَّرِقَةِ.

The person was convicted as a criminal after his involvement in the theft was proven.

investigator

مُحَقِّقٌ

قادَ المُحَقِّقُ التَّحْقيقَ في قَضِيَّةِ الاخْتِلاسِ الكَبيرَةِ.

The investigator led the investigation into the major embezzlement case.

informant

مُخْبِرٌ

قَدَّمَ المُخْبِرُ مَعْلوماتٍ حاسِمَةً أَدَّتْ إِلى القَبْضِ عَلى عِصابَةِ المُخَدِّراتِ.

The informant provided crucial information that led to the arrest of the drug gang.

> While مُرْشِدٌ can also translate as 'informant,' it specifically refers to a civilian who helps the police undercover, whereas مُخْبِرٌ is someone who works directly for the police.

special prosecutor

مُدَّعٍ خاصٌّ

عَيَّنَتِ المَحْكَمَةُ مُدَّعِيًا خاصًّا لِلنَّظَرِ في القَضِيَّةِ السِّياسِيَّةِ الحَسّاسَةِ.

The court appointed a special prosecutor to look into the sensitive political case.

arrest warrant

مُذَكِّرَةُ تَوْقيفٍ

صَدَرَتْ مُذَكِّرَةُ تَوْقيفٍ بِحَقِّ السِّياسِيِّ المُتَّهَمِ بِالفَسادِ.

An arrest warrant was issued for the politician accused of corruption.

guilty
مُذْنِبٌ

أُدِينَ المُتَّهَمُ وَوُجِدَ مُذْنِبًا في قَضِيَّةِ الاحْتِيالِ.

The accused was convicted and found guilty in the fraud case.

surveillance
مُراقَبَةٌ

تَمَّتْ مُراقَبَةُ المُشْتَبَهِ بِهِ عَلى مَدارِ السَّاعَةِ لِجَمْعِ الأَدِلَّةِ ضِدَّهُ.

The suspect was under 24-hour surveillance to gather evidence against him.

police station
• مَراكِزُ   مَرْكَزُ شُرْطَةٍ

تَمَّ اسْتِجْوابُ الشَّاهِدِ في مَرْكَزِ الشُّرْطَةِ لِجَمْعِ المَزيدِ مِنَ المَعْلوماتِ.

The witness was interrogated at the police station to gather more information.

crime scene
• مَسارِحُ   مَسْرَحُ جَريمَةٍ

قامَ الخُبَراءُ بِفَحْصِ مَسْرَحِ الجَريمَةِ لِجَمْعِ الأَدِلَّةِ.

Experts examined the crime scene to collect evidence.

suspect
مُشْتَبَهٌ بِهِ

يُعْتَبَرُ الشَّخْصُ مُشْتَبَهًا بِهِ إلى أَنْ يَثْبُتَ العَكْسُ وَفْقًا لِلْقانونِ.

A person is considered a suspect until proven otherwise, according to the law.

inspector
مُفَتِّشٌ

قادَ المُفَتِّشُ فَريقَ التَّحْقيقِ في قَضِيَّةِ القَتْلِ الغامِضَةِ.

The inspector led the investigation team in the mysterious murder case.

counter-terrorism
مُكافَحَةُ الإرْهابِ

تَخَصَّصَتِ الوَحَدَةُ في مُكافَحَةِ الإرْهابِ وَتَحْليلِ التَّهْديداتِ.

The unit specialized in counter-terrorism and threat analysis.

to prevent, prohibit	مَنَعَ • مَنْعٌ

مَنَعَتِ الشُّرْطَةُ تَجَمُّعًا غَيْرَ قانونيٍّ في وَسَطِ المَدينَةِ.

The police prevented an illegal gathering in the city center.

court approval	مُوافَقَةُ مَحْكَمَةٍ

تَمَّتِ المُوافَقَةُ عَلَى التَّفْتيشِ بَعْدَ حُصولِ الضُّبّاطِ عَلَى مُوافَقَةِ المَحْكَمَةِ.

The search was approved after the officers obtained court approval.

to coordinate	نَسَّقَ • تَنْسيقٌ

نَسَّقَتِ الأَجْهِزَةُ الأَمْنِيَّةُ جُهودَها لِلْقَبْضِ عَلَى العِصابَةِ.

The security agencies coordinated their efforts to arrest the gang.

to regulate, organize	نَظَّمَ • تَنْظيمٌ

نَظَّمَتِ الشُّرْطَةُ حَمْلَةً لِتَوْعِيَةِ المُواطِنينَ حَوْلَ مَخاطِرِ المُخَدِّراتِ.

The police organized a campaign to educate citizens about the dangers of drugs.

to implement, carry out, execute	نَفَّذَ • تَنْفيذٌ

نَفَّذَ الفَريقُ الأَمْنِيُّ عَمَلِيَّةً خاصَّةً لِاسْتِرْدادِ الرَّهائِنِ.

The security team executed a special operation to recover the hostages.

checkpoint	نُقْطَةُ تَفْتيشٍ • نِقاطٌ

أَقامَتِ السُّلُطاتُ نُقْطَةَ تَفْتيشٍ لِمُراقَبَةِ الدُّخولِ وَالخُروجِ مِنَ المِنْطَقَةِ.

The authorities set up a checkpoint to monitor entry and exit in the area.

special unit	وَحْدَةٌ خاصَّةٌ

تَدَخَّلَتْ وَحْدَةٌ خاصَّةٌ لِلتَّعامُلِ مَعَ الوَضْعِ الأَمْنِيِّ الطَّارِئِ.

A special unit intervened to handle the emergency security situation.

في عَمَلِيَّةٍ نَوْعِيَّةٍ، أَعْلَنَتِ الشُّرْطَةُ عَنْ تَفْكِيكِ شَبَكَةِ تَهْرِيبٍ دَوْلِيَّةٍ بَعْدَ تَحْقِيقٍ جِنائِيٍّ مُعَمَّقٍ اسْتَمَرَّ لِأَشْهُرٍ. اُسْتُخْدِمَتْ في التَّحْقيقِ تَحْليلاتُ الحَمْضِ النَّوَوِيِّ وَتَحْليلُ البَصَماتِ لِتَحْديدِ هُوِيَّةِ المُتَوَرِّطينَ، وَتَمَّ اعْتِقالُ عَدَدٍ مِنَ المُشْتَبَهِ بِهِمْ بِناءً عَلَى مُذَكِّراتِ تَوْقيفٍ قَضائِيَّةٍ.

In a special operation, the police announced the dismantling of an international smuggling network following an in-depth criminal investigation that lasted for months. DNA analysis and fingerprint analysis were used in the investigation to identify those involved, and several suspects were arrested based on judicial arrest warrants.

شَهِدَتِ المَدينَةُ مَوْجَةً مِنَ الاحْتِجاجاتِ عَقِبَ احْتِجازٍ قانونِيٍّ لِناشِطٍ مَعْروفٍ في مَجالِ الحُقوقِ المَدَنِيَّةِ. اِتَّهَمَتْ جَماعاتُ حُقوقِ الإنْسانِ الشُّرْطَةَ بِانْتِهاكِ الخُصوصِيَّةِ وَالتَّدَخُّلِ السَّريعِ دونَ مُوافَقَةِ المَحْكَمَةِ، مُطالِبَةً بِإِجْراءِ تَحْقيقٍ نَزيهٍ وَالإفْراجِ بِكَفالَةٍ عَنِ الناشِطِ.

The city witnessed a wave of protests following the lawful detention of a well-known civil rights activist. Human rights groups accused the police of violating privacy and rapid intervention without court approval, demanding a fair investigation and the activist's release on bail.

نَفَّذَتْ وَحْدَةٌ خاصَّةٌ مِنَ الشُّرْطَةِ عَمَلِيَّةَ إِنْقاذٍ سَريعَةً لِضَحايا خَطْفٍ تَمَّ تَحْديدُ مَوْقِعِهِمْ بِاسْتِخْدامِ كاميراتِ المُراقَبَةِ. أَثْبَتَتِ الدَّوْرِيَّةُ الشُّرْطِيَّةُ فَعالِيَّتَها في التَّعَقُّبِ وَالتَّحَرّي، مِمّا أَدّى إِلى إِنْقاذِ الضَّحايا بِسَلامٍ وَاعْتِقالِ المُجْرِمينَ.

A special police unit carried out a swift rescue operation for kidnapping victims, located using surveillance cameras. The police patrol proved effective in tracking and investigating, leading to the safe rescue of the victims and the arrest of the criminals.

في إِطارِ التَّعاوُنِ الدَّوْلِيِّ في مَجالِ إِنْفاذِ القانونِ، تَمَكَّنَتِ الأَجْهِزَةُ الأَمْنِيَّةُ مِنْ إِسْقاطِ شَبَكَةٍ إِرْهابِيَّةٍ كانَتْ تُخَطِّطُ لِعِدَّةِ هَجَماتٍ. تَمَّ جَمْعُ الأَدِلَّةِ وَرَصْدُ الأَنْشِطَةِ الإِرْهابِيَّةِ عَبْرَ تَحْقيقاتٍ مُشْتَرَكَةٍ، مِمّا أَدّى إِلى اعْتِقالاتٍ كَبيرَةٍ وَمَنْعِ تَنْفيذِ الهَجَماتِ.

In the context of international law enforcement cooperation, security agencies succeeded in taking down a terrorist network that was planning several attacks. Evidence was collected and terrorist activities were monitored through joint investigations, leading to significant arrests and preventing the execution of the attacks.

إِحْتَجَزَ مُسَلَّحٌ عَدَدًا مِنَ الأَشْخاصِ كَرَهائِنَ في مَرْكَزٍ تِجارِيٍّ، مِمَّا اسْتَدْعى تَدَخُّلَ قُوَّةِ مُكافَحَةِ شَغَبٍ. اسْتَطاعَتِ الشُّرْطَةُ التَّفاوُضَ مَعَ المُسَلَّحِ وَإِنْهاءَ الأَزْمَةِ دونَ إِصاباتٍ، حَيْثُ تَمَّ تَحْريرُ الرَّهائِنِ وَاعْتِقالُ الجاني بِطَريقَةٍ قانونِيَّةٍ.

An armed individual detained several people as hostages in a shopping center, necessitating the intervention of a riot control force. The police managed to negotiate with the armed individual and end the crisis without injuries, freeing the hostages and legally arresting the perpetrator.

10.1.1.2 Article: Honor Killings

تَحْقيقاتٌ في جَريمَةِ شَرَفٍ تَهُزُّ قَرْيَةً سورِيَّةً

في قَرْيَةٍ نائِيَةٍ بِريفِ سوريا، هَزَّتْ جَريمَةُ شَرَفٍ الأَوْساطَ الاجْتِماعِيَّةَ وَأَثارَتْ تَحْقيقًا شامِلًا مِنْ قِبَلِ قُوّاتِ الأَمْنِ العامِّ. الضَّحِيَّةُ، شابَّةٌ تُدْعى لينا الزَّهْرانيّ، وُجِدَتْ مَقْتولَةً بِطَريقَةٍ وَحْشِيَّةٍ مِمّا اسْتَدْعى التَّدَخُّلَ الفَوْرِيَّ مِنَ السُّلُطاتِ المَحَلِّيَّةِ.

أَثارَتِ الجَريمَةُ الصّادِمَةُ انْتِباهَ المُحَقِّقِ الخاصِّ عُمَرَ الفاروقِ، الَّذي تَوَلّى مُهِمَّةَ تَقَصّي الحَقائِقِ وَكَشْفِ مُلابَساتِ الحادِثِ. بَدَأَتِ التَّحْقيقاتُ بِجَمْعِ الأَدِلَّةِ مِنْ مَسْرَحِ الجَريمَةِ، حَيْثُ تَمَّ العُثورُ عَلى بَصَماتٍ وَآثارِ حَمْضٍ نَوَوِيٍّ سُجِّلَتْ كَأَدِلَّةٍ رَئيسِيَّةٍ في القَضِيَّةِ.

بِاسْتِجْوابِ الشُّهودِ وَتَحْليلِ السِّجِلّاتِ، تَبَيَّنَ أَنَّ لينا كَهَدَّدَتْها بِسَبَبِ عَلاقَتِها غَيْرِ اللائِقَةِ مَعَ جارِها. أَشارَتْ شَهاداتُ الجيرانِ إِلى أَنَّ أَخاها، ياسِرَ الزَّهْرانيّ، كانَ يُعَبِّرُ عَنِ الغَضَبِ تُجاهَ سُلوكِها "غَيْرِ المَقْبولِ"، مِمّا جَعَلَهُ مُشْتَبَهًا بِهِ رَئيسِيًّا في القَضِيَّةِ.

تَعَقَّبَ الضّابِطُ اتِّصالاتِ ياسِرَ وَراقَبَ تَحَرُّكاتِهِ، مُسْتَخْدِمًا تَحْليلَ الحَمْضِ النَّوَوِيِّ وَتَفْتيشَ المُمْتَلَكاتِ لِإِحْكامِ القَضِيَّةِ ضِدَّهُ. بَعْدَ تَحْقيقٍ دامَ عِدَّةَ أَسابيعَ، تَمَكَّنَ الفَريقُ مِنْ جَمْعِ أَدِلَّةٍ كافِيَةٍ لِإِثْباتِ ذَنْبِ ياسِرَ في ارْتِكابِ جَريمَةِ الشَّرَفِ.

في نِهايَةِ المَطافِ، أَصْدَرَتِ المَحْكَمَةُ مُذَكِّرَةَ تَوْقيفٍ بِحَقِّ ياسِرَ الزَّهْرانيّ، مُتَّهِمَةً إِيّاهُ بِقَتْلِ شَقيقَتِهِ. وَأَعْلَنَ أَنَّهُ سَيُواجِهُ مُحاكَمَةً قانونِيَّةً تَحْتَرِمُ الإِجْراءاتِ الشُّرْطِيَّةَ وَتَضْمَنُ تَحْقيقًا نَزيهًا وَشَفافِيَّةً في العَمَلِيَّةِ القَضائِيَّةِ، مِمّا يَعْكِسُ جُهودَ القِطاعِ الأَمْنِيِّ في مُكافَحَةِ الجَرائِمِ المَبْنِيَّةِ عَلى الشَّرَفِ وَحِمايَةِ حُقوقِ الضَّحايا في القُرى السّورِيَّةِ.

In a remote village in rural Syria, an honor killing has shaken the social fabric and sparked a comprehensive investigation by the public security forces. The victim, a young woman named Lina Al-Zahrani, was found brutally murdered, prompting immediate intervention from the local authorities.

The shocking crime caught the attention of the special investigator, Omar Al-Farouq, who undertook the task of uncovering the facts and revealing the circumstances of the incident. The investigations began with the collection of evidence from the crime scene, where fingerprints and DNA traces were recorded as key evidence in the case.

Through interrogating witnesses and analyzing records, it was revealed that Lina lived in fear of her family, who threatened her due to her improper relationship with a neighbor. Testimonies from neighbors indicated that her brother, Yaser Al-Zahrani, expressed anger towards her "unacceptable" behavior, making him a prime suspect in the case.

The officer tracked Yaser's communications and monitored his movements, using DNA analysis and property searches to strengthen the case against him. After several weeks of investigation, the team managed to gather enough evidence to prove Yaser's guilt in the honor killing.

Ultimately, the court issued an arrest warrant for Yaser Al-Zahrani, accusing him of murdering his sister. It was announced that he would face a legal trial that respects police procedures and ensures a fair and transparent judicial process, reflecting the security sector's efforts to combat honor-based crimes and protect the rights of victims in Syrian villages.

10.1.1.3 Article: Police Investigation

Track 4

تَحْقيقٌ شُرْطِيٌّ في قَطَرَ يَكْشِفُ شَبَكَةَ تَجَسُّسٍ دَوْلِيَّةٍ

الدَّوْحَةُ، قَطَرَ - في تَطَوُّرٍ مُثيرٍ لِلْأَحْداثِ الْأَمْنِيَّةِ في قَطَرَ، أَعْلَنَتْ قُوَّةُ الْأَمْنِ العامِّ عَنِ اخْتِتامِ تَحْقيقٍ جِنائِيٍّ كَبيرٍ أَسْفَرَ عَنْ كَشْفِ شَبَكَةِ تَجَسُّسٍ دَوْلِيَّةٍ كانَتْ تَعْمَلُ سِرًّا داخِلَ البِلادِ. القَضِيَّةُ، الَّتي بَدَأَتْ بِتَحَرِّياتٍ عَقِبَ اسْتِجْوابِ الْمُشْتَبَهِ بِهِ الرَّئيسِيِّ، سَعيدِ النَّجّارِ، قادَتْ إلى اعْتِقالاتٍ مُتَعَدِّدَةٍ وإفْراجٍ بِكَفالَةٍ عَنْ بَعْضِ الْأَفْرادِ ذَوي الصِّلاتِ الضَّعيفَةِ بِالْقَضِيَّةِ.

التَّحْقيقُ، الَّذي اسْتَمَرَّ لِعِدَّةِ أَشْهُرٍ، تَمَيَّزَ بِتَعاوُنٍ دَوْلِيٍّ مُكَثَّفٍ في مَجالِ إنْفاذِ القانونِ، حَيْثُ اسْتَعانَتِ الشُّرْطَةُ القَطَرِيَّةُ بِخُبَراءَ مِنْ دُوَلٍ مُجاوِرَةٍ لِتَحْليلِ البَياناتِ الرَّقْمِيَّةِ وَتَعَقُّبِ تَحَرُّكاتِ أَفْرادِ الشَّبَكَةِ. وَفْقًا لِلْمُحَقِّقِ الرَّئيسِيِّ، عُمَرَ الخالِدِيِّ، فَإِنَّ "العَمَلِيَّةَ الاسْتِخْباراتِيَّةَ تَضَمَّنَتْ تَحْليلَ البَصَماتِ، وَتَحْليلَ الحَمْضِ النَّوَوِيِّ، وَمُراقَبَةً مُكَثَّفَةً بِاسْتِخْدامِ كاميراتِ المُراقَبَةِ المُنْتَشِرَةِ في مَناطِقَ حَيَوِيَّةٍ."

أَدَّتِ التَّحْقِيقَاتُ إِلَى تَحْدِيدِ هُوِيَّةِ عَنَاصِرِ الشَّبَكَةِ، حَيْثُ أَظْهَرَتْ أَنَّهُمْ يَتْبَعُونَ تَنْظِيمًا أَجْنَبِيًّا كَانَ يَهْدُفُ إِلَى جَمْعِ مَعْلُومَاتٍ حَسَّاسَةٍ تَتَعَلَّقُ بِالْأَمْنِ الْقَطَرِيِّ. تَمَكَّنَتِ الشُّرْطَةُ مِنَ احْتِجَازِ الْعَدِيدِ مِنَ الْمُشْتَبَهِ بِهِمْ فِي انْتِظَارِ الْمُحَاكَمَةِ، وَذَلِكَ بَعْدَ الْحُصُولِ عَلَى إِذْنِ تَفْتِيشٍ مِنَ الْقَضَاءِ الْقَطَرِيِّ لِمُدَاهَمَةِ مَوَاقِعَ يُشْتَبَهُ بِأَنَّهَا مَرَاكِزُ لِلشَّبَكَةِ.

تَابَعَ الْجُمْهُورُ الْقَطَرِيُّ التَّطَوُّرَاتِ عَنْ كَثَبٍ، حَيْثُ أَكَّدَتِ الشُّرْطَةُ الْتِزَامَهَا بِالشَّفَافِيَّةِ وَحِمَايَةِ الْحُقُوقِ الْمَدَنِيَّةِ أَثْنَاءَ الْعَمَلِيَّاتِ. وَقَدْ أَشَادَتِ السُّلُطَاتُ بِالْجُهُودِ الْمَبْذُولَةِ فِي سَبِيلِ تَأْمِينِ الْبِلَادِ ضِدَّ أَيِّ تَهْدِيدَاتٍ خَارِجِيَّةٍ، مُشِيرَةً إِلَى أَهَمِّيَّةِ التَّعَاوُنِ الدَّوْلِيِّ فِي مُكَافَحَةِ الْجَرَائِمِ الْمُنَظَّمَةِ وَالتَّجَسُّسِ.

تُعَدُّ هَذِهِ الْقَضِيَّةُ وَاحِدَةً مِنْ أَكْبَرِ الْعَمَلِيَّاتِ الْأَمْنِيَّةِ فِي تَارِيخِ قَطَرَ الْحَدِيثِ، وَتُظْهِرُ مَدَى الْكَفَاءَةِ وَالْجِدِّيَّةِ الَّتِي تَتَعَامَلُ بِهَا قُوَّاتُ الْأَمْنِ الْقَطَرِيَّةُ مَعَ تَهْدِيدَاتِ الْأَمْنِ الدَّاخِلِيِّ وَالْخَارِجِيِّ.

Police Investigation in Qatar Unveils International Espionage Network

Doha, Qatar - In a thrilling development in Qatar's security events, the Public Security Force announced the conclusion of a major criminal investigation that uncovered an international espionage network operating secretly within the country. The case, initiated by inquiries following the interrogation of the main suspect, Saeed Al-Najjar, led to multiple arrests and the release on bail of some individuals with weak links to the case.

The investigation, which lasted for several months, was marked by intense international cooperation in law enforcement, with Qatari police enlisting experts from neighboring countries to analyze digital data and track the movements of the network members. According to the lead investigator, Omar Al-Khaldi, "the intelligence operation included fingerprint analysis, DNA analysis, and intensive monitoring using surveillance cameras deployed in vital areas."

The investigations identified the network members, revealing that they belonged to a foreign organization aiming to collect sensitive information related to Qatari security. The police were able to detain many suspects pending trial after obtaining a search warrant from the Qatari judiciary to raid locations suspected to be network centers.

The Qatari public closely followed the developments, as the police affirmed their commitment to transparency and the protection of civil rights during the operations. Authorities praised the efforts made to secure the country against external threats, highlighting the importance of international cooperation in combating organized crime and espionage.

This case is one of the largest security operations in modern Qatari history, demonstrating the efficiency and seriousness with which the Qatari security forces handle internal and external security threats.

10.1.2 Trial Procedures and Sentencing

to convict

أدانَ

• إدانَةٌ

أَدانَتِ المَحْكَمَةُ المُتَّهَمَ بَعْدَ ثُبوتِ تَوَرُّطِهِ في الجَريمَةِ.

The court convicted the accused after proving his involvement in the crime.

to issue a verdict

أَصْدَرَ حُكْمًا

• إصْدارٌ

أَصْدَرَ القاضي حُكْمًا بِالسَّجْنِ لِمُدَّةِ خَمْسِ سَنَواتٍ عَلى المُتَّهَمِ.

The judge issued a five-year prison sentence for the accused.

legal procedure

إجْراءٌ قانونيٌّ

تَتَطَلَّبُ العَمَليَّةُ القَضائيَّةُ اتِّباعَ إجْراءاتٍ قانونيَّةٍ صارِمَةٍ لِضَمانِ العَدالَةِ.

The judicial process requires following strict legal procedures to ensure justice.

trial proceedings

إجْراءاتُ مُحاكَمَةٍ

pl.

تَتَضَمَّنُ إجْراءاتُ المُحاكَمَةِ عِدَّةَ خُطُواتٍ كالِاسْتِماعِ لِلشُّهودِ وَتَقْديمِ الأَدِلَّةِ.

Trial procedures include several steps such as listening to witnesses and presenting evidence.

> The noun إجْراءاتُ is always plural in this context. When used in the singular (إجْراءُ مُحاكَمَةٍ), it refers to '(the act of) holding a trial.'

conviction

إدانَةٌ

جاءَتِ الإدانَةُ بِتُهْمَةِ السَّرِقَةِ بَعْدَ عَرْضِ الأَدِلَّةِ القاطِعَةِ.

The conviction for theft came after presenting conclusive evidence.

retrial

إعادَةُ مُحاكَمَةٍ

أَمَرَتِ المَحْكَمَةُ بِإعادَةِ المُحاكَمَةِ بِناءً عَلى الأَدِلَّةِ الجَديدَةِ الَّتي قُدِّمَتْ.

The court ordered a retrial based on the new evidence presented.

إِدَّعَى   • إِدِّعَاءٌ   to claim, argue

اِدَّعَى المُتَّهَمُ بِأَنَّهُ كانَ في مَكانٍ آخَرَ وَقْتَ وُقوعِ الجَرِيمَةِ، مُقَدِّمًا حُجَّةَ غِيابٍ.

The accused claimed he was elsewhere at the time of the crime, providing an alibi.

اِسْتَأْنَفَ   • اِسْتِئْنافٌ   to appeal

اِسْتَأْنَفَ المَحْكومُ عَلَيْهِ الحُكْمَ لِلْمُطالَبَةِ بِإعادَةِ النَّظَرِ في القَضِيَّةِ.

The sentenced individual appealed the verdict to request a review of the case.

اِسْتَجْوَبَ شاهِدًا   • اِسْتِجْوابٌ   to question a witness

اِسْتَجْوَبَ الدِّفاعُ شاهِدًا قَدَّمَ شَهادَةً مُهِمَّةً تُؤَكِّدُ عَلى بَراءَةِ المُتَّهَمِ.

The defense interrogated a witness who provided crucial testimony affirming the accused's innocence.

اِسْتَدْعى شاهِدًا   • اِسْتِدْعاءٌ   to call a witness

اِسْتَدْعَتِ النِّيابَةُ شاهِدًا لِإثْباتِ الدَّليلِ ضِدَّ المُتَّهَمِ.

The prosecution summoned a witness to prove the evidence against the accused.

بَرَّأَ   • تَبْرِئَةٌ   to acquit

بَرَّأَتِ المَحْكَمَةُ المُتَّهَمَ بَعْدَ عَدَمِ ثُبوتِ الأَدِلَّةِ ضِدَّهُ.

The court acquitted the accused after the evidence against him was not proven.

بَراءَةٌ   acquittal

حَصَلَ المُتَّهَمُ عَلى بَراءَةٍ مِنَ التُّهَمِ المُوَجَّهَةِ إلَيْهِ بِفَضْلِ شَهادَةِ الشُّهودِ الأَساسِيّينَ.

The accused was exonerated from the charges against him thanks to the testimony of key witnesses.

بَريءٌ   • أَبْرِياءُ   innocent

بَعْدَ المُحاكَمَةِ، أَعْلَنَ القاضي أَنَّ المُتَّهَمَ بَريءٌ مِنْ جَميعِ التُّهَمِ المُوَجَّهَةِ ضِدَّهُ.

After the trial, the judge declared the accused innocent of all charges against him.

تَعْوِيضٌ

compensation, reparation

حَكَمَتِ الْمَحْكَمَةُ بِتَعْوِيضِ الْمُتَّهَمِ عَنِ الْأَضْرَارِ النَّفْسِيَّةِ وَالْمَادِّيَّةِ الَّتِي لَحِقَتْ بِهِ.

The court ruled compensation for the accused for the psychological and material damages he suffered.

تَنْظِيمُ مَحاكِمَ

court organization

يُعْتَبَرُ تَنْظِيمُ الْمَحاكِمِ جُزْءًا حاسِمًا فِي نِظامِ الْعَدالَةِ لِضَمانِ سَيْرِ الْإِجْراءاتِ بِفَعالِيَّةٍ.

The organization of courts is a crucial part of the justice system to ensure the proceedings run effectively.

تُهْمَةٌ • تُهَمٌ

charge

وُجِّهَتْ لِلْمُتَّهَمِ تُهْمَةُ الِاحْتِيالِ وَالِاخْتِلاسِ مِنَ الشَّرِكَةِ.

The accused was charged with fraud and embezzlement from the company.

The example sentence more literally translates as 'a charge of fraud... was faced by the accused.'

جَزائِيٌّ

punitive, penal

تُفَكِّرُ الْحُكومَةُ فِي تَنْفِيذِ إِجْراءاتٍ جَزائِيَّةٍ جَدِيدَةٍ لِمُواجَهَةِ ارْتِفاعِ مُعَدَّلاتِ الْجَرِيمَةِ.

The government is considering implementing new penal measures to address rising crime rates.

جِنائِيٌّ

criminal

فِي النِّظامِ الْجِنائِيِّ، يَتِمُّ التَّعامُلُ مَعَ الْجَرائِمِ بِجِدِّيَّةٍ تامَّةٍ وَفْقًا لِلْقانونِ.

In the criminal system, crimes are dealt with seriously and according to the law.

Note that this is an adjective describing something related to crime or criminal matters. The noun 'criminal' is مُجْرِمٌ, which is covered in Unit 2 (Book 1).

حاكَمَ • مُحاكَمَةٌ

to try

حاكَمَتِ الْمَحْكَمَةُ الْعَدِيدَ مِنَ الْأَشْخاصِ فِي قَضايا مُخْتَلِفَةٍ، مِنَ السَّرِقَةِ إِلَى الْجَرائِمِ الْجِنائِيَّةِ الْكُبْرَى.

The court tried many individuals in various cases, from theft to major criminal offenses.

detention

حَبْسٌ

أَمَرَ القاضي بِحَبْسِ المُتَّهَمِ احْتِياطِيًّا حَتّى مَوْعِدِ المُحاكَمَةِ.

The judge ordered the accused to be detained in custody until the trial date.

> The word حَبْسٌ is usually used to refer to short periods of time or temporary detention. On the other hand, سَجْنٌ is used when a verdict is made and typically refers to longer periods of imprisonment.

pretrial detention

حَبْسٌ عَلى ذِمَّةِ قَضِيَّةٍ

تُواجِهُ سُلُطاتُ القَضاءِ انْتِقاداتٍ بِشَأْنِ اسْتِخْدامِها المُتَزايِدِ لِلْحَبْسِ عَلى ذِمَّةِ القَضايا.

The judiciary authorities are facing criticism over their increasing use of pretrial detention.

free

حُرٌّ • أَحْرارٌ

أُطْلِقَ سَراحُ النّاشِطِ السِّياسِيِّ لِيَكونَ حُرًّا بَعْدَ قَضاءِ عامٍ في السِّجْنِ.

The political activist was released to be free after spending a year in prison.

human rights

pl.

حُقوقُ إنْسانٍ

تَناوَلَتِ المُنَظَّماتُ الدَّوْلِيَّةُ مَوْضوعَ حُقوقِ الإنْسانِ خِلالَ الاجْتِماعِ السَّنَوِيِّ.

International organizations addressed the issue of human rights during the annual meeting.

witnesses' rights

pl.

حُقوقُ الشُّهودِ

يَجِبُ ضَمانُ حُقوقِ الشُّهودِ لِحِمايَتِهِمْ عِنْدَ تَقْديمِ الشَّهادَةِ في المَحْكَمَةِ.

Witness rights must be ensured to protect them when providing testimony in court.

children's rights

pl.

حُقوقُ الطِّفْلِ

تَضَمَنُ حُقوقُ الطِّفْلِ الحِمايَةَ مِنَ الإساءَةِ وَتَوْفيرَ التَّعْليمِ وَالرِّعايَةِ الصِّحِّيَّةِ.

Children's rights include protection from abuse and the provision of education and health care.

women's rights   *pl.*   حُقوقُ المَرْأَةِ

يَشْمَلُ تَعْزيزُ حُقوقِ المَرْأَةِ مُكافَحَةَ العُنْفِ الأُسَرِيِّ وَتَوْفيرَ فُرَصٍ مُتَساوِيَةٍ في العَمَلِ.

Advancing women's rights includes combating domestic violence and providing equal employment opportunities.

death sentence   أَحْكامٌ •   حُكْمٌ بِالإعْدامِ

أَصْدَرَتِ المَحْكَمَةُ حُكْمًا بِالإعْدامِ ضِدَّ القاتِلِ المُتَسَلْسِلِ.

The court issued a death sentence against the serial killer.

prison sentence   حُكْمٌ بِالسَّجْنِ

تَمَّ تَأْكيدُ الحُكْمِ النِّهائِيِّ بِالسَّجْنِ المُؤَبَّدِ لِلْمُتَّهَمِ في قَضِيَّةِ الخِيانَةِ.

The final life imprisonment sentence for the accused in the treason case was confirmed.

to sentence to   حُكْمٌ •   حَكَمَ عَلى

حَكَمَ القاضي عَلى المُتَّهَمِ بِالسَّجْنِ لِمُدَّةِ عَشْرِ سَنَواتٍ بَعْدَ ثُبوتِ الجَريمَةِ.

The judge sentenced the accused to ten years in prison after proving the crime.

final verdict   حُكْمٌ نِهائِيٌّ

أَصْبَحَ الحُكْمُ نِهائِيًّا بَعْدَ رَفْضِ الاسْتِئْنافِ الأَخيرِ مِنَ المُتَّهَمِ.

The sentence became final after the accused's last appeal was rejected.

witness protection   حِمايَةُ الشُّهودِ

تُوَفِّرُ بَرامِجُ حِمايَةِ الشُّهودِ الأَمانَ وَالسِّرِّيَّةَ لِلشُّهودِ المُعَرَّضينَ لِلْخَطَرِ.

Witness protection programs provide safety and confidentiality for witnesses at risk.

to reduce a sentence   تَخْفيفٌ •   خَفَّفَ عُقوبَةً

خَفَّفَ القاضي العُقوبَةَ بِناءً عَلى كَوْنِ المُتَّهَمِ مُتَّهَمًا لِلْمَرَّةِ الأولى بِجَريمَةٍ غَيْرِ عَنيفَةٍ، وَعَدَمِ وُجودِ سِجِلٍّ إجْرامِيٍّ سابِقٍ.

The judge reduced the sentence because the defendant is a first-time offender of a non-violent crime with no prior criminal record.

to defend	دِفاعٌ / مُدافَعَةٌ •	دافَعَ

دافَعَ المُحامي بِقُوَّةٍ عَنْ مُوَكِّلِهِ في المَحْكَمَةِ لِإِثْباتِ بَراءَتِه.

The lawyer vigorously defended his client in court to prove his innocence.

public defense	دِفاعٌ عامٌّ

تَمَّ تَعْيينُ مُحامٍ مِنَ الدِّفاعِ العامِّ لِلْمُتَّهَمِ الَّذي لا يَسْتَطيعُ تَحَمُّلَ تَكاليفِ التَّمْثيلِ القانونيِّ.

A public defender was appointed for the accused, who could not afford legal representation.

legal defense	دِفاعٌ قانونيٌّ

كانَ الدِّفاعُ القانونيُّ المُقَدَّمُ قَوِيًّا، حَيْثُ اسْتَنَدَ إلى الأَدِلَّةِ وَالشَّهاداتِ لِتَبْرِئَةِ المُتَّهَمِ.

The legal defense presented was strong, based on evidence and testimonies to exonerate the accused.

to pay compensation	دَفَعَ •	دَفَعَ تَعْويضًا

أُمِرَ المُتَّهَمُ بِدَفْعِ تَعْويضٍ لِلضَّحِيَّةِ عَنِ الأَضْرارِ النَّفْسِيَّةِ وَالمادِّيَّةِ.

The accused was ordered to pay compensation to the victim for psychological and material damages.

criminal evidence	أَدِلَّةٌ •	دَليلٌ جِنائيٌّ

اِسْتَخْدَمَ الاِدِّعاءُ دَليلًا جِنائيًّا مَلْموسًا لِإِثْباتِ تَوَرُّطِ المُتَّهَمِ في الجَريمَةِ.

The prosecution used concrete criminal evidence to prove the accused's involvement in the crime.

imprisonment	سَجْنٌ

حُكِمَ عَلى المُجْرِمِ بِالسَّجْنِ لِمُدَّةِ خَمْسِ سَنَواتٍ بَعْدَ إِدانَتِهِ بِالسَّرِقَةِ.

The criminal was sentenced to five years in prison after being convicted of theft.

> This term is سَجْنٌ, a verbal noun meaning 'imprisonment'. → Compare with سِجْنٌ (p. 41), which refers to a prison or jail (the place).

سَجَنَ • سِجْنٌ

to be imprisoned

سُجِنَ المُديرُ التَّنْفيذِيُّ لِلشَّرِكَةِ بَعْدَ إِدانَتِهِ بِالاحْتِيالِ المالِيِّ.

The company's CEO was imprisoned after being convicted of financial fraud.

سِجْنٌ مُؤَبَّدٌ

life imprisonment

حُكِمَ بِالسِّجْنِ المُؤَبَّدِ عَلَى المُتَّهَمِ بِدونِ إِمْكانِيَّةِ الإِفْراجِ المَشْروطِ في قَضِيَّةِ القَتْلِ العَمْدِ.

The accused was sentenced to life imprisonment without the possibility of parole in the premeditated murder case.

شاهِدٌ • شُهودٌ

witness

أَدْلَى الشّاهِدُ بِشَهادَتِهِ أَمامَ المَحْكَمَةِ، مِمّا أَدّى إِلى تَغْييرِ مَسارِ القَضِيَّةِ.

The witness testified before the court, leading to a change in the course of the case.

شاهِدُ عِيانٍ

eyewitness

شَهِدَ شاهِدُ العِيانِ في المُحاكَمَةِ، حَيْثُ قَدَّمَ تَفاصيلَ حَيَوِيَّةً حَوْلَ الحادِثِ.

The eyewitness testified in the trial, providing vital details about the incident.

شَهادَةٌ

testimony, witness statement

اُسْتُدْعِيَ شاهِدُ إِثْباتٍ لِتَقْديمِ شَهادَتِهِ ضِدَّ المُتَّهَمِ.

A prosecution witness was summoned to give his testimony against the accused.

طَلَبُ اسْتِئْنافٍ

appeal

قَدَّمَ الدِّفاعُ طَلَبَ اسْتِئْنافٍ ضِدَّ حُكْمِ المَحْكَمَةِ الابْتِدائِيِّ.

The defense filed an appeal against the initial court decision.

عاقَبَ • مُعاقَبَةٌ / عِقابٌ

to sentence

عاقَبَ القاضي المُتَّهَمَ بِالحَبْسِ ثَلاثَةَ أَشْهُرٍ بِسَبَبِ الشَّغَبِ العامِّ.

The judge sentenced the accused to three months of imprisonment for public disturbance.

justice   عَدالَةٌ

تَهْدُفُ العَدالَةُ إلى ضَمانِ مُعامَلَةِ جَميعِ الأَطْرافِ في النِّزاعِ بِإِنْصافٍ وَحِيادِيَّةٍ.

Justice aims to ensure that all parties in a dispute are treated fairly and impartially.

transitional justice   عَدالَةٌ انْتِقالِيَّةٌ

ساهَمَتِ العَدالَةُ الانْتِقالِيَّةُ في مُعالَجَةِ الجَرائِمِ الَّتي وَقَعَتْ خِلالَ النِّزاعاتِ السِّياسِيَّةِ السّابِقَةِ.

Transitional justice contributed to addressing crimes committed during past political conflicts.

> This term refers to measures employed to address human rights abuses and promote reconciliation after periods of conflict or dictatorship. Transitional justice aims to provide accountability, serve justice, and achieve reconciliation, often through mechanisms such as truth commissions, reparations, and institutional reforms.

punishment, sentence   عُقوبَةٌ

فَرَضَتِ المَحْكَمَةُ عُقوبَةَ الخِدْمَةِ العامَّةِ كَبَديلٍ لِلسَّجْنِ.

The court imposed community service as an alternative to imprisonment.

fine   غَرامَةٌ

فُرِضَتْ غَرامَةٌ كَبيرَةٌ عَلى الشَّرِكَةِ بِسَبَبِ مُخالَفاتِها البيئِيَّةِ.

A large fine was imposed on the company for its environmental violations.

illegal   غَيْرُ قانونِيٍّ

يُعْتَبَرُ التَّنْقيبُ عَنِ الآثارِ دونَ تَرْخيصٍ غَيْرَ قانونِيٍّ وَيُعاقِبُ عَلَيْهِ القانونُ.

Excavating archaeological sites without a license is illegal and punishable by law.

not convicted   غَيْرُ مُدانٍ

بَعْدَ المُحاكَمَةِ، وُجِدَ المُتَّهَمُ غَيْرَ مُدانٍ بِالتُّهَمِ المُوَجَّهَةِ إِلَيْهِ.

After the trial, the accused was found not convicted of the charges against him.

غَيْرُ مُذْنِبٍ

not guilty

أَعْلَنَ المُتَّهَمُ بَراءَتَهُ قائِلًا "أَنا غَيْرُ مُذْنِبٍ" أَمامَ المَحْكَمَةِ.

The accused declared his innocence, stating "I am not guilty" in court.

فَرَضَ غَرامَةً • فَرْضٌ

to impose a fine

فَرَضَتِ المَحْكَمَةُ غَرامَةً عَلَى الشَّرِكَةِ لِانْتِهاكِها قَوانينَ العَمَلِ.

The court imposed a fine on the company for violating labor laws.

قاسٍ

harsh

وَصَفَ المُنْتَقِدونَ الحُكْمَ الصّادِرَ بِأَنَّهُ قاسٍ لِلْغايَةِ، مُشيرينَ إلى العُقوبَةِ الطَّويلَةِ بِدونِ أَيِّ فُرْصَةٍ لِلْإِفْراجِ المَشْروطِ.

Critics described the sentence as harsh, pointing to the lengthy punishment without any chance for parole.

قاضٍ • قُضاةٌ

judge

قَرَّرَ القاضي تَأْجيلَ الجَلْسَةِ لِمَزيدٍ مِنَ التَّحْقيقِ.

The judge decided to postpone the session for further investigation.

قانونُ أَحْوالٍ شَخْصِيَّةٍ • قَوانينٌ

personal status law

يُنَظِّمُ قانونُ الأَحْوالِ الشَّخْصِيَّةِ قَضايا مِثْلَ الزَّواجِ، والطَّلاقِ، وَحَضانَةِ الأَطْفالِ.

Personal status law regulates issues such as marriage, divorce, and child custody.

قانونُ أَحْوالٍ شَخْصِيَّةٍ regulates family matters like marriage, divorce, and inheritance. In the Arab world, it is often based on Islamic law (Sharia) and enforced by religious courts or legal bodies.

قانونٌ جِنائِيٌّ

criminal law

يُنَظِّمُ القانونُ الجِنائِيُّ العُقوباتِ المُرْتَبِطَةَ بِالجَرائِمِ كالسَّرِقَةِ وَالقَتْلِ.

Criminal law regulates the penalties associated with crimes such as theft and murder.

international law

قانونٌ دَوْلِيٌّ

يُعالِجُ القانونُ الدَّوْلِيُّ القَضايا بَيْنَ الدُّوَلِ وَيَشْمَلُ المُعاهَداتِ وَالِاتِّفاقِيّاتِ الدَّوْلِيَّةِ.

International law addresses issues between states and includes treaties and international agreements.

penal code

قانونُ عُقوباتٍ

يُحَدِّدُ قانونُ العُقوباتِ الجَزاءاتِ وَالعُقوباتِ لِمُخْتَلِفِ الجَرائِمِ.

The penal code specifies the sanctions and penalties for various crimes.

labor law

قانونُ عَمَلٍ

يُوَفِّرُ قانونُ العَمَلِ الحِمايَةَ لِلعُمّالِ وَيُنَظِّمُ العَلاقَةَ بَيْنَ أَصْحابِ العَمَلِ وَالمُوَظَّفينَ.

Labor law provides protection for workers and regulates the relationship between employers and employees.

civil law

قانونٌ مَدَنِيٌّ

يُنَظِّمُ القانونُ المَدَنِيُّ المَسائِلَ المُتَعَلِّقَةَ بِالحُقوقِ وَالواجِباتِ الشَّخْصِيَّةِ كالمِلْكِيَّةِ وَالعُقودِ.

Civil law regulates matters related to personal rights and duties, such as property and contracts.

anti-corruption law

قانونُ مُكافَحَةِ فَسادٍ

يَهْدُفُ قانونُ مُكافَحَةِ الفَسادِ إلى الحَدِّ مِنَ السُّلوكِيّاتِ غَيْرِ الأَخْلاقِيَّةِ وَتَعْزيزِ الشَّفافِيَّةِ في الإدارَةِ العامَّةِ.

Anti-corruption law aims to curb unethical behaviors and promote transparency in public administration.

legal

قانونِيٌّ

يَتَطَلَّبُ العَمَلُ القانونِيُّ الِالْتِزامَ بِالمَعاييرِ وَالإجْراءاتِ المُحَدَّدَةِ في التَّشْريعاتِ.

Legal work requires adherence to the standards and procedures set forth in legislation.

to present evidence

قَدَّمَ إِثْباتًا • تَقْديمٌ

قَدَّمَ المُحامي إِثْباتًا قَوِيًّا دَعْمًا لِقَضِيَّةِ مُوَكِّلِهِ خِلالَ المُحاكَمَةِ.

The lawyer presented strong evidence in support of his client's case during the trial.

قَرِينَةُ البَرَاءَةِ   • قَرَائِنُ

presumption of innocence

تَسْتَنِدُ قَرِينَةُ البَرَاءَةِ إِلَى مَبْدَأٍ أَنَّ الشَّخْصَ يُعْتَبَرُ بَرِيئًا إِلَى أَنْ تَثْبُتَ إِدَانَتُهُ.

The presumption of innocence is based on the principle that a person is considered innocent until proven guilty.

كَفَالَةٌ

bail

دَفَعَ المُتَّهَمُ كَفَالَةً مُرْتَفِعَةً لِلْإِفْرَاجِ عَنْهُ مُؤَقَّتًا حَتَّى مَوْعِدِ المُحَاكَمَةِ.

The accused paid a high bail to be temporarily released until the trial date.

مُؤَقَّتٌ

temporary

صَدَرَ الحُكْمُ المُؤَقَّتُ لِلسَّمَاحِ بِمَزِيدٍ مِنَ الوَقْتِ لِجَمْعِ الأَدِلَّةِ.

The temporary ruling was given to allow more time for gathering evidence.

مَالِيٌّ

financial

تُنَظِّمُ القَوَانِينُ المَالِيَّةُ كَيْفِيَّةَ جَمْعِ الضَّرَائِبِ وَإِدَارَةَ الأَمْوَالِ العَامَّةِ.

Financial laws regulate how taxes are collected and public funds are managed.

مُتَّهَمٌ

accused

فِي المُحَاكَمَةِ، وُجِّهَتْ لِلْمُتَّهَمِ تُهْمَةُ التَّجَسُّسِ وَالخِيَانَةِ الوَطَنِيَّةِ.

In the trial, the accused was charged with espionage and national treason.

مُحَاكَمَةٌ

trial

بَدَأَتْ مُحَاكَمَةُ الرَّئِيسِ السَّابِقِ لِتَوَرُّطِهِ فِي فَضِيحَةِ فَسَادٍ كُبْرَى.

The trial of the former president began for his involvement in a major corruption scandal.

مُحَاكَمَةٌ عَلَنِيَّةٌ

public trial

انْعَقَدَتْ مُحَاكَمَةٌ عَلَنِيَّةٌ لِضَمَانِ شَفَافِيَّةِ الإِجْرَاءَاتِ وَثِقَةِ العَامَّةِ.

A public trial was held to ensure transparency of the proceedings and public trust.

attorney, lawyer

مُحامٍ

وَكَّلَ المُتَّهَمُ مُحامِيًا بارِزًا لِلدِّفاعِ عَنْهُ في قَضِيَّةِ الِاخْتِلاسِ المالِيِّ.

The accused appointed a prominent lawyer to defend him in the financial embezzlement case.

international criminal court

مَحْكَمَةٌ جِنائِيَّةٌ دَوْلِيَّةٌ   •   مَحاكِمُ

قَدَّمَتِ المَحْكَمَةُ الجِنائِيَّةُ الدَّوْلِيَّةُ لائِحَةَ اتِّهامٍ ضِدَّ الدِّيكْتاتورِ لِارْتِكابِهِ جَرائِمَ حَرْبٍ.

The International Criminal Court issued an indictment against the dictator for committing war crimes.

sentenced

مَحْكومٌ عَلَيْهِ

يُواجِهُ الشَّخْصُ المَحْكومُ عَلَيْهِ بِالسَّجْنِ لِمُدَّةٍ طَويلَةٍ تَحَدِّياتٍ عَديدَةً في إعادَةِ التَّأْهيلِ وَالِانْدِماجِ في المُجْتَمَعِ.

The person sentenced to a long prison term faces many challenges in rehabilitation and reintegration into society.

convicted

مُدانٌ

حُكِمَ عَلى المُدانِ بِالسَّجْنِ المُؤَبَّدِ دونَ إمْكانِيَّةِ الإفْراجِ المَشْروطِ بِسَبَبِ جَريمَتِهِ الشَّنْعاءِ.

The convicted was sentenced to life imprisonment without the possibility of parole for his heinous crime.

prison term

مُدَّةُ سَجْنٍ   •   مُدَدٌ

تَمَّ تَحْديدُ مُدَّةِ السَّجْنِ لِلمُتَّهَمِ بِخَمْسَةَ عَشَرَ عامًا بَعْدَ إدانَتِهِ بِالِاحْتِيالِ الجَسيمِ.

The prison term for the accused was set at fifteen years after his conviction for major fraud.

prosecutor

مُدَّعٍ عامٌّ

أَقْنَعَ المُدَّعي العامُّ هَيْئَةَ المُحَلَّفينَ بِأَدِلَّةٍ لا تَقْبَلُ الشَّكَّ عَلى إدانَةِ المُتَّهَمِ.

The public prosecutor convinced the jury with irrefutable evidence of the accused's guilt.

civil

مَدَنِيٌّ

تَمَّ التَّعامُلُ مَعَ القَضِيَّةِ في مَحْكَمَةٍ مَدَنِيَّةٍ حَيْثُ جَرى النَّظَرُ في نِزاعٍ عَقارِيٍّ بَيْنَ جيرانٍ.

The case was handled in a civil court where a property dispute between neighbors was considered.

guilty

مُذْنِبٌ

أَقَرَّ الطَّرَفُ المُذْنِبُ بِجَرائِمِهِ أَمامَ القاضي، مِمّا ساهَمَ في تَسْريعِ عَمَلِيَّةِ المُحاكَمَةِ.

The guilty party confessed his crimes in front of the judge, helping to expedite the trial process.

guaranteed (as in guaranteed rights)

مَكْفولٌ

يَهْدُفُ التَّشْريعُ الجَديدُ الَّذي تَمَّ اعْتِمادُهُ إلى ضَمانِ الحُقوقِ المَكْفولَةِ لِجَميعِ المُواطِنينَ.

The newly passed legislation aims to ensure guaranteed rights for all citizens.

to grant amnesty

مَنَحَ عَفْوًا • مَنْحٌ

مَنَحَ الرَّئيسُ عَفْوًا لِلنّاشِطِ السِّياسِيِّ بَعْدَ ضُغوطٍ دَوْلِيَّةٍ.

The president granted amnesty to the political activist following international pressure.

to pronounce a verdict

نَطَقَ بِحُكْمٍ • نُطْقٌ

نَطَقَ القاضي بِالحُكْمِ في قَضِيَّةِ القَتْلِ، مُحَدِّدًا عُقوبَةَ الإعْدامِ لِلْمُتَّهَمِ.

The judge pronounced the sentence in the murder case, determining the death penalty for the accused.

final

نِهائِيٌّ

بَعْدَ مُرورِ عِدَّةِ سَنَواتٍ، أَصْبَحَ الحُكْمُ نِهائِيًّا وَغَيْرَ قابِلٍ لِلطَّعْنِ.

After several years, the verdict became final and unappealable.

jury

هَيْئَةُ مُحَلَّفينَ

قَرَّرَتْ هَيْئَةُ المُحَلَّفينَ بِالإجْماعِ إدانَةَ المُتَّهَمِ بَعْدَ تَقْييمِ جَميعِ الأَدِلَّةِ.

The jury unanimously decided to convict the accused after evaluating all the evidence.

10.1.2.1 Mini-Articles

Track **6**

في مَحْكَمَةِ العَدْلِ العُلْيا، أَدانَ قاضٍ مَسْؤُولاً حُكومِيًّا سابِقًا بِتُهَمِ الفَسادِ المالِيّ بَعْدَ مُحاكَمَةٍ عَلَنِيّةٍ اسْتَمَرَّتْ لِأَسابيعَ. اِسْتَدْعى الاِدِّعاءُ شُهودَ عِيانٍ وَقَدَّمَ أَدِلّةً جِنائِيّةً مُقْنِعَةً، مِمّا أَسْفَرَ عَنْ حُكْمٍ بِالسَّجْنِ لِمُدّةِ عَشْرِ سَنَواتٍ وَفَرْضِ غَرامَةٍ مالِيّةٍ كَبيرةٍ كَتَعْويضٍ لِلْخِزانَةِ العامّةِ.

At the Supreme Court, a judge convicted a former government official of financial corruption charges following a public trial that lasted for weeks. The prosecution summoned eyewitnesses and presented compelling criminal evidence, resulting in a ten-year prison sentence and a significant fine as compensation to the public treasury.

بَعْدَ مُحاكَمَةٍ شَهِدَتْ تَقَلُّباتٍ عَديدةً، بَرَّأَتِ المَحْكَمَةُ شابًا مِنْ تُهْمَةِ ارْتِكابِ جَريمَةِ شَرَفٍ. اِسْتَنَدَ قَرارُ البَراءَةِ إلى نَقْصِ الأَدِلّةِ الجِنائِيّةِ وَتَضارُبِ شَهاداتِ شُهودِ العِيانِ. أَكَّدَ الدِّفاعُ عَلى حُقوقِ المُتَّهَمِ وَقَرينَةِ البَراءَةِ، مِمّا دَفَعَ القاضِيَ لِإصْدارِ حُكْمٍ بِالبَراءَةِ.

After a trial with many twists, the court acquitted a young man of an honor crime charge. The acquittal was based on the lack of criminal evidence and conflicting eyewitness testimonies. The defense emphasized the accused's rights and the presumption of innocence, leading the judge to issue an acquittal verdict.

أَصْدَرَتِ المَحْكَمَةُ حُكْمًا بِالإعْدامِ عَلى مُدانٍ بِارْتِكابِ جَريمَةِ قَتْلٍ بَشِعَةٍ. جاءَ الحُكْمُ النِّهائِيُّ بَعْدَ مُداوَلاتٍ طَويلَةٍ مِنْ هَيْئَةِ المُحَلَّفينَ وَتَقْديمِ دَليلٍ جِنائِيٍّ دامِغٍ. كانَتْ حِمايَةُ الشُّهودِ أَوْلَوِيّةً خِلالَ المُحاكَمَةِ، وَسُمِحَ لِلْمَحْكومِ عَلَيْهِ بِطَلَبِ الاِسْتِئْنافِ ضِدَّ الحُكْمِ.

The court issued a death sentence for a convict found guilty of committing a heinous murder. The final verdict came after lengthy deliberations by the jury and the presentation of conclusive criminal evidence. Witness protection was a priority during the trial, and the convicted was allowed to appeal the sentence.

في حادِثَةٍ غَيْرِ مَأْلوفَةٍ، خَفَّفَتِ المَحْكَمَةُ عُقوبَةَ سَجينٍ مَحْكومٍ عَلَيْهِ بِالسَّجْنِ المُؤَبَّدِ إلى 15 عامًا بَعْدَ إعادَةِ مُحاكَمَةٍ بِناءً عَلى أَدِلّةٍ جَديدةٍ. كَشَفَ الاِسْتِجْوابُ الجَديدُ لِشاهِدٍ رَئيسِيٍّ عَنْ مَعْلوماتٍ أَدَّتْ إلى إعادَةِ تَقْييمِ القَضِيّةِ، مِمّا نَتَجَ عَنْهُ تَخْفيفُ العُقوبَةِ.

In an unusual incident, the court reduced the life sentence of a prisoner to 15 years after a retrial based on new evidence. The new interrogation of a key witness revealed information that led to a reassessment of the case, resulting in the sentence reduction.

أَدانَتِ المَحْكَمَةُ اثْنَيْنِ مِنَ المُوَظَّفِينَ العُمومِيِّينَ بِخَرْقِ قانونِ مُكافَحَةِ الفَسادِ، وَحَكَمَتْ عَلَيْهِما بِالسَّجْنِ لِمُدَّةِ خَمْسِ سَنَواتٍ وَدَفْعِ تَعْويضاتٍ مالِيَّةٍ لِلدَّوْلَةِ. جاءَ الحُكْمُ بَعْدَ تَحْقيقٍ دَقيقٍ كَشَفَ عَنِ اسْتِغْلالِ المَناصِبِ العامَّةِ لِأَغْراضٍ شَخْصِيَّةٍ، وَأَكَّدَ المُدَّعي العامُّ عَلى ضَرورَةِ تَنْفيذِ القانونِ بِحَزْمٍ لِحِمايَةِ المالِ العامِّ.

The court convicted two public officials of breaching the anti-corruption law, sentencing them to five years in prison and ordering them to pay financial compensation to the state. The verdict followed a thorough investigation that exposed the exploitation of public positions for personal gain, with the prosecutor general emphasizing the necessity of strictly enforcing the law to protect public funds.

10.1.2.2 Article: Corruption Case

Track **7**

مَحْكَمَةٌ أُرْدُنِّيَّةٌ تُصْدِرُ حُكْمًا تاريخِيًّا في قَضِيَّةِ فَسادٍ كَبيرَةٍ

عَمّانُ، الأُرْدُنُ - في حَدَثٍ لافِتٍ حَظِيَ بِاهْتِمامِ الرَّأْيِ العامِّ الأُرْدُنِّيِّ وَالدَّوْلِيِّ، أَصْدَرَتْ مَحْكَمَةٌ أُرْدُنِّيَّةٌ حُكْمًا بِالسَّجْنِ المُؤَبَّدِ عَلى رَجُلِ الأَعْمالِ البارِزِ، عِمادِ الرّاشِد، بَعْدَ إِدانَتِهِ في قَضِيَّةِ فَسادٍ مالِيٍّ وَإِداريٍّ كَبيرَةٍ شَهِدَتْها البِلادُ.

المُحاكَمَةُ الَّتي اسْتَمَرَّتْ لِعِدَّةِ أَشْهُرٍ، شَهِدَتِ اسْتِدْعاءَ عِدَّةِ شُهودِ عِيانٍ وَاسْتِجوابَهُمْ، حَيْثُ قَدَّموا شَهاداتٍ حاسِمَةً أَثْبَتَتْ تَوَرُّطَ الرّاشِد في مُمارَساتٍ غَيْرِ قانونِيَّةٍ تَضَمَّنَتْ تَبْديدَ المالِ العامِّ واسْتِغْلالَ السُّلْطَةِ لِأَغْراضٍ شَخْصِيَّةٍ. القاضي، خالِدِ النَّسورِ، نَطَقَ بِالحُكْمِ مُعْلِنًا أَنَّ الأَدِلَّةَ المُقَدَّمَةَ في المَحْكَمَةِ كانَتْ كافِيَةً لِإِثْباتِ ذَنْبِ المُتَّهَمِ.

جَرَتِ المُحاكَمَةُ في جَوٍّ مِنَ الشَّفافِيَّةِ وَالعَدالَةِ، مَعَ ضَمانِ حُقوقِ الدِّفاعِ العامِّ لِلْمُتَّهَمِ. كَما أَشادَ المُدَّعي العامُّ، يوسُفُ الخَوالِدَة، بِالإِجْراءاتِ القانونِيَّةِ الَّتي اتُّخِذَتْ لِضَمانِ مُحاكَمَةٍ عادِلَةٍ وَنَزيهَةٍ.

أَثارَ الحُكْمُ الصّادِرُ رُدودَ فِعْلٍ واسِعَةً في الأَوْساطِ القانونِيَّةِ وَالمُجْتَمَعِيَّةِ، حَيْثُ اعْتَبَرَهُ كَثيرونَ خُطْوَةً هامَّةً نَحْوَ تَرْسيخِ مَبادِئِ العَدالَةِ وَمُكافَحَةِ الفَسادِ في الأُرْدُنِّ. تَأْتي هذِهِ القَضِيَّةُ لِتُؤَكِّدَ الْتِزامَ الأُرْدُنِّ بِتَطْبيقِ القانونِ وَمُحاسَبَةِ المُخالِفينَ بِغَضِّ النَّظَرِ عَنْ مَراكِزِهِمْ أَوْ نُفوذِهِمْ.

في نِهايَةِ المُحاكَمَةِ، أَكَّدَ القاضي النَّسور عَلى أَهَمِّيَّةِ الحِفاظِ عَلى حُقوقِ الإِنْسانِ وَحُقوقِ الشُّهودِ، مُشَدِّدًا عَلى أَنَّ القَضاءَ الأُرْدُنِّيَّ مُسْتَمِرٌّ في سَعْيِهِ لِتَحْقيقِ العَدالَةِ وَتَطْبيقِ القانونِ بِكُلِّ شَفافِيَّةٍ وَحَزْمٍ.

Jordanian Court Issues Historic Verdict in Major Corruption Case

Amman, Jordan - In a significant event that garnered attention both nationally and internationally, a Jordanian court has sentenced the prominent businessman, Imad Al-Rashid, to life imprisonment after his conviction in a major financial and administrative corruption case that the country witnessed.

The trial, which lasted for several months, involved summoning and interrogating several eyewitnesses who provided crucial testimonies proving Al-Rashid's involvement in illegal practices including the embezzlement of public funds and the abuse of power for personal gain. Judge Khalid Al-Nasoor announced the verdict, stating that the evidence presented in court was sufficient to prove the guilt of the accused.

The trial took place in an atmosphere of transparency and justice, ensuring the public defense rights of the accused. The public prosecutor, Youssef Al-Khawaldeh, praised the legal procedures adopted to guarantee a fair and impartial trial.

The verdict sparked widespread reactions in legal and social circles, with many considering it a significant step towards establishing principles of justice and combating corruption in Jordan. This case affirms Jordan's commitment to enforcing the law and holding violators accountable, regardless of their positions or influence.

At the end of the trial, Judge Al-Nasoor emphasized the importance of preserving human rights and the rights of witnesses, asserting that the Jordanian judiciary continues its pursuit of justice and the application of the law with transparency and determination.

10.1.2.3 Historical Account: Mubarak's Trial

Track **8**

مُحاكَمَةُ مُبارَك: اسْتِعْراضٌ تاريخِيٌّ لِلْعَدالَةِ وَالجَدَلِ في مِصْرَ

في الرّابِعِ وَالعِشرينَ مِنْ مايو 2011، أَمَرَ الرَّئيسُ المِصرِيُّ الأَسْبَقُ، حُسني مُبارَك، بِالْوُقوفِ أَمامَ المَحْكَمَةِ، مُواجِهًا تُهَمَ القَتْلِ العَمْدِ لِلْمُتَظاهِرينَ السَّلْمِيّينَ خِلالَ الثَّوْرَةِ، وَهِيَ جَريمَةٌ قَدْ تُؤَدّي إِلى الحُكْمِ بِالإِعْدامِ. كَما وُجِّهَتْ إِلَيْهِ تُهَمُ الفَسادِ، وَإِساءَةِ اسْتِخْدامِ النُّفوذِ، وَالجَرائِمِ الماليَّةِ. في الثّامِنِ وَالعِشرينَ مِنْ مايو، تَمَّ تَغْريمُهُ لِإِلْحاقِهِ الضَّرَرَ بِالاِقْتِصادِ المِصْرِيِّ عَبْرَ إِغْلاقِ خِدْماتِ الإِنْتَرْنِتْ وَالهاتِفِ خِلالَ الاِحْتِجاجاتِ.

بَدَأَتْ مُحاكَمَةُ مُبارَك في الثّالِثِ مِنْ أَغُسْطُسَ 2011، حَيْثُ أَعْلَنَ بَراءَتَهُ. كانَتِ الجَلَساتُ الأولى لِلْمُحاكَمَةِ عَلَنِيَّةً، لَكِنْ تَمَّ إِغْلاقُ الجَلَساتِ لاحِقًا أَمامَ وَسائِلِ الإِعْلامِ. في يونيو 2012، حُكِمَ عَلَيْهِ بِالسِّجْنِ المُؤَبَّدِ لِعَدَمِ إيقافِهِ قَتْلَ المُتَظاهِرينَ، عَلى الرَّغْمِ مِنْ عَدَمِ إِدانَتِهِ بِإِصْدارِ أَوامِرِ القَمْعِ. تَمَّ رَفْضُ التُّهَمِ المُتَعَلِّقَةِ بِالاِحْتِيالِ الاِقْتِصادِيِّ وَالفَسادِ، وَبُرِّئَتْ ساحَةُ أَبْنائِهِ لِعَدَمِ كِفايَةِ الأَدِلَّةِ.

في يَنايَرَ 2013، أَلْغَتْ مَحْكَمَةُ الاِسْتِئْنافِ حُكْمَهُ المُؤَبَّدَ، مِمّا أَدّى إِلى إِعادَةِ المُحاكَمَةِ. تَمَّ إِطْلاقُ سَراحِ مُبارَك لِفَتْرَةٍ وَجيزَةٍ في أُغُسْطُسَ 2013 وَلَكِنْ تَمَّ وَضْعُهُ قَيْدَ الإِقامَةِ الجَبْرِيَّةِ. في مايو 2014، أُدينَ بِالاِخْتِلاسِ وَحُكِمَ عَلَيْهِ بِالسِّجْنِ لِمُدَّةِ ثَلاثِ سَنَواتٍ، مَعَ فَرْضِ غَراماتٍ إِضافيَّةٍ.

في نوفَمْبَرَ 2014، تَمَّ إِسْقاطُ تُهَمِ المُؤامَرَةِ لِقَتْلِ المُتَظاهِرينَ، وَأَسْفَرَتْ إِعادَةُ المُحاكَمَةِ حَوْلَ تُهَمِ الاِخْتِلاسِ في مايو 2015 عَنْ حُكْمٍ بِالسِّجْنِ لِثَلاثِ سَنَواتٍ عَلى مُبارَك وَأَرْبَعِ سَنَواتٍ لِأَبْنائِهِ، مَعَ إِمْكانِيَّةِ احْتِسابِ الوَقْتِ الَّذي

قَضَوْهُ بِالْفِعْلِ فِي الحَبْسِ. أَدَّى هَذَا الحُكْمُ إِلَى امْتِعاضٍ عامٍّ، مِمَّا يَعْكِسُ الجَدَلَ وَالِانْقِسامَ المُسْتَمِرَّ فِي المُجْتَمَعِ المِصْرِيِّ بِشَأْنِ إِرْثِ مُبارَك وَالمُساءَلَةِ.

Mubarak's Trial: A Historical Review of Justice and Controversy in Egypt

On May 24, 2011, the former Egyptian President, Hosni Mubarak, was ordered to stand trial, facing charges of premeditated murder of peaceful protesters during the revolution, a crime that could lead to the death penalty. He was also charged with corruption, abuse of power, and financial crimes. On May 28, he was fined for damaging the Egyptian economy by shutting down internet and telephone services during the protests.

Mubarak's trial began on August 3, 2011, when he declared his innocence. The initial sessions of the trial were public, but later sessions were closed to the media. In June 2012, he was sentenced to life imprisonment for not stopping the killing of protesters, despite not being convicted of issuing orders for suppression. Charges related to economic fraud and corruption were dismissed, and his sons were acquitted due to insufficient evidence.

In January 2013, an appeals court overturned his life sentence, leading to a retrial. Mubarak was briefly released in August 2013 but was then placed under house arrest. In May 2014, he was convicted of embezzlement and sentenced to three years in prison, along with additional fines.

In November 2014, charges of conspiracy to kill protesters were dropped, and the retrial on embezzlement charges in May 2015 resulted in a three-year prison sentence for Mubarak and four years for his sons, with the possibility of crediting the time already spent in detention. This verdict led to public discontent, reflecting the ongoing debate and division in Egyptian society regarding Mubarak's legacy and accountability.

10.1.3 Prisons and Corrections

Track **9**

أَعادَ تَأْهِيلًا

to rehabilitate　　　　　إِعادَةٌ •

أَعادَ البَرْنامَجُ التَّأْهِيلِيُّ تَأْهِيلَ السُّجَناءِ، مِمَّا ساعَدَهُمْ عَلَى تَطْوِيرِ مَهاراتٍ جَدِيدَةٍ لِلْحَياةِ بَعْدَ الإِفْراجِ.

The rehabilitation program rehabilitated the prisoners, helping them develop new life skills for after their release.

أُعِيدَ تَأْهِيلُهُ

to be rehabilitated　　　　إِعادَةٌ •

بَعْدَ عَمَلِيَّةِ التَّأْهِيلِ الطَّوِيلَةِ، أُعِيدَ تَأْهِيلُ السَّجِينِ وَأَصْبَحَ نَمُوذَجًا لِلسُّلُوكِ الإِيجابِيِّ.

After the lengthy rehabilitation process, the prisoner was rehabilitated and became a model of positive behavior.

to be released

• إِفْراجٌ

أُفْرِجَ عَنْهُ

أُفْرِجَ عَنِ السَّجينِ بَعْدَ قَضاءِ ثُلُثَيْ مُدَّةِ عُقوبَتِهِ نَظيرَ حُسْنِ سُلوكِهِ.

The prisoner was released after serving two-thirds of his sentence due to good behavior.

to rehabilitate

• تَأْهيلٌ

أَهَّلَ

خَصَّصَتِ الحُكومَةُ تَمْويلًا لِإِعادَةِ تَأْهيلِ الأَفْرادِ المُدانينَ وَإِدْماجِهِمْ مَرَّةً أُخْرى في المُجْتَمَعِ.

The government has allocated funds to rehabilitate convicted individuals and integrate them back into society.

reform

إِصْلاحٌ

يَهْدُفُ الإِصْلاحُ في نِظامِ السُّجونِ إِلى تَحْسينِ ظُروفِ الاحْتِجازِ وَتَقْليلِ مُعَدَّلاتِ العَوْدَةِ لِلْجَريمَةِ.

The reform in the prison system aims to improve detention conditions and reduce recidivism rates.

rehabilitation of prisoners

إِصْلاحُ وَتَأْهيلُ سُجَناءَ

تَمَّ إِنْشاءُ بَرامِجِ إِصْلاحٍ وَتَأْهيلِ السُّجَناءِ لِمُساعَدَتِهِمْ عَلى اكْتِسابِ مَهاراتٍ جَديدَةٍ.

Programs for the reform and rehabilitation of prisoners were established to help them acquire new skills.

correctional

إِصْلاحِيٌّ

تَتَبَنّى بَعْضُ السُّجونِ نَموذَجًا إِصْلاحِيًّا يُرَكِّزُ عَلى التَّعْليمِ وَالعَمَلِ كَوَسائِلَ لِلتَّأْهيلِ.

Some prisons adopt a reformative model focusing on education and work as means of rehabilitation.

correctional facility

إِصْلاحِيَّةٌ

تَمَّ نَقْلُ السُّجَناءِ إِلى الإِصْلاحِيَّةِ الجَديدَةِ الَّتي تُوَفِّرُ بَرامِجَ تَعْليمِيَّةً وَتَدْريبًا مِهْنِيًّا.

The prisoners were transferred to the new correctional facility that offers educational programs and vocational training.

إِعَادَةُ تَأْهِيلٍ

rehabilitation

تُعْتَبَرُ إِعَادَةُ تَأْهِيلِ السُّجَنَاءِ جُزْءًا أَسَاسِيًّا مِنْ عَمَلِيَّةِ الإِصْلَاحِ العِقَابِيِّ لِلْحَدِّ مِنَ الجَرِيمَةِ.

Rehabilitating prisoners is considered a fundamental part of the correctional reform process to reduce crime.

إِفْرَاجٌ

release

قَرَّرَتِ اللَّجْنَةُ الإِفْرَاجَ عَنِ السَّجِينِ بَعْدَ مُرَاجَعَةِ سُلُوكِهِ دَاخِلَ السِّجْنِ.

The committee decided to release the prisoner after reviewing his behavior inside the prison.

إِفْرَاجٌ مَشْرُوطٌ

parole

تَمَّ مَنْحُ الإِفْرَاجِ المَشْرُوطِ لِلْمُدَانِ بِنَاءً عَلَى تَقْيِيمٍ إِيجَابِيٍّ لِتَحَسُّنِ سُلُوكِهِ.

Conditional release was granted to the convict based on a positive assessment of his improved behavior.

اِحْتَجَزَ • اِحْتِجَازٌ

to detain

اِحْتَجَزَتِ الشُّرْطَةُ عَدَدًا مِنَ المُشْتَبَهِ بِهِمْ بَعْدَ سِلْسِلَةٍ مِنَ الحَمَلَاتِ المُنَسَّقَةِ فِي جَمِيعِ أَنْحَاءِ المَدِينَةِ.

The police detained several suspects following a series of coordinated raids across the city.

أُعْتُقِلَ • اِعْتِقَالٌ

to be arrested

أُعْتُقِلَ الفَاعِلُ بَعْدَ تَحْقِيقٍ أَظْهَرَ دَلَائِلَ عَلَى ارْتِكَابِهِ لِلْجَرِيمَةِ.

The perpetrator was arrested after an investigation revealed evidence of his crime.

بَرْنَامَجُ إِعَادَةِ تَأْهِيلٍ • بَرَامِجُ

rehabilitation program

يُشَارِكُ السُّجَنَاءُ فِي بَرْنَامَجِ إِعَادَةِ تَأْهِيلٍ لِتَعَلُّمِ مَهَارَاتٍ جَدِيدَةٍ وَتَحْسِينِ سُلُوكِيَّاتِهِمْ.

Prisoners participate in a rehabilitation program to learn new skills and improve their behavior.

discipline

تَأْدِيبٌ

تَمَّ تَأْدِيبُ السُّجَناءِ المُتَوَرِّطِينَ في الشَّغَبِ لِضَمانِ النِّظامِ داخِلَ السِّجْنِ.

Prisoners involved in the riot were disciplined to ensure order within the prison.

correspondence

تَبادُلُ رَسائِلَ

تَبادَلَ السُّجَناءُ الرَّسائِلَ مَعَ عائِلاتِهِمْ كَجُزْءٍ مِنْ بَرْنامَجِ دَعْمٍ نَفْسِيٍّ.

Prisoners exchanged letters with their families as part of a psychological support program.

improving prison conditions

تَحْسِينُ ظُروفِ السُّجونِ

تُرَكِّزُ الجُهودُ عَلَى تَحْسِينِ ظُروفِ السُّجونِ لِتَوْفِيرِ بيئَةٍ أَكْثَرَ إِنْسانِيَّةً لِلسُّجَناءِ.

Efforts are focused on improving prison conditions to provide a more humane environment for prisoners.

to rebel, riot

تَمَرُّدَ • تَمَرُّدٌ

وَقَعَ تَمَرُّدٌ داخِلَ السِّجْنِ كَرَدِّ فِعْلٍ عَلَى الظُّروفِ القاسِيَةِ وَالمُعامَلَةِ غَيْرِ العادِلَةِ.

A rebellion occurred inside the prison as a reaction to harsh conditions and unfair treatment.

execution of a sentence

تَنْفِيذُ حُكْمٍ

تَمَّ تَنْفِيذُ حُكْمِ السِّجْنِ بِحَقِّ الجاني بَعْدَ إِدانَتِهِ بِجَرِيمَةِ القَتْلِ العَمْدِ.

The prison sentence was executed against the perpetrator after his conviction for premeditated murder.

prison guard

حارِسُ سِجْنٍ • حُرّاسٌ

عَمِلَ حارِسُ السِّجْنِ لِأَكْثَرَ مِنْ عِشْرِينَ عامًا في السِّجْنِ، مُشْرِفًا عَلَى أَمْنِ الزَّنازِينِ.

The guard worked in the prison for over twenty years, overseeing the security of the cells.

solitary confinement

حَبْسٌ انْفِرادِيٌّ

أُمِرَ بِالْحَبْسِ الانْفِرادِيِّ لِلسَّجينِ بِسَبَبِ مُحاوَلَتِهِ الهُروبَ مِنَ السِّجْنِ.

Solitary confinement was ordered for the prisoner due to his escape attempt.

guarding, custody

حِراسَةٌ

أُوكِلَتْ حِراسَةُ المُتَّهَمِ الخَطيرِ إلى فَريقٍ مُتَخَصِّصٍ داخِلَ السِّجْنِ.

The custody of the dangerous accused was entrusted to a specialized team inside the prison.

to guard

حَرَسَ • حِراسَةٌ

حَرَسَ الضّابِطُ مَدْخَلَ المَحْكَمَةِ خِلالَ المُحاكَمَةِ الهامَّةِ.

The officer guarded the entrance of the court during the important trial.

to sentence

حَكَمَ • حُكْمٌ

حَكَمَ القاضي عَلى الفاعِلِ بِالسَّجْنِ المُؤَبَّدِ بِدونِ إمْكانِيَّةِ الإفْراجِ المَشْروطِ.

The judge sentenced the perpetrator to life imprisonment without the possibility of parole.

to be sentenced

حُكِمَ عَلَيْهِ • حُكْمٌ

حُكِمَ عَلى المُتَّهَمِ بِالخِدْمَةِ العامَّةِ كَعُقوبَةٍ بَديلَةٍ لِلْحَبْسِ.

The accused was sentenced to community service as an alternative punishment to imprisonment.

to be under surveillance

خَضَعَ لِمُراقَبَةٍ • خُضوعٌ

خَضَعَ المُجْرِمُ السّابِقُ لِلْمُراقَبَةِ بَعْدَ إطْلاقِ سَراحِهِ المَشْروطِ.

The former criminal was under surveillance after his conditional release.

to correspond

راسَلَ • مُراسَلَةٌ

راسَلَ السَّجينُ عائِلَتَهُ بِانْتِظامٍ لِلْحِفاظِ عَلى الاتِّصالِ خِلالَ فَتْرَةِ حَبْسِهِ.

The prisoner corresponded with his family regularly to maintain contact during his incarceration.

to monitor, watch

مُراقَبَة •

راقَبَ

راقَبَتِ الشُّرْطَةُ تَحَرُّكاتِ العِصابَةِ لِعِدَّةِ أَشْهُرٍ قَبْلَ القِيامِ بِالمُداهَمَةِ.

The police monitored the gang's movements for several months before conducting the raid.

surveillance

رِقابَةٌ

تَمَّتِ الرِّقابَةُ عَلى السُّجَناءِ لِضَمانِ عَدَمِ وُجودِ أَنْشِطَةٍ مُخالِفَةٍ داخِلَ السِّجْنِ.

Prisoners were surveilled to ensure no illicit activities occurred within the prison.

to visit

زِيارَةٌ •

زارَ

زارَ المُحامي مُوَكِّلَهُ في السِّجْنِ لِمُناقَشَةِ تَفاصيلِ الاسْتِئْنافِ.

The lawyer visited his client in prison to discuss the details of the appeal.

cell

زِنْزاناتٌ / زَنازينَ •

زِنْزانَةٌ

أُغْلِقَتْ زِنْزانَةُ السَّجينِ بَعْدَ إعادَتِهِ إلَيْها عَقِبَ جَلْسَةِ المُحاكَمَةِ.

The prisoner's cell was locked after he was returned to it following the court session.

increasing prison capacity

زِيادَةُ السَّعَةِ الاسْتيعابِيَّةِ لِلسُّجونِ

تُواجِهُ السُّلُطاتُ تَحَدِّيًا في زِيادَةِ السَّعَةِ الاسْتيعابِيَّةِ لِلسُّجونِ دونَ المَساسِ بِالظُّروفِ المَعيشِيَّةِ.

Authorities face a challenge in increasing prison capacity without compromising living conditions.

visit

زِيارَةٌ

جَرَتْ زِيارَةُ السَّجينِ مِنْ قِبَلِ أَفْرادِ عائِلَتِهِ في يَوْمِ الزِّيارَةِ المُخَصَّصِ.

The prisoner was visited by his family members on the designated visiting day.

> Note the use of the verb جَرى to form a passive structure in the example sentence above. (→ Refer to the note on p. 117 of Book 2 for more on this structure.)

to imprison

سَجْنٌ •

سَجَنَ

تَمَّ سَجْنُ المُشْتَبَهِ بِهِ لِمُدَّةِ عَشْرِ سَنواتٍ بَعْدَ إدانَتِهِ بِتُهَمِ احْتِيالٍ مُتَعَدِّدَةٍ.

The suspect was imprisoned for ten years following conviction on multiple charges of fraud.

prison, jail

سِجْنٌ • سُجونٌ

نُقِلَ المُتَّهَمُ إلى السِّجْنِ لِبَدْءِ تَنْفيذِ عُقوبَتِهِ بَعْدَ النُّطْقِ بِالحُكْمِ.

The accused was transferred to prison to begin serving his sentence after the sentencing.

life imprisonment

سِجْنٌ مُؤَبَّدٌ

قَضى السَّجينُ سَجْنًا مُؤَبَّدًا خَلْفَ القُضْبانِ بَعْدَ إدانَتِهِ في جَريمَةِ قَتْلٍ.

The inmate served a life sentence behind bars after being convicted of murder.

incarcerated

سَجينٌ • سُجَناءُ / سَجينونَ

يُواجِهُ الأَفْرادُ السُّجَناءُ تَحَدِّياتٍ كَبيرَةً في الحِفاظِ عَلى العَلاقاتِ الأُسَرِيَّةِ وَالاجْتِماعِيَّةِ.

Incarcerated individuals face significant challenges in maintaining family and social relationships.

political prisoner

سَجينٌ سِياسِيٌّ

أُفْرِجَ عَنِ السَّجينِ السِّياسِيِّ بَعْدَ حَمْلَةٍ دَوْلِيَّةٍ ضَغَطَتْ لِإطْلاقِ سَراحِهِ.

The political prisoner was released after an international campaign pressured for his release.

to participate in a program

شارَكَ في بَرْنامَجٍ • مُشارَكَةٌ

شارَكَ السَّجينُ في بَرْنامَجِ إعادَةِ التَّأْهيلِ لِتَحْسينِ فُرَصِهِ في الإفْراجِ المَشْروطِ.

The inmate participated in a rehabilitation program to improve his chances of parole.

to enforce the law

طَبَّقَ القانونَ • تَطْبيقٌ

طَبَّقَ القاضي القانونَ بِحَزْمٍ خِلالَ المُحاكَمَةِ، مُؤَكِّدًا عَلى أَهَمِّيَّةِ العَدالَةِ.

The judge applied the law firmly during the trial, emphasizing the importance of justice.

fair

عادِلٌ

وُصِفَتِ المُحاكَمَةُ بِأَنَّها عادِلَةٌ نَظَرًا لِاعْتِمادِها عَلى الأَدِلَّةِ المَوْثوقَةِ وَشَفافِيَّةِ الإجْراءاتِ.

The trial was described as fair due to its reliance on reliable evidence and transparency of procedures.

to punish	• عِقابٌ / مُعاقَبَةٌ	عاقَبَ

عاقَبَ القاضي السَّجينَ الهارِبَ بِإضافَةِ سِتَّةِ أَشْهُرٍ إلى مُدَّةِ عُقوبَتِهِ.

The judge punished the escaping prisoner by adding six months to his sentence.

riot, rebellion	عِصْيانٌ

وَقَعَ عِصْيانٌ داخِلَ السِّجْنِ حَيْثُ حاوَلَ السُّجَناءُ الاِحْتِجاجَ عَلى الظُّروفِ القاسِيَةِ.

A rebellion occurred in the prison as inmates tried to protest against harsh conditions.

punishment, sentence	عُقوبَةٌ

تَمَّ تَحْديدُ عُقوبَةِ السَّرِقَةِ بِخَمْسِ سَنَواتٍ مِنَ السِّجْنِ وَغَرامَةٍ مالِيَّةٍ.

The punishment for theft was set at five years in prison and a financial fine.

violent	• عُنْفٌ	عَنيفٌ

اِنْدَلَعَتْ أَعْمالٌ عَنيفَةٌ داخِلَ السِّجْنِ، مِمّا اسْتَدْعى تَدَخُّلَ الحُرّاسِ بِسُرْعَةٍ.

Violent acts broke out inside the prison, necessitating quick intervention by the guards.

to impose a penalty	• فَرْضٌ	فَرَضَ عُقوبَةً

فَرَضَ القاضي عُقوبَةً قاسِيَةً عَلى المُتَّهَمِ بِسَبَبِ خُطورَةِ الجَريمَةِ.

The judge imposed a harsh penalty on the accused due to the severity of the crime.

prison yard	• أَفْنِيَةٌ	فِناءٌ

يُسْتَخْدَمُ فِناءُ السِّجْنِ لِتَوْفيرِ وَقْتٍ تَرْفيهِيٍّ لِلسُّجَناءِ، لَكِنَّهُ تَحْتَ المُراقَبَةِ الدَّقيقَةِ.

The prison yard is used to provide recreational time for inmates, but it is under close surveillance.

harsh	قاسٍ

وَصَفَ المُنْتَقِدونَ الحُكْمَ بِأَنَّهُ قاسٍ لِلْغايَةِ وَغَيْرُ مُتَناسِبٍ مَعَ الجُرْمِ المُرْتَكَبِ.

Critics described the sentence as excessively harsh and disproportionate to the committed offense.

قَضى عُقوبَةً
• قَضاءٌ

to serve a sentence

قَضى السَّجينُ عُقوبَتَهُ البالِغَةَ عَشْرَ سَنَواتٍ وَأُطْلِقَ سَراحُهُ بَعْدَ ذَلِكَ.

The prisoner served his ten-year sentence and was released thereafter.

مُؤْسِفٌ

regrettable

وُصِفَ الحادِثُ داخِلَ السَّجْنِ بِأَنَّهُ مُؤْسِفٌ، مِمّا دَعا إلى مُراجَعَةِ إجْراءاتِ الأَمانِ.

The incident inside the prison was described as unfortunate, calling for a review of safety procedures.

مُدانٌ

convict

قَضى المُدانُ في قَضِيَّةِ الاِحْتِيالِ المالِيِّ سَنَتَيْنِ في السِّجْنِ قَبْلَ الإفْراجِ المَشْروطِ.

The convict in the financial fraud case spent two years in prison before being paroled.

مُراقِبٌ

watchman, guard

يَعْمَلُ المُراقِبُ في السِّجْنِ عَلى ضَمانِ الأَمانِ وَالنِّظامِ بَيْنَ السُّجَناءِ.

The watchman in the prison works to ensure safety and order among the inmates.

مُراقَبَةٌ

surveillance

تُعَدُّ مُراقَبَةُ السُّجَناءِ جُزْءًا أَساسِيًّا مِنْ إجْراءاتِ الأَمانِ داخِلَ السُّجونِ.

Monitoring prisoners is an essential part of security procedures inside prisons.

مَسْجونٌ
• مَسْجونونَ / مَساجينَ

imprisoned

تَمَّ الاِحْتِفاظُ بِالمَسْجونِ في الزِّنْزانَةِ الاِنْفِرادِيَّةِ بَعْدَ مُحاوَلَتِهِ العُنْفَ ضِدَّ حارِسِ السِّجْنِ.

The imprisoned individual was kept in solitary confinement after attempting violence against a prison guard.

detainee

مُعْتَقَلٌ

تَمَّ احْتِجازُ المُعْتَقَلِ في مَرْكَزٍ لِلتَّوْقيفِ الأَوَّلِيِّ قَبْلَ نَقْلِهِ إلى السِّجْنِ الرَّسْمِيِّ.

The detainee was held in a preliminary detention center before being transferred to the official prison.

prison inmate

نَزيلُ سِجْنٍ • نُزَلاءُ

طَلَبَ نَزيلُ السِّجْنِ مُراجَعَةَ قَضِيَّتِهِ بِسَبَبِ وُجودِ أَدِلَّةٍ جَديدَةٍ قَدْ تُثْبِتُ بَراءَتَهُ.

The prison inmate requested a review of his case due to new evidence that might prove his innocence.

to advise

نَصَحَ • نُصْحٌ

نَصَحَ الطَّبيبُ النَّفْسِيُّ النَّزيلَ بِالمُشارَكَةِ في بَرامِجِ إعادَةِ التَّأْهيلِ داخِلَ السِّجْنِ.

The psychologist advised the inmate to participate in rehabilitation programs inside the prison.

to organize (activities or protests)

نَظَّمَ • تَنْظيمٌ

نَظَّمَ السُّجَناءُ داخِلَ السِّجْنِ مُظاهَرَةً سِلْمِيَّةً لِلاحْتِجاجِ عَلى ظُروفِ الاحْتِجازِ.

The inmates organized a peaceful protest inside the prison to object to the detention conditions.

to carry out a sentence

نَفَّذَ حُكْمًا • تَنْفيذٌ

اِتَّخَذَتِ السُّلُطاتُ قَرارًا بِتَنْفيذِ الحُكْمِ الصّادِرِ مِنَ المَحْكَمَةِ، مِمّا يُمَثِّلُ نِهايَةً لِعَمَلِيَّةٍ قانونِيَّةٍ طَويلَةٍ.

The authorities have decided to carry out the sentence handed down by the court, marking the culmination of a lengthy legal process.

to escape

هَرَبَ • هُروبٌ

هَرَبَ السَّجينُ مِنَ السِّجْنِ بِاسْتِخْدامِ أَدَواتٍ بِدائِيَّةٍ لِقَطْعِ الأَسْلاكِ الشّائِكَةِ.

The prisoner escaped from the prison using primitive tools to cut through the barbed wire.

escape

هُروبٌ

وَقَعَ حادِثُ هُروبٍ كَبيرٍ مِنَ السِّجْنِ، مِمّا أَدّى إلى تَشْديدِ الإجْراءاتِ الأَمْنِيَّةِ.

A major prison break occurred, leading to tightened security measures.

10.1.3.1 Mini-Articles

أَعْلَنَتِ السُّلُطاتُ الأُرْدُنِيَّةُ عَنْ تَبَنِّي بَرْنامَجٍ جَديدٍ لِإِصْلاحِ وَتَأْهيلِ السُّجَناءِ، يَهْدُفُ إِلى تَحْسينِ ظُروفِ السُّجونِ وَتَأْهيلِ النُّزَلاءِ لِإِعادَةِ دَمْجِهِمْ في المُجْتَمَعِ. يَشْمَلُ البَرْنامَجُ وَرَشَ عَمَلٍ تَعْليمِيَّةً وَتَدْريبًا مِهْنِيًّا لِتَمْكينِ السُّجَناءِ مِنَ اكْتِسابِ مَهاراتٍ جَديدَةٍ.

The Jordanian authorities have announced the adoption of a new program for the reform and rehabilitation of prisoners, aimed at improving prison conditions and preparing inmates for reintegration into society. The program includes educational workshops and vocational training to enable prisoners to acquire new skills.

في سِجْنٍ مِصْرِيٍّ، فُرِضَتْ حِراسَةٌ مُشَدَّدَةٌ بَعْدَ مُحاوَلَةِ هُروبٍ فاشِلَةٍ قامَ بِها عَدَدٌ مِنَ السُّجَناءِ. وَقَدْ تَمَّ إِحْباطُ المُحاوَلَةِ بِفَضْلِ يَقَظَةِ حُرّاسِ السِّجْنِ، مِمّا دَفَعَ الإِدارَةَ إِلى تَعْزيزِ الإِجْراءاتِ الأَمْنِيَّةِ وَزِيادَةِ السَّعَةِ الاسْتيعابِيَّةِ لِمَنْعِ أَيِّ عِصْيانٍ مُسْتَقْبَلِيٍّ.

In an Egyptian prison, tight security was imposed after a failed escape attempt by several inmates. The attempt was thwarted thanks to the vigilance of the prison guards, prompting the administration to strengthen security measures and increase capacity to prevent future insurrections.

في تَطَوُّرٍ مُؤْسِفٍ، حُكِمَ عَلى ناشِطٍ سِياسِيٍّ في سوريا بِالسِّجْنِ المُؤَبَّدِ بَعْدَ مُحاكَمَةٍ أَثارَتْ جَدَلًا واسِعًا. النّاشِطُ، الَّذي خَضَعَ لِلْمُراقَبَةِ الدَّقيقَةِ قَبْلَ الاعْتِقالِ، أُدينَ بِتُهَمٍ تَتَعَلَّقُ بِالعِصْيانِ وَالتَّحْريضِ عَلى العُنْفِ، وَسَطَ انْتِقاداتٍ دَوْلِيَّةٍ لِعَدَمِ عَدالَةِ الإِجْراءاتِ.

In a regrettable development, a political activist in Syria was sentenced to life imprisonment after a trial that sparked widespread controversy. The activist, who was closely monitored before being arrested, was convicted on charges related to dissent and inciting violence, amid international criticism of the unfair proceedings.

في لُبْنانَ، أَظْهَرَ بَرْنامَجُ إِعادَةِ تَأْهيلٍ مُطَبَّقٍ في أَحَدِ السُّجونِ نَتائِجَ إيجابِيَّةً، حَيْثُ شارَكَ عَدَدٌ مِنَ النُّزَلاءِ في أَنْشِطَةٍ تَعْليمِيَّةٍ واجْتِماعِيَّةٍ تَهْدُفُ إِلى تَأْهيلِهِمْ وَإِصْلاحِ سُلوكِهِمْ. تَمَّ رَصْدُ تَحَسُّنٍ مَلْحوظٍ في تَصَرُّفاتِ السُّجَناءِ الَّذينَ شارَكوا في البَرْنامَجِ.

In Lebanon, a rehabilitation program implemented in one of the prisons showed positive results, with several inmates participating in educational and social activities aimed at rehabilitating and reforming their behavior. A noticeable improvement in the behavior of prisoners who participated in the program was observed.

أُفْرِجَ عَنْ عِدَّةِ مُدانينَ في الإمارات بِموجِبِ حُكْمِ الإفْراجِ المَشْروطِ، بَعْدَ أَنْ أَثْبَتوا حُسْنَ السُّلوكِ وَالِالْتِزامِ بِالْقَوانينِ خِلالَ فَتْرَةِ حَبْسِهِمْ. تَمَّتِ المُوافَقَةُ عَلى إطْلاقِ سَراحِهِمْ بَعْدَ تَقْييمٍ دَقيقٍ مِنْ قِبَلِ لَجْنَةِ المُراقَبَةِ، وَسَيَسْتَمِرّونَ في خُضوعِهِمْ لِلْمُراقَبَةِ خارِجَ السِّجْنِ لِضَمانِ اسْتِمْرارِيَّةِ إصْلاحِهِمْ.

Several convicts in the United Arab Emirates were released on parole after they demonstrated good behavior and compliance with laws during their incarceration. Their release was approved after a thorough evaluation by the monitoring committee, and they will continue to be under surveillance outside the prison to ensure the continuity of their reform.

10.1.3.2 Informative Article: Harsh Prison Conditions

الظُّروفُ القاسِيَةُ في سِجْنِ العَقْرَبِ: تَحَدِّياتُ حُقوقِ الإنْسانِ في مِصْرَ

في الأَعْماقِ القاتِمَةِ لِسِجْنِ العَقْرَبِ، المَعْروفِ رَسْمِيًّا بِاسْمِ سِجْنِ طُرَةَ 992 ذي الحِراسَةِ المُشَدَّدَةِ، بَرَزَتْ تَقاريرُ مُثيرَةٌ لِلْقَلَقِ تُفيدُ بِوُقوعِ انْتِهاكاتٍ حادَّةٍ لِحُقوقِ الإنْسانِ، شَمِلَتِ التَّعْذيبَ، الِاعْتِداءَ الجِنْسِيَّ، وَالِاعْتِداءُ البَدَنِيُّ الشَّديدَ الَّذي أَدّى إلى إصاباتٍ وَكُسورٍ عَظيمَةٍ بَيْنَ السُّجَناءِ السِّياسِيّينَ. يُعَدُّ هَذا السِّجْنُ العالِيَ الأَمانِ رَمْزًا لِلنَّهْجِ القاسي في الِاحْتِجازِ وَمُعامَلَةِ المُعْتَقَلينَ في مِصْرَ.

تَحْتَ إشْرافِ وَزيرِ الداخِلِيَّةِ حَسَنٍ الأَلْفي خِلالَ عَهْدِ حُسْني مُبارَك، صُمِّمَ سِجْنُ العَقْرَبِ لِيَكونَ مَكانًا لِلْعُقوبَةِ الشَّديدَةِ، مَعَ مِعْمارِهِ الَّذي يَشْمَلُ أَرْبَعَةَ مَبانٍ رَئيسِيَّةٍ لِلِاحْتِجازِ مُرَتَّبَةٍ بِشَكْلِ حَرْفِ H ، مِمّا يُسَهِّلُ السَّيْطَرَةَ الصّارِمَةَ وَمُراقَبَةَ النُّزَلاءِ. زَنازينُهُ الضَّيِّقَةُ، وَالوُصولُ المَحْدودُ لِلضَّوْءِ الطَّبيعِيِّ، وَالساحاتُ المُغْلَقَةُ ذاتُ الحِراسَةِ المُكَثَّفَةِ، تُجَسِّدُ مُؤَسَّسَةً تُرَكِّزُ عَلى التَّأْديبِ أَكْثَرَ مِنْ إعادَةِ التَّأْهيلِ.

تَكْشِفُ شَهاداتٌ مِنْ مُعْتَقَلينَ سابِقينَ صورَةً مُرَوِّعَةً مِنَ الْحَياةِ داخِلَ العَقْرَبِ. تَصِفُ الرِّواياتُ المُعامَلَةَ اللّاإنْسانِيَّةَ، الَّتي تَشْمَلُ الضَّرْبَ، وَالحِرْمانَ مِنَ الضَّرورِيّاتِ كالطَّعامِ، وَتَقْييدَ الوُصولِ إلى فِناءِ السِّجْنِ لِلتَّمارينِ، مِمّا أَدّى إلى تَدَهْوُرِ الحالَةِ الصِّحِّيَّةِ وَالصَّدْمَةِ النَّفْسِيَّةِ لِلنُّزَلاءِ. تَتَناقَضُ هَذِهِ الظُّروفُ مَعَ المَبادِئِ الإصْلاحِيَّةِ، الَّتي تُؤَكِّدُ عَلى إعادَةِ تَأْهيلِ السُّجَناءِ، والمُعامَلَةِ الإنْسانِيَّةِ، وَتَوْفيرِ الفُرَصِ لِإعادَةِ دَمْجِهِمْ في المُجْتَمَعِ.

رَغْمَ أَنَّهُ يُعْتَبَرُ مُنْشَأَةً تَصْحيحِيَّةً، يَعْمَلُ سِجْنُ العَقْرَبِ بِوَصْفِهِ أَداةً لِلْقَمْعِ، تَخْدُمُ أَغْراضَ الأَمْنِ القَوْمِيِّ وَالسَّيْطَرَةِ السِّياسِيَّةِ. غِيابُ بَرامِجِ إعادَةِ التَّأْهيلِ المُؤَثِّرَةِ، مَعَ مُمارَسَةِ الحَبْسِ الِانْفِرادِيِّ وَالمُعامَلَةِ القاسِيَةِ لِلْمُعْتَقَلينَ، يُبْرِزُ الِانْحِرافَ عَنِ المَعاييرِ الدَّوْلِيَّةِ لِمُعامَلَةِ السُّجَناءِ.

يَجْري الإلْحاحُ عَلى ضَرورَةِ الإصْلاحاتِ العاجِلَةِ لِتَحْسينِ ظُروفِ السُّجونِ، وَضَمانِ مُعامَلَةٍ عادِلَةٍ لِلْمُعْتَقَلينَ، وَدَمْجِ بَرامِجِ إعادَةِ التَّأْهيلِ الَّتي تُهَيِّئُ النُّزَلاءِ لِإعادَةِ الِانْدِماجِ النِّهائِيِّ في المُجْتَمَعِ. الفَجْوَةُ الكَبيرَةُ بَيْنَ مَبادِئِ العَدالَةِ

التَّصْحِيحِيَّةِ وَوَاقِعِ سِجْنِ العَقْرَبِ تُبْرِزُ الحَاجَةَ إلى تَجْدِيدٍ شَامِلٍ في نِظَامِ السُّجونِ المِصْرِيِّ، مَعَ التَّوَجُّهِ نَحْوَ المُعَامَلَةِ الإِنْسَانِيَّةِ، واحْتِرَامِ حُقوقِ الإِنْسَانِ، وَإِعَادَةِ تَأْهِيلِ الجُنَاةِ.

يَظَلُّ سِجْنُ العَقْرَبِ في مِصْرَ مِثَالًا صَارِخًا عَلى التَّحَدِّيَاتِ الَّتي تُوَاجِهُ النِّظَامَ القَضَائِيَّ وَنِظَامَ السُّجونِ في البِلادِ، مِمَّا يَسْتَدْعِي نَظْرَةً مُعَمَّقَةً وَتَدَخُّلَاتٍ فَعَّالَةً لِضَمَانِ حُقوقِ السُّجَنَاءِ وَإِحْلَالِ نَهْجٍ إِصْلاحِيٍّ يَلِيقُ بِمَعَايِيرِ العَدَالَةِ الدَّوْلِيَّةِ.

Harsh Conditions in Al-Aqrab Prison: Human Rights Challenges in Egypt

In the dark depths of Al-Aqrab Prison, officially known as Tora 992 Maximum Security Prison, alarming reports have emerged of severe human rights violations, including torture, sexual assault, and severe physical abuse, leading to injuries and bone fractures among political prisoners. This high-security prison symbolizes the harsh approach to detention and treatment of detainees in Egypt.

Under the supervision of Minister of Interior Hassan Al-Alfi during Hosni Mubarak's regime, Al-Aqrab Prison was designed to be a place for severe punishment, with its architecture featuring four main detention buildings arranged in an H-shape, facilitating strict control and monitoring of inmates. Its narrow cells, limited access to natural light, and heavily guarded enclosed yards embody an institution focused more on discipline than rehabilitation.

Testimonies from former detainees reveal a horrifying picture of life inside Al-Aqrab. Accounts describe inhumane treatment, including beatings, deprivation of essentials like food, and restricted access to the prison yard for exercise, leading to deteriorating health conditions and psychological trauma for the inmates. These conditions are in stark contrast to reformative principles, which emphasize the rehabilitation of prisoners, humane treatment, and providing opportunities for their reintegration into society.

Although it is considered a correctional facility, Al-Aqrab Prison functions as a tool of repression, serving national security purposes and political control. The absence of effective rehabilitation programs, along with the practice of solitary confinement and harsh treatment of detainees, highlights a deviation from international standards for prisoner treatment.

Urgent reforms are called for to improve prison conditions, ensure fair treatment of detainees, and integrate rehabilitation programs that prepare inmates for eventual reintegration into society. The significant gap between the principles of correctional justice and the reality of Al-Aqrab Prison underscores the need for a comprehensive overhaul of the Egyptian prison system, with a shift towards humane treatment, respect for human rights, and the rehabilitation of offenders.

Al-Aqrab Prison in Egypt remains a glaring example of the challenges facing the country's judicial and prison systems, necessitating a thorough review and effective interventions to ensure prisoners' rights and the establishment of a reformative approach that meets international justice standards.

10.2 Legal Terminology and Court Procedures

10.2.1 Civil and Criminal Law

Track **12**

to issue a verdict   إِصْدَارٌ •   أَصْدَرَ حُكْمًا

أَصْدَرَ القاضي حُكْمًا بِتَعْويضِ الضَّحِيَّةِ في قَضِيَّةِ الإِهْمالِ الطِّبِّيِّ.

The judge issued a verdict to compensate the victim in the medical negligence case.

to accuse   اِدِّعاءٌ •   اِدَّعى

اِدَّعى المُدَّعي أَنَّ الشَّرِكَةَ اِنْتَهَكَتْ عَقْدَ العَمَلِ، مِمّا تَسَبَّبَ في خَسائِرَ مالِيَّةٍ لَهُ.

The plaintiff claimed that the company breached the employment contract, causing him financial losses.

to appeal   اِسْتِئْنافٌ •   اِسْتَأْنَفَ

اِسْتَأْنَفَ المَحْكومُ عَلَيْهِ القَرارَ أَمامَ مَحْكَمَةٍ أَعْلى طالِبًا إِعادَةَ النَّظَرِ في القَضِيَّةِ.

The convicted person appealed the decision to a higher court seeking a review of the case.

to cross-examine   اِسْتِجْوابٌ •   اِسْتَجْوَبَ

اِسْتَجْوَبَ المُحَقِّقونَ الشّاهِدَ الرَّئيسِيَّ في التَّحْقيقِ الجِنائِيِّ لِلْحُصولِ عَلى مَعْلوماتٍ هامَّةٍ.

The investigators interrogated the key witness in the criminal investigation to obtain crucial information.

criminal investigation   تَحْقيقٌ جِنائِيٌّ

يُعْتَبَرُ التَّحْقيقُ الجِنائِيُّ مُهِمًّا لِجَمْعِ الأَدِلَّةِ وَتَحْديدِ مُلابَساتِ الجَريمَةِ.

Criminal investigations are important for gathering evidence and determining the circumstances of the crime.

to undertake a legal obligation   تَعَهُّدٌ •   تَعَهَّدَ

تَعَهَّدَ المُتَّهَمُ بِالاِمْتِثالِ لِجَميعِ شُروطِ الإِفْراجِ المَشْروطِ.

The accused pledged to comply with all the conditions of parole.

to negotiate
تَفاوُضٌ •
تَفاوَضَ المُحامي عَلى تَسْوِيَةٍ خارِجَ المَحْكَمَةِ لِتَجَنُّبِ مُحاكَمَةٍ طَويلَةٍ وَمُكَلِّفَةٍ.

The lawyer negotiated an out-of-court settlement to avoid a lengthy and costly trial.

to mediate
تَوَسُّطٌ •
تَوَسَّطَ القاضي بَيْنَ الطَّرَفَيْنِ لِتَسْهيلِ حَلِّ النِّزاعِ في قَضِيَّةِ الطَّلاقِ.

The judge mediated between the parties to facilitate the resolution of the divorce case.

crime
جَرائِمُ •
في القَضِيَّةِ، وُجِّهَتْ تُهْمَةُ الاخْتِلاسِ ضِمْنَ الجَرائِمِ المَنْظورَةِ أمامَ المَحْكَمَةِ.

In the case, embezzlement was charged as part of the crimes considered by the court.

felony
جِنايَةٌ
تُعْتَبَرُ الجِنايَةُ جَريمَةً خَطيرَةً تَسْتَوْجِبُ عُقوبَةً أشَدَّ مُقارَنَةً بِالجُنْحَةِ.

A felony is considered a serious crime warranting a harsher punishment compared to a misdemeanor.

misdemeanor
جُنَحٌ •
تُمَثِّلُ الجُنْحَةُ مُخالَفَةً قانونِيَّةً أقَلَّ خُطورَةً وَعادَةً ما تُؤَدّي إلى عُقوباتٍ أخَفَّ.

A misdemeanor represents a less serious legal offense and usually results in lighter penalties.

human rights
pl.
جَرى الدِّفاعُ عَنْ حُقوقِ الإنْسانِ في المَحْكَمَةِ الدَّوْلِيَّةِ، مَعَ التَّرْكيزِ عَلى الحُرِّيّاتِ الأساسِيَّةِ.

Human rights were defended in the international court, focusing on fundamental freedoms.

verdict
أحْكامٌ •
أصْدَرَ القاضي حُكْمًا بِالسَّجْنِ لِمُدَّةِ عَشْرِ سَنَواتٍ في قَضِيَّةِ الاحْتِيالِ المالِيِّ.

The judge issued a ten-year prison sentence in the financial fraud case.

legal dispute — خِلافٌ قَضائِيٌّ

نَشَأَ خِلافٌ قَضائِيٌّ بَيْنَ الشَّرِكَتَيْنِ بِسَبَبِ بَراءاتِ الاِخْتِراعِ.

A legal dispute arose between the two companies over patents.

to defend — دافَعَ عَنْ • دِفاعٌ / مُدافَعَةٌ

دافَعَ المُحامي عَنِ المُتَّهَمِ، مُؤَكِّدًا عَلى ضَعْفِ الأَدِلَّةِ ضِدَّهُ.

The lawyer defended the accused, emphasizing the weakness of the evidence against him.

lawsuit — دَعْوى • دَعاوَى

رُفِعَتْ دَعْوى ضِدَّ البَلَدِيَّةِ بِسَبَبِ الإهْمالِ الَّذي أَدّى إلى حَوادِثَ خَطيرَةٍ.

A lawsuit was filed against the municipality due to negligence that led to serious accidents.

criminal case — دَعْوى جِنائِيَّةٌ

تَمَّتْ مُعالَجَةُ دَعْوى جِنائِيَّةٍ ضِدَّ المُتَّهَمِ بِتُهْمَةِ القَتْلِ العَمْدِ في المَحْكَمَةِ العُلْيا.

A criminal lawsuit against the accused for premeditated murder was handled in the Supreme Court.

civil suit — دَعْوى مَدَنِيَّةٌ

في الدَّعْوى المَدَنِيَّةِ، طالَبَ المُدَّعي بِتَعْويضٍ كَبيرٍ بِسَبَبِ الأَضْرارِ الَّتي لَحِقَتْ بِهِ.

In the civil lawsuit, the plaintiff demanded substantial compensation for the damages incurred.

public defense — دِفاعٌ عامٌّ

تَوَلّى مُحامي الدِّفاعِ العامّ قَضِيَّةَ الفُقَراءِ الَّذينَ لا يَسْتَطيعونَ تَحَمُّلَ تَكاليفِ التَّمْثيلِ القانونِيِّ.

The public defense attorney took on the case of the poor who cannot afford legal representation.

to pay compensation — دَفَعَ تَعْويضًا • دَفْعٌ

دَفَعَ المُتَّهَمُ تَعْويضًا لِلضَّحِيَّةِ بِناءً عَلى حُكْمِ المَحْكَمَةِ.

The accused paid compensation to the victim based on the court's judgment.

شَهادَةٌ

testimony

أَدَّتْ شَهادَةُ الشّاهِدِ الرَّئيسِيِّ إلى تَغْييرِ مَسارِ القَضِيَّةِ بِشَكْلٍ كَبيرٍ.

The testimony of the key witness significantly altered the course of the case.

قاضٍ • قُضاةٌ

judge

تَوَلَّى القاضي مَسْؤوليَّةَ النَّظَرِ في الأَدِلَّةِ وَإِصْدارِ الحُكْمِ النِّهائِيِّ.

The judge took responsibility for examining the evidence and issuing the final verdict.

قاضى • مُقاضاةٌ

to sue

قاضى النُّشَطاءُ البيئيُّون مَجْلِسَ المَدينَةِ بِسَبَبِ المُوافَقَةِ عَلى مَشْروعِ بِناءٍ مُثيرٍ لِلْجَدَلِ.

Environmental activists sued the city council over the approval of a controversial construction project.

قانونُ أَحْوالٍ شَخْصِيَّةٍ • قَوانينُ

personal status law

يُنَظِّمُ قانونُ الأَحْوالِ الشَّخْصِيَّةِ مَسائِلَ مِثلَ الزَّواجِ والطَّلاقِ والميراثِ.

Personal status law governs matters such as marriage, divorce, and inheritance.

قانونٌ جِنائِيٌّ • قَوانينُ

criminal law

يُعالِجُ القانونُ الجِنائِيُّ الجَرائِمَ وَالعُقوباتِ المُتَرَتِّبَةَ عَلَيْها، مِثلَ السَّرِقَةِ وَالاعْتِداءِ.

Criminal law deals with crimes and the penalties associated with them, such as theft and assault.

قانونٌ دَوْلِيٌّ

international law

يَضَعُ القانونُ الدَّوْلِيُّ الأُطُرَ القانونيَّةَ لِلْعَلاقاتِ بَيْنَ الدُّوَلِ وَيَشْمَلُ مُعاهَداتٍ مِثلَ حُقوقِ الإِنْسانِ.

International law sets the legal frameworks for relations between countries and includes treaties like human rights.

قانونُ شَرِكاتٍ

company law

يُنَظِّمُ قانونُ الشَّرِكاتِ تَأْسيسَ وَتَشْغيلَ وَتَصْفِيَةَ الشَّرِكاتِ في السّوقِ التِّجارِيِّ.

Corporate law regulates the formation, operation, and dissolution of companies in the commercial market.

civil law

قانونٌ مَدَنيٌّ

يَهْتَمُّ القانونُ المَدَنيُّ بِالنِّزاعاتِ بَيْنَ الأَفْرادِ وَالمُؤَسَّساتِ، كَالعُقودِ وَالمِلْكِيَّةِ.

Civil law focuses on disputes between individuals and institutions, such as contracts and property.

legal

قانونيٌّ

يَتَطَلَّبُ التَّحَرُّكُ القانونيُّ مَعْرِفَةً بِالقَوانينِ وَالإجراءاتِ لِضَمانِ تَنْفيذِ العَدالَةِ بِشَكْلٍ صَحيحٍ.

Legal action requires knowledge of laws and procedures to ensure justice is correctly executed.

to file a lawsuit

قَدَّمَ دَعْوى • تَقْديمٌ

قَدَّمَ المُحامي دَعْوى جَديدَةً ضِدَّ الشَّرِكَةِ بِسَبَبِ انْتِهاكاتٍ مَزْعومَةٍ لِلْعَقْدِ.

The lawyer filed a new lawsuit against the company for alleged contract violations.

judgment

قَرارٌ

أَصْدَرَتِ المَحْكَمَةُ قَرارًا بِإعادَةِ فَتْحِ القَضِيَّةِ اسْتِنادًا إلى أَدِلَّةٍ جَديدَةٍ.

The court issued a decision to reopen the case based on new evidence.

accused

مُتَّهَمٌ

واجَهَ المُتَّهَمُ تُهَمًا بِالْاخْتِلاسِ في المَحْكَمَةِ الجِنائِيَّةِ.

The accused faced embezzlement charges in the criminal court.

criminal

مُجْرِمٌ

أُدينَ المُجْرِمُ بَعْدَ سِلْسِلَةٍ مِنَ الجَرائِمِ الَّتي ارْتَكَبَها.

The criminal was convicted after a series of crimes he committed.

lawyer, advocate

مُحامٍ

اِسْتَعانَ المُتَّهَمُ بِمُحامٍ مُتَمَرِّسٍ لِلدِّفاعِ عَنْهُ في المُحاكَمَةِ.

The accused hired an experienced lawyer to defend him in the trial.

the practice of law

مُحاماةٌ

تُعْتَبَرُ المُحاماةُ في مَجالِ القانونِ المَدَنِيِّ تَخَصُّصًا يَتَطَلَّبُ فَهْمًا عَميقًا لِلْقَوانينِ المَعْمولِ بِها.

Practicing in civil law is a specialization that requires a deep understanding of applicable laws.

court

مَحْكَمَةٌ

• مَحاكِمُ

عُقِدَتِ الجَلْسَةُ في المَحْكَمَةِ لِلنَّظَرِ في الدَّعْوى المُقَدَّمَةِ ضِدَّ الشَّرِكَةِ.

The session was held in the court to consider the lawsuit filed against the company.

court of appeals

مَحْكَمَةُ اسْتِئْنافٍ

تَقَدَّمَ الدِّفاعُ بِطَلَبِ اسْتِئْنافٍ لِلْحُكْمِ الصّادِرِ في مَحْكَمَةِ الاسْتِئْنافِ.

The defense filed an appeal against the verdict issued in the court of appeals.

criminal court

مَحْكَمَةُ جِناياتٍ

نَظَرَتْ مَحْكَمَةُ الجِناياتِ في قَضايا الجَرائِمِ الخَطيرَةِ.

The criminal court considered cases of serious crimes.

convicted

مَحْكومٌ عَلَيْهِ

قَدَّمَ الشَّخْصُ المَحْكومُ عَلَيْهِ بِالسَّجْنِ المُؤَبَّدِ طَلَبًا لِإعادَةِ النَّظَرِ في قَضِيَّتِهِ.

The person sentenced to life imprisonment submitted a request for a retrial of his case.

prosecutor

مُدَّعٍ عامٌّ

تَوَلّى المُدَّعي العامُّ قيادَةَ التَّحْقيقِ في الفَسادِ الحُكومِيِّ.

The public prosecutor led the investigation into government corruption.

defendant

مُدَّعى عَلَيْهِ

كانَ المُدَّعى عَلَيْهِ شَرِكَةً كُبْرى في قَضِيَّةٍ تِجارِيَّةٍ مُعَقَّدَةٍ.

The defendant was a major company in a complex commercial case.

civil

مَدَنِيٌّ

تَناوَلَتِ الدَّعْوى المَدَنِيَّةُ نِزاعًا عَلى حُقوقِ المِلْكِيَّةِ.

The civil lawsuit dealt with a property rights dispute.

contentiousness

مَوْضوعُ النِّزاعِ • مَواضيعُ

حُدِّدَ مَوْضوعُ النِّزاعِ في الجَلْسَةِ وَتَمَّ العَمَلُ عَلى حَلِّ الخِلافِ قَضائِيًّا.

The cause of the dispute was identified in the session, and efforts were made to resolve the conflict judicially.

10.2.1.1 Mini-Articles

Track **13**

في قَضِيَّةٍ شَغَلَتِ الرَّأْيَ العامَّ، أَصْدَرَتْ مَحْكَمَةُ الجِناياتِ حُكْمًا بِإِدانَةِ رَجُلِ الأَعْمالِ المَعْروفِ، أَميرِ الزُّهَيْري، بِتُهْمَةِ ارْتِكابِ جَريمَةٍ كُبْرى تَتَعَلَّقُ بِالاحْتِيالِ الماليِّ. اِسْتَجْوَبَ القاضي عِدَّةَ شُهودٍ قَبْلَ أَنْ يُقَرِّرَ إِصْدارَ حُكْمِهِ، مُسْتَنِدًا إِلى أَدِلَّةِ تَحْقيقٍ جِنائيٍّ دامَ لِأَشْهُرٍ.

In a case that captivated public opinion, the criminal court convicted the well-known businessman, Amir Al-Zuhairi, of committing a major crime related to financial fraud. The judge interrogated several witnesses before deciding to issue his verdict, based on evidence from a criminal investigation that lasted for months.

في خِلافٍ قَضائيٍّ مُعَقَّدٍ بَيْنَ شَرِكَتَيْنِ كَبيرَتَيْنِ، أَسْفَرَتْ دَعْوى مَدَنِيَّةٌ عَنْ تَسْوِيَةٍ بِمَلايينِ الدّولاراتِ. شَهِدَتِ المَحْكَمَةُ جَلَساتِ تَفاوُضٍ طَويلَةً، حَيْثُ تَوَسَّطَ مُحامو الطَّرَفَيْنِ لِلوُصولِ إِلى اتِّفاقٍ يُرْضي جَميعَ الأَطْرافِ المُتَنازِعَةِ.

In a complex legal dispute between two large companies, a civil lawsuit resulted in a settlement worth millions of dollars. The court witnessed lengthy negotiation sessions, where lawyers from both sides mediated to reach an agreement satisfactory to all disputing parties.

رَفَضَتْ مَحْكَمَةُ الاسْتِئْنافِ طَلَبَ اسْتِئْنافٍ قَدَّمَهُ مُحَمَّدُ العِرْيان، الَّذي حُكِمَ عَلَيْهِ في قَضِيَّةِ جُنْحَةٍ تَتَعَلَّقُ بِالسَّرِقَةِ البَسيطَةِ. وَجَدَتِ المَحْكَمَةُ أَنَّ الأَدِلَّةَ كافِيَةٌ وَالحُكْمَ الابْتِدائيَّ صَحيحٌ، مُؤَكِّدَةً عَلى قَرارِها النِّهائيِّ.

The appellate court rejected an appeal filed by Mohamed Al-Aryan, who was convicted in a misdemeanor case related to petty theft. The court found the evidence sufficient and the initial judgment correct, reaffirming its final decision.

عَقَدَتْ مَحْكَمَةٌ دَوْلِيَّةٌ جَلْسَةَ اسْتِماعٍ حَوْلَ انْتِهاكاتِ حُقوقِ الإِنْسانِ في مِنْطَقَةِ نِزاعٍ، حَيْثُ دافَعَ عِدَّةُ مُحامينَ عَنْ ضَحايا الانْتِهاكاتِ. جَذَبَتِ القَضِيَّةُ انْتِباهَ المُجْتَمَعِ الدَّوْلِيِّ، وَاسْتَدْعَتِ القِيامَ بِإِجْراءاتٍ قانونِيَّةٍ لِمُحاسَبَةِ المَسْؤولينَ.

An international court held a hearing on human rights violations in a conflict zone, where several lawyers defended the victims of the violations. The case attracted international attention and called for legal proceedings to hold the responsible parties accountable.

في قَضِيَّةٍ هَزَّتِ الأَوْساطَ القانونِيَّةَ، أُدينَ المُحامي سَليم الجوهري بِتَزْويرِ وَثائِقَ قَضائِيَّةٍ في مَحْكَمَةٍ مَدَنِيَّةٍ. أَصْدَرَ القَضاءُ حُكْمًا قاسِيًا بِحَقِّ الجوهري، مُعْتَبِرًا فَعْلَتَهُ خِيانَةً لِلْأَمانَةِ القانونِيَّةِ وَاسْتِهْتارًا بِالعَدالَةِ.

In a case that shook the legal community, lawyer Salim Al-Johari was convicted of forging judicial documents in a civil court. The judiciary issued a severe sentence against Al-Johari, considering his act a betrayal of legal trust and a disregard for justice.

10.2.1.2 Informative Article: The Justice System in Saudi Arabia

النِّظامُ القَضائِيُّ في المَمْلَكَةِ العَرَبِيَّةِ السُّعودِيَّةِ: الشَّريعَةُ وَالعَدالَةُ

في السُّعودِيَّةِ، يُعَدُّ النِّظامُ القَضائِيُّ جُزْءًا لا يَتَجَزَّأُ مِنَ النِّظامِ الإِسْلامِيِّ، حَيْثُ تُطَبَّقُ أَحْكامُ الشَّريعَةِ الإِسْلامِيَّةِ في القَضايا الجِنائِيَّةِ، وَالمَدَنِيَّةِ، وَحالاتِ الأَحْوالِ الشَّخْصِيَّةِ. يَضُمُّ النِّظامُ مَحاكِمَ مُتَعَدِّدَةَ المُسْتَوَياتِ، بَدْءًا مِنَ المَحاكِمِ الابْتِدائِيَّةِ وُصولًا إِلى مَحاكِمِ الاسْتِئْنافِ.

المَحاكِمُ الابْتِدائِيَّةُ: تُعْتَبَرُ البَوّابَةَ الأولى لِلنِّظامِ القَضائِيِّ، حَيْثُ تَنْظُرُ في مُخْتَلِفِ الدَّعاوى الجِنائِيَّةِ وَالمَدَنِيَّةِ. في القَضايا الجِنائِيَّةِ، يَقومُ قاضٍ بِالتَّحْقيقِ الجِنائِيِّ وَيُدافِعُ المُتَّهَمُ عَنْ نَفْسِهِ أَوْ يَسْتَعينُ بِمُحامٍ لِلدِّفاعِ عَنْهُ.

مَحاكِمُ الاسْتِئْنافِ: تَسْتَقْبِلُ الطُّعونَ في الأَحْكامِ الصّادِرَةِ عَنِ المَحاكِمِ الابْتِدائِيَّةِ. تَتِمُّ مُراجَعَةُ الأَحْكامِ وَالإِجْراءاتِ القانونِيَّةِ لِضَمانِ العَدالَةِ وَالتَّقَيُّدِ بِأَحْكامِ الشَّريعَةِ.

المَحْكَمَةُ العُلْيا: تُعَدُّ أَعْلى سُلْطَةٍ في النِّظامِ القَضائِيِّ السُّعودِيِّ، تَنْظُرُ في الطُّعونِ القانونِيَّةِ الكُبْرى وَتُصْدِرُ القَراراتِ النِّهائِيَّةَ غَيْرَ القابِلَةِ لِلاسْتِئْنافِ.

بِجانِبِ هَذِهِ المَحاكِمِ، يوجَدُ "ديوانُ المَظالِمِ"، وَهُوَ مَحْكَمَةٌ خاصَّةٌ تَنْظُرُ في الشَّكاوى ضِدَّ الأَجْهِزَةِ الحُكومِيَّةِ وَالإِدارِيَّةِ لِضَمانِ حُقوقِ الأَفْرادِ وَمُحاسَبَةِ الجِهاتِ الإِدارِيَّةِ.

تَتَعامَلُ المَحاكِمُ الشَّرْعِيَّةُ مَعَ قَضايا الأَحْوالِ الشَّخْصِيَّةِ مِثْلِ الزَّواجِ، وَالطَّلاقِ، وَالميراثِ، وَالوَصايا، بَيْنَما تُعْنى المَحاكِمُ التِّجارِيَّةُ بِالنِّزاعاتِ التِّجارِيَّةِ وَقَضايا الشَّرِكاتِ.

يُشْرِفُ عَلَى النِّظامِ القَضائِيِّ مَجْلِسُ القَضاءِ الأَعْلى، الَّذي يَعْمَلُ عَلَى تَعْزيزِ العَدالَةِ، ومُراقَبَةِ أَداءِ المَحاكِمِ، وَضَمانِ تَطْبيقِ القَوانينِ وَفْقًا لِمَبادِئِ الشَّريعَةِ.

في النِّهايَةِ، فَإِنَّ النِّظامَ القَضائِيَّ في السُّعوديَّةِ يَعْكِسُ التِزامَ المَمْلَكَةِ بِمَبادِئِ الشَّريعَةِ الإِسْلاميَّةِ كَأَساسٍ لِلْقانونِ، مَعَ تَوْفيرِ إِطارٍ قانونِيٍّ يَضْمَنُ العَدالَةَ والنَّزاهَةَ.

The Judicial System in Saudi Arabia: Sharia and Justice

In Saudi Arabia, the judicial system is an integral part of the Islamic framework, where Islamic Sharia laws are applied in criminal, civil, and personal status cases. The system comprises multi-tiered courts, ranging from primary courts to courts of appeal.

Primary Courts: These are the entry points to the judicial system, handling various criminal and civil lawsuits. In criminal cases, a judge conducts the investigation, and the accused defends themselves or hires a lawyer.

Courts of Appeal: They handle appeals against judgments issued by primary courts. Judgments and legal procedures are reviewed to ensure justice and adherence to Sharia laws.

The Supreme Court: This is the highest authority in the Saudi judicial system, dealing with major legal appeals and issuing final, unappealable decisions.

Besides these courts, there is the "Board of Grievances," a special court that looks into complaints against governmental and administrative bodies to ensure individual rights and hold administrative entities accountable.

Sharia courts deal with personal status issues like marriage, divorce, inheritance, and wills, while commercial courts handle business disputes and corporate cases.

The Supreme Judicial Council oversees the judicial system, enhancing justice, monitoring court performance, and ensuring laws are applied according to Sharia principles.

In conclusion, Saudi Arabia's judicial system reflects the kingdom's commitment to the principles of Islamic Sharia as the basis of law, providing a legal framework that ensures justice and integrity.

10.2.2 International Law and Human Rights

Track **15**

basic, fundamental

أَساسِيٌّ

حُقوقُ الإِنْسانِ هِيَ مَعاييرُ أَساسِيَّةٌ يَجِبُ حِمايَتُها واحْتِرامُها عالَمِيًّا.

Human rights are fundamental standards that must be protected and respected globally.

ethnic minority

أَقَلِّيَّةٌ عِرْقِيَّةٌ

تَعْمَلُ الْهَيْئَاتُ الدَّوْلِيَّةُ عَلَى حِمَايَةِ الْأَقَلِّيَّاتِ الْعِرْقِيَّةِ مِنَ التَّمْيِيزِ وَالِاضْطِهَادِ.

International bodies work on the protection of ethnic minorities from discrimination and persecution.

genocide

إِبَادَةٌ جَمَاعِيَّةٌ

صَنَّفَتِ الْمَحَاكِمُ الدَّوْلِيَّةُ الْجَرَائِمَ ضِدَّ الْأَقَلِّيَّةِ كَإِبَادَةٍ جَمَاعِيَّةٍ.

The international courts classified the crimes against the minority as genocide.

human rights convention

اِتِّفَاقِيَّةُ حُقوقِ إِنْسَانٍ

وَقَّعَتِ الدُّوَلُ عَلَى اتِّفَاقِيَّةِ حُقوقِ الْإِنْسانِ لِضَمانِ حِمايَةِ الْحُرِّيّاتِ الْأَساسِيَّةِ.

Countries signed the Human Rights Convention to ensure the protection of fundamental freedoms.

international convention/agreement

اِتِّفَاقِيَّةٌ دَوْلِيَّةٌ

تُعْتَبَرُ الِاتِّفَاقِيَّةُ الدَّوْلِيَّةُ حَوْلَ تَغَيُّرِ الْمُنَاخِ جُزْءًا مِنَ الْجُهودِ الْعالَمِيَّةِ لِحِمايَةِ البيئَةِ.

The international agreement on climate change is part of global efforts to protect the environment.

to admit to a crime

• اِعْتِرافٌ اِعْتَرَفَ بِجَريمَةٍ

اِعْتَرَفَ الزَّعيمُ بِجَريمَةِ الحَرْبِ أمامَ المَحْكَمَةِ الدَّوْلِيَّةِ.

The leader acknowledged the war crime before the international court.

the United Nations

pl.

الأُمَمُ المُتَّحِدَةُ

تَلْعَبُ الأُمَمُ المُتَّحِدَةُ دَوْرًا مِحْوَرِيًّا في تَعْزيزِ السَّلامِ وَحُقوقِ الإنْسانِ عَلى مُسْتَوى العالَمِ.

The United Nations plays a pivotal role in promoting peace and human rights worldwide.

commitment to international law

الِالتِزامُ بِالْقانونِ الدَّوْلِيّ

يَجِبُ عَلى الدُّوَلِ الِالتِزامُ بِالْقانونِ الدَّوْلِيِّ لِضَمانِ العَدالَةِ وَالأَمانِ العالَمِيَّيْنِ.

States must adhere to international law to ensure global justice and security.

human rights abuse

اِنْتِهاكُ حُقوقِ الإِنْسانِ

تَنْشُرُ الْمُنَظَّماتُ غَيْرُ الْحُكومِيّةِ تَقاريرَ دَوْرِيَّةً عَنِ انْتِهاكاتِ حُقوقِ الإِنْسانِ في مَناطِقِ النِّزاعِ.

Non-governmental organizations publish periodic reports on human rights abuses in conflict zones.

to violate human rights

اِنْتَهَكَ حُقوقَ الإِنْسانِ   •   اِنْتِهاكٌ

اِنْتَهَكَتِ الْحُكومَةُ حُقوقَ الإِنْسانِ بِفَرْضِ الرَّقابَةِ وَالِاعْتِقالاتِ التَّعَسُّفِيَّةِ.

The government violated human rights by imposing censorship and arbitrary detentions.

international investigation

تَحْقيقٌ دَوْلِيٌّ

تَمَّ الْبَدْءُ في تَحْقيقٍ دَوْلِيٍّ لِلنَّظَرِ في الِادِّعاءاتِ بِشَأْنِ اسْتِخْدامِ الأَسْلِحَةِ الكيميائِيَّةِ.

An international investigation was launched to examine allegations of chemical weapons use.

investigate violations

تَحْقيقٌ في انْتِهاكاتٍ

تَقودُ مُنَظَّمَةٌ حُقوقِيَّةٌ تَحْقيقًا في انْتِهاكاتِ حُقوقِ الإِنْسانِ في مِنْطَقَةِ النِّزاعِ.

A human rights organization is leading an investigation into human rights violations in the conflict zone.

law enforcement

تَطْبيقُ قانونٍ

يَعْمَلُ النِّظامُ الْقَضائِيُّ عَلى تَطْبيقِ القانونِ بِشَكْلٍ عادِلٍ لِضَمانِ العَدالَةِ.

The judicial system works to apply the law fairly to ensure justice.

racial discrimination

تَمييزٌ عُنْصُرِيٌّ

واجَهَتِ الأَقَلِّيّاتُ العِرْقِيَّةُ تَمييزًا عُنْصُرِيًّا مُمَنْهَجًا يُؤَثِّرُ عَلى فُرَصِهِمْ في التَّعْليمِ وَالعَمَلِ.

Ethnic minorities faced systematic racial discrimination, affecting their opportunities in education and employment.

war crime

جَريمَةُ حَرْبٍ   •   جَرائِمُ

تُجْرى تَحْقيقاتٌ دَوْلِيَّةٌ في جَرائِمِ الحَرْبِ لِضَمانِ تَقْديمِ المَسْؤولينَ لِلْعَدالَةِ.

International investigations into war crimes are conducted to ensure that those responsible are brought to justice.

crime against humanity

جَرِيمَةٌ ضِدَّ الإِنْسانِيَّةِ • جَرائِمُ

تَمَّتْ مُحاكَمَةُ الزَّعِيمِ السِّياسِيِّ بِتُهْمَةِ ارْتِكابِ جَرائِمَ ضِدَّ الإِنْسانِيَّةِ خِلالَ النِّزاعِ المُسَلَّحِ.

The political leader was tried for committing crimes against humanity during the armed conflict.

freedom of expression

حُرِّيَّةُ تَعْبِيرٍ

تُعْتَبَرُ حُرِّيَّةُ التَّعْبِيرِ حَقًّا أَساسِيًّا تَحْمِيهِ القَوانِينُ الدَّوْلِيَّةُ لِحُقوقِ الإِنْسانِ.

Freedom of expression is a fundamental right protected by international human rights laws.

human rights

حُقوقُ الإِنْسانِ

pl.

تَشْمَلُ حُقوقُ الإِنْسانِ الحَقَّ في الحَياةِ، وَالحُرِّيَّةِ، وَالأَمانِ الشَّخْصِيِّ.

Human rights include the right to life, liberty, and personal security.

women's rights

حُقوقُ المَرْأَةِ

pl.

تَهْدُفُ حُقوقُ المَرْأَةِ إلى القَضاءِ عَلى التَّمْيِيزِ الجِنْسِيِّ وَتَعْزِيزِ المُساواةِ بَيْنَ الجِنْسَيْنِ.

Women's rights aim to eliminate gender discrimination and promote gender equality.

protection of human rights

حِمايَةُ حُقوقِ الإِنْسانِ

تُعَدُّ حِمايَةُ حُقوقِ الإِنْسانِ مَسْؤولِيَّةً عالَمِيَّةً تَتَطَلَّبُ التَّعاوُنَ بَيْنَ الدُّوَلِ وَالمُنَظَّماتِ.

Protecting human rights is a global responsibility requiring cooperation among nations and organizations.

to support basic freedoms

دَعَمَ حُرِّيّاتٍ أَساسِيَّةٍ • دَعْمٌ

تَعْمَلُ المُنَظَّماتُ غَيْرُ الحُكومِيَّةِ عَلى دَعْمِ الحُرِّيّاتِ الأَساسِيَّةِ وَضَمانِ احْتِرامِها.

NGOs work to support fundamental freedoms and ensure their respect.

international

دَوْلِيٌّ

يُشيرُ البُعْدُ الدَّوْلِيُّ إلى التَّعاوُنِ وَالتَّفاعُلِ بَيْنَ الدُّوَلِ في مَجالاتٍ مُتَعَدِّدَةٍ كالسِّياسَةِ وَالاقْتِصادِ.

The international dimension refers to cooperation and interaction among nations in various fields like politics and economics.

oppressive

ظالِمٌ

وُصِفَ النِّظامُ الحاكِمُ بِأَنَّهُ ظالِمٌ بِسَبَبِ مُمارَساتِهِ في انْتِهاكِ حُقوقِ الإنْسانِ.

The ruling regime was described as oppressive due to its practices in violating human rights.

racial

عُنْصُرِيٌّ

يُعْتَبَرُ الفِعْلُ عُنْصُرِيًّا عِنْدَما يُبْنى عَلى مُعْتَقَداتِ التَّفَوُّقِ العِرْقِيِّ أَوِ التَّمْييزِ ضِدَّ جَماعاتٍ عِرْقِيَّةٍ.

An act is considered racist when it is based on beliefs of racial superiority or discrimination against ethnic groups.

violent

عُنْفٌ •   عَنيفٌ

اِسْتَخْدَمَتْ قُوّاتُ الأَمْنِ تَدابيرَ عَنيفَةً ضِدَّ المُتَظاهِرينَ المُطالِبينَ بِالدّيمُقْراطِيَّةِ.

The security forces used violent measures against protesters demanding democracy.

unlawful

غَيْرُ قانونِيٍّ

أُدينَ التَّوْقيفُ التَّعَسُّفِيُّ للصَّحَفِيّينَ كَإِجْراءٍ غَيْرِ قانونِيٍّ يُقَوِّضُ حُرِّيَّةَ الصَّحافَةِ.

The arbitrary detention of journalists was condemned as an illegal action undermining press freedom.

unreasonable

غَيْرُ مَعقولٍ

وَصَفَتِ المُنَظَّماتُ الحُقوقِيَّةُ الظُّروفَ في مُعَسْكَراتِ الاحْتِجازِ بِأَنَّها غَيْرُ مَعقولَةٍ وَتَنْتَهِكُ كَرامَةَ الإنْسانِ.

Human rights organizations described the conditions in detention camps as unreasonable and violating human dignity.

قانونٌ دَوْليٌّ
international law
• قوانينُ

يُعالِجُ القانونُ الدَّوْليُّ النِّزاعاتِ بَيْنَ الدُّوَلِ وَيَضَعُ المَعايِيرَ لِلْعَلاقاتِ الدَّوْلِيَّةِ.

International law addresses conflicts between states and sets standards for international relations.

قانونُ لاجِئِينَ
refugee law

يُوَفِّرُ قانونُ اللَّاجِئِينَ الحِمايَةَ لِلْأَشْخاصِ الَّذِينَ يَفِرّونَ مِنَ الِاضْطِهادِ وَالنِّزاعاتِ في بِلادِهِمْ.

Refugee law provides protection for individuals fleeing persecution and conflicts in their countries.

مُجْرِمٌ
criminal

تَمَّ تَسْلِيمُ المُجْرِمِ لِلْعَدالَةِ بَعْدَ سَنَواتٍ مِنَ التَّحْقِيقاتِ الدَّوْلِيَّةِ.

The criminal was brought to justice after years of international investigations.

مَحْكَمَةٌ جِنائِيَّةٌ دَوْلِيَّةٌ
international criminal court
• مَحاكِمُ

تَنْظُرُ المَحْكَمَةُ الجِنائِيَّةُ الدَّوْلِيَّةُ في جَرائِمِ الحَرْبِ وَالإبادَةِ الجَماعِيَّةِ وَالجَرائِمِ ضِدَّ الإنْسانِيَّةِ.

The International Criminal Court deals with war crimes, genocide, and crimes against humanity.

مُخْزٍ
shameful

وُصِفَتِ الحالاتُ الإنْسانِيَّةُ في مَناطِقِ النِّزاعِ بِأَنَّها مُخْزِيَةٌ وَتَتَطَلَّبُ تَدَخُّلًا دَوْلِيًّا فَوْرِيًّا.

The humanitarian situations in conflict zones were described as disgraceful and requiring immediate international intervention.

مَدَنِيٌّ
civilian

يَجِبُ حِمايَةُ المَدَنِيِّينَ في مَناطِقِ النِّزاعِ وَعَدَمُ اسْتِهْدافِهِمْ بِموجِبِ القانونِ الإنْسانِيِّ الدَّوْلِيِّ.

Civilians must be protected in conflict zones and not targeted, in accordance with international humanitarian law.

مُساواةٌ
equality

تُعْتَبَرُ المُساواةُ أمامَ القانونِ مَبْدَأً أساسِيًّا يَضْمَنُ العَدالَةَ لِلْجَمِيعِ بِغَضِّ النَّظَرِ عَنِ الخَلْفِيَّةِ أَوِ الوَضْعِ الِاجْتِماعِيِّ.

Equality before the law is a fundamental principle that ensures justice for everyone regardless of background or social status.

aggressor مُعْتَدٍ

تَمَّ تَحْديدُ الدَّوْلَةِ كَمُعْتَدِيَةٍ بَعْدَ انْتِهاكِها سِيادَةَ الدُّوَلِ الأُخْرى.

The state was identified as the aggressor after violating the sovereignty of other countries.

political prisoner مُعْتَقَلٌ سِياسِيٌّ

تُطالِبُ الجَماعاتُ الحُقوقِيَّةُ بِإِطْلاقِ سَراحِ المُعْتَقَلينَ السِّياسِيّينَ الَّذينَ سُجِنوا لِمُجَرَّدِ تَعْبيرِهِمْ عَنْ آرائِهِمْ.

Human rights groups demand the release of political prisoners who have been jailed merely for expressing their opinions.

Amnesty International مُنَظَّمَةُ العَفْوِ الدَّوْلِيَّةُ

تَعْمَلُ مُنَظَّمَةُ العَفْوِ الدَّوْلِيَّةُ عَلى تَسْليطِ الضَّوْءِ عَلى انْتِهاكاتِ حُقوقِ الإِنْسانِ وَالدِّفاعِ عَنِ المَظْلومينَ.

Amnesty International works to highlight human rights violations and advocate for the oppressed.

to enforce international law نَفَّذَ القانونَ الدَّوْلِيَّ • تَنْفيذٌ

يُطالِبُ زُعَماءُ العالَمِ باتِّخاذِ إِجْراءاتٍ أَقْوى لِفَرْضِ القانُونِ الدَّوْلِيِّ.

Global leaders are calling for stronger measures to enforce international law.

10.2.2.1 Mini-Articles

Track **16**

أَطْلَقَتِ الأُمَمُ المُتَّحِدَةُ تَحْقيقًا دَوْلِيًّا في الاتِّهاماتِ المُوَجَّهَةِ ضِدَّ إِحْدى الحُكوماتِ لِتَوَرُّطِها في جَرائِمَ حَرْبٍ وَجَرائِمَ ضِدَّ الإِنْسانِيَّةِ. تَشْمَلُ الاتِّهاماتُ الإِبادَةَ الجَماعِيَّةَ وَالتَّمْييزَ العُنْصُرِيَّ ضِدَّ أَقَلِّيّاتٍ عِرْقِيَّةٍ، حَيْثُ تَسْعى المُنَظَّمَةُ لِتَطْبيقِ القانونِ الدَّوْلِيِّ وَحِمايَةِ حُقوقِ الإِنْسانِ.

The United Nations launched an international investigation into accusations against a government for its involvement in war crimes and crimes against humanity. The allegations include genocide and racial discrimination against ethnic minorities, as the organization aims to enforce international law and protect human rights.

خِلالَ مُؤْتَمَرٍ دَوْلِيٍّ عُقِدَ مُؤَخَّرًا، تَمَّ التَّأْكِيدُ عَلَى ضَرُورَةِ دَعْمِ وَحِمَايَةِ حُقُوقِ المَرْأَةِ وَمُكَافَحَةِ التَّمْيِيزِ العُنْصُرِيِّ. نَاقَشَ المُشَارِكُونَ كَيْفِيَّةَ تَعْزِيزِ حُرِّيَّةِ التَّعْبِيرِ وَضَمَانِ المُسَاوَاةِ فِي الحُقُوقِ، وَفْقًا لِلاتِّفَاقِيَّاتِ الدَّوْلِيَّةِ وَمَعَايِيرِ الأُمَمِ المُتَّحِدَةِ.

During a recent international conference, the necessity of supporting and protecting women's rights and combating racial discrimination was emphasized. Participants discussed how to enhance freedom of expression and ensure equality of rights in accordance with international agreements and United Nations standards.

أَصْدَرَتِ المَحْكَمَةُ الجِنَائِيَّةُ الدَّوْلِيَّةُ حُكْمًا بِإِدَانَةِ قَائِدٍ عَسْكَرِيٍّ سَابِقٍ بِتُهْمَةِ ارْتِكَابِ جَرَائِمِ حَرْبٍ وَانْتِهَاكَاتٍ جَسِيمَةٍ لِحُقُوقِ الإِنْسَانِ. أَكَّدَ القَضَاءُ الدَّوْلِيُّ أَنَّ الأَفْعَالَ الَّتِي قَامَ بِهَا المُتَّهَمُ تُمَثِّلُ جَرَائِمَ ضِدَّ الإِنْسَانِيَّةِ وَأَظْهَرَ الْتِزَامًا بِالقَانُونِ الدَّوْلِيِّ فِي مُحَاسَبَةِ المَسْؤُولِينَ.

The International Criminal Court issued a verdict convicting a former military commander of committing war crimes and severe human rights violations. The international judiciary confirmed that the actions of the accused constitute crimes against humanity and demonstrated a commitment to international law in holding those responsible accountable.

دَعَتْ مُنَظَّمَةُ العَفْوِ الدَّوْلِيَّةُ إِلَى إِجْرَاءِ تَحْقِيقٍ دَوْلِيٍّ فِي الانْتِهَاكَاتِ المَنْهَجِيَّةِ لِحُقُوقِ الإِنْسَانِ فِي دَوْلَةٍ تَشْهَدُ نِزَاعًا مُسَلَّحًا. أَبْرَزَتِ المُنَظَّمَةُ حَالَاتِ التَّعْذِيبِ، وَالاحْتِجَازِ التَّعَسُّفِيِّ، وَحِرْمَانِ المَدَنِيِّينَ مِنَ الحُقُوقِ الأَسَاسِيَّةِ كَأَمْثِلَةٍ عَلَى الانْتِهَاكَاتِ الصَّارِخَةِ الَّتِي تَسْتَدْعِي الرَّدَّ القَانُونِيَّ.

Amnesty International called for an international investigation into systematic human rights violations in a country experiencing armed conflict. The organization highlighted cases of torture, arbitrary detention, and deprivation of basic rights for civilians as examples of blatant violations that necessitate legal response.

تَمَّ التَّوْقِيعُ عَلَى اتِّفَاقِيَّةٍ دَوْلِيَّةٍ جَدِيدَةٍ تَهْدُفُ إِلَى تَعْزِيزِ حِمَايَةِ حُقُوقِ اللَّاجِئِينَ وَدَعْمِ حُرِّيَّاتِهِمُ الأَسَاسِيَّةِ. الاتِّفَاقِيَّةُ، الَّتِي شَارَكَتْ فِيهَا عِدَّةُ دُوَلٍ وَمُنَظَّمَاتٍ حُقُوقِيَّةٍ، تَسْعَى لِتَحْسِينِ ظُرُوفِ اسْتِقْبَالِ اللَّاجِئِينَ وَضَمَانِ حُصُولِهِمْ عَلَى العَدَالَةِ وَالمُعَامَلَةِ الإِنْسَانِيَّةِ.

A new international agreement aimed at enhancing the protection of refugee rights and supporting their fundamental freedoms was signed. The agreement, participated in by various countries and human rights organizations, seeks to improve the conditions for receiving refugees and ensure their access to justice and humane treatment.

مَجْلِسُ الأَمْنِ يَدْعو لِوَقْفِ إِطْلاقِ النارِ في غَزَّةَ

في تَطَوُّرٍ بارِزٍ عَلى صَعيدِ القانونِ الدَّوْليِّ، أَقَرَّ مَجْلِسُ الأَمْنِ التابِعُ لِلأُمَمِ المُتَّحِدَةِ قَرارًا يَدْعو إلى وَقْفٍ فَوْريٍّ لِإطْلاقِ النارِ في النِّزاعِ المُسْتَمِرِّ بَيْنَ إِسْرائيلَ وَحَماسَ في غَزَّةَ. يُعْتَبَرُ هذا القَرارُ تَحْقيقًا دَوْليًّا في انْتِهاكاتِ حُقوقِ الإنْسانِ وَيُشَكِّلُ خُطْوَةً نَحْوَ الالْتِزامِ بِالْقانونِ الدَّوْليِّ.

القَرارُ الَّذي حازَ عَلى دَعْمٍ دَوْليٍّ، يُطالِبُ بِالْإفْراجِ الفَوْريِّ عَنْ جَميعِ الرَّهائِنِ وَيُناشِدُ وَقْفَ الأَعْمالِ العَدائيَّةِ، خاصَّةً خِلالَ شَهْرِ رَمَضانَ. السَّفيرَةُ الأَمْريكيَّةُ، ليندا توماس - غرينفيلد، أَشارَتْ إلى أَنَّ امْتِناعَ الولاياتِ المُتَّحِدَةِ عَنِ التَّصْويتِ يَأْتي في ضَوْءِ عَدَمِ تَضْمينِ إِدانَةٍ صَريحَةٍ لِحَماسَ في النَّصِّ.

مِنْ جِهَتِهِ، اعْتَبَرَ مَكْتَبُ رَئيسِ الوُزَراءِ الإسْرائيليِّ هذا الإجْراءَ بِمَثابَةِ تَراجُعٍ عَنِ الدَّعْمِ السابِقِ، مُحَذِّرًا مِنْ تَأْثيرِهِ عَلى جُهودِ الحَرْبِ وَالمَساعي لِإطْلاقِ سَراحِ الإسْرائيليّينَ المُحْتَجَزينَ.

عَلى الصَّعيدِ الدَّوْليِّ، تَسْتَمِرُّ الدَّعَواتُ لِحِمايَةِ حُقوقِ الإنْسانِ وَمَنْعِ جَرائِمِ الحَرْبِ، حَيْثُ يُنْظَرُ إلى القَرارِ كَفُرْصَةٍ لِتَعْزيزِ الحُرِّيّاتِ الأَساسيَّةِ وَضَمانِ تَنْفيذِ القانونِ الدَّوْليِّ لِحِمايَةِ المَدَنيّينَ في مَناطِقِ النِّزاعِ.

بِالرَّغْمِ مِنْ هذا القَرارِ، تَسْتَمِرُّ التَّحَدِّياتُ في تَحْقيقِ السَّلامِ الدَّائِمِ، مَعَ التَّأْكيدِ عَلى ضَرورَةِ التَّحْقيقِ في انْتِهاكاتِ حُقوقِ الإنْسانِ وَالجَرائِمِ ضِدَّ الإنْسانيَّةِ الَّتي ارْتُكِبَتْ خِلالَ الصِّراعِ. الأَيّامُ القادِمَةُ سَتَكونُ حاسِمَةً في تَحْديدِ مَدى فَعّاليَّةِ القَرارِ وَقُدْرَتِهِ عَلى وَضْعِ حَدٍّ لِلأَعْمالِ العَدائيَّةِ وَدَعْمِ مَبادِئِ العَدالَةِ وَالمُساواةِ.

The Security Council calls for a ceasefire in Gaza

In a significant development in international law, the United Nations Security Council passed a resolution calling for an immediate ceasefire in the ongoing conflict between Israel and Hamas in Gaza. This resolution is considered an international inquiry into human rights violations and represents a step towards adherence to international law.

The resolution, which gained international support, demands the immediate release of all hostages and appeals for a cessation of hostilities, especially during the month of Ramadan. The U.S. Ambassador, Linda Thomas-Greenfield, indicated that the United States' abstention from voting was due to the absence of an explicit condemnation of Hamas in the text.

The Israeli Prime Minister's office viewed this measure as a step back from previous support, warning of its impact on war efforts and the endeavor to release detained Israelis.

Internationally, there are ongoing calls to protect human rights and prevent war crimes, with the resolution seen as an opportunity to strengthen fundamental freedoms and ensure the enforcement of international law to protect civilians in conflict zones.

Despite this resolution, challenges in achieving lasting peace continue, with emphasis on the necessity of investigating alleged human rights violations and crimes against humanity committed during the conflict. The coming days will be crucial in determining the effectiveness of the resolution and its ability to end hostilities and support principles of justice and equality.

10.2.3 Contracts and Business Law

Track **18**

أَداءُ عَقْدٍ

contract performance

أَوْفَتِ الشَّرِكَةُ بِجَمِيعِ الْتِزاماتِها وَفْقًا لِأَداءِ الْعَقْدِ الْمُبْرَمِ مَعَ الطَّرَفِ الآخَرِ.

The company fulfilled all its obligations according to the performance of the contract agreed with the other party.

أَنْهى اتِّفاقِيَّةً • إِنْهاءٌ

to terminate an agreement

قَرَّرَتِ الشَّرِكَتانِ بِالتَّراضي إِنْهاءَ الاتِّفاقِيَّةِ قَبْلَ الْمَوْعِدِ الْمُحَدَّدِ بِسَبَبِ تَغَيُّرِ الظُّروفِ.

The two companies mutually decided to terminate the agreement ahead of schedule due to changing circumstances.

إِفْلاسٌ

bankruptcy

أَعْلَنَتِ الشَّرِكَةُ إِفْلاسَها بَعْدَ فَشَلِها في سَدادِ دُيونِها الْمُتَراكِمَةِ.

The company declared bankruptcy after failing to repay its accumulated debts.

اتِّفاقٌ تِجارِيٌّ

commercial agreement

وَقَّعَتِ الشَّرِكاتُ اتِّفاقًا تِجارِيًّا لِتَوْسيعِ نِطاقِ التَّعاوُنِ وَزِيادَةِ الأَرْباحِ.

The companies signed a commercial agreement to expand cooperation and increase profits.

اتِّفاقُ تَعاوُنٍ

cooperation agreement

تَمَّ التَّوَصُّلُ إلى اتِّفاقِ تَعاوُنٍ بَيْنَ الجامِعاتِ لِتَبادُلِ الأَبْحاثِ وَالْمَوارِدِ.

A cooperation agreement was reached between universities for the exchange of research and resources.

اِتِّفَاقِيَّة

agreement, treaty

دَخَلَتِ الشَّرِكَتانِ في اتِّفاقِيَّةٍ لِمُشارَكَةِ التِّكْنولوجْيا وَتَحْسينِ الِابْتِكاراتِ.

The two companies entered into an agreement to share technology and enhance innovations.

اِتِّفَاقِيَّة إيجار

lease agreement

تَمَّ تَجْديدُ اتِّفاقِيَّةِ إيجارِ المَكْتَبِ لِمُدَّةِ خَمْسِ سَنَواتٍ إِضافِيَّةٍ مَعَ المالِكِ.

The office lease agreement was renewed for an additional five years with the landlord.

اِتِّفَاقِيَّة بَيْع

sales agreement

وَقَّعَتِ الشَّرِكَةُ اتِّفاقِيَّةَ بَيْعٍ لِتَصْريفِ مَخْزونِ المُنْتَجاتِ الزّائِدِ عَنِ الحاجَةِ.

The company signed a sale agreement to dispose of excess inventory.

اِتِّفَاقِيَّة تِجارِيَّة

commercial agreement

تَهْدُفُ الِاتِّفاقِيَّةُ التِّجارِيَّةُ الجَديدَةُ إلى تَعْزيزِ التَّبادُلِ التِّجارِيِّ بَيْنَ الدُّوَلِ الأَعْضاءِ.

The new trade agreement aims to enhance commercial exchange between the member countries.

اِتِّفَاقِيَّة تَحْكيم

arbitration agreement

تَضَمَّنَتِ اتِّفاقِيَّةُ التَّحْكيمِ بَنْدًا يَقْضي بِأَنَّ أَيَّ نِزاعٍ يَجِبُ أَنْ يُحَلَّ عَنْ طَريقِ التَّحْكيمِ.

The arbitration agreement included a clause stating that any dispute should be resolved through arbitration.

اِتِّفَاقِيَّة تَوْظيف

employment agreement

وَقَّعَ المُوَظَّفُ عَلى اتِّفاقِيَّةِ تَوْظيفٍ تُحَدِّدُ الرّاتِبَ وَالواجِباتِ وَشُروطَ العَمَلِ.

The employee signed an employment agreement specifying the salary, duties, and terms of employment.

اِلْتِزامُ عَقْدٍ

contractual obligation

يَتَعَيَّنُ عَلى الطَّرَفَيْنِ الوَفاءُ بِالْتِزاماتِ العَقْدِ لِضَمانِ حِمايَةِ حُقوقِهِمْ وَمَصالِحِهِمْ.

Both parties must fulfill the contract obligations to ensure their rights and interests are protected.

اِنْتَهَتْ صَلاحِيَّتُهُ • اِنْتِهاءٌ

to expire, to become invalid

اِنْتَهَتْ صَلاحِيَّةُ العَقْدِ المُبْرَمِ بَيْنَ الطَّرَفَيْنِ، مِمّا اسْتَوْجَبَ التَّفاوُضَ عَلى شُروطٍ جَديدَةٍ.

The contract between the parties expired, necessitating negotiation of new terms.

اِنْتَهَكَ • اِنْتِهاكٌ

to violate

اِنْتَهَكَتِ الشَّرِكَةُ البُنودَ المُتَّفَقَ عَلَيْها، مِمّا أَدّى إلى فَسْخِ الاِتِّفاقِ.

The company violated the agreed-upon terms, leading to the termination of the agreement.

اِنْتَهَكَ عَقْدًا • اِنْتِهاكٌ

to breach a contract

اُتُّهِمَتِ الشَّرِكَةُ بِأَنَّها اِنْتَهَكَتْ عَقْدًا مَعَ شَريكٍ تِجارِيٍّ، مِمّا أَدّى إلى دَعْوى قَضائِيَّةٍ.

The company was accused of breaching a contract with a business partner, resulting in a lawsuit.

باطِلٌ

void

أُعْلِنَ العَقْدُ باطِلًا بِسَبَبِ عَدَمِ الاِمْتِثالِ لِلشُّروطِ القانونِيَّةِ الأَساسِيَّةِ.

The contract was declared void due to non-compliance with essential legal terms.

تِجارِيٌّ

commercial

ناقَشَ الطَّرَفانِ شُروطَ الاِتِّفاقِ التِّجارِيِّ الجَديدِ لِلشَّراكَةِ.

The parties discussed the terms of the new commercial agreement for the partnership.

تَعاقُدِيٌّ

contractual

الاِلْتِزامُ التَّعاقُدِيُّ يُحَتِّمُ عَلى الطَّرَفَيْنِ الوَفاءَ بِوُعودِهِما حَسْبَ ما هُوَ مُوَضَّحٌ في العَقْدِ.

Contractual obligation requires both parties to fulfill their promises as outlined in the contract.

contract interpretation

تَفْسيرُ عَقْدٍ

اِسْتَعانَتِ الشَّرِكَةُ بِمُحامٍ لِتَفْسيرِ عَقْدٍ مُعَقَّدٍ وَضَمانِ الِامْتِثالِ لِجَميعِ بُنودِهِ.

The company hired a lawyer to interpret a complex contract and ensure compliance with all its clauses.

to waive

تَنازَلَ • تَنازُلٌ

تَنازَلَ المُديرُ عَنْ حُقوقِهِ في الِاتِّفاقِيَّةِ بِموجِبِ وَثيقَةٍ رَسْمِيَّةٍ.

The manager waived his rights in the agreement under an official document.

intellectual property rights

حُقوقُ مِلْكِيَّةٍ فِكْرِيَّةٍ   pl.

حِمايَةُ حُقوقِ المِلْكِيَّةِ الفِكْرِيَّةِ أَساسِيَّةٌ لِلْحِفاظِ عَلَى الِابْتِكاراتِ وَالِاخْتِراعاتِ.

Protecting intellectual property rights is essential for preserving innovations and inventions.

ruling, judgment

حُكْمٌ • أَحْكامٌ

أَصْدَرَتِ المَحْكَمَةُ حُكْمًا يَفُضُّ النِّزاعَ بَيْنَ الشَّرِكاتِ بِشَأْنِ التَّعَدّي عَلَى بَراءَةِ الِاخْتِراعِ.

The court issued a judgment resolving the dispute between companies over patent infringement.

private

خاصٌّ

تَتَعامَلُ القَوانينُ الخاصَّةُ مَعَ العَلاقاتِ بَيْنَ الأَفْرادِ وَالمُؤَسَّساتِ دونَ تَدَخُّلِ الدَّوْلَةِ.

Private laws deal with relationships between individuals and institutions without state intervention.

debt

دَيْنٌ • دُيونٌ

تُواجِهُ شَرِكَةُ الجَبَلِ الأَخْضَرِ دَيْنًا مُتَزايِدًا بَعْدَ فَشَلِ الِاسْتِثْماراتِ الأَخيرَةِ.

Green Mountain Company faces increasing debt after recent investment failures.

established, firm

راسِخٌ

تَظَلُّ مُؤَسَّسَةُ النَّهْضَةِ راسِخَةً في السّوقِ رَغْمَ الخِلافاتِ القانونِيَّةِ المُسْتَمِرَّةِ مَعَ مُنافِسيها.

Renaissance Corporation remains firmly in the market despite ongoing legal disputes with competitors.

تَسْوِيَةٌ •

سَوَّى

to settle

تَمَّتْ تَسْوِيَةُ النِّزاعِ بَيْنَ شَرِكَةِ أَوْراقِ اللُّوتَسِ وَشَرِكَةِ البِحارِ السَّبْعَةِ بِشَأْنِ حُقوقِ الطَّبْعِ والنَّشْرِ.

The dispute between Lotus Papers Ltd. and Seven Seas Corp. over copyright rights was settled.

شُروطٌ •

شَرْطٌ

clause

في القَضِيَّةِ ضِدَّ شَرِكَةِ التَّكْنولوجْيا العُلْيا، أَكَّدَتِ المَحْكَمَةُ عَلى أَهَمِّيَّةِ الشُّروطِ المَنْصوصِ عَلَيْها في العُقودِ التِّجارِيَّةِ.

In the case against HighTech Co., the court emphasized the importance of conditions stated in business contracts.

شُروطٌ •

شَرْطٌ جَزائِيٌّ

penalty clause

تَدْفَعُ شَرِكَةُ بِناءِ المُسْتَقْبَلِ شَرْطًا جَزائِيًّا كَبيرًا بَعْدَ تَأْخيرِ تَسْليمِ المَشْروعِ.

Future Builders Co. pays a large penalty clause after delaying the project delivery.

pl.

شُروطٌ وَأَحْكامُ عَقْدٍ

contract terms and conditions

تَحْتَدِمُ المَعْرَكَةُ القانونِيَّةُ حَوْلَ تَفْسيرِ شُروطٍ وَأَحْكامِ العَقْدِ بَيْنَ زَيْتونِ العَقارِيَّةِ وَمُسْتَثْمِريها.

The legal battle over the interpretation of contract terms and conditions intensifies between Olive Real Estate and its investors.

شَهادَةٌ شَرْعِيَّةٌ إِسْلامِيَّةٌ

Islamic legal certificate

أَطْلَقَتْ بُنوكُ النَّخيلِ مَجْموعَةً مِنَ المُنْتَجاتِ المالِيَّةِ الجَديدَةِ مَعَ شَهادَةٍ شَرْعِيَّةٍ إِسْلامِيَّةٍ.

Palm Banks launched a new range of financial products with an Islamic legality certificate.

شَهادَةُ مُحاماةٍ

lawyer's certificate

تُكَرِّمُ جامِعَةُ القانونِ الدَّوْلِيِّ خِرِّيجيها بِشَهادَةِ مُحاماةٍ في حَفْلِ تَخَرُّجٍ مَهيبٍ.

International Law University honors its graduates with a law degree in a grand graduation ceremony.

deed صَكٌّ • صُكوكٌ

صَدَرَ صَكُّ الإِدانَةِ ضِدَّ مُديرِ شَرِكَةِ الأَنْهارِ الذَّهَبِيَّةِ بِتُهْمَةِ التَّلاعُبِ المالِيِّ.

The conviction deed was issued against the manager of Golden Rivers Company for financial manipulation.

rights deed صَكُّ حُقوقٍ

تَمَّ الاِعْتِرافُ رَسْمِيًّا بِصَكِّ حُقوقٍ لِلْمُخْتَرِعِ أَميرٍ خالِدٍ لِتَطْويرِهِ تِقْنِيَّةً رائِدَةً لِتَنْقِيَةِ المِياهِ.

A rights deed was officially recognized for inventor Amir Khaled for developing pioneering water purification technology.

public عامٌّ

تُعْتَبَرُ المَصْلَحَةُ العامَّةُ عُنْصُرًا أَساسِيًّا في تَحْديدِ شُروطِ العُقودِ وَفْقَ قَوانينِ الأَعْمالِ.

The public interest is considered a fundamental element in determining contract terms according to business laws.

offer and acceptance عَرْضٌ وَقَبولٌ

تَمَّ التَّوَصُّلُ إِلى عَرْضٍ وَقَبولٍ بَيْنَ شَرِكَةِ المَرْجانِ البَحْرِيِّ وَشَرِكَةِ الأَصْدافِ لِتَطْويرِ مَرْسى جَديدٍ.

An offer and acceptance were reached between Coral Marine Co. and Shells Corp. for the development of a new marina.

contract عَقْدٌ • عُقودٌ

وَقَّعَتْ شَرِكَةُ النُّجومِ الصّاعِدَةُ عَقْدًا ضَخْمًا مَعَ شَرِكَةِ تِكْنوفيجِنْ لِتَوْريدِ أَحْدَثِ التِّقْنِيّاتِ الذَّكِيَّةِ.

Rising Stars Company signed a huge contract with TechnoVision to supply the latest smart technologies.

consultancy contract عَقْدُ اسْتِشارَةٍ

أَبْرَمَتْ شَرِكَةُ الزُّمُرُّدِ لِلتَّطْويرِ العَقارِيِّ عَقْدَ اسْتِشارَةٍ مَعَ خُبَراءَ عالَمِيّينَ لِتَطْويرِ مَشْروعِها الجَديدِ.

Emerald Development Company entered into a consultancy contract with global experts to develop its new project.

عَقْدُ بَيْعٍ

sales contract

أَتَمَّتْ شَرِكَةُ الأَزْهَارِ عَقْدَ بَيْعٍ مَعَ مُوَزِّعِينَ دَوْلِيِّينَ لِتَصْدِيرِ مُنْتَجَاتِها الزِّرَاعِيَّةِ.

Al-Azhaar Company finalized a sales contract with international distributors to export its agricultural products.

عَقْدُ تَأْجِيرٍ

lease agreement

تَمَّ تَوْقِيعُ عَقْدِ تَأْجِيرٍ بَيْنَ شَرِكَةِ المَرَاعِي الخَضْرَاءِ وَالمُزَارِعِينَ المَحَلِّيِّينَ لِاسْتِخْدَامِ الأَرَاضِي الزِّرَاعِيَّةِ.

A leasing contract was signed between Green Meadows Company and local farmers for the use of agricultural land.

عَقْدُ تَوْرِيدٍ

supply contract

وَقَّعَتْ شَرِكَةُ المُعَدَّاتِ الثَّقِيلَةِ عَقْدَ تَوْرِيدٍ مَعَ الحُكُومَةِ لِتَزْوِيدِها بِالآلِيَّاتِ اللَّازِمَةِ لِلمَشَارِيعِ الإِنْشَائِيَّةِ.

Heavy Equipment Company signed a supply contract with the government to provide the necessary machinery for construction projects.

عَقْدُ شَرَاكَةٍ

partnership contract

أَعْلَنَتْ شَرِكَتَا غَالَاكْسِي تِكْ وَسَايَبَر سُولْيوشَنْزْ عَنْ عَقْدِ شَرَاكَةٍ لِتَطْوِيرِ بَرْمَجِيَّاتِ الأَمْنِ السَّيْبَرَانِيِّ.

Galaxy Tech and Cyber Solutions announced a partnership contract to develop cybersecurity software.

عَقَدَ صَفْقَةً • عَقْدٌ

to make a deal

عَقَدَتْ شَرِكَةُ المُحِيطِ الأَزْرَقِ صَفْقَةً مَعَ شَرِكَةِ سُفُنِ العَالَمِ لِشِرَاءِ سَفِينَةٍ جَدِيدَةٍ.

Blue Ocean Company struck a deal with World Ships Inc. to purchase a new vessel.

عَقْدُ عَمَلٍ

employment contract

وَقَّعَ جَلَالُ الدِّينِ مُعَمَّر عَقْدَ عَمَلٍ مَعَ مُؤَسَّسَةِ الأَبْحَاثِ المُتَقَدِّمَةِ لِمُدَّةِ ثَلَاثِ سَنَوَاتٍ.

Jalaluddin Muammar signed an employment contract with the Advanced Research Institute for three years.

to compensate	• تَعْويضٌ	عَوَّضَ

عَوَّضَتْ شَرِكَةُ الوادي الأَخْضَرِ السُّكَّانَ المَحَلِّيِّينَ عَنِ الأَراضي الَّتي اسْتَخْدَمَتْها في مَشْروعِها الجَديدِ.

Green Valley Company compensated the local residents for the land used in its new project.

to authorize	• تَفْويضٌ	فَوَّضَ

فَوَّضَتْ شَرِكَةُ البَرْمَجِيّاتِ النّاشِئَةُ مُحاميها لِلتَّفاوُضِ بِشَأْنِ عُقودِ التَّرْخيصِ مَعَ الشَّرِكاتِ الكُبْرى.

The startup software company authorized its lawyer to negotiate licensing contracts with major firms.

contract law	• قَوانينُ	قانونُ العُقودِ

دَرَّسَتِ الجامِعَةُ قانونَ العُقودِ كَجُزْءٍ مِنَ البَرْنامَجِ الأَكاديمِيِّ لِطُلّابِ القانونِ.

The university taught contract law as part of the academic program for law students.

company law	• قَوانينُ	قانونُ شَرِكاتٍ

تَعْمَلُ شَرِكَةُ المُسْتَقْبَلِ لِلتَّطْويرِ عَلى الامْتِثالِ لِقانونِ الشَّرِكاتِ الجَديدِ الَّذي يَفْرِضُ مَعايِيرَ أَعْلى لِلشَّفافِيَّةِ.

Future Development Company is working to comply with the new corporate law that imposes higher standards for transparency.

legal	قانونِيٌّ

تَمَّ تَقْديمُ المُسْتَنَدِ القانونِيِّ لِلمَحْكَمَةِ لِإِثْباتِ شَرْعِيَّةِ الإِجْراءاتِ المُتَّخَذَةِ مِنْ قِبَلِ الشَّرِكَةِ.

A legal document was submitted to the court to prove the legitimacy of the procedures taken by the company.

void	لاغٍ

أَعْلَنَتِ المَحْكَمَةُ العَقْدَ لاغِيا بِسَبَبِ تَوْقيعِهِ تَحْتَ الإِكْراهِ.

The court declared the contract void due to it being signed under duress.

to cancel	• إِلْغاءٌ	أَلْغى

أَلْغَتْ إِدارَةُ الشَّرِكَةِ الاِتِّفاقَ السّابِقَ بِسَبَبِ عَدَمِ تَحْقيقِ الأَهْدافِ المُتَّفَقِ عَلَيْها.

The company's management canceled the previous agreement due to failure to achieve the agreed-upon objectives.

breach of contract terms مُخالَفَةُ شُروطِ عَقْدٍ

أُتُّهِمَتِ الشَّرِكَةُ بِمُخالَفَةِ شُروطِ العَقْدِ، مِمّا أَدّى إلى خَسائِرَ مالِيَّةٍ كَبيرَةٍ لِلطَّرَفِ الآخَرِ.

The company was accused of breaching the contract terms, leading to significant financial losses for the other party.

civil مَدَنِيٌّ

تَمَّتْ تَسْوِيَةُ النِّزاعِ المَدَنِيِّ بِشَأْنِ حُدودِ الأَرْضِ بَيْنَ الجارَيْنِ خارِجَ المَحْكَمَةِ.

The civil dispute over land boundaries between the neighbors was settled out of court.

decree مَرْسومٌ • مَراسيمُ

أَصْدَرَتِ الحُكومَةُ مَرْسومًا يَتَضَمَّنُ تَعْديلاتٍ جَديدَةً عَلى قانونِ الضَّرائِبِ لِلشَّرِكاتِ.

The government issued a decree containing new amendments to the corporate tax law.

civil liability مَسْؤولِيَّةٌ مَدَنِيَّةٌ

تَحْمِلُ الشَّرِكَةُ مَسْؤولِيَّةً مَدَنِيَّةً نَتيجَةَ الأَضْرارِ الَّتي سَبَّبَتْها لِلْبيئَةِ.

The company bears civil liability for the environmental damage it caused.

commercial document مُسْتَنَدٌ تِجارِيٌّ

قَدَّمَتِ الشَّرِكَةُ مُسْتَنَدًا تِجارِيًّا لِإِثْباتِ تَفاصيلِ الصَّفْقَةِ المُبْرَمَةِ مَعَ المُوَرِّدينَ.

The company provided a commercial document to prove the details of the deal made with suppliers.

legal document مُسْتَنَدٌ قانونِيٌّ

يُعْتَبَرُ العَقْدُ مُسْتَنَدًا قانونِيًّا مُلْزِمًا يُحَدِّدُ حُقوقَ وَواجِباتِ كُلِّ طَرَفٍ.

The contract is considered a legally binding document that specifies the rights and duties of each party.

conditional مَشْروطٌ

تم تحديدُ الشُّروطِ المَشْروطَةِ في العَقدِ لِضَمانِ الالتزاماتِ المُتَبادَلَةِ بَيْنَ الأَطْرافِ.

The conditional terms in the contract have been specified to ensure mutual obligations between the parties.

compliant with the law مُطابِقٌ لِلْقانون

تَأَكَّدَتِ الشَّرِكَةُ مِنْ أَنَّ جَميعَ عَمَلِيّاتِها مُطابِقَةٌ لِلْقانونِ لِتَجَنُّبِ أَيِّ مُساءَلَةٍ قانونِيَّةٍ.

The company ensured that all its operations were in accordance with the law to avoid any legal accountability.

pending مُعَلَّقٌ

القَضِيَّةُ مُعَلَّقَةٌ في المَحْكَمَةِ في انْتِظارِ المَزيدِ مِنَ الأَدِلَّةِ لِتَقْديمِ الحُكْمِ النِّهائِيِّ.

The case is pending in court, awaiting further evidence to deliver the final judgment.

valid, enforceable مَعْمولٌ بِهِ

تَتَطَلَّبُ القَوانينُ المَعْمولُ بِها مِنَ الشَّرِكاتِ الالْتِزامَ بِمَعاييرَ مُحَدَّدَةٍ لِلتَّشْغيلِ.

The laws in force require companies to adhere to specific operational standards.

commercial dispute نِزاعٌ تِجارِيٌّ

يَتِمُّ التَّعامُلُ مَعَ النِّزاعِ التِّجارِيِّ بَيْنَ شَرِكَةِ الأَلْفِيَّةِ الجَديدَةِ وَشَرِكَةِ التِّقْنِيّاتِ العالَمِيَّةِ مِنْ خِلالِ مَحْكَمَةِ التَّحْكيمِ الدَّوْلِيَّةِ.

The commercial dispute between New Millennium Co. and Global Technologies Inc. is being handled through the International Arbitration Court.

to transfer ownership نَقَلَ مِلْكِيَّةً • نَقَلَ

أَكْمَلَتْ شَرِكَةُ العَقاراتِ الكُبْرى إِجْراءاتِ نَقْلِ مِلْكِيَّةِ الأَرْضِ إِلى المُطَوِّرِ الجَديدِ بِنَجاحٍ.

The major real estate company successfully completed the procedures for transferring ownership of the land to the new developer.

وَثَّقَ عَقْدًا

to notarize a contract

تَوْثِيقٌ •

وَثَّقَ المُحامِي عَقْدَ الشَّراكَةِ بَيْنَ الشَّرِكَتَيْنِ لِضَمانِ صِحَّةِ الاتِّفاقِ وَفْقًا لِلْقَوانِينِ المَحَلِّيَّةِ.

The lawyer notarized the partnership contract between the two companies to ensure the agreement's validity according to local laws.

وَقَّعَ عَقْدًا

to sign a contract

تَوْقِيعٌ •

وَقَّعَ الرَّئِيسُ التَّنْفِيذِيُّ لِشَرِكَةِ زينونْ لِلطَّاقَةِ عَقْدًا لِبَدْءِ مَشْرُوعِ الطَّاقَةِ الشَّمْسِيَّةِ الجَدِيدِ في المِنْطَقَةِ.

The CEO of Zenon Energy signed a contract to initiate the new solar power project in the region.

10.2.3.1 Mini-Articles

Track **19**

أَنْهَتْ شَرِكَةُ زينونْ لِلتِّكْنولوجْيا اتِّفاقِيَّةَ بَيْعٍ مَعَ شَرِكَةِ أوريكس لِلطَّاقَةِ بَعْدَ أَنِ انْتَهَكَتِ الأَخِيرَةُ شُروطَ العَقْدِ. تَصاعَدَ النِّزاعُ التِّجارِيُّ بَعْدَ أَنْ فَشِلَتْ أوريكس في تَحْقِيقِ الأَداءِ المُتَّفَقِ عَلَيْهِ، مِمّا أَدّى إلى فَسْخِ الاتِّفاقِيَّةِ وَتَسْوِيَةِ الدُّيونِ عَبْرَ التَّحْكِيمِ.

Xenon Technology Corporation terminated a sales agreement with Oryx Energy after the latter violated the contract terms. The commercial dispute escalated after Oryx failed to achieve the agreed performance, leading to the termination of the agreement and debt settlement through arbitration.

وَقَّعَتْ شَرِكَتا بِتروميد لِلنِّفْطِ وَتيكْسول لِلطَّاقَةِ اتِّفاقَ تَعاوُنٍ لِتَطْوِيرِ حُقولٍ نِفْطِيَّةٍ جَدِيدَةٍ. الاتِّفاقِيَّةُ تَشْمَلُ شُروطَ وَأَحْكامَ عَقْدٍ تَفْصِيلِيَّةً تَضْمَنُ حُقوقَ المِلْكِيَّةِ الفِكْرِيَّةِ المُشْتَرَكَةِ وَتَقاسُمَ الأَرْباحِ.

Petromed Oil Company and Texsol Energy signed a cooperation agreement to develop new oil fields. The agreement includes detailed contractual terms and conditions that ensure shared intellectual property rights and profit sharing.

أَشْهَرَتْ شَرِكَةُ الإعْمارِ لِلْبِناءِ إفْلاسَها، مِمّا أَدّى إلى انْتِهاكِ عُقودِ التَّوْرِيدِ مَعَ الشُّرَكاءِ التِّجارِيِّينَ. يَسْعى دائِنو الشَّرِكَةِ لِلْحُصولِ عَلى تَعْوِيضاتٍ مالِيَّةٍ عَبْرَ المَحاكِمِ الخاصَّةِ، مُتَّهِمِينَ الإدارَةَ بِالإهْمالِ وَمُخالَفَةِ قانونِ العُقودِ.

Al-Emaar Construction Company declared bankruptcy, resulting in the breach of supply contracts with business partners. The company's creditors are seeking financial compensation through specialized courts, accusing the management of negligence and contract law violations.

شَرِكَةُ إِنُوفِيتْ لِلْبَرْمَجِيّاتِ راجَعَتْ وَوَثَّقَتْ عُقودَ العَمَلِ لِتَتَطابَقَ مَعَ قانونِ العَمَلِ الجَديدِ وَحِمايَةِ حُقوقِ المُوَظَّفينَ. تَتَضَمَّنُ العُقودُ المُحَدَّثَةُ شُروطًا جَزائِيَّةً مُحَدَّدَةً لِضَمانِ الِالْتِزامِ التَّعاقُدِيِّ وَالحِفاظِ عَلى سِرِّيَّةِ المَعْلوماتِ.

Innovate Software Company reviewed and documented employment contracts to comply with the new labor law and protect employees' rights. The updated contracts include specific penalty clauses to ensure contractual commitment and maintain information confidentiality.

بَدَأَتْ مَحْكَمَةُ التِّجارَةِ جَلَساتِ الِاسْتِماعِ في نِزاعٍ بَيْنَ شَرِكَةِ عَقاراتِ الخَليجِ وَمَجموعَةِ المُنْتَزَهاتِ العَقارِيَّةِ بِشَأْنِ عَقْدِ شَراكَةٍ تَمَّ إِلْغاؤُهُ. تَدورُ القَضِيَّةُ حَوْلَ المَسْؤولِيَّةِ المَدَنِيَّةِ وَالمُطالَباتِ بِتَعْويضاتٍ ناتِجَةٍ عَنْ فَواتِ الفُرَصِ التِّجارِيَّةِ بِسَبَبِ التَّعاقُدِ المُعَلَّقِ.

The commercial court began hearing sessions in a dispute between Gulf Real Estate Company and Al-Montazah Real Estate Group regarding a partnership contract that was canceled. The case revolves around civil liability and claims for compensation due to missed business opportunities caused by the suspended contract.

10.3 Intellectual Property and Copyright Law

10.3.1 Patents, Trademarks, and Copyrights

Track **20**

to be issued — • إِصْدارٌ — أُصْدِرَ

أُصْدِرَتْ بَراءَةُ اخْتِراعٍ لِلْمُخْتَرِعِ بَعْدَ أَنْ أَثْبَتَ تَفَرُّدَ اخْتِراعِهِ وَفائِدَتَهُ.

A patent was issued to the inventor after he proved the uniqueness and utility of his invention.

copyright infringement — انْتِهاكُ حُقوقِ طَبْعٍ وَنَشْرٍ

يُعَدُّ نَسْخُ الكُتُبِ دونَ إِذْنٍ انْتِهاكًا لِحُقوقِ المُؤَلِّفِ لِلطَّبْعِ وَالنَّشْرِ.

Copying books without permission constitutes a violation of the author's copyright.

registered patent — اخْتِراعٌ مُسَجَّلٌ

يَحْظى الِاخْتِراعُ المُسَجَّلُ بِحِمايَةٍ قانونِيَّةٍ لِمَنْعِ الِاسْتِخْدامِ غَيْرِ المُصَرَّحِ بِهِ.

The registered invention is legally protected to prevent unauthorized use.

اِسْتِخْدامٌ حُرٌّ وَعامٌّ

free and public use

تَسْمَحُ بَعْضُ الأَعْمالِ بِالاسْتِخْدامِ الحُرِّ وَالعامِّ دونَ الحاجَةِ إلى إِذْنٍ مُسْبَقٍ.

Some works allow for free and public use without the need for prior permission.

اِسْتِخْدامٌ عادِلٌ لِحُقوقِ نَشْرٍ

fair use of copyright

يُعْتَبَرُ اسْتِخْدامُ مُقْتَطَفاتٍ مِنَ الكُتُبِ في التَّقْييماتِ التَّعْليمِيَّةِ اسْتِخْدامًا عادِلًا لِحُقوقِ النَّشْرِ.

Using excerpts from books in educational reviews is considered fair use of copyright.

اِسْتَخْدَمَ بِطَريقَةٍ عادِلَةٍ   • اِسْتِخْدامٌ

to use fairly

اِسْتَخْدَمَ الباحِثُ الصّورَةَ في دِراسَتِهِ بِطَريقَةٍ عادِلَةٍ مُحْتَرِمًا حُقوقَ المُؤَلِّفِ الأَصْلِيِّ.

The researcher used the image in his study fairly, respecting the original author's rights.

اِسْتَخْدَمَ عَلامَةً تِجارِيَّةً   • اِسْتِخْدامٌ

to use a trademark

اِسْتَخْدَمَتِ الشَّرِكَةُ النّاشِئَةُ عَلامَةً تِجارِيَّةً مَعْروفَةً دونَ إِذْنٍ، مِمّا أَدّى إلى نِزاعٍ قانونِيٍّ.

The startup used a well-known trademark without permission, leading to a legal dispute.

اِنْتِهاكٌ

infringement

تُعْتَبَرُ أَفْعالُ القَرْصَنَةِ انْتِهاكًا جَسيمًا لِحُقوقِ المِلْكِيَّةِ الفِكْرِيَّةِ.

Acts of piracy are considered a serious violation of intellectual property rights.

اِنْتَهَكَ حُقوقَ طَبْعٍ وَنَشْرٍ   • اِنْتِهاكٌ

to violate copyright

اِنْتَهَكَ الشَّخْصُ حُقوقَ طَبْعٍ وَنَشْرِ الأُغْنِيَةِ بِنَشْرِها عَلى مَواقِعِ الإِنْتَرْنِتِّ دونَ إِذْنٍ.

The individual violated the song's copyright by posting it on internet sites without permission.

اِنْتَهَكَ حُقوقَ مِلْكِيَّةٍ فِكْرِيَّةٍ   • اِنْتِهاكٌ

to infringe on intellectual property rights

اِنْتَهَكَتِ الشَّرِكَةُ حُقوقَ المِلْكِيَّةِ الفِكْرِيَّةِ عِنْدَما اسْتَخْدَمَتْ بَرْمَجِيّاتٍ ذاتَ بَراءاتِ اخْتِراعٍ دونَ الحُصولِ عَلى تَرْخيصٍ.

The company infringed on intellectual property rights when it used patented software without obtaining a license.

patent

بَرَاءَةُ اخْتِرَاع

حَصَلَ المُبْتَكِرُ عَلَى بَرَاءَةِ اخْتِرَاعٍ لِجِهَازِهِ الجَدِيد، مِمّا مَنَحَهُ حُقوقًا حَصْرِيَّةً لاسْتِخْدامِهِ وَبَيْعِهِ.

The innovator obtained a patent for his new device, granting him exclusive rights to its use and sale.

copyright scope determination

تَحْدِيدُ نِطاقِ حُقوقِ طَبْعٍ وَنَشْر

تَحْدِيدُ نِطاقِ حُقوقِ الطَّبْعِ وَالنَّشْرِ يُساعِدُ في تَوْضيحِ الاسْتِخْداماتِ المَسْموحِ بِها لِلْعَمَلِ.

Defining the scope of copyright helps clarify the permitted uses of the work.

copyright registration

تَسْجِيلُ حُقوقِ مُؤَلِّف

يَجِبُ تَسْجِيلُ حُقوقِ المُؤَلِّفِ لِحِمايَةِ العَمَلِ الأَدَبِيِّ أَوِ الفَنِّيِّ مِنَ الاسْتِخْدامِ غَيْرِ المُصَرَّحِ بِهِ.

Copyrights must be registered to protect literary or artistic works from unauthorized use.

trademark registration

تَسْجِيلُ عَلامَةٍ تِجارِيَّة

يَضْمَنُ تَسْجِيلُ العَلامَةِ التِّجارِيَّةِ حَقَّ الشَّرِكَةِ في اسْتِخْدامِها حَصْرِيًّا وَيَمْنَعُ الآخَرينَ مِنَ اسْتِغْلالِها تِجارِيًّا.

Registering a trademark ensures a company's right to use it exclusively and prevents others from commercially exploiting it.

fair use statement

تَصْرِيحٌ بِالاسْتِخْدامِ العادِل

يَمْنَحُ التَّصْرِيحُ بِالاسْتِخْدامِ العادِلِ الحَقَّ في اسْتِخْدامِ المُحْتَوى المَحْمِيِّ بِحُقوقِ الطَّبْعِ وَالنَّشْرِ تَحْتَ ظُروفٍ مُحَدَّدَةٍ.

A fair use authorization allows the use of copyrighted content under specific conditions.

copyright

حَقُّ طَبْعٍ وَنَشْر • حُقوقٌ

يُوَفِّرُ حَقُّ الطَّبْعِ وَالنَّشْرِ لِلْمُؤَلِّفِ الحِمايَةَ القانونِيَّةَ لِمُصَنَّفاتِهِ الأَدَبِيَّةِ وَالفَنِّيَّةِ.

Copyright provides legal protection for an author's literary and artistic works.

author's right

حَقُّ مُؤَلِّفٍ

تَمْنَحُ حُقوقُ المُؤَلِّفِ لِلْكاتِبِ السَّيْطَرَةَ عَلى نَشْرٍ وَتَوْزيعٍ وَعَرْضِ عَمَلِهِ.

Author's rights give the writer control over the publication, distribution, and display of their work.

intellectual property rights

حَقُّ مِلْكِيَّةٍ فِكْرِيَّةٍ

تَمَّ تَوْقيعُ اتِّفاقِيّاتٍ جَديدَةٍ لِحِمايَةِ حَقِّ المِلْكِيَّةِ الفِكْرِيَّةِ في المُؤْتَمَرِ الدَّوْلِيِّ الأَخيرِ.

New agreements to protect intellectual property rights were signed at the recent international conference.

to protect copyrights

• حِمايَةٌ   حَمى حُقوقَ مُؤَلِّفٍ

تَضْمَنُ حِمايَةُ حُقوقِ المُؤَلِّفِ لِلْكُتّابِ والفَنّانينَ الحُصولَ عَلى عَوائِدَ مادِّيَّةٍ وَمَعْنَوِيَّةٍ مِنْ أَعْمالِهِمْ.

Protecting copyrights ensures that writers and artists receive material and moral rewards for their works.

to register a patent

• تَسْجيلٌ   سَجَّلَ اخْتِراعًا

تم تَسْجيلُ اخْتِراعٍ جديدٍ في مَجالِ الذَّكاءِ الاصْطِناعِيِّ بِواسِطَةِ فَريقٍ بَحْثِيٍّ مُبْتَكِرٍ.

A new invention has been registered in the field of artificial intelligence by an innovative research team.

to register a trademark

• تَسْجيلٌ   سَجَّلَ عَلامَةً تِجارِيَّةً

سَجَّلَتِ الشَّرِكَةُ عَلامَتَها التِّجارِيَّةَ لِحِمايَتِها مِنَ الاسْتِخْدامِ غَيْرِ المَشْروعِ في السّوقِ.

The company registered its trademark to protect it from unlawful use in the market.

copyright certificate

شَهادَةُ حُقوقِ الطَّبْعِ والنَّشْرِ

تُظْهِرُ شَهادَةُ حُقوقِ الطَّبْعِ والنَّشْرِ الحُقوقَ القانونِيَّةَ لِلْمُؤَلِّفِ عَلى عَمَلِهِ.

The copyright certificate shows the legal rights of the author over their work.

trademark

عَلامَةٌ تِجارِيَّةٌ

اِسْتَخْدَمَتِ الشَّرِكَةُ عَلامَةً تِجارِيَّةً مُمَيَّزَةً لِتَحْديدِ مُنْتَجاتِها في السّوقِ.

The company used a distinctive trademark to identify its products in the market.

unlicensed

غَيْرُ مُرَخَّصٍ

تَمَّ التَّعامُلُ مَعَ المُنْتَجاتِ غَيْرِ المُرَخَّصَةِ كانْتِهاكاتٍ خَطيرَةٍ لِلْقانونِ.

Unlicensed products were treated as serious violations of the law.

unauthorized

غَيْرُ مُصَرَّحٍ بِهِ

الوُصولُ غَيْرُ المُصَرَّحِ بِهِ إلى البَياناتِ الشَّخْصِيَّةِ يُعْتَبَرُ خَرْقًا لِلْخُصوصِيَّةِ.

Unauthorized access to personal data is considered a breach of privacy.

legal

قانونيٌّ

تَمَّ اتِّخاذُ الإجْراءاتِ القانونِيَّةِ لِضَمانِ الْتِزامِ الشَّرِكاتِ بِالْمَعاييرِ القانونِيَّةِ.

Legal actions were taken to ensure that companies comply with legal standards.

protected by a patent

مَحْمِيٌّ بِبَراءَةِ اخْتِراعٍ

المُنْتَجُ مَحْمِيٌّ بِبَراءَةِ اخْتِراعٍ، مِمّا يَمْنَعُ الآخَرينَ مِنَ اسْتِنْساخِهِ أَوْ بَيْعِهِ بِدونِ إِذْنٍ.

The product is protected by a patent, preventing others from copying or selling it without permission.

protected by copyrights

مَحْمِيٌّ بِحُقوقِ طَبْعٍ وَنَشْرٍ

الكِتابُ مَحْمِيٌّ بِحُقوقِ طَبْعٍ وَنَشْرٍ، مِمّا يَحْظُرُ نَسْخَهُ وَتَوْزيعَهُ بِشَكْلٍ غَيْرِ قانونيٍّ.

The book is protected by copyright, prohibiting its unauthorized copying and distribution.

violative

مُخالِفٌ

تُعْتَبَرُ الأَعْمالُ المُخالِفَةُ لِقَوانينِ المِلْكِيَّةِ الفِكْرِيَّةِ جَريمَةً يُمْكِنُ أَنْ تُؤَدِّيَ إلى إجْراءاتٍ قانونِيَّةٍ.

Acts that violate intellectual property laws are considered crimes that can lead to legal action.

licensed

مُرَخَّصٌ

يُتيحُ المُحْتَوى المُرَخَّصُ لِلْمُسْتَخْدِمينَ اسْتِعْمالَهُ ضِمْنَ الشُّروطِ المُتَّفَقِ عَلَيْها.

Licensed content allows users to use it within the agreed terms.

مُصَرَّحٌ بِهِ

authorized

يَضْمَنُ الِاسْتِخْدامُ المُصَرَّحُ بِهِ احْتِرامَ حُقوقِ المِلْكِيَّةِ وَيُجَنِّبُ المُسْتَخْدِمينَ المُساءَلَةَ القانونِيَّةَ.

Authorized use ensures respect for property rights and prevents users from legal accountability.

مِلْكِيَّةٌ فِكْرِيَّةٌ

intellectual property

تُعْتَبَرُ المِلْكِيَّةُ الفِكْرِيَّةُ جُزْءًا حَيَوِيًّا مِنَ الأُصولِ الَّتي تَحْتاجُ الشَّرِكاتُ إلى حِمايَتِها.

Intellectual property is a vital part of the assets that companies need to protect.

مَنَعَ الِاسْتِخْدامَ غَيْرَ المُصَرَّحِ بِهِ • مَنْعُ

to prohibit unauthorized use

تَمَّ مَنْعُ الِاسْتِخْدامِ غَيْرِ المُصَرَّحِ بِهِ لِلْبَرْمَجِيّاتِ لِحِمايَةِ حُقوقِ المُطَوِّرينَ.

The use of software without authorization was prohibited to protect the developers' rights.

10.3.1.1 Mini-Articles

حَصَلَتْ شَرِكَةُ تِكْنوفيجَنْ الرّائِدَةُ في مَجالِ التِّكْنولوجْيا مُؤَخَّرًا عَلى بَراءَةِ اخْتِراعٍ لِاخْتِراعِها الجَديدِ في أَنْظِمَةِ الذَّكاءِ الِاصْطِناعِيِّ. هَذا الِاخْتِراعُ المُسَجَّلُ يُمَثِّلُ طَفْرَةً في الصِّناعَةِ وَيُعَزِّزُ مَوْقِفَ الشَّرِكَةِ في سوقِ المِلْكِيَّةِ الفِكْرِيَّةِ.

TechnoVision, a leader in technology, recently obtained a patent for its new invention in artificial intelligence systems. This registered invention represents a breakthrough in the industry and enhances the company's position in the intellectual property market.

رَفَعَتْ دارُ نَشْرٍ كَبيرَةٌ دَعْوى قانونِيَّةً ضِدَّ مَوْقِعٍ إلِكْترونِيٍّ بِتُهْمَةِ انْتِهاكِ حُقوقِ الطَّبْعِ والنَّشْرِ. اِسْتَخْدَمَ المَوْقِعُ مُحْتَوًى مَحْمِيًّا بِحُقوقِ الطَّبْعِ والنَّشْرِ دونَ تَصْريحٍ، مِمّا أَثارَ جَدَلًا حَوْلَ الِاسْتِخْدامِ العادِلِ لِلْمُحْتَوى المَحْمِيِّ.

A major publishing house filed a legal suit against a website for copyright infringement. The site used copyrighted content without permission, sparking debate over the fair use of protected content.

أَطْلَقَتْ شَرِكَةُ بيفِريجِز العالَمِيَّةُ مَشْروبًا جَديدًا مَحْمِيًّا بِعَلامَةٍ تِجارِيَّةٍ مُسَجَّلَةٍ في أَكْثَرَ مِنْ 50 دَوْلَةً. يُؤَكِّدُ تَسْجيلُ العَلامَةِ التِّجارِيَّةِ عَلى الهُوِيَّةِ الفَريدَةِ لِلْمُنْتَجِ وَيَحْميهِ مِنَ التَّقْليدِ والِاسْتِخْدامِ غَيْرِ المُرَخَّصِ.

Beverages International launched a new drink protected by a trademark registered in over 50 countries. The trademark registration emphasizes the product's unique identity and protects it against imitation and unauthorized use.

أَعْلَنَتِ الحُكُومَةُ عَنْ تَشْدِيدِ القَوانِينِ لِحِمايَةِ حُقوقِ المِلْكِيَّةِ الفِكْرِيَّةِ في قِطاعِ البَرْمَجِيّاتِ. تَهْدُفُ هَذِهِ الخُطْوَةُ إلى حِمايَةِ الابْتِكاراتِ وَضَمانِ حُصولِ المُطَوِّرِينَ عَلى حُقوقِهِمِ الكامِلَةِ وَتَحْدِيدِ نِطاقِ حُقوقِ الطَّبْعِ وَالنَّشْرِ بِشَكْلٍ واضِحٍ.

The government announced the tightening of laws to protect intellectual property rights in the software sector. This move aims to protect innovations and ensure developers receive their full rights, clearly defining the scope of copyright.

حَكَمَتْ مَحْكَمَةٌ لِصالِحِ مُؤَلِّفٍ مَعْروفٍ في قَضِيَّةِ حَقِّ مُؤَلِّفٍ ضِدَّ شَرِكَةِ نَشْرٍ اسْتَخْدَمَتْ أَعْمالَهُ دونَ مُوافَقَةٍ. يُؤَكِّدُ الحُكْمُ عَلى أَهَمِّيَّةِ حِمايَةِ حُقوقِ المُؤَلِّفِ وَيُعَزِّزُ مَبْدَأَ المِلْكِيَّةِ الفِكْرِيَّةِ في البِيئَةِ الإبْداعِيَّةِ.

A court ruled in favor of a well-known author in a copyright case against a publishing company that used his works without consent. The verdict underscores the importance of protecting copyright and reinforces the principle of intellectual property in the creative environment.

10.3.2 Digital Rights and Privacy

Track **22**

secure

آمِنٌ

يَتَطَلَّبُ ضَمانُ بِيئَةٍ آمِنَةٍ عَلى الإنْتَرْنِتِّ اسْتِخْدامَ بُروتوكولاتِ أَمانٍ سَيْبَرانِيٍّ مُتَطَوِّرَةٍ.

Ensuring a safe online environment requires the use of advanced cybersecurity protocols.

cybersecurity

أَمْنٌ سَيْبَرانِيٌّ

في نِزاعٍ حَوْلَ الأَمْنِ السَّيْبَرانِيِّ، حَكَمَتِ المَحْكَمَةُ بِأَنَّ الشَّرِكَةَ فَشِلَتْ في حِمايَةِ بَياناتِ العُمَلاءِ بِسَبَبِ نَقْصِ تَدابِيرِ الأَمْنِ السَّيْبَرانِيِّ.

In a dispute over cybersecurity, the court ruled that the company failed to protect customer data due to insufficient cybersecurity measures.

to violate privacy

انْتِهاكٌ • إِنْتَهَكَ خُصوصِيَّةً

انْتَهَكَتِ الشَّرِكَةُ خُصوصِيَّةَ المُسْتَخْدِمِينَ بِجَمْعِ بَياناتِهِمِ الشَّخْصِيَّةِ دونَ مُوافَقَةٍ.

The company violated users' privacy by collecting their personal data without consent.

antivirus software

بَرامِجٌ • بَرْنامَجُ مُكافَحَةِ فَيْروساتٍ

بَعْدَ الهُجومِ السَّيْبَرانِيِّ، أَمَرَتِ المَحْكَمَةُ الشَّرِكَةَ المُتَضَرِّرَةَ بِتَنْصيبِ بَرامِجِ مُكافَحَةِ فَيْروساتٍ عَلى جَميعِ أَجْهِزَتِها لِمَنْعِ المَزيدِ مِنَ الخُروقاتِ الأَمْنِيَّةِ.

After the cyberattack, the court ordered the affected company to install antivirus software on all its devices to prevent further security breaches.

personal data

pl. بَياناتٌ شَخْصِيَّةٌ

تَتَضَمَّنُ البَياناتُ الشَّخْصِيَّةُ مَعْلوماتٍ حَسّاسَةً تَحْتاجُ إِلى حِمايَةٍ مِنَ التَّسْريباتِ وَالاِسْتِخْدامِ غَيْرِ المَشْروعِ.

Personal data includes sensitive information that needs protection from leaks and unauthorized use.

to track electronic violations

تَتَبُّعٌ • تَتَبُّعُ اِنْتِهاكاتٍ إِلِكْتِرونِيَّةٍ

يَتِمُّ تَتَبُّعُ الاِنْتِهاكاتِ الإِلِكْتِرونِيَّةِ لِتَحْديدِ وَمُكافَحَةِ التَّهْديداتِ الأَمْنِيَّةِ عَلى الإِنْتَرْنِتِ.

Electronic violations are tracked to identify and combat online security threats.

data encryption

تَشْفيرُ بَياناتٍ

يُساعِدُ تَشْفيرُ البَياناتِ في حِمايَةِ المَعْلوماتِ مِنَ الوُصولِ غَيْرِ المُصَرَّحِ بِهِ وَالاِخْتِراقِ.

Data encryption helps protect information from unauthorized access and breaches.

right to access information

حُقوقٌ • حَقٌّ في الحُصولِ عَلى مَعْلوماتٍ

يُعْتَبَرُ الحَقُّ في الحُصولِ عَلى المَعْلوماتِ جُزْءًا مِنَ الحُقوقِ الأَساسِيَّةِ، مِمّا يَسْمَحُ بِالشَّفافِيَّةِ وَالمُساءَلَةِ.

The right to access information is part of fundamental rights, allowing for transparency and accountability.

intellectual property rights

pl. حُقوقُ مِلْكِيَّةٍ فِكْرِيَّةٍ

تُشَكِّلُ حُقوقُ المِلْكِيَّةِ الفِكْرِيَّةِ قَضِيَّةً مُهِمَّةً في العالَمِ الرَّقْمِيِّ، حَيْثُ يَجِبُ حِمايَتُها مِنَ الاِسْتِخْدامِ غَيْرِ القانونِيِّ.

Intellectual property rights are a significant issue in the digital world, where they must be protected from illegal use.

strong password protection

حِمايَةٌ جَيِّدَةٌ لِكَلِماتِ مُرورٍ

شَدَّدَتِ الشَّرِكَةُ عَلَى الحِمايَةِ الجَيِّدَةِ لِكَلِماتِ المُرورِ لِمَنْعِ الوُصولِ غَيْرِ المُصَرَّحِ بِهِ إلى الحِساباتِ.

The company emphasized good password protection to prevent unauthorized access to accounts.

privacy protection

حِمايَةُ خُصوصِيَّةٍ

يُطالِبُ النُّشَطاءُ بِحِمايَةِ خُصوصِيَّةِ الأَفْرادِ عَلَى الإنْتَرْنِتَّ لِضَمانِ سَلامَتِهِمِ الرَّقْمِيَّةِ.

Activists demand individual privacy protection online to ensure their digital safety.

protection against malware

حِمايَةٌ مِنْ بَرْمَجِيّاتٍ خَبيثَةٍ

اِعْتَمَدَتِ المُؤَسَّسَةُ الحِمايَةَ مِنَ البَرْمَجِيّاتِ الخَبيثَةِ لِلدِّفاعِ ضِدَّ الهَجَماتِ السَّيْبَرانِيَّةِ.

The institution adopted protection against malware to defend against cyber attacks.

privacy

خُصوصِيَّةٌ

تَمَّ رَفْعُ دَعْوى قَضائِيَّةٍ بِسَبَبِ اِنْتِهاكِ خُصوصِيَّةِ العُمَلاءِ مِنْ خِلالِ التَّجَسُّسِ الإلِكْترونِيِّ.

A lawsuit was filed due to customer privacy violations through electronic spying.

confidential

سِرِّيٌّ

يَجِبُ أَنْ تَكونَ الوَثائِقُ الحُكومِيَّةُ سِرِّيَّةً لِحِمايَةِ المَعْلوماتِ الحَسّاسَةِ.

Government documents must be kept confidential to protect sensitive information.

privacy policy

سِياسَةُ خُصوصِيَّةٍ

قامَتِ الشَّرِكَةُ بِتَحْديثِ سِياسَةِ الخُصوصِيَّةِ لِتَعْكِسَ مُمارَساتٍ أَفْضَلَ في حِمايَةِ بَياناتِ المُسْتَخْدِمينَ.

The company updated its privacy policy to reflect better practices in protecting user data.

modifiable

قابِلٌ لِلتَّعْديلِ

أَصْبَحَتِ البَياناتُ الشَّخْصِيَّةُ قابِلَةً لِلتَّعْديلِ بِموجِبِ القانونِ الجَديدِ لِحِمايَةِ حُقوقِ الأَفْرادِ.

Personal data became modifiable under the new law to protect individuals' rights.

encrypted

إِنَّ البَيَاناتِ المُرْسَلَةَ عَبْرَ الإِنْتَرْنِتْ مُشَفَّرَةٌ لِضَمانِ الأَمانِ وَالحِمايَةِ مِنَ الِاعْتِراضِ.

Data transmitted over the internet is encrypted to ensure security and protection from interception.

مُهَدَّدٌ بِالِاخْتِراقِ

vulnerable to hacking

يُعْتَبَرُ النِّظامُ مُهَدَّدًا بِالِاخْتِراقِ عِنْدَما تَكونُ الإِجْراءاتُ الأَمْنِيَّةُ غَيْرَ كافِيَةٍ.

The system is considered vulnerable to hacking when security measures are inadequate.

10.3.2.1 Mini-Articles

كَشَفَتِ السُّلْطاتُ الأَمْنِيَّةُ عَنْ شَبَكَةٍ مَعْلوماتِيَّةٍ تَعْمَلُ داخِلَ إِحْدى المَدارِسِ الثَّانَوِيَّةِ، حَيْثُ كانَتْ تَنْخَرِطُ في انْتِهاكاتٍ إِلِكْترونِيَّةٍ وَتَنْتَهِكُ خُصوصِيَّةَ الطُّلّابِ وَالمُعَلِّمينَ. تَمَّ اسْتِخْدامُ بَرامِجِ تَشْفيرِ البَياناتِ لِحِمايَةِ المَعْلوماتِ مِنَ التَّسْريبِ، وَلَكِنْ تَمَّ اكْتِشافُ أَنَّ بَعْضَ البَياناتِ الشَّخْصِيَّةِ كانَتْ قابِلَةً لِلتَّعْديلِ وَمُعَرَّضَةً لِلِاخْتِراقِ.

Security authorities revealed a computer network operating within a high school, which was involved in electronic violations and breached the privacy of students and teachers. Data encryption programs were used to protect information from leaks, but it was discovered that some personal data was modifiable and vulnerable to hacking.

أَعْلَنَتْ شَرِكَةٌ تِكْنولوجِيَّةٌ رائِدَةٌ عَنْ إِطْلاقِ بَرْنامَجٍ مُكافَحَةِ فَيْروساتٍ جَديدٍ يَتَضَمَّنُ مَيِّزاتِ تَشْفيرِ بَياناتٍ مُتَقَدِّمَةً لِتَوْفيرِ أَمانٍ سَيْبَرانِيٍّ فائِقٍ. يَهْدُفُ البَرْنامَجُ إِلى حِمايَةِ البَياناتِ الشَّخْصِيَّةِ وَضَمانِ الخُصوصِيَّةِ لِلْمُسْتَخْدِمينَ مِنْ خِلالِ الحِمايَةِ الجَيِّدَةِ لِكَلِماتِ المُرورِ وَالدِّفاعِ ضِدَّ البَرْمَجِيّاتِ الخَبيثَةِ.

A leading technology company announced the launch of a new antivirus program featuring advanced data encryption capabilities to provide superior cybersecurity. The program aims to protect personal data and ensure user privacy through strong password protection and defense against malware.

أُقيمَ مُؤْتَمَرٌ دَوْلِيٌّ حَوْلَ حُقوقِ المِلْكِيَّةِ الفِكْرِيَّةِ وَناقَشَ قَضايا الحِمايَةِ الرَّقْمِيَّةِ وَالخُصوصِيَّةِ. ناقَشَ خُبَراءُ الأَمانِ السَّيْبَرانِيِّ وَالمُحامونَ كَيْفَ يُمْكِنُ لِلتَّشْفيرِ وَسِياساتِ الخُصوصِيَّةِ تَعْزيزِ الأَمانِ لِلْمُسْتَهْلِكينَ وَالشَّرِكاتِ عَلى حَدٍّ سَواءٍ، مُؤَكِّدينَ عَلى الحَقِّ في الحُصولِ عَلى مَعْلوماتٍ آمِنَةٍ وَمَحْمِيَّةٍ.

An international conference on intellectual property rights discussed digital protection and privacy issues. Cybersecurity experts and lawyers debated how encryption and privacy policies could enhance security for both consumers and businesses, emphasizing the right to secure and protected information.

أَطْلَقَتْ مُنَظَّمَةٌ غَيْرُ رِبْحِيَّةٍ حَمْلَةَ تَوْعِيَةٍ لِتَعْلِيمِ العامَّةِ عَنْ أَهَمِّيَّةِ حِمايَةِ الخُصوصِيَّةِ الرَّقْمِيَّةِ وَحُقوقِ المِلْكِيَّةِ الفِكْرِيَّةِ. تَشْمَلُ الحَمْلَةُ وَرَشَ عَمَلٍ حَوْلَ تَأْمينِ البَياناتِ الشَّخْصِيَّةِ واسْتِخْدامِ بَرامِجِ مُكافَحَةِ الفَيْروساتِ وَالبَرْمَجِيّاتِ المُشَفَّرَةِ لِضَمانِ سِرِّيَّةِ المَعْلوماتِ.

A non-profit organization launched an awareness campaign to educate the public on the importance of protecting digital privacy and intellectual property rights. The campaign includes workshops on securing personal data, using antivirus programs, and encrypted software to ensure information confidentiality.

Unit 11
Media and Journalism

Media and Journalism are pivotal in disseminating information and influencing public discourse. In this unit, you will acquire a robust set of vocabulary related to different facets of media and journalism in Arabic, enabling you to better understand and interact with news content, whether you are reading, listening, or discussing it.

We begin with **Types of Media and Journalism**, starting with **Print Media**. Here, you will learn the vocabulary used in newspapers, magazines, and other print publications. Next, **Broadcast Media** covers the terms associated with television and radio journalism, giving you the tools to understand and discuss broadcast news. The section concludes with **Online and Social Media**, where you will explore the language of digital journalism, social networks, and online news platforms.

The focus then shifts to **Reporting and Writing**, a core aspect of journalism. **News Values and Ethics** introduces you to the principles guiding journalistic integrity and the ethical considerations that journalists must navigate. **Story Structure and News Writing** covers the elements of crafting a news story, from the lead to the conclusion, ensuring you understand the mechanics of news writing. **Opinion Writing and Editorializing** explains the language used in opinion pieces, editorials, and commentary, helping you to differentiate between objective reporting and subjective analysis.

Investigative Journalism delves into the terminology of in-depth reporting, exposing hidden truths and holding power to account. This section provides the language needed to discuss investigative methods and the challenges faced by investigative journalists. Finally, **Feature Writing and Long-Form Journalism** explores the vocabulary of detailed, narrative-driven journalism, focusing on storytelling techniques and the language of extended articles.

The language taught in this unit is invaluable not only for passively reading or listening to the news but also for actively discussing media and journalism. This ability to engage in conversations about the media is important for learners, as it enables them to critically analyze news sources, understand media biases, and participate in informed discussions about the role of journalism in society. By mastering this vocabulary, you will be well-equipped to navigate the ever-evolving landscape of media and journalism in Arabic-speaking contexts.

news- **إِخْبارِيٌّ**

يُقَدِّمُ البَرْنامَجُ الإِخْبارِيُّ تَحْليلاتٍ عَميقَةً لِلْأَحْداثِ الجارِيَةِ.

The news program provides in-depth analyses of current events.

media- **إِعْلامِيٌّ**

يُعْتَبَرُ الإِعْلامِيُّ مَسْؤولًا عَنْ تَقْديمِ المَعْلوماتِ بِطَريقَةٍ مَوْضوعِيَّةٍ.

The media professional is responsible for presenting information objectively.

advertisement **إِعْلانٌ**

أَطْلَقَتِ الشَّرِكَةُ إِعْلانًا جَديدًا لِمُنْتَجِها الأَخيرِ عَلى التِّلِفِزْيونِ.

The company launched a new advertisement for its latest product on television.

news editing **تَحْريرُ أَخْبارٍ**

يَلْعَبُ تَحْريرُ الأَخْبارِ دَوْرًا حَيَوِيًّا في تَقْديمِ قِصَصٍ مُؤَثِّرَةٍ ومَوْثوقَةٍ لِلْجُمْهورِ.

News editing plays a pivotal role in delivering impactful and credible stories to the audience.

media coverage **تَغْطِيَةٌ إِعْلامِيَّةٌ**

كانَتِ التَّغْطِيَةُ الإِعْلامِيَّةُ لِلِانْتِخاباتِ شامِلَةً ومُفَصَّلَةً.

The media coverage of the elections was comprehensive and detailed.

comprehensive coverage **تَغْطِيَةٌ شامِلَةٌ**

قَدَّمَتِ القَناةُ تَغْطِيَةً شامِلَةً لِلْأَلْعابِ الأُولِمْبِيَّةِ، شَمِلَتِ المُسابَقاتِ والمُقابَلاتِ.

The channel provided extensive coverage of the Olympics, including the competitions and interviews.

news **خَبَرٌ • أَخْبارٌ**

نَشَرَتِ الجَريدَةُ خَبَرَ اسْتِقالَةِ رَئيسِ الوُزَراءِ.

The newspaper published the news of the prime minister's resignation.

breaking news

خَبَرٌ عاجِلٌ

أَذاعَتِ الْقَناةُ خَبَرًا عاجِلًا عَنْ زِلْزالٍ ضَرَبَ الْمِنْطَقَةَ الْجَنوبِيَّةَ.

The channel broadcasted breaking news about an earthquake that hit the southern region.

journalism

صِحافَةٌ

تُعَدُّ الصِّحافَةُ رَكيزَةً أَساسِيَّةً في الْمُجْتَمَعِ لِتَوْفيرِ الْمَعْلوماتِ وَالتَّحْليلاتِ.

Journalism is a fundamental pillar in society for providing information and analysis.

journalist

صَحَفِيٌّ

الصَّحَفِيُّ مُكَلَّفٌ بِإِجْراءِ الْمُقابَلاتِ وَجَمْعِ الْأَخْبارِ مِنْ مَصادِرَ مُتَعَدِّدَةٍ.

The journalist is tasked with conducting interviews and collecting news from multiple sources.

journalistic

صَحَفِيٌّ

تَتَمَيَّزُ التَّقاريرُ الصَّحَفِيَّةُ بِدِقَّتِها وَمَوْضوعِيَّتِها في تَقْديمِ الْأَخْبارِ.

Journalistic reports are characterized by their accuracy and objectivity in presenting news.

> صَحَفِيٌّ is a nisba adjective, which can function both as an adjective and as a noun referring to a person. This usage is illustrated in the two preceding examples. → Refer to p. 68 of Book 1 for further details.

to cover

غَطّى • تَغْطِيَةٌ

غَطّى الْمُراسِلُ الْأَحْداثَ السِّياسِيَّةَ الْأَخيرَةَ في الْعاصِمَةِ.

The correspondent covered the recent political events in the capital.

news brief

موجَزٌ إِخْبارِيٌّ

يَبْدَأُ الْموجَزُ الْإِخْبارِيُّ بِأَهَمِّ الْأَحْداثِ الْعالَمِيَّةِ وَالْمَحَلِّيَّةِ.

The news summary begins with the most important global and local events.

> A synonym is موجَزُ أَنْباءٍ.

11.1 Types of Media and Journalism

11.1.1 Print Media

to manage • إِدارَةٌ أَدارَ

أَدارَ النّاشِرُ الحَمْلَةَ التَّرويجِيَّةَ لِإِطْلاقِ العَدَدِ الجَديدِ مِنَ الصَّحيفَةِ.

The publisher managed the promotional campaign for launching the new issue of the newspaper.

weekly أُسْبوعِيٌّ

تَصْدُرُ المَجَلَّةُ الأُسْبوعِيَّةُ كُلَّ يَوْمِ جُمْعَةٍ مَعَ تَحْديثاتٍ وَتَقاريرَ خاصَّةٍ.

The weekly magazine is issued every Friday with updates and special reports.

to prepare • إِعْدادٌ أَعَدَّ

أَعَدَّ الصَّحَفِيُّ تَقريرًا مُفَصَّلًا عَنِ الوَضْعِ الاِقْتِصادِيِّ الحالِيِّ.

The journalist prepared a detailed report on the current economic situation.

edition, issue إِصْدارٌ

صَدَرَ الإِصْدارُ الأَخيرُ مِنَ المَجَلَّةِ مَعَ مَقالاتٍ مُفَصَّلَةٍ حَوْلَ التِّكْنولوجْيا الحَديثَةِ.

The latest issue of the magazine was released with detailed articles on modern technology.

classified ad إِعْلانٌ مُبَوَّبٌ

تَجِدُ العَديدَ مِنَ الإِعْلاناتِ المُبَوَّبَةِ في الصَّفَحاتِ الأَخيرَةِ لِلصَّحيفَةِ، تَشْمَلُ بَيْعَ السَّيّاراتِ والعَقاراتِ.

Many classified ads are found in the last pages of the newspaper, including car and property sales.

to edit • تَحْريرٌ حَرَّرَ

حَرَّرَ المُحَرِّرُ المَقالَ الرَّئيسِيَّ في الصَّحيفَةِ لِتَسْليطِ الضَّوْءِ عَلى قَضايا العَدالَةِ الاِجْتِماعِيَّةِ.

The editor edited the lead article in the newspaper to highlight issues of social justice.

دَوْرِيٌّ

periodical

تُصْدِرُ المَجَلَّةُ الدَّوْرِيَّةُ تَقارِيرَ عَنِ التَّطَوُّراتِ الأَخيرَةِ في عالَمِ العُلومِ.

The periodical magazine publishes reports on recent developments in the world of science.

دَوْرِيَّةٌ

periodical

تُقَدِّمُ الدَّوْرِيَّةُ العِلْمِيَّةُ مَقالاتٍ مُتَخَصِّصَةً حَوْلَ الأَبْحاثِ البَيولوجِيَّةِ.

The scientific periodical offers specialized articles on biological research.

→ See note on p. 37.

رَئِيسُ تَحْريرٍ • رُؤَساءُ

editor-in-chief

يَتَمَتَّعُ رَئِيسُ التَّحْريرِ بِسُلْطَةِ تَحْديدِ الخَطِّ التَّحْريرِيِّ لِلْمَطْبوعَةِ.

The editor-in-chief has the authority to set the editorial line of the publication.

شَهْرِيٌّ

monthly

تَنْشُرُ الصَّحيفَةُ الشَّهْرِيَّةُ تَحْليلاتٍ عَميقَةً حَوْلَ السِّياسَةِ الدَّوْلِيَّةِ.

The monthly newspaper publishes in-depth analyses of international politics.

صَحيفَةٌ • صُحُفٌ

newspaper

تُعَدُّ الصَّحيفَةُ مَصْدَرًا يَوْمِيًّا لِلْأَخْبارِ العاجِلَةِ والمَعْلوماتِ الهامَّةِ.

The newspaper is a daily source of breaking news and important information.

صَحيفَةٌ يَوْمِيَّةٌ

daily newspaper

تُعْتَبَرُ الصَّحيفَةُ اليَوْمِيَّةُ مَصْدَرًا رَئِيسِيًّا لِلْأَخْبارِ العاجِلَةِ والتَّحْديثاتِ.

The daily newspaper is a primary source for breaking news and updates.

صَفْحَةٌ

page

كُلُّ صَفْحَةٍ مِنَ الصَّحيفَةِ تَحْمِلُ مَوْضوعاتٍ مُخْتَلِفَةً تُلَبّي اهْتِماماتِ القُرّاءِ.

Each page of the newspaper carries different topics to meet readers' interests.

صَمَّمَ • تَصْمِيمٌ

to design

صَمَّمَ المُصَمِّمُ الغِلافَ الجَديدَ لِلْمَجَلَّةِ بِأَلْوانٍ زاهِيَةٍ وَجَذّابَةٍ.

The designer designed the new cover of the magazine with bright and attractive colors.

عُنْوانٌ • عَناوينُ

headline, title

جَذَبَ العُنْوانُ الرَّئيسيُّ في الصَّحيفَةِ انْتِباهَ الجُمْهورِ بِشَكْلٍ كَبيرٍ.

The headline in the newspaper greatly attracted public attention.

مُتَخَصِّصٌ

specialized

تُناقِشُ المَجَلَّةُ المُتَخَصِّصَةُ قَضايا مُعَقَّدَةً في مَجالِ الهَنْدَسَةِ الوِراثِيَّةِ.

The specialized magazine discusses complex issues in the field of genetic engineering.

مَجَلَّةٌ

magazine

تَنْشُرُ المَجَلَّةُ مَوْضوعاتٍ مُتَنَوِّعَةً تَتَراوَحُ بَيْنَ الثَّقافَةِ والسِّياسَةِ والتِّكْنولوجْيا.

The magazine publishes a variety of topics ranging from culture and politics to technology.

مَجَلَّةٌ شَهْرِيَّةٌ

monthly magazine

تُعْتَبَرُ المَجَلَّةُ الشَّهْرِيَّةُ مَصْدَرًا مُمْتازًا لِلتَّحْليلاتِ الإِخْبارِيَّةِ المُعَمَّقَةِ.

The monthly magazine is an excellent source for in-depth news analysis.

مَقالٌ = مَقالَةٌ

article

تَحْتَوي المَجَلَّةُ الشَّهْرِيَّةُ عَلى مَقالاتٍ مُتَنَوِّعَةٍ تُغَطّي مَواضيعَ مِثْلَ الفَنِّ والثَّقافَةِ.

The monthly magazine contains diverse articles covering topics such as art and culture.

مَقالَةُ رَأْي

opinion piece

كَتَبَ الصَّحَفِيُّ مَقالَةَ رَأْيٍ حَوْلَ تَأْثيرِ التَّغَيُّرِ المُناخِيِّ عَلى الاقْتِصادِ.

The journalist wrote an opinion article on the impact of climate change on the economy.

supplement

مُلْحَقٌ

يَتَضَمَّنُ المُلْحَقُ الأُسْبُوعِيُّ لِلصَّحِيفَةِ قِصَصًا مُمَيَّزَةً وَمُقابَلاتٍ مَعَ شَخْصِيّاتٍ مَعْروفَةٍ.

The weekly supplement of the newspaper includes feature stories and interviews with well-known personalities.

printed edition

نُسْخَةٌ مَطْبوعَةٌ • نُسَخٌ

اِحْتَفَظَ القارِئُ بِنُسْخَةٍ مَطْبوعَةٍ مِنَ المَقالِ الَّذي أَثَّرَ فيهِ بِشَكْلٍ كَبيرٍ.

The reader kept a printed edition of the article that greatly influenced him.

to lay out, format

نَسَّقَ • تَنْسيقٌ

نَسَّقَ الفَريقُ التَّحْريرِيُّ المُحْتَوى بِشَكْلٍ يُسَهِّلُ القِراءَةَ وَالفَهْمَ.

The editorial team formatted the content to be easy to read and understand.

to coordinate

نَسَّقَ • تَنْسيقٌ

يَجِبُ تَنْسيقُ الجُهودِ بَيْنَ أَقْسامِ الصَّحيفَةِ لِضَمانِ تَغْطِيَةٍ شامِلَةٍ.

Efforts must be coordinated between the newspaper's departments to ensure comprehensive coverage.

to publish

نَشَرَ • نَشْرٌ

نَشَرَ الباحِثُ مَقالًا في مَجَلَّةٍ مُتَخَصِّصَةٍ حَوْلَ الإِبْتِكاراتِ العِلْمِيَّةِ.

The researcher published an article about scientific innovations in a specialized magazine.

to distribute

وَزَّعَ • تَوْزيعٌ

وَزَّعَتِ الصَّحيفَةُ اليَوْمِيَّةُ عَدَدًا خاصًّا بِمُناسَبَةِ الذِّكْرى السَّنَوِيَّةِ لِلْمَدينَةِ.

The daily newspaper distributed a special edition on the city's anniversary.

daily

يَوْمِيٌّ

يُقَدِّمُ الإِصْدارُ اليَوْمِيُّ مِنَ الصَّحيفَةِ آخَرَ التَّحْديثاتِ عَلى مَدارِ السّاعَةِ.

The daily edition of the newspaper provides the latest updates around the clock.

11.1.1.1 Mini-Articles

Track **26**

اِحْتَفَلَتْ صَحِيفَةُ "التَّقَدُّمُ" اليَوْمِيَّةُ بِذِكْرَى تَأْسِيسِها الخَمْسِينَ مِنْ خِلالِ إِصْدارٍ خاصٍّ غَنِيٍّ بِالمَقالاتِ التَّحْلِيلِيَّةِ وَالمُقابَلاتِ الحَصْرِيَّةِ مَعَ شَخْصِيّاتٍ بارِزَةٍ. تَضَمَّنَ الإِصْدارُ تَغْطِيَةً شامِلَةً لِتارِيخِ الصَّحِيفَةِ وَتَطَوُّرِ الصَّحافَةِ المَحَلِّيَّةِ، مَعَ إِبْرازِ أَهَمِّ الأَخْبارِ وَالأَحْداثِ الَّتي غَطَّتْها عَبْرَ العُقُودِ.

The daily newspaper "Al-Taqaddum" celebrated its fiftieth anniversary by issuing a special edition rich with analytical articles and exclusive interviews with prominent figures. The edition provided comprehensive coverage of the newspaper's history and the development of local journalism, highlighting the major news and events it has covered over the decades.

نَظَّمَتْ مَجْموعَةٌ مِنَ الصَّحَفِيِّينَ البارِزِينَ وَرْشَةَ عَمَلٍ حَوْلَ تَحْرِيرِ الأَخْبارِ العاجِلَةِ، مُسْتَهْدِفَةً تَعْزِيزَ مَهاراتِ العامِلِينَ في المَجالِ الإِخْبارِيِّ. تُرَكِّزُ الوَرْشَةُ عَلَى كَيْفِيَّةِ جَمْعِ الأَخْبارِ بِسُرْعَةٍ وَدِقَّةٍ، وَتَحْرِيرِها بِطَرِيقَةٍ تُلَبِّي حاجَةَ الجُمْهُورِ لِلْمَعْلوماتِ الفَوْرِيَّةِ، مَعَ الحِفاظِ عَلَى المَعايِيرِ الصَّحَفِيَّةِ العالِيَةِ.

A group of distinguished journalists organized a workshop on editing breaking news, aimed at enhancing the skills of those in the news field. The workshop focused on how to quickly and accurately gather news and edit it in a way that meets the public's need for immediate information while maintaining high journalistic standards.

أَعْلَنَتْ دارُ نَشْرٍ مَعْروفَةٌ عَنْ إِطْلاقِ مَجَلَّةٍ شَهْرِيَّةٍ مُتَخَصِّصَةٍ تُرَكِّزُ عَلَى الأَدَبِ وَالثَّقافَةِ، تَهْدُفُ إِلَى تَوْفِيرِ تَغْطِيَةٍ إِعْلامِيَّةٍ عَمِيقَةٍ لِلْمَشْهَدِ الثَّقافِيِّ العَرَبِيِّ. تَضُمُّ المَجَلَّةُ مَقالاتٍ نَقْدِيَّةً، وَمُراجَعاتِ كُتُبٍ، وَحِواراتٍ مَعَ كُتّابٍ وَمُثَقَّفِينَ، وَتَعِدُ بِتَقْدِيمِ مُحْتَوًى غَنِيٍّ يُلَبِّي تَطَلُّعاتِ القُرّاءِ المُهْتَمِّينَ بِالثَّقافَةِ.

A well-known publishing house announced the launch of a monthly magazine focused on literature and culture, aimed at providing in-depth media coverage of the Arab cultural scene. The magazine includes critical articles, book reviews, and interviews with writers and intellectuals, promising to deliver rich content that meets the aspirations of readers interested in culture.

أَطْلَقَتْ "الأُسْبوعُ البِيئِيُّ"، الدَّوْرِيَّةُ الأُسْبوعِيَّةُ المُتَخَصِّصَةُ، عَدَدَها الجَدِيدَ مَعَ تَرْكِيزٍ كَبِيرٍ عَلَى القَضايا البِيئِيَّةِ المَحَلِّيَّةِ وَالعالَمِيَّةِ. تُقَدِّمُ التَّغْطِيَةُ تَقارِيرَ مُفَصَّلَةً حَوْلَ التَّحَدِّياتِ البِيئِيَّةِ، وَالمَشْروعاتِ المُسْتَدامَةِ، وَأَثَرِ التَّغَيُّرِ المُناخِيِّ، مُسَلِّطَةً الضَّوْءَ عَلَى جُهودِ المُنَظَّماتِ وَالأَفْرادِ في مُكافَحَةِ الأَزْمَةِ البِيئِيَّةِ.

"The Environmental Week," the specialized weekly periodical, released its new issue with a major focus on local and global environmental issues. The coverage provides detailed reports on environmental challenges, sustainable projects, and the impact of climate change, highlighting the efforts of organizations and individuals in combating the environmental crisis.

أَعْلَنَتِ اليَوْمُ الإخْبارِيُّ، الصَّحيفَةُ اليَوْمِيَّةُ الرَّائِدَةُ، عَنْ تَعْزيزِ وُجودِها الرَّقْمِيِّ مِنْ خِلالِ إطْلاقِ مُلْحَقٍ تِكْنولوجِيٍّ جَديدٍ. يَهْدُفُ المُلْحَقُ إلى تَوْفيرِ تَغْطِيَةٍ مُعَمَّقَةٍ لِأَحْدَثِ التَّوَجُّهاتِ التِّكْنولوجِيَّةِ، وَالابْتِكاراتِ، وَتَأْثيرِها عَلى المُجْتَمَعِ، مَعَ تَقْديمِ مَقالاتٍ تَحْليلِيَّةٍ، تَقاريرَ خاصَّةً، وَمُقابَلاتٍ مَعَ خُبَراءَ في المَجالِ.

Al-Yawm Al-Ikhbari, a leading daily newspaper, announced the enhancement of its digital presence by launching a new technology supplement. The supplement aims to provide in-depth coverage of the latest technological trends, innovations, and their impact on society, with analytical articles, special reports, and interviews with experts in the field.

11.1.1.2 Reference: Arabic Newspapers

Track **27**

الصُّحُفُ العَرَبِيَّةُ البارِزَةُ وَمَوْقِفُها الإعْلامِيُّ

في عَصْرٍ تَتَسارَعُ فيهِ وَتيرَةُ الأَحْداثِ العالَمِيَّةِ، تَلْعَبُ وَسائِلُ الإعْلامِ دَوْرًا حاسِمًا في تَشْكيلِ وِجْهاتِ نَظَرِنا وَفَهْمِنا لِلْعالَمِ. في الوَطَنِ العَرَبِيِّ، تَبْرُزُ مَجْموعَةٌ مِنَ الصُّحُفِ وَالمَواقِعِ الإخْبارِيَّةِ كَبَعْضٍ مِنْ أَبْرَزِ المَنابِرِ الإعْلامِيَّةِ الَّتي تُؤَثِّرُ في الرَّأْيِ العامِّ وَتُقَدِّمُ تَغْطِيَةً شامِلَةً لِلْأَحْداثِ المَحَلِّيَّةِ وَالعالَمِيَّةِ. نُقَدِّمُ لَكُمْ نَظْرَةً عَلى بَعْضٍ مِنْ أَبْرَزِ الصُّحُفِ وَالمَواقِعِ الإخْبارِيَّةِ العَرَبِيَّةِ وَمَواقِفِها الإعْلامِيَّةِ.

الدُّسْتورُ (الأُرْدُنُّ): صَحيفَةُ "الدُّسْتور"، الَّتي تَأَسَّسَتْ في عام 1967، تُعَدُّ مِنَ الصُّحُفِ الرَّئيسِيَّةِ في الأُرْدُنِّ. تَمْتازُ بِمَوْقِفِها الوِدِّيِّ تِجاهَ الحُكومَةِ، وَتُقَدِّمُ تَغْطِيَةً إعْلامِيَّةً لِلْأَحْداثِ السِّياسِيَّةِ وَالاقْتِصادِيَّةِ الأُرْدُنِّيَّةِ وَالدَّوْلِيَّةِ. تَحْرِصُ الصَّحيفَةُ عَلى نَشْرِ مَقالاتٍ وَتَحْليلاتٍ تَتَوافَقُ مَعَ السِّياساتِ الوَطَنِيَّةِ وَتُسْهِمُ في تَعْزيزِ الوَعْيِ العامِّ.

اليَوْمُ السّابِعُ (مِصْرُ): يُعَدُّ مَوْقِعُ "اليَوْمِ السّابِعِ"، الَّذي أُطْلِقَ في عام 2008، مِنْ أَهَمِّ المَواقِعِ الإخْبارِيَّةِ الإلِكْترونِيَّةِ في مِصْرَ. يَتَمَيَّزُ بِتَغْطِيَتِهِ الواسِعَةِ وَالمُتَنَوِّعَةِ لِلْأَخْبارِ العاجِلَةِ، وَالسِّياسَةِ، وَالاقْتِصادِ، وَالثَّقافَةِ، وَالرِّياضَةِ، وَيُعْرَفُ بِسُرْعَةِ تَحْديثِهِ لِلْأَخْبارِ وَالتَّحْليلاتِ العَميقَةِ الَّتي تُلَبّي احْتِياجاتِ القارِئِ العَرَبِيِّ الباحِثِ عَنْ مَعْلوماتٍ دَقيقَةٍ وَمُوَثَّقَةٍ.

الرَّأْيُ (الأُرْدُنُّ): تَأَسَّسَتْ صَحيفَةُ "الرَّأْي" في عام 1971 وَتُعْتَبَرُ مِنْ أَعْرَقِ الصُّحُفِ في الأُرْدُنِّ. كَصَحيفَةِ "الدُّسْتور"، تَتَّخِذُ مَوْقِفًا داعِمًا لِلْحُكومَةِ، مَعَ تَرْكيزٍ قَوِيٍّ عَلى الأَخْبارِ الوَطَنِيَّةِ وَالشُّؤونِ العَرَبِيَّةِ. تَسْعى الصَّحيفَةُ إلى تَقْديمِ تَغْطِيَةٍ إعْلامِيَّةٍ دَقيقَةٍ وَمُتَوازِنَةٍ، مَعَ التَّرْكيزِ عَلى القَضايا الاجْتِماعِيَّةِ وَالاقْتِصادِيَّةِ.

أَخْبارُ اليَوْمِ (مِصْرُ): "أَخْبارُ اليَوْمِ"، وَالَّتي تُعْرَفُ أَيْضًا باسْمِ "الأَخْبارِ"، هِيَ واحِدَةٌ مِنْ أَقْدَمِ الصُّحُفِ المِصْرِيَّةِ، تَأَسَّسَتْ في عام 1944. تَعْمَلُ كَذِراعٍ إعْلامِيٍّ شِبْهِ رَسْمِيٍّ لِلدَّوْلَةِ، تَعْكِسُ وِجْهاتِ نَظَرِ الحُكومَةِ وَتُناقِشُ السِّياساتِ العامَّةَ. تُقَدِّمُ الصَّحيفَةُ تَحْليلاتٍ مُعَمَّقَةً وَتَغْطِيَةً مُوَسَّعَةً لِلْأَخْبارِ المَحَلِّيَّةِ وَالعَرَبِيَّةِ.

القُدْسُ العَرَبِيُّ (المَمْلَكَةُ المُتَّحِدَةُ): تَأَسَّسَتِ "القُدْسُ العَرَبِيُّ" في لَنْدَنَ عامَ 1989، وَهِيَ صَحِيفَةٌ مُسْتَقِلَّةٌ تُغَطِّي الشُّؤُونَ العَرَبِيَّةَ وَالدَّوْلِيَّةَ. تَشْتَهِرُ بِتَوَجُّهِها النَّقْدِيِّ وَالتَّحْرِيرِ الجَرِيءِ، وَتُعْتَبَرُ مِنْبَرًا لِلْأَصْواتِ المُسْتَقِلَّةِ وَالمُعارِضَةِ. تَلْتَزِمُ الصَّحِيفَةُ بِمَعايِيرِ الصَّحافَةِ الحُرَّةِ وَتُوَفِّرُ مَنْظُورًا مُتَعَدِّدَ الأَوْجُهِ لِلْأَحْداثِ الجارِيَةِ.

الأَهْرامُ (مِصْرُ): تَأَسَّسَتِ "الأَهْرامُ"، الَّتِي تُعَدُّ واحِدَةً مِنْ أَقْدَمِ وَأَكْبَرِ الصُّحُفِ في العالَمِ العَرَبِيِّ، في عامِ 1875. كَصَحِيفَةٍ مَمْلُوكَةٍ لِلدَّوْلَةِ، تَعْكِسُ بِشَكْلٍ كَبِيرٍ الرُّؤْيَةَ الحُكُومِيَّةَ، وَتُقَدِّمُ تَغْطِيَةً مُتَنَوِّعَةً تَشْمَلُ الأَخْبارَ المَحَلِّيَّةَ وَالدَّوْلِيَّةَ، وَالثَّقافَةَ، وَالرِّياضَةَ.

الأَخْبارُ (لُبْنانُ): تُعَدُّ "الأَخْبارُ"، الَّتِي تَأَسَّسَتْ في عامِ 2006، مِنَ الصُّحُفِ اللُّبْنانِيَّةِ الرّائِدَةِ ذاتِ التَّوَجُّهِ اليَسارِيِّ. تَشْتَهِرُ بِتَحْلِيلاتِها النَّقْدِيَّةِ لِلسِّياسَةِ اللُّبْنانِيَّةِ وَالعَرَبِيَّةِ، وَتُعْرَفُ بِمَوْقِفِها الجَرِيءِ وَالصَّرِيحِ في تَناوُلِ القَضايا المَحَلِّيَّةِ وَالإِقْلِيمِيَّةِ.

الوَطَنُ (السُّعُودِيَّةُ): مُنْذُ تَأْسِيسِها في عامِ 2000، بَرَزَتِ "الوَطَنُ" كَواحِدَةٍ مِنَ الصُّحُفِ السُّعُودِيَّةِ البارِزَةِ. تُغَطِّي مَجْمُوعَةً واسِعَةً مِنَ المَواضِيعِ مِنَ السِّياسَةِ إِلى الِاقْتِصادِ وَالثَّقافَةِ، مُعَبِّرَةً عَنِ التَّوَجُّهاتِ وَالسِّياساتِ السُّعُودِيَّةِ.

Prominent Arab Newspapers and Their Media Stance

In an era of rapidly evolving global events, media plays a crucial role in shaping our perspectives and understanding of the world. In the Arab world, a group of newspapers and news websites stand out as leading media platforms that influence public opinion and provide comprehensive coverage of local and international events. Here is a look at some of the prominent Arab newspapers and their media stances.

Al-Dustour (Jordan): Established in 1967, "Al-Dustour" is one of the main newspapers in Jordan. It is known for its government-friendly stance, offering media coverage of Jordanian and international political and economic events. The newspaper strives to publish articles and analyses that align with national policies and contribute to public awareness.

Al-Youm Al-Sabea (Egypt): Launched in 2008, "Al-Youm Al-Sabea" is one of Egypt's leading online news portals. It is distinguished by its broad and diverse coverage of breaking news, politics, economy, culture, and sports, and it is known for its rapid news updates and in-depth analyses that cater to the needs of the Arab reader seeking accurate and reliable information.

Al-Rai (Jordan): Founded in 1971, "Al-Rai" is one of the oldest newspapers in Jordan. Like "Al-Dustour," it adopts a pro-government stance, with a strong focus on national news and Arab affairs. The newspaper aims to provide accurate and balanced media coverage, focusing on social and economic issues.

Akhbar Al-Youm (Egypt): Also known as "Al-Akhbar," this is one of Egypt's oldest newspapers, established in 1944. It acts as a semi-official media arm of the state, reflecting government views and discussing public policies. The newspaper offers in-depth analyses and extensive coverage of local and Arab news.

Al-Quds Al-Arabi (United Kingdom): Established in London in 1989, "Al-Quds Al-Arabi" is an independent newspaper covering Arab and international affairs. Known for its critical approach and bold editing, it serves as a platform for independent and dissenting voices. The newspaper is committed to the standards of a free press and provides a multifaceted perspective on current events.

Al-Ahram (Egypt): One of the oldest and largest newspapers in the Arab world, "Al-Ahram" was founded in 1875. As a state-owned newspaper, it largely reflects the governmental vision, offering a variety of coverage, including local and international news, culture, and sports.

Al-Akhbar (Lebanon): Established in 2006, "Al-Akhbar" is a leading Lebanese newspaper with a leftist orientation. It is renowned for its critical analyses of Lebanese and Arab politics and is known for its bold and outspoken stance on local and regional issues.

Al-Watan (Saudi Arabia): Since its inception in 2000, "Al-Watan" has emerged as one of the prominent Saudi newspapers. It covers a wide range of topics from politics to economy and culture, expressing Saudi orientations and policies.

11.1.2 Broadcast Media

Track 28

to broadcast

أَذاعَ • إذاعَةٌ

أَذاعَتِ القَناةُ تَقْريرًا خاصًّا عَنِ الأَزْمَةِ الاِقْتِصادِيَّةِ.

The channel broadcasted a special report on the economic crisis.

to produce

أَنْتَجَ • إِنْتاجٌ

أَنْتَجَتِ الشَّرِكَةُ سِلْسِلَةً تِلِفِزْيونِيَّةً جَديدَةً تَحْكي قِصَّةَ اسْتِكْشافِ الفَضاءِ.

The company produced a new television series narrating the story of space exploration.

radio; radio station

إذاعَةٌ

تَبُثُّ الإذاعَةُ بَرامِجَ مُتَنَوِّعَةً تَشْمَلُ الموسيقى، وَالأَخْبارَ، وَالبَرامِجَ التَّعْليمِيَّةَ.

The radio station broadcasts a variety of programs, including music, news, and educational shows.

FM radio

إِذَاعَةُ الـ FM

تَحْظى إِذَاعَةُ الـ FM بِشَعْبِيَّةٍ كَبِيرَةٍ بِسَبَبِ جودَةِ الصَّوْتِ العالِيَةِ وَتَنَوُّعِ المُحْتَوى.

FM radio is very popular due to its high sound quality and diverse content.

news radio

إِذَاعَةُ أَخْبارٍ

تُرَكِّزُ إِذَاعَةُ الأَخْبارِ عَلى تَقْديمِ آخِرِ التَّطَوُّراتِ العالَمِيَّةِ وَالمَحَلِّيَّةِ لِلْمُسْتَمِعينَ.

The news radio station focuses on delivering the latest global and local developments to listeners.

Islamic radio

إِذَاعَةٌ إِسْلامِيَّةٌ

تَبُثُّ الإِذَاعَةُ الإِسْلامِيَّةُ بَرامِجَ تَعْليمِيَّةً وَدينِيَّةً لِتَعْزيزِ الوَعْي الرّوحِيِّ.

The Islamic radio station broadcasts educational and religious programs to enhance spiritual awareness.

talk radio

إِذَاعَةٌ حِوارِيَّةٌ

تُعْتَبَرُ الإِذَاعَةُ الحِوارِيَّةُ مِنَصَّةً لِلنِّقاشاتِ العَميقَةِ حَوْلَ القَضايا الاِجْتِماعِيَّةِ وَالسِّياسِيَّةِ.

The talk radio station is a platform for in-depth discussions on social and political issues.

school radio

إِذَاعَةٌ مَدْرَسِيَّةٌ

تُقَدِّمُ الإِذَاعَةُ المَدْرَسِيَّةُ فُرْصَةً لِلطُّلّابِ لِتَطْويرِ مَهاراتِهِمْ في الإِلْقاءِ وَالتَّقْديمِ.

The school radio offers students an opportunity to develop their speaking and presentation skills.

radio-

إِذاعِيٌّ

يَعْمَلُ المُذيعُ الإِذاعِيُّ عَلى إِعْدادِ وَتَقْديمِ البَرامِجِ الإِخْبارِيَّةِ وَالثَّقافِيَّةِ.

The radio broadcaster prepares and presents news and cultural programs.

TV studio

إِسْتوديو تِلِفِزْيونيٌّ

يَحْتَوي الاِسْتوديو التِّلِفِزْيونيُّ عَلى المُعَدّاتِ اللّازِمَةِ لِإِنْتاجِ وَتَسْجيلِ بَرامِجِ البَثِّ الحَيِّ.

The television studio contains the necessary equipment for producing and recording live broadcast programs.

بَثَّ • to broadcast

بَثَّتِ القَناةُ الوَثائِقِيَّةُ سِلْسِلَةً مِنَ البَرامِجِ التَّعْليمِيَّةِ عَنِ التّاريخِ الطَّبيعِيِّ.

The documentary channel broadcasted a series of educational programs about natural history.

بَثٌّ تِلِفِزْيونِيٌّ مُباشِرٌ

live TV broadcast

شاهَدَ الجُمْهورُ البَثَّ التِّلِفِزْيونِيَّ المُباشِرَ لِلْحَفْلِ الِافْتِتاحِيِّ لِلْأَلْعابِ الأولِمْبِيَّةِ.

The audience watched the live television broadcast of the Olympic opening ceremony.

بَثٌّ مُباشِرٌ

live broadcast

يُفَضِّلُ الكَثيرُ مِنَ النّاسِ مُشاهَدَةَ البَثِّ المُباشِرِ لِلْأَحْداثِ الرِّياضِيَّةِ لِمُتابَعَةِ الإثارَةِ لَحْظَةً بِلَحْظَةٍ.

Many people prefer watching live broadcasts of sports events to follow the excitement moment by moment.

بَثَّ • to broadcast live

بَثٌّ مُباشَرَةً

بَثَّتِ القَناةُ التِّلِفِزْيونِيَّةُ الحَدَثَ الرِّياضِيَّ مُباشَرَةً، مِمّا سَمَحَ لِلْمُشاهِدينَ بِمُتابَعَةِ اللُّعْبَةِ لَحْظَةً بِلَحْظَةٍ.

The television channel broadcast the sports event live, allowing viewers to follow the game moment by moment.

بَرْنامَجٌ (تِلِفِزْيونِيٌّ)

(TV) program

بَرامِج •

يَعْرِضُ البَرْنامَجُ التِّلِفِزْيونِيُّ مَجْموعَةً مُتَنَوِّعَةً مِنَ المَواضيعِ مِثْلَ العُلومِ وَالثَّقافَةِ.

The television program features a variety of topics, such as science and culture.

بَرْنامَجٌ إخْبارِيٌّ

news program

يُقَدِّمُ البَرْنامَجُ الإخْبارِيُّ تَحْليلاتٍ مُعَمَّقَةً لِلْأَحْداثِ الجارِيَةِ حَوْلَ العالَمِ.

The news program provides in-depth analyses of current events around the world.

تابَع • مُتابَعَةٌ

to follow, to tune in to

تابَعَ المُشاهِدونَ السِّلسِلَةَ الوَثائِقِيَّةَ بِشَغَفٍ لِمَعرِفَةِ تَطَوُّراتِ القِصَّةِ.

Viewers followed the documentary series eagerly to learn about the story's developments.

تَحَدَّث • تَحَدَّثَ

to speak, talk

تَحَدَّثَ المُحَلِّلُ السِّياسِيُّ عَنِ التَّوَتُّراتِ الدَّوْلِيَّةِ في البَثِّ الحَيِّ.

The political analyst spoke about international tensions in the live broadcast.

تَصويرٌ

filming

اِستَخدَمَ المُخرِجُ تِقنِيّاتِ تَصويرٍ مُتَطَوِّرَةً لِإنتاجِ الفيلْمِ الجَديدِ.

The director used advanced filming techniques to produce the new movie.

تَعْليقٌ

commentary

قَدَّمَ التَّعْليقُ الفَعّالُ تَحْليلًا قَيِّمًا خِلالَ المُباراةِ.

The insightful commentary provided valuable analysis during the match.

تَغْطِيَةٌ

coverage

شَمِلَتْ تَغْطِيَةُ الاِنتِخاباتِ مُقابَلاتٍ مَعَ المُرَشَّحينَ وَتَحْليلًا لِلنَّتائِجِ.

The coverage of the elections included interviews with the candidates and analysis of the results.

تَغْطِيَةٌ تِلِفِزْيونِيَّةٌ

TV coverage

تابَعَ المَلايينُ حَوْلَ العالَمِ التَّغْطِيَةَ التِّلِفِزْيونِيَّةَ لِحَفْلِ تَوْزيعِ جَوائِزِ الأوسكارِ.

Millions worldwide followed the television coverage of the Oscar awards ceremony.

تِقْنِيَّةُ بَثٍّ

broadcasting technology

تَتَطَلَّبُ تِقْنِيَّةُ البَثِّ اِستِخدامَ مُعَدّاتٍ مُتَطَوِّرَةٍ لِنَقْلِ الصّورَةِ وَالصَّوْتِ بِوُضوحٍ.

Broadcasting technology requires advanced equipment to transmit clear images and sound.

television

تِلِفِزْيُونٌ

أَصْبَحَ التِّلِفِزْيُونُ وَسِيلَةَ تَرْفِيهٍ رَئِيسِيَّةً فِي المَنازِلِ حَوْلَ العالَمِ.

Television has become a major entertainment medium in homes around the world.

reality TV

تِلِفِزْيُونُ واقِعٍ

يَعْرِضُ تِلِفِزْيُونُ الواقِعِ بَرامِجَ تَتَناوَلُ حَياةَ الأَشْخاصِ اليَوْمِيَّةَ وَتَجارِبَهُمُ الشَّخْصِيَّةَ.

Reality television shows programs that explore people's daily lives and personal experiences.

television-

تِلِفِزْيُونِيٌّ

يَشْمَلُ المُحْتَوى التِّلِفِزْيُونِيُّ مَجْموعَةً واسِعَةً مِنَ الأَنْواعِ مِثْلَ الأَخْبارِ، وَالدِّراما، وَالبَرامِجِ التَّعْليمِيَّةِ.

Television content includes a wide range of genres, such as news, drama, and educational programs.

to receive

تَلَقَّى • تَلَقٍّ

تَلَقَّى البَرْنامَجُ التِّلِفِزْيُونِيُّ رُدودَ فِعْلٍ إيجابِيَّةً مِنَ الجُمْهورِ بَعْدَ العَرْضِ الأَوَّلِ.

The television program received positive feedback from the audience after its premiere.

to edit

حَرَّرَ • تَحْريرٌ

حَرَّرَ الصَّحَفِيُّ المَقالَةَ بِعِنايَةٍ، مُضيفًا تَفاصيلَ دَقيقَةً وَمَعْلوماتٍ مُوَثَّقَةً.

The journalist carefully edited the article, adding precise details and verified information.

vital, essential

حَيَوِيٌّ

يُعْتَبَرُ النَّقْلُ المُباشِرُ لِلْأَحْداثِ الرِّياضِيَّةِ مِنَ العَناصِرِ الحَيَوِيَّةِ فِي البَثِّ التِّلِفِزْيُونِيِّ.

Live broadcasting of sports events is a vital element of television broadcasting.

to film, record

صَوَّرَ • تَصْويرٌ

صَوَّرَ المُخْرِجُ مَشاهِدَ الفيلْمِ فِي عِدَّةِ مَواقِعَ حَوْلَ العالَمِ.

The director filmed the movie scenes in various locations around the world.

to air, show

عَرْضٌ • عَرَضَ

عَرَضَتِ القَناةُ التِّلِفِزْيونيَّةُ الفيلْمَ الجَديدَ في سَهْرَةِ نِهايَةِ الأُسْبوعِ، جاذِبَةً جُمْهورًا كَبيرًا.

The television channel aired the new movie during the weekend evening, attracting a large audience.

to commentate

تَعْليقٌ • عَلَّقَ

عَلَّقَ المُذيعُ على الأَحْداثِ الرِّياضِيَّةِ مُباشَرَةً، مُوَفِّرًا تَحْليلا فَوْرِيًّا للْمُبارَياتِ.

The broadcaster commented on the sports events live, providing instant analysis of the matches.

to present

تَقْديمٌ • قَدَّمَ

قَدَّمَ الصَّحَفِيُّ تَقْريرًا مُفَصَّلًا عَنِ الوَضْعِ الإِنْسانِيِّ في المَناطِقِ المُتَأَثِّرَةِ بِالحَرْبِ.

The journalist presented a detailed report on the humanitarian situation in war-affected areas.

(TV) channel

قَنَواتٌ • قَناةٌ (تِلِفِزْيونيَّةٌ)

تَبُثُّ القَناةُ التِّلِفِزْيونيَّةُ مَجْموعَةً مُتَنَوِّعَةً مِنَ البَرامِجِ لِجَذْبِ جُمْهورٍ عَريضٍ.

The television channel broadcasts a variety of programs to attract a wide audience.

news channel

قَناةٌ إِخْبارِيَّةٌ

تُوَفِّرُ القَناةُ الإِخْبارِيَّةُ تَحْديثاتٍ مُسْتَمِرَّةً حَوْلَ الأَحْداثِ العالَمِيَّةِ والمَحَلِّيَّةِ.

The news channel provides continuous updates on global and local events.

satellite channel

قَناةٌ فَضائيَّةٌ

تَصِلُ القَنَواتُ الفَضائِيَّةُ إلى جُمْهورٍ عالَمِيٍّ، مِمّا يُوَسِّعُ نِطاقَ تَأْثيرِها الإِعْلامِيِّ.

Satellite channels reach a global audience, expanding their media influence.

live, direct

مُباشِرٌ

يُفَضِّلُ العَديدُ مِنَ المُشاهِدينَ مُتابَعَةَ البَرامِجِ المُباشِرَةِ لِمُشاهَدَةِ الأَحْداثِ لَحْظَةَ وُقوعِها.

Many viewers prefer watching live programs to see events as they happen.

مُذيعٌ (الأَخْبارِ)

(news) anchor

يَعْمَلُ مُذيعُ الأَخْبارِ عَلى تَقْديمِ الأَخْبارِ وَتَحْليلِها بِطَريقَةٍ مَوْضوعِيَّةٍ لِلمُشاهِدينَ.

The news anchor works on presenting and analyzing the news objectively for viewers.

مُراسِلٌ

correspondent

يَقومُ المُراسِلُ بِنَقْلِ الأَخْبارِ مِنْ مَوْقِعِ الحَدَثِ مُباشَرَةً إلى الجُمْهورِ.

The correspondent reports the news directly from the event location to the audience.

مُسَجَّلٌ

recorded

تَمَّ بَثُّ البَرْنامَجِ المُسَجَّلِ عَلى القَناةِ التِّلِفِزْيونِيَّةِ بَعْدَ إجْراءِ المونْتاجِ اللّازِمِ.

The recorded program was broadcast on the television channel after necessary editing.

مَشْهورٌ

popular; famous

أَصْبَحَ الفَنّانُ مَشْهورًا بَعْدَ ظُهورِهِ في عِدَّةِ بَرامِجَ تِلِفِزْيونِيَّةٍ شَعْبِيَّةٍ.

The artist became famous after appearing in several popular television shows.

مُقَدِّمُ بَرْنامَجٍ

program host

يَجْذِبُ مُقَدِّمُ البَرْنامَجِ المُشاهِدينَ بِأُسْلوبِهِ الفَريدِ وَطَريقَةِ تَقْديمِهِ المُمْتِعَةِ.

The program host attracts viewers with his unique style and entertaining presentation.

مُقَدِّمُ نَشْرَةٍ جَوِّيَّةٍ

weather presenter

يُقَدِّمُ مُقَدِّمُ النَّشْرَةِ الجَوِّيَّةِ تَوَقُّعاتٍ جَوِّيَّةً دَقيقَةً وَمُفَصَّلَةً لِلْجُمْهورِ.

The weather bulletin presenter provides accurate and detailed weather forecasts to the audience.

مونْتاجٌ

editing, montage

اِسْتَخْدَمَ المُحَرِّرُ مَهاراتِ المونْتاجِ لِإنْشاءِ فيلْمٍ قَصيرٍ مُؤَثِّرٍ.

The editor used editing skills to create an impactful short film.

news bulletin

نَشْرَةٌ إِخْبارِيَّةٌ

تُقَدِّمُ النَّشْرَةُ الإِخْبارِيَّةُ آخِرَ الأَخْبارِ وَالتَّحْليلاتِ حَوْلَ الأَحْداثِ الجارِيَةِ.

The news bulletin provides the latest news and analysis of current events.

live news bulletin

نَشْرَةٌ إِخْبارِيَّةٌ حَيَّةٌ

شَهِدَتِ النَّشْرَةُ الإِخْبارِيَّةُ الحَيَّةُ تَغْطِيَةً لِلانْتِخاباتِ الرِّئاسِيَّةِ بِمُشارَكَةِ مُراسِلينَ مِنْ مَواقِعَ مُخْتَلِفَةٍ.

The live news bulletin featured coverage of the presidential elections with correspondents from various locations.

to transmit, broadcast, relay نَقَلَ • نَقْلٌ

نَقَلَ المُراسِلُ آخِرَ الأَخْبارِ مِنْ مَرْكَزِ الحَدَثِ، مِمّا سَمَحَ لِلْمُشاهِدينَ بِمُتابَعَةِ التَّطَوُّراتِ لَحْظَةً بِلَحْظَةٍ.

The correspondent relayed the latest news from the event center, allowing viewers to follow the developments moment by moment.

broadcast media *pl.* وَسائِلُ بَثٍّ إِعْلامِيٍّ

تَشْمَلُ وَسائِلُ البَثِّ الإِعْلامِيِّ التِّلِفِزْيونَ، وَالرّادْيو، وَالإِنْتَرْنِتَّ.

Broadcast media include television, radio, and the internet.

11.1.2.1 Mini-Articles

Track **29**

أَعْلَنَتْ مَجْموعَةٌ إِعْلامِيَّةٌ كُبْرى عَنْ إِطْلاقِ قَناةٍ إِخْبارِيَّةٍ فَضائِيَّةٍ جَديدَةٍ تَسْتَخْدِمُ أَحْدَثَ تِقْنِيّاتِ البَثِّ لِتَقْديمِ تَغْطِيَةٍ تِلِفِزْيونِيَّةٍ شامِلَةٍ وَمُباشِرَةٍ لِلْأَحْداثِ العالَمِيَّةِ. القَناةُ، الَّتي تَمَيَّزَتْ بِتَقْديمِ بَرامِجَ إِخْبارِيَّةٍ حَيَّةٍ وَتَحْليلاتٍ مُعَمَّقَةٍ، أَصْبَحَتْ سَريعًا مَصْدَرًا مَوْثوقًا لِلْأَخْبارِ بِفَضْلِ جَوْدَةِ الصّورَةِ وَدِقَّةِ المَعْلوماتِ.

A major media group announced the launch of a new satellite news channel that utilizes the latest broadcasting technology to provide comprehensive and live television coverage of global events. The channel, known for its live news programs and in-depth analyses, quickly became a trusted source for news thanks to its high-quality imagery and accurate information.

أَطْلَقَ اسْتودْيو تِلِفِزْيونِيٌّ مَعْروفٌ بَرْنامَجًا جَديدًا يُرَكِّزُ عَلى القَضايا البيئِيَّةِ وَالاسْتِدامَةِ. البَرْنامَجُ، الَّذي يُبَثُّ مُباشَرَةً، يَعْرِضُ تَقاريرَ مَيْدانِيَّةً وَلِقاءاتٍ مَعَ خُبَراءَ لِمُناقَشَةِ التَّحَدِّياتِ البيئِيَّةِ الرّاهِنَةِ واسْتِكْشافِ الحُلولِ المُسْتَدامَةِ، مِمّا يُعَزِّزُ الوَعْيَ البيئِيَّ بَيْنَ المُشاهِدينَ.

A well-known television studio launched a new program focusing on environmental issues and sustainability. The live program features field reports and interviews with experts to discuss current environmental challenges and explore sustainable solutions, enhancing environmental awareness among viewers.

نَقَلَتْ قَناةٌ رِياضِيَّةٌ فَضائِيَّةٌ مُباشَرَةً إِحْدى المُبارَياتِ الهامَّةِ في دَوْرِيِّ كُرَةِ القَدَمِ، مُحَقِّقَةً أَعْلى نِسَبِ مُشاهَدَةٍ في تاريخِ القَناةِ. شَمِلَتِ التَّغْطِيَةُ الحَيَّةُ تَعْليقاتٍ مُفَصَّلَةً مِنْ مُعَلِّقينَ رِياضِيّينَ مَشْهورينَ وَتَحْليلاتِ ما بَعْدَ المُباراةِ، مِمّا أَثْرى تَجْرِبَةَ المُشاهَدَةِ لِلْجُمْهورِ.

A sports satellite channel broadcasted a major football league match live, achieving the highest viewership in the channel's history. The live coverage included detailed commentary from famous sports commentators and post-match analyses, enriching the viewing experience for the audience.

قَدَّمَتْ إِذاعَةُ FM شَهيرَةٌ بَرْنامَجًا حِوارِيًّا تَناوَلَ التَّحَوُّلاتِ السِّياسِيَّةِ الرَّئيسِيَّةِ في المِنْطَقَةِ. اسْتَضافَ البَرْنامَجُ مَجْموعَةً مِنَ الخُبَراءِ وَالمُحَلِّلينَ السِّياسِيّينَ لِتَقْديمِ تَعْليقاتٍ عَميقَةٍ وَنِقاشاتٍ مُسْتَفيضَةٍ حَوْلَ الأَحْداثِ الجارِيَةِ، مُوَفِّرًا لِلْمُسْتَمِعينَ فَهْمًا أَعْمَقَ لِلسِّياقِ السِّياسِيِّ.

A popular FM radio station presented a talk show that addressed major political transformations in the region. The program hosted a group of experts and political analysts to provide in-depth comments and extensive discussions on ongoing events, offering listeners a deeper understanding of the political context.

أَطْلَقَتْ قَناةُ تِلِفِزْيونِ واقِعٍ جَديدَةٌ بَرْنامَجًا يَعْرِضُ حَياةَ المَشاهيرِ بَعيدًا عَنْ دائِرَةِ الضَّوْءِ، يُبَثُّ مُباشَرَةً وَيُوَفِّرُ لِلْمُشاهِدينَ نَظْرَةً خاصَّةً عَلى الجَوانِبِ الشَّخْصِيَّةِ وَاليَوْمِيَّةِ لِحَياةِ النُّجومِ. يُقَدِّمُ البَرْنامَجُ مُحْتَوًى حَيَوِيًّا وَتَفاعُلِيًّا، مِمّا يَجْذِبُ اهْتِمامَ جُمْهورٍ واسِعٍ وَيُعَزِّزُ مِنْ شَعْبِيَّةِ القَناةِ.

A new reality TV channel launched a program showcasing the lives of celebrities away from the limelight, broadcasted live and offering viewers a special look at the personal and daily aspects of the stars' lives. The program provides dynamic and interactive content, attracting a wide audience and enhancing the channel's popularity.

11.1.2.2 Informative Article: Satellite News Channels

Track **30**

قَنَواتُ الأَخْبارِ الفَضائِيَّةُ في العالَمِ العَرَبِيِّ: التّاريخُ، الأَهَمِّيَّةُ، وَالتَّأْثيرُ

في العالَمِ العَرَبِيِّ، تُعَدُّ قَنَواتُ الأَخْبارِ الفَضائِيَّةُ رَكيزَةً أَساسِيَّةً لِوَسائِلِ الإِعْلامِ، تُساهِمُ في إِثْراءِ المَشْهَدِ الإِعْلامِيِّ وَتَعْزيزِ حُرِّيَّةِ الإِعْلامِ وَتَدَفُّقِ المَعْلوماتِ بَيْنَ الدُّوَلِ وَالشُّعوبِ العَرَبِيَّةِ، وَقَدْ شَهِدَتْ هَذِهِ القَنَواتُ تَطَوُّرًا مَلْحوظًا عَلى مَدى العُقودِ الماضِيَةِ. بَدَأَ ظُهورُها في أَوائِلِ التِّسْعينِيّاتِ، حَيْثُ مَثَّلَتْ نُقْطَةَ تَحَوُّلٍ في طَريقَةِ تَلَقّي النّاسِ لِلْأَخْبارِ وَالمَعْلوماتِ عَبْرَ الوَطَنِ العَرَبِيِّ.

كَانَتْ بِدَايَةُ الْبَثِّ التِّلِفِزْيُونِيِّ فِي الْعَالَمِ الْعَرَبِيِّ مَحْدُودَةً بِالْقَنَوَاتِ الْأَرْضِيَّةِ الَّتِي كَانَتْ تُسَيْطِرُ عَلَيْهَا الْحُكُومَاتُ بِشَكْلٍ كَامِلٍ. مَعَ ظُهُورِ الْقَنَوَاتِ الْفَضَائِيَّةِ، تَغَيَّرَ الْمَشْهَدُ الْإِعْلَامِيُّ جِذْرِيًّا. أَصْبَحَتِ الْأَخْبَارُ مُتَاحَةً عَلَى مَدَارِ السَّاعَةِ، وَزَادَتِ الْمُنَافَسَةُ لِتَوْفِيرِ تَغْطِيَةٍ إِخْبَارِيَّةٍ شَامِلَةٍ وَمُبَاشِرَةٍ لِلْأَحْدَاثِ الْعَالَمِيَّةِ الْجَارِيَةِ.

تَلْعَبُ قَنَوَاتُ الْأَخْبَارِ الْفَضَائِيَّةُ دَوْرًا حَيَوِيًّا فِي تَشْكِيلِ الرَّأْيِ الْعَامِّ وَنَقْلِ الْأَحْدَاثِ الْعَاجِلَةِ. تُوَفِّرُ هَذِهِ الْقَنَوَاتُ لِلْجُمْهُورِ تَغْطِيَةً مُبَاشِرَةً لِلْأَحْدَاثِ الْهَامَّةِ، مِنَ السِّيَاسَةِ إِلَى الِاقْتِصَادِ وَالثَّقَافَةِ. كَمَا تُعَدُّ مِنْبَرًا لِلنِّقَاشِ وَالْحِوَارِ، حَيْثُ تُقَدِّمُ بَرَامِجَ تَحْلِيلِيَّةً وَحِوَارِيَّةً تَسْتَضِيفُ خُبَرَاءَ وَمُحَلِّلِينَ لِمُنَاقَشَةِ مُخْتَلِفِ الْقَضَايَا.

أَثَّرَتْ قَنَوَاتُ الْأَخْبَارِ الْفَضَائِيَّةُ بِشَكْلٍ كَبِيرٍ عَلَى الْمُجْتَمَعَاتِ الْعَرَبِيَّةِ، حَيْثُ سَاهَمَتْ فِي رَفْعِ مُسْتَوَى الْوَعْيِ وَالْمَعْرِفَةِ بَيْنَ النَّاسِ. أَدَّتِ الْقُدْرَةُ عَلَى بَثِّ الْأَخْبَارِ بِشَكْلٍ فَوْرِيٍّ وَمُسْتَمِرٍّ إِلَى تَسْرِيعِ وَتِيرَةِ تَلَقِّي الْمَعْلُومَاتِ وَرُدُودِ الْفِعْلِ عَلَى الْأَحْدَاثِ السِّيَاسِيَّةِ وَالِاجْتِمَاعِيَّةِ.

رَغْمَ أَهَمِّيَّتِهَا، تُوَاجِهُ الْقَنَوَاتُ الْفَضَائِيَّةُ الْإِخْبَارِيَّةُ تَحَدِّيَاتٍ مُتَعَدِّدَةً، مِثْلَ الضُّغُوطِ السِّيَاسِيَّةِ وَالصُّعُوبَاتِ التِّقْنِيَّةِ. كَمَا يَتَعَيَّنُ عَلَيْهَا التَّعَامُلُ مَعَ قَضَايَا الْحِيَادِ وَالْمَوْضُوعِيَّةِ فِي تَغْطِيَةِ الْأَخْبَارِ، حَيْثُ تُتَّهَمُ أَحْيَانًا بِالتَّحَيُّزِ أَوِ التَّأْثِيرِ عَلَى الرَّأْيِ الْعَامِّ.

تَسْتَمِرُّ قَنَوَاتُ الْأَخْبَارِ الْفَضَائِيَّةُ فِي التَّطَوُّرِ، مَعَ التَّرْكِيزِ الْمُتَزَايِدِ عَلَى اسْتِخْدَامِ تِقْنِيَاتِ بَثٍّ مُتَطَوِّرَةٍ وَالِاسْتِفَادَةِ مِنْ وَسَائِلِ الْإِعْلَامِ الْجَدِيدَةِ وَالرَّقْمِيَّةِ. يُتَوَقَّعُ أَنْ تُوَاصِلَ هَذِهِ الْقَنَوَاتُ لَعِبَ دَوْرٍ مِحْوَرِيٍّ فِي الْمَشْهَدِ الْإِعْلَامِيِّ الْعَرَبِيِّ، مُوَاكِبَةً لِلتَّغَيُّرَاتِ السَّرِيعَةِ وَالتَّطَوُّرَاتِ الْعَالَمِيَّةِ.

Satellite News Channels in the Arab World: History, Importance, and Impact

In the Arab world, satellite news channels are a fundamental pillar of broadcast media, contributing to enriching the media landscape and enhancing media freedom and the flow of information among Arab countries and peoples. These channels have experienced significant development over the past decades. Their emergence in the early 1990s represented a turning point in how people receive news and information across the Arab world.

The beginning of television broadcasting in the Arab world was limited to terrestrial channels, which were completely controlled by governments. With the advent of satellite channels, the media landscape changed radically. News became available around the clock, and competition increased to provide comprehensive and live coverage of ongoing global events.

Satellite news channels play a vital role in shaping public opinion and broadcasting urgent events. These channels offer the audience live coverage of important events, from politics to economics and culture. They also serve as a platform for discussion and dialogue, presenting analytical and talk shows that host experts and analysts to discuss various issues.

Satellite news channels have significantly impacted Arab societies by raising awareness and knowledge among people. The ability to broadcast news instantly and continuously has accelerated the pace of information reception and reaction to political and social events.

Despite their importance, satellite news channels face multiple challenges, such as political pressure and technical difficulties. They also have to deal with issues of neutrality and objectivity in news coverage, sometimes being accused of bias or influencing public opinion.

Satellite news channels continue to evolve, with an increasing focus on using advanced broadcasting technologies and leveraging new and digital media. These channels are expected to continue playing a pivotal role in the Arab media landscape, keeping pace with rapid changes and global developments.

11.1.3 Online and Social Media

Track 31

أَعْجَبَ (بِ) • إِعْجابٌ

to like

أَعْجَبَ المُسْتَخْدِمُ بِالصّورَةِ، فَضَغَطَ عَلى زِرِّ الإعْجابِ لِيُظْهِرَ تَقْديرَهُ.

The user liked the picture, clicking the like button to show appreciation.

إِعْجابٌ

like

حَصَلَ المَنْشورُ عَلى آلافِ الإعْجاباتِ في غُضونِ ساعاتٍ.

The post received thousands of likes within hours.

اِجْتِماعِيٌّ

social

يَتَمَيَّزُ المُحْتَوى الاِجْتِماعِيُّ بِقُدْرَتِهِ عَلى رَبْطِ الأَشْخاصِ مِنْ خَلْفِيّاتٍ مُتَنَوِّعَةٍ.

Social content is characterized by its ability to connect people from diverse backgrounds.

اِفْتِراضِيٌّ

virtual

يُتيحُ العالَمُ الاِفْتِراضِيُّ إِمْكانِيّاتٍ لا حَصْرَ لَها لِلتَّفاعُلِ وَالتَّعَلُّمِ.

The virtual world offers endless possibilities for interaction and learning.

اِنْتَشَرَ • اِنْتِشارٌ

to spread

اِنْتَشَرَ الفيْديو بِسُرْعَةٍ عَلى مِنَصّاتِ التَّواصُلِ الاِجْتِماعِيِّ، مُحَقِّقًا مَلايينَ المُشاهَداتِ.

The video spread quickly on social media platforms, achieving millions of views.

to follow
• مُتَابَعَةٌ

تابَعَ
تابَعَ الآلافُ الحِسابَ لِمُتابَعَةِ آخِرِ الأَخْبارِ وَالتَّحْديثاتِ.

Thousands followed the account to keep up with the latest news and updates.

social media analytics
pl.

تَحْليلاتُ وَسائِلِ تَواصُلٍ اجْتِماعِيٍّ
تُسْتَخْدَمُ تَحْليلاتُ وَسائِلِ التَّواصُلِ الاجْتِماعِيِّ لِفَهْمِ سُلوكِ المُسْتَخْدِمينَ وَتَفْضيلاتِهِمْ.

Social media analytics are used to understand user behavior and preferences.

blog post

تَدوينَةٌ
نَشَرَ المُدَوِّنُ تَدوينَةً جَديدَةً تُناقِشُ التَّغَيُّراتِ الاقْتِصادِيَّةَ الأَخيرَةَ.

The blogger posted a new post discussing recent economic changes.

social media marketing

تَسْويقٌ عَبْرَ وَسائِلِ تَواصُلٍ اجْتِماعِيٍّ
أَصْبَحَ التَّسْويقُ عَبْرَ وَسائِلِ التَّواصُلِ الاجْتِماعِيِّ طَريقَةً فَعّالَةً لِلْوُصولِ إِلى جُمْهورٍ أَوْسَعَ.

Marketing through social media has become an effective way to reach a broader audience.

application, app

تَطْبيقٌ
يَسْتَخْدِمُ المَلايينُ التَّطْبيقَ لِلتَّواصُلِ مَعَ الأَصْدِقاءِ وَمُشارَكَةِ اللَّحَظاتِ.

Millions use the app to connect with friends and share moments.

comment

تَعْليقٌ
كَتَبَ المُسْتَخْدِمُ تَعْليقًا تَحْتَ المَنْشورِ لِلتَّعْبيرِ عَنْ رَأْيِهِ في المَوْضوعِ.

The user wrote a comment under the post to express his opinion on the topic.

to interact

تَفاعَلَ • تَفاعُلٌ

شَجَّعَتِ المَيزاتُ الجَديدَةُ لِلتَّطْبيقِ عَلى تَفاعُلٍ أَكْبَرَ بَيْنَ المُسْتَخْدِمينَ.

The new app features encouraged greater interaction among users.

social interaction

تَفاعُلٌ اجْتِماعِيٌّ

شَهِدَ التَّفاعُلُ الاجْتِماعِيُّ زِيادَةً كَبيرَةً بِفَضْلِ مِنَصّاتِ التَّواصُلِ عَبْرَ الإنْتَرْنِتِ.

Social interaction has significantly increased thanks to online communication platforms.

social media account

حِسابُ تَواصُلٍ اجْتِماعِيٌّ

يُديرُ المُمَثِّلُ حِسابَ التَّواصُلِ الاجْتِماعِيِّ بِنَفْسِهِ لِلتَّواصُلِ المُباشِرِ مَعَ المُعْجَبينَ.

The actor manages their social media account personally to directly connect with fans.

digital

رَقْمِيٌّ

تَحَوَّلَتِ الكَثيرُ مِنَ الخِدْماتِ إلى النِّظامِ الرَّقْمِيِّ لِتَسْهيلِ الوُصولِ وَالاسْتِخْدامِ.

Many services have transitioned to digital to facilitate access and usage.

to share

شارَكَ • مُشارَكَةٌ

شارَكَ المُسْتَخْدِمونَ الصُّوَرَ وَالقِصَصَ عَبْرَ شَبَكاتِهِمِ الاجْتِماعِيَّةِ لِلتَّعْبيرِ عَنْ تَجارِبِهِمِ اليَوْمِيَّةِ.

Users shared photos and stories through their social networks to express their daily experiences.

social network

شَبَكَةٌ اجْتِماعِيَّةٌ

يُعْتَبَرُ فيسْبوك وَتيك توك مِنْ أَشْهَرِ الشَّبَكاتِ الاجْتِماعِيَّةِ المُسْتَخْدَمَةِ حَوْلَ العالَمِ.

Facebook and TikTok are among the most famous social networks used worldwide.

personal

شَخْصِيٌّ

يُفَضِّلُ الكَثيرُ مِنَ الأَشْخاصِ اسْتِخْدامَ حِساباتِهِمِ الشَّخْصِيَّةِ لِمُشارَكَةِ لَحَظاتِهِمِ الخاصَّةِ.

Many people prefer using their personal accounts to share their private moments.

صانِعُ المُحْتَوى content creator

يُشارِكُ صانِعُ المُحْتَوى الشَّهيرُ نَصائِحَهُ حَوْلَ كَيْفِيَّةِ النَّجاحِ في مِنَصّاتِ التَّواصُلِ الاِجْتِماعِيِّ.

The famous content creator shares his tips on how to succeed on social media platforms.

صَفْحَةٌ page

تَحْتَوي الصَّفْحَةُ عَلى مَعْلوماتٍ مُفَصَّلَةٍ عَنِ الخِدْماتِ المُقَدَّمَةِ.

The page contains detailed information about the services offered.

عَلَّقَ • تَعْليقٌ to comment

عَلَّقَ المُسْتَخْدِمُ عَلى المَنْشورِ مُعَبِّرًا عَنْ تَأْييدِهِ لِلْآراءِ الوارِدَةِ فيهِ.

The user commented on the post, expressing his support for the opinions presented.

مُتابِعٌ follower

زادَ عَدَدُ المُتابِعينَ بِشَكْلٍ كَبيرٍ بَعْدَ نَشْرِ الفيديو الأَخيرِ.

The number of followers significantly increased after posting the latest video.

مُتَداوَلٌ trending, circulated, shared

أَصْبَحَ المَوْضوعُ مُتَداوَلًا عَلى الإِنْتَرِنتِّ بَعْدَ الجَدَلِ الَّذي أَثارَهُ.

The topic became trending on the internet after the controversy it sparked.

مُتَداوِلٌ sharer

يُعَدُّ المُسْتَخْدِمُ مُتَداوِلًا نَشِطًا عِنْدَما يُشارِكُ المُحْتَوى بِانْتِظامٍ مَعَ الآخَرينَ.

A user is considered an active sharer when they regularly share content with others.

مُتَّصِلٌ connected

يَظَلُّ المُسْتَخْدِمُ مُتَّصِلًا بِالإِنْتَرِنتِّ لِتَلَقّي التَّحْديثاتِ الفَوْرِيَّةِ.

The user stays connected to the internet to receive instant updates.

digital content

مُحْتَوًى رَقْمِيٌّ

تَشْمَلُ المَكْتَبَةُ الرَّقْمِيَّةُ مُحْتَوًى رَقْمِيًّا مُتَنَوِّعًا يَتَرَاوَحُ مِنَ الكُتُبِ إِلَى الأَفْلَامِ.

The digital library includes diverse digital content ranging from books to movies.

blog

مُدَوَّنَةٌ

أَصْبَحَتِ المُدَوَّنَةُ وَسِيلَةً شَعْبِيَّةً لِلْأَفْرَادِ لِنَشْرِ أَفْكَارِهِمْ وَتَجَارِبِهِمْ عَلَى الإِنْتَرْنِتِّ.

Blogs have become a popular means for individuals to publish their ideas and experiences on the internet.

share

مُشَارَكَةٌ

تُشَجِّعُ مَيزَةُ المُشَارَكَةِ عَلَى الشَّبَكَاتِ الاِجْتِمَاعِيَّةِ الأَشْخَاصَ عَلَى تَوْزِيعِ المُحْتَوى بَيْنَ دَوَائِرِهِمْ.

The sharing feature on social networks encourages people to distribute content within their circles.

shared

مُشَارَكٌ

تَحْظَى المَعْلُوماتُ المُشَارَكَةُ عَلَى مِنَصَّاتِ التَّواصُلِ بِقُدْرَةٍ عَلَى الوُصولِ إِلى جُمْهورٍ واسِعٍ.

Shared information on social platforms has the potential to reach a wide audience.

video clip

مَقْطَعُ فيديو

اِنْتَشَرَ مَقْطَعُ الفيديو عَلَى الإِنْتَرْنِتَّ بِسُرْعَةٍ وَحَقَّقَ مَلايينَ المُشاهَدات.

The video clip went viral on the internet and garnered millions of views.

viral

مُنْتَشِرٌ

أَصْبَحَ الفيديو مُنْتَشِرًا بِسُرْعَةٍ، مُحَقِّقًا مَلايينَ المُشاهَداتِ خِلالَ ساعاتٍ.

The video went viral quickly, achieving millions of views within hours.

post

مَنْشورٌ

تَمَّ تَحْديثُ المَنْشورِ عَلَى الفيسْبوك لِيَشْمَلَ المَعْلوماتِ الجَديدَةَ حَوْلَ الحَدَثِ.

The post on Facebook was updated to include new information about the event.

social media platform

مِنَصَّةُ تَواصُلٍ اجْتِماعِيٍّ

تُعَدُّ مِنَصَّةُ التَّواصُلِ الاجْتِماعِيِّ كَإِنْسْتَغْرامْ مَكانًا شائِعًا لِمُشارَكَةِ الصُّوَرِ وَالقِصَصِ.

A social media platform like Instagram is a popular place for sharing photos and stories.

social media website

مَواقِع • مَوقِعُ تَواصُلٍ اجْتِماعِيٍّ

يَسْتَخْدِمُ النَّاسُ مَواقِعَ التَّواصُلِ الاجْتِماعِيِّ لِلْبَقاءِ عَلى اتِّصالٍ مَعَ الأَصْدِقاءِ وَالعائِلَةِ.

People use social networking sites to stay in touch with friends and family.

to post, to publish

نَشَرَ • نَشْرُ

نَشَرَ النَّاشِطُ مَقالَتَهُ عَلى الإِنْتَرْنِتْ لِجَذْبِ الانْتِباهِ إلى القَضايا البيئِيَّةِ.

The activist published his article online to draw attention to environmental issues.

online media content publishing

نَشْرُ مُحْتَوًى إعْلامِيٍّ عَلى الإِنْتَرْنِتْ

باتَ نَشْرُ المُحْتَوى الإعْلامِيِّ عَلى الإِنْتَرْنِتْ أداةً قَوِيَّةً لِلتَّأْثيرِ العامِّ وَالتَّوْعِيَةِ.

Publishing media content online has become a powerful tool for public influence and awareness.

hashtag

هاشْتاج

أُسْتُخْدِمَ الهاشْتاجُ لِلتَّرْويجِ لِلْحَمْلَةِ عَلى تويتَرْ وَزِيادَةِ الوَعْيِ حَوْلَ المَوْضوعِ.

The hashtag was used to promote the campaign on Twitter and raise awareness about the topic.

> هاشْتاج, also spelled هاشْتاغ, illustrates the regional variation in using ج vs. غ to represent the hard 'g' sound in loanwords.

11.1.3.1 Mini-Articles

Track **32**

أُطْلِقَتْ مُبادَرَةٌ عَبْرَ مِنَصّاتِ التَّواصُلِ الاجْتِماعِيِّ تَهْدُفُ إلى دَعْمِ الشَّبابِ المُبْدِعينَ في مُخْتَلِفِ المَجالاتِ. تُشَجِّعُ المُبادَرَةُ المُسْتَخْدِمينَ عَلى مُشارَكَةِ أَعْمالِهِمْ بِاسْتِخْدامِ هاشْتاج خاصٍّ، وَسُرْعانَ ما انْتَشَرَتِ التَّدْوِيناتُ وَمَقاطِعُ الفيديو، مِمّا أدّى إلى تَفاعُلٍ اجْتِماعِيٍّ كَبيرٍ وَتَسْليطِ الضَّوْءِ عَلى المَواهِبِ الجَديدَةِ.

An initiative was launched on social media platforms aimed at supporting creative youth in various fields. The initiative encourages users to share their work using a specific hashtag, and quickly, posts and video clips spread, leading to significant social interaction and highlighting new talents.

أُطْلِقَتْ شَبَكَةٌ اجْتِمَاعِيَّةٌ جَدِيدَةٌ تُرَكِّزُ عَلَى المُحْتَوَى الرَّقْمِيِّ التَّفَاعُلِيِّ وَسُرْعَانَ ما أَصْبَحَتْ شَائِعَةً بَيْنَ المُسْتَخْدِمِينَ. تَتَمَيَّزُ الشَّبَكَةُ بِتَطْبِيقٍ سَهْلِ الاسْتِخْدَامِ يُمَكِّنُ المُسْتَخْدِمِينَ مِنْ نَشْرِ مُحْتَوَاهُم وَالتَّفَاعُلِ مَعَ مُتَابِعِيهِم بِطُرُقٍ مُبْتَكَرَةٍ، مِمَّا جَذَبَ مَلَايِينَ المُشْتَرِكِينَ فِي فَتْرَةٍ قَصِيرَةٍ.

A new social network focused on interactive digital content was launched and quickly became popular among users. The network features an easy-to-use application that allows users to publish their content and interact with their followers in innovative ways, attracting millions of subscribers in a short period.

أَطْلَقَتْ شَرِكَةٌ تِجَارِيَّةٌ كُبْرَى حَمْلَةً تَسْوِيقِيَّةً عَبْرَ مِنَصَّاتِ التَّوَاصُلِ الاجْتِمَاعِيِّ لِمُنْتَجِها الجَدِيد، مُسْتَخْدِمَةً مَقَاطِعَ فِيدْيو مُبْتَكَرَةً وَتَفَاعُلِيَّةً. حَقَّقَتِ الحَمْلَةُ إِعْجَابًا وَتَفَاعُلًا ضَخْمًا مِنَ المُسْتَخْدِمِينَ، مِمَّا سَاهَمَ فِي انْتِشَارِ العَلَامَةِ التِّجَارِيَّةِ وَزِيَادَةِ الوَعْيِ بِالمُنْتَجِ.

A major commercial company launched a marketing campaign on social media for its new product, using innovative and interactive video clips. The campaign achieved massive likes and interactions from users, contributing to the spread of the brand and increasing awareness of the product.

حَقَّقَتْ مُدَوَّنَةٌ تَعْلِيمِيَّةٌ افْتِرَاضِيَّةٌ إِنْجَازًا بَارِزًا بِوُصُولِها إِلَى مِلْيُونِ مُتَابِعٍ عَلَى إِحْدَى مِنَصَّاتِ التَّوَاصُلِ الاجْتِمَاعِيِّ. المُدَوَّنَةُ، الَّتِي تُشَارِكُ مُحْتَوًى تَعْلِيمِيًّا وَتَثْقِيفِيًّا بِانْتِظَامٍ، أَصْبَحَتْ مَصْدَرًا مَوْثُوقًا لِلْمَعْلُومَاتِ وَنَمُوذَجًا لِلنَّجَاحِ فِي اسْتِخْدَامِ الوَسَائِطِ الاجْتِمَاعِيَّةِ لِلتَّعْلِيمِ وَالتَّعَلُّمِ.

A virtual educational blog achieved a significant milestone by reaching a million followers on one of the social media platforms. The blog, which regularly shares educational and informative content, has become a reliable source of information and a model for success in using social media for education and learning.

انْتَشَرَ فِيدْيو تَوْعَوِيٌّ عَنْ أَهَمِّيَّةِ الحِفَاظِ عَلَى البِيئَةِ بِسُرْعَةٍ فَائِقَةٍ عَلَى مَوَاقِعِ التَّوَاصُلِ الاجْتِمَاعِيِّ، مُحَقِّقًا مَلَايِينَ المُشَاهَدَاتِ وَآلَافَ التَّعْلِيقَاتِ. الفِيدْيو، الَّذِي تَمَّ تَصْوِيرُهُ بِجَوْدَةٍ عَالِيَةٍ وَمُحْتَوًى مُؤَثِّرٍ، لَفَتَ انْتِبَاهَ الجُمْهُورِ وَحَفَّزَ حَرَكَةَ تَفَاعُلٍ اجْتِمَاعِيٍّ وَاسِعَةٍ حَوْلَ قَضَايَا الاسْتِدَامَةِ.

An awareness video about the importance of environmental conservation spread rapidly on social media, achieving millions of views and thousands of comments. The high-quality and impactful video attracted public attention and stimulated a broad social interaction movement around sustainability issues.

دَوْرُ وَسائِلِ التَّواصُلِ الاِجْتِماعِيِّ خِلالَ الثَّوْرَةِ المِصْريَّةِ

خِلالَ الثَّوْرَةِ المِصْريَّةِ في عام 2011، لَعِبَتْ وَسائِلُ التَّواصُلِ الاِجْتِماعِيِّ دَوْرًا حاسِمًا في تَشْكيلِ الأَحْداثِ وَنَقْلِها لِلعالَمِ. شَهِدَتْ تِلْكَ الفَتْرَةُ تَحَوُّلًا اِسْتِثْنائيًّا في كَيْفيَّةِ اِسْتِخْدامِ المِصْريّينَ لِلإِنْتَرْنِتَ، خاصَّةً مِنَصّاتٍ كَفيسبوكْ وَتويتَرْ، لِتَنْظيمِ التَّظاهُراتِ وَنَشْرِ الأَخْبارِ العاجِلَةِ وَتَنْظيمِ التَّجَمُّعاتِ الاِحْتِجاجيَّةِ.

مَكَّنَتِ الشَّبَكاتُ الاِجْتِماعيَّةُ المُتَظاهِرينَ مِنْ تَنْسيقِ جُهودِهِمْ بِشَكْلٍ فَعّالٍ، حَيْثُ اسْتَخْدَموا الهاشتاجاتِ لِتَعْزيزِ تَحَرُّكاتِهِمْ وَتَنْظيمِ المَسيراتِ في مُخْتَلِفِ أَنْحاءِ البِلادِ. كَما ساهَمَتْ في تَغْطِيَةِ الأَحْداثِ لَحْظَةً بِلَحْظَةٍ، مِمّا أَعْطى الثَّوْرَةَ زَخْمًا كَبيرًا وَجَذَبَ انْتِباهَ العالَمِ.

أَصْبَحَتْ وَسائِلُ التَّواصُلِ الاِجْتِماعِيِّ مِنْبَرًا لِلتَّعْبيرِ عَنِ الرَّأْيِ وَتَبادُلِ الأَفْكارِ وَالمَعْلوماتِ بِسُرْعَةٍ وَعَلى نِطاقٍ واسِعٍ. المَنْشوراتُ وَالمَقاطِعُ المُصَوَّرَةُ الَّتي تَمَّ نَشْرُها عَلى الإِنْتَرْنِتَ ساعَدَتْ في تَوْثيقِ الاِنْتِهاكاتِ وَحَشْدِ الدَّعْمِ الدَّوْليِّ.

رَغْمَ مُحاوَلاتِ قَطْعِ الإِنْتَرْنِتَ وَحَجْبِ المَواقِعِ الاِجْتِماعيَّةِ مِنْ قِبَلِ الحُكومَةِ، إِلّا أَنَّ النُّشَطاءَ تَمَكَّنوا مِنْ إِيجادِ طُرُقٍ بَديلَةٍ لِلبَقاءِ مُتَّصِلينَ وَتابَعوا نَشْرَ الأَخْبارِ وَالتَّحْديثاتِ. أَظْهَرَتْ هَذِهِ الأَحْداثُ القُوَّةَ الهائِلَةَ لِوَسائِلِ التَّواصُلِ الاِجْتِماعِيِّ كَأَداةٍ لِلتَّغْييرِ السِّياسِيِّ وَالاِجْتِماعِيِّ.

في الخِتامِ، أَثْبَتَتِ الثَّوْرَةُ المِصْريَّةُ أَنَّ وَسائِلَ التَّواصُلِ الاِجْتِماعِيِّ لَيْسَتْ مُجَرَّدَ مِنَصّاتٍ لِلتَّفاعُلِ الشَّخْصِيِّ، بَلْ هِيَ أَيْضًا أَدَواتٌ قَوِيَّةٌ لِلتَّعْبيرِ الجَماعِيِّ وَالحَراكِ الشَّعْبِيِّ، حَيْثُ لَعِبَتْ دَوْرًا لا يُمْكِنُ إِنْكارُهُ في تَشْكيلِ المَشْهَدِ السِّياسِيِّ في مِصْرَ وَالعالَمِ العَرَبِيِّ.

The Role of Social Media During the Egyptian Revolution

During the Egyptian Revolution in 2011, social media played a crucial role in shaping and broadcasting the events to the world. This period marked an extraordinary transformation in how Egyptians used the internet, especially platforms like Facebook and Twitter, to organize demonstrations, spread breaking news, and coordinate protest gatherings.

Social networks enabled protesters to coordinate their efforts effectively, using hashtags to boost their movements and organize marches throughout the country. They also contributed to covering the events in real time, giving the revolution significant momentum and drawing global attention.

Social media became a platform for expressing opinions, exchanging ideas, and rapidly disseminating information on a wide scale. The posts and videos shared online helped document violations and garner international support.

Despite the government's attempts to cut off the internet and block social sites, activists managed to find alternative ways to stay connected and continued to publish news and updates. These events showcased the immense power of social media as a tool for political and social change.

In conclusion, the Egyptian Revolution demonstrated that social media is not just a platform for personal interaction but also a powerful tool for collective expression and popular mobilization, playing an undeniable role in shaping the political landscape in Egypt and the Arab world.

11.1.3.3 Essay: Social Media and Mental Health

تَأْثِيرُ وَسائِلِ التَّواصُلِ الاجْتِماعِيِّ عَلَى الصِّحَّةِ النَّفْسِيَّةِ

في عَصْرِنا الرَّقْمِيِّ، تَحَوَّلَتْ وَسائِلُ التَّواصُلِ الاجْتِماعِيِّ إلى جُزْءٍ لا يَتَجَزَّأُ مِنْ حَياتِنا اليَوْمِيَّةِ، مِمّا أَثَّرَ بِشَكْلٍ مَلْحوظٍ عَلَى الصِّحَّةِ النَّفْسِيَّةِ لِلمُسْتَخْدِمينَ. تُظْهِرُ الدِّراساتُ أَنَّ التَّفاعُلَ المُسْتَمِرَّ عَلَى هَذِهِ المِنَصّاتِ يُمْكِنُ أَنْ يَكونَ لَهُ تَأْثيراتٌ سَلْبِيَّةٌ وَإيجابِيَّةٌ عَلَى السَّلامَةِ العاطِفِيَّةِ وَالنَّفْسِيَّةِ.

التَّأْثيراتُ السَّلْبِيَّةُ: ازْدادَ القَلَقُ وَالاكْتِئابُ بَيْنَ مُسْتَخْدِمي شَبَكاتِ التَّواصُلِ، حَيْثُ يَرْتَبِطُ الإفْراطُ في اسْتِخْدامِ هَذِهِ المِنَصّاتِ بِمَشاعِرِ الوَحْدَةِ وانْخِفاضِ الثِّقَةِ بِالنَّفْسِ. يَعودُ ذَلِكَ جُزْئِيًّا إلى ظاهِرَةِ المُقارَنَةِ الاجْتِماعِيَّةِ، حَيْثُ يُقارِنُ الأَفْرادُ حَياتَهُمْ بِما يُنْشَرُ عَلَى الإنْتَرْنِتَّ مِنْ قِبَلِ الآخَرينَ، مِمّا يُؤَدّي إلى الشُّعورِ بِعَدَمِ الكَفاءَةِ وَعَدَمِ الرِّضا.

التَّأْثيراتُ الإيجابِيَّةُ: مِنْ جِهَةٍ أُخْرى، تُعَدُّ وَسائِلُ التَّواصُلِ الاجْتِماعِيِّ أَداةً فَعّالَةً لِبِناءِ العَلاقاتِ وَتَعْزيزِ الدَّعْمِ الاجْتِماعِيِّ. فَهِيَ تَسْمَحُ لِلأَفْرادِ بِالتَّواصُلِ وَمُشارَكَةِ الخِبْراتِ وَالاهْتِماماتِ، وَبِالتّالي يُمْكِنُ أَنْ تُسْهِمَ في تَحْسينِ الصِّحَّةِ النَّفْسِيَّةِ عِنْدَ اسْتِخْدامِها بِشَكْلٍ مُتَوازِنٍ.

دَعْوَةٌ لِلتَّوْعِيَةِ وَالتَّدَخُّلِ: يَدْعو الخُبَراءُ إلى زِيادَةِ التَّوْعِيَةِ حَوْلَ الاسْتِخْدامِ الصِّحِّيِّ لِوَسائِلِ التَّواصُلِ الاجْتِماعِيِّ، مُشَدِّدينَ عَلَى أَهَمِّيَّةِ التَّوازُنِ بَيْنَ الحَياةِ الرَّقْمِيَّةِ وَالواقِعِيَّةِ. كَما يُؤَكِّدونَ عَلَى ضَرورَةِ تَطْويرِ بَرامِجَ تَعْليمِيَّةٍ تَهْدُفُ إلى تَعْزيزِ مَهاراتِ التَّفاعُلِ الاجْتِماعِيِّ وَإدارَةِ الوَقْتِ الرَّقْمِيِّ بِفَعالِيَّةٍ.

في الخِتامِ، تُظْهِرُ الأَدِلَّةُ أَنَّ وَسائِلَ التَّواصُلِ الاجْتِماعِيِّ لَها تَأْثيرٌ قَوِيٌّ عَلَى الصِّحَّةِ النَّفْسِيَّةِ، مِمّا يَسْتَلْزِمُ نَهْجًا مُتَوازِنًا وَواعِيًا لاسْتِخْدامِها، بِهَدَفِ الحِفاظِ عَلَى صِحَّةٍ نَفْسِيَّةٍ جَيِّدَةٍ وَتَعْزيزِ جَوْدَةِ الحَياةِ الاجْتِماعِيَّةِ.

The Impact of Social Media on Mental Health

In our digital age, social media has become an integral part of our daily lives, significantly affecting users' mental health. Studies show that continuous engagement on these platforms can have both negative and positive effects on emotional and mental well-being.

Negative Impacts: There has been an increase in anxiety and depression among social media users, as excessive use of these platforms is associated with feelings of loneliness and low self-esteem. This is partly due to the phenomenon of social comparison, where individuals compare their lives with the idealized lives posted online by others, leading to feelings of inadequacy and dissatisfaction.

Positive Impacts: On the other hand, social media can be an effective tool for building relationships and enhancing social support. It allows individuals to connect and share experiences and interests, which can contribute to improved mental health when used in a balanced manner.

Call for Awareness and Intervention: Experts call for increased awareness about healthy social media use, emphasizing the importance of balancing digital and real-life experiences. They also stress the need to develop educational programs aimed at enhancing social interaction skills and effectively managing digital time.

In conclusion, evidence shows that social media has a profound impact on mental health, necessitating a balanced and conscious approach to its use, with the goal of maintaining good mental health and enhancing the quality of social life.

11.2 Reporting and Writing

11.2.1 News Values and Ethics

fake news

pl.

أَخْبارٌ زائِفَةٌ

اِنْتَشَرَتِ الأَخْبارُ الزّائِفَةُ بِسُرْعَةٍ عَلَى الإِنْتَرْنِتْ، مِمّا أَدّى إلى سوءِ فَهْمٍ واسِعِ النِّطاقِ.

Fake news spread rapidly on the internet, leading to widespread misunderstanding.

ethical

أَخْلاقِيٌّ

يَجِبُ عَلى الصَّحَفِيّينَ اتِّباعُ المَعايِيرِ الأَخْلاقِيَّةِ عِنْدَ تَغْطِيَةِ الأَخْبارِ لِلْحِفاظِ عَلى مِصداقِيَّتِهِمْ.

Journalists should adhere to ethical standards when covering news to maintain their credibility.

sensationalism

إِثارَةٌ مُتَعَمَّدَةٌ

تَجَنَّبَتِ الصَّحيفَةُ الإِثارَةَ المُتَعَمَّدَةَ في تَقارِيرِها لِتَقْديمِ مَعْلوماتٍ مَوْثوقَةٍ.

The newspaper avoided deliberate sensationalism in its reports to provide reliable information.

free press

إِعْلَامٌ حُرٌّ

الإِعْلَامُ الحُرُّ ضَرُورِيٌّ لِدِيمُقْرَاطِيَّةٍ سَلِيمَةٍ لِأَنَّهُ يَسْمَحُ بِتَدَفُّقِ المَعْلُومَاتِ بِحُرِّيَّةٍ.

A free press is essential for a healthy democracy because it allows for the free flow of information.

to verify, fact-check

تَحَقَّقَ • تَحَقُّقٌ

يَتَحَقَّقُ الصَّحَفِيّونَ مِنْ صِحَّةِ الأَخْبَارِ قَبْلَ نَشْرِها لِضَمانِ نَقْلِ الحَقَائِقِ بِدِقَّةٍ.

Journalists verify the accuracy of news before publishing to ensure the facts are accurately conveyed.

bias

تَحَيُّزٌ

يَنْبَغِي عَلَى الوَسَائِلِ الإِعْلَامِيَّةِ تَجَنُّبُ التَّحَيُّزِ لِتَقْدِيمِ تَغْطِيَةٍ مَوْضوعِيَّةٍ.

Media outlets should avoid bias to provide objective coverage.

media bias

تَحَيُّزٌ إِعْلَامِيٌّ

يُمْكِنُ أَنْ يُؤَدِّيَ التَّحَيُّزُ الإِعْلَامِيُّ إِلَى تَشْوِيهِ الحَقِيقَةِ وَالتَّأْثِيرِ سَلْبًا عَلَى الرَّأْيِ العامِّ.

Media bias can lead to the distortion of truth and negatively affect public opinion.

conflict of interest

تَضَارُبُ مَصَالِحَ

يَجِبُ عَلَى الصَّحَفِيِّينَ الإِفْصَاحُ عَنْ أَيِّ تَضَارُبِ مَصَالِحَ لِلْحِفَاظِ عَلَى الشَّفَافِيَّةِ.

Journalists should disclose any conflicts of interest to maintain transparency.

to edit

حَرَّرَ • تَحْرِيرٌ

حَرَّرَ الصَّحَفِيُّ المَقَالَ بِعِنَايَةٍ لِضَمَانِ دِقَّةِ المَعْلُومَاتِ وَحِيَادِيَّتِها.

The journalist carefully edited the article to ensure the accuracy and impartiality of the information.

freedom of expression

حُرِّيَّةُ تَعْبِيرٍ

تُعْتَبَرُ حُرِّيَّةُ التَّعْبِيرِ حَقًّا أَسَاسِيًّا يَسْمَحُ لِلْأَفْرَادِ مُشَارَكَةَ آرَائِهِمْ بِدونِ خَوْفٍ مِنَ الرِّقَابَةِ.

Freedom of expression is a fundamental right that allows individuals to share their opinions without fear of censorship.

press freedom

حُرِّيَّةُ صِحافَةٍ

حُرِّيَّةُ الصَّحافَةِ ضَرورِيَّةٌ لِتَوْفيرِ تَغْطِيَةٍ مُسْتَقِلَّةٍ وَنَقْدِيَّةٍ تُساهِمُ في المُساءَلَةِ الاجْتِماعِيَّةِ وَالسِّياسِيَّةِ.

Press freedom is essential for providing independent and critical reporting that contributes to social and political accountability.

source protection

حِمايَةُ مَصْدَرٍ

الصَّحَفِيّونَ مُلْتَزِمونَ بِحِمايَةِ مَصادِرِهِمْ لِضَمانِ تَدَفُّقِ المَعْلوماتِ دونَ تَعْريضِ الأَشْخاصِ لِلْخَطَرِ.

Journalists are committed to protecting their sources to ensure the flow of information without endangering individuals.

impartial, neutral

حِيادِيٌّ

يَجِبُ أَنْ يَظَلَّ المُراسِلُ حِيادِيًّا أَثْناءَ تَغْطِيَةِ الأَحْداثِ لِتَقْديمِ تَقْريرٍ مُتَوازِنٍ.

The reporter should remain impartial while covering events to provide a balanced report.

impartiality

حِيادِيَّةٌ

يَجِبُ عَلَى الصَّحَفِيّينَ الحِفاظُ عَلَى الحِيادِيَّةِ وَالمَوْضوعِيَّةِ لِتَقْديمِ تَقاريرَ غَيْرِ مُتَحَيِّزَةٍ وَدَقيقَةٍ.

Journalists must maintain impartiality and objectivity to provide unbiased and accurate reports.

plagiarism

سَرِقَةٌ أَدَبِيَّةٌ

تُعْتَبَرُ السَّرِقَةُ الأَدَبِيَّةُ انْتِهاكًا خَطيرًا لِلْأَخْلاقِيّاتِ المِهْنِيَّةِ، وَيُمْكِنُ أَنْ تُقَوِّضَ مِصْداقِيَّةَ الصَّحَفِيِّ.

Plagiarism is a serious violation of professional ethics and can undermine a journalist's credibility.

editorial policy

سِياسَةُ تَحْريرٍ

تُحَدِّدُ سِياسَةُ التَّحْريرِ المَعاييرَ وَالقِيَمَ الَّتي يَجِبُ عَلَى النّاشِرينَ وَالمُحَرِّرينَ اتِّباعُها.

Editorial policy outlines the standards and values that publishers and editors should follow.

شَفافِيَّةٌ

transparency

تُعَزِّزُ الشَّفافِيَّةُ في العَمَلِ الصَّحَفِيِّ الثِّقَةَ وَتَسْمَحُ بِالْمُحاسَبَةِ.

Transparency in journalism enhances trust and allows for accountability.

صادِقٌ

truthful, honest

يَجِبُ أَنْ يَكونَ الصَّحَفِيُّ صادِقًا في تَغْطِيَتِهِ لِتَقْديمِ صورَةٍ دَقيقَةٍ لِلْأَحْداثِ.

The journalist should be honest in his reporting to provide an accurate picture of events.

صِحافَةٌ صَفْراءُ

yellow journalism

تَتَّسِمُ الصِّحافَةُ الصَّفْراءُ بِالْإِثارَةِ وَالْمُبالَغَةِ لِجَذْبِ الِانْتِباهِ، مِمّا يُؤَثِّرُ سَلْبًا عَلى جَوْدَةِ المَعْلوماتِ.

Yellow journalism is characterized by sensationalism and exaggeration to attract attention, negatively affecting the quality of information.

عَلَّقَ • تَعْليقٌ

to comment

عَلَّقَ الصَّحَفِيُّ عَلى النَّقْدِ بِمِهْنِيَّةٍ، مُؤَكِّدًا عَلى الِتِزامِهِ بِالْمَعاييرِ الْأَخْلاقِيَّةِ.

The journalist responded to the criticism professionally, emphasizing his commitment to ethical standards.

غَيْرُ مُنْحازٍ

unbiased

يَجِبُ عَلى الصَّحَفِيّينَ الحِفاظُ عَلى مَوْقِفٍ غَيْرِ مُنْحازٍ لِضَمانِ التَّقْديمِ النَّزيهِ لِلْأَخْبارِ.

Journalists must maintain an unbiased stance to ensure the fair presentation of news.

قابِلٌ لِلتَّحَقُّقِ

verifiable

يَجِبُ أَنْ تَكونَ المَعْلوماتُ المُقَدَّمَةُ في التَّقاريرِ قابِلَةً لِلتَّحَقُّقِ لِتَعْزيزِ الشَّفافِيَّةِ وَالمِصْداقِيَّةِ.

The information provided in reports should be verifiable to enhance transparency and credibility.

قَدَّمَ الْأَخْبارَ • تَقْديمٌ

to present the news

يَقومُ المُذيعُ بِتَقْديمِ الْأَخْبارِ يَوْمِيًّا، مُزَوِّدًا الجُمْهورَ بِأَحْدَثِ المَعْلوماتِ وَالتَّحْليلاتِ.

The anchor presents the news daily, providing the audience with the latest information and analyses.

to uncover facts

كَشْفٌ • كَشَفَ حَقائِقَ

عَمِلَ الصَّحَفِيُّ عَلى كَشْفِ حَقائِقَ مُهِمَّةٍ مِنْ خِلالِ تَحْقيقِهِ الاسْتِقْصائِيِّ.

The journalist worked to uncover important facts through his investigative report.

to expose corruption

كَشْفٌ • كَشَفَ عَنْ فَسادٍ

تُساهِمُ التَّحْقيقاتُ الصَّحَفِيَّةُ في الكَشْفِ عَنِ الفَسادِ وَالمُمارَساتِ غَيْرِ الأَخْلاقِيَّةِ في القِطاعاتِ المُخْتَلِفَةِ.

Journalistic investigations contribute to exposing corruption and unethical practices in various sectors.

balanced

مُتَوازِنٌ

يَجِبُ أَنْ يَكونَ التَّقْريرُ الإِخْبارِيُّ مُتَوازِنًا، مُعْتَمِدًا عَلى مَصادِرَ مُتَعَدِّدَةٍ لِتَقْديمِ جَميعِ جَوانِبِ القِصَّةِ.

The news report should be balanced, relying on multiple sources to present all sides of the story.

media watchdogs

مُراقِبو وَسائِلِ إِعْلام

يَقومُ مُراقِبو وَسائِلِ الإِعْلامِ بِتَقْييمِ الأَخْبارِ وَالبَرامِجِ لِضَمانِ الامْتِثالِ لِلْمَعاييرِ الأَخْلاقِيَّةِ وَالمِهْنِيَّةِ.

Media monitors evaluate news and programs to ensure compliance with ethical and professional standards.

accountability

مُساءَلَةٌ

تُعَزِّزُ الصَّحافَةُ المُساءَلَةَ مِنْ خِلالِ تَسْليطِ الضَّوْءِ عَلى القَضايا العامَّةِ وَتَحَدّي السُّلُطاتِ عِنْدَ الضَّرورَةِ.

Journalism promotes accountability by highlighting public issues and challenging authorities when necessary.

credibility

مِصْداقِيَّةٌ

مِصْداقِيَّةُ الصَّحَفِيِّ تَعْتَمِدُ عَلى نَزاهَتِهِ وَقُدْرَتِهِ عَلى نَقْلِ الحَقائِقِ بِدِقَّةٍ.

A journalist's credibility depends on their integrity and ability to accurately convey facts.

مَصْدَرٌ مَوْثُوقٌ • مَصَادِرُ

credible source, reliable source

اِسْتَخْدَمَ الصَّحَفِيُّ مَصَادِرَ مَوْثُوقَةً لِتَعْزِيزِ دِقَّةِ التَّقْرِيرِ وَمِصْداقِيَّتِهِ.

The journalist used reliable sources to enhance the accuracy and credibility of the report.

مَصْلَحَةٌ عامَّةٌ • مَصَالِحُ

public interest

يَعْمَلُ الصَّحَفِيّونَ عَلَى تَسْلِيطِ الضَّوْءِ عَلَى القَضَايا ذاتِ المَصْلَحَةِ العامَّةِ لِإِبْلاغِ الجُمْهورِ وَتَوْعِيَتِهِ.

Journalists work to highlight issues of public interest to inform and educate the public.

مَعايِيرُ مِهْنِيَّةٌ   pl.

professional standards

يَلْتَزِمُ الصَّحَفِيّونَ بِمَعايِيرَ مِهْنِيَّةٍ لِضَمانِ تَقْدِيمِ تَغْطِيَةٍ دَقِيقَةٍ وَعادِلَةٍ.

Journalists adhere to professional standards to ensure accurate and fair reporting.

مَوْثوقٌ

credible, reliable

يُعْتَبَرُ المَوْقِعُ مَوْثوقًا عِنْدَما يُقَدِّمُ مَعْلوماتٍ مُدَقَّقَةً وَمُؤَكَّدَةً مِنْ مَصادِرَ رَسْمِيَّةٍ.

A website is considered credible when it provides verified information from official sources.

مِيثاقُ شَرَفٍ • مَواثِيقُ

code of ethics

يَتْبَعُ الصَّحَفِيّونَ مِيثاقَ شَرَفٍ يُحَدِّدُ الأَخْلاقِيّاتِ وَالمَبادِئَ التَّوْجِيهِيَّةَ لِمِهْنَتِهِمْ.

Journalists follow a code of ethics that outlines the morals and guidelines for their profession.

نَزاهَةٌ

Integrity

تُعْتَبَرُ النَّزاهَةُ في الصَّحافَةِ أَساسِيَّةً لِكَسْبِ ثِقَةِ الجُمْهورِ وَبِناءِ سُمْعَةِ المُؤَسَّسَةِ الإِعْلامِيَّةِ.

Integrity in journalism is essential for gaining public trust and building the media organization's reputation.

نَشَرَ الأَخْبارَ • نَشْرٌ

to disseminate the news

تَهْدِفُ وَسائِلُ الإِعْلامِ إلى نَشْرِ الأَخْبارِ لِإِبْقاءِ الجُمْهورِ مُطَّلِعًا عَلَى الأَحْداثِ الجارِيَةِ.

The media aims to disseminate the news to keep the public informed about current events.

أَطْلَقَتْ إِحْدَى المُؤَسَّساتِ الإِعْلامِيَّةِ الكُبْرَى بَرْنامَجًا تَدْرِيبِيًّا لِلصَّحَفِيِّينَ يُرَكِّزُ عَلَى تِقْنِيّاتِ التَّحَقُّقِ مِنَ الأَخْبارِ لِمُكافَحَةِ انْتِشارِ الأَخْبارِ الزَّائِفَةِ. يَهْدُفُ البَرْنامَجُ إِلَى تَعْزِيزِ المَعايِيرِ المِهْنِيَّةِ وَضَمانِ النَّزاهَةِ وَالشَّفافِيَّةِ فِي العَمَلِ الصَّحَفِيِّ.

One of the major media institutions launched a training program for journalists focusing on news verification techniques to combat the spread of fake news. The program aims to enhance professional standards and ensure integrity and transparency in journalistic work.

فِي تَحْقِيقٍ اسْتِقْصائِيٍّ حَدِيثٍ، كَشَفَ صَحَفِيّونَ عَنْ قَضايا فَسادٍ كَبِيرَةٍ فِي إِحْدَى الهَيْئاتِ الحُكُومِيَّةِ، مِمّا سَلَّطَ الضَّوْءَ عَلَى أَهَمِّيَّةِ حُرِّيَّةِ الصَّحافَةِ وَدَوْرِها الحاسِمِ فِي المُساءَلَةِ وَحِمايَةِ المَصْلَحَةِ العامَّةِ.

In a recent investigative report, journalists exposed major corruption issues within a governmental body, highlighting the importance of press freedom and its crucial role in accountability and protecting the public interest.

نَظَّمَتْ جامِعَةٌ مَعْرُوفَةٌ نَدْوَةً حَوْلَ الحِيادِيَّةِ وَالتَّوازُنِ فِي الإِعْلامِ، جَمَعَتْ خُبَراءَ فِي الصَّحافَةِ وَالإِعْلامِ لِمُناقَشَةِ التَّحَدِّياتِ الَّتِي تُواجِهُ الإِعْلامَ فِي ظِلِّ التَّحَيُّزِ الإِعْلامِيِّ المُتَزايِدِ وَتَضارُبِ المَصالِحِ، مَعَ التَّأْكِيدِ عَلَى أَهَمِّيَّةِ النَّزاهَةِ وَمِصْداقِيَّةِ المَصادِرِ.

A well-known university organized a seminar on neutrality and balance in media, bringing together experts in journalism and media to discuss the challenges faced by the media amid increasing media bias and conflicting interests, emphasizing the importance of integrity and source credibility.

أَعْلَنَتْ مُنَظَّمَةٌ غَيْرُ رِبْحِيَّةٍ عَنْ مُبادَرَةٍ جَدِيدَةٍ لِتَعْزِيزِ الشَّفافِيَّةِ فِي الإِعْلامِ، تَتَضَمَّنُ تَطْوِيرَ سِياسَةٍ تَّحْرِيرِيَّةٍ تَضْمَنُ حِمايَةَ المَصادِرِ وَتُحَقِّقُ التَّوازُنَ وَالحِيادَ فِي تَقْدِيمِ الأَخْبارِ، مِمّا يُعَزِّزُ الثِّقَةَ بَيْنَ الجُمْهُورِ وَوَسائِلِ الإِعْلامِ.

A non-profit organization announced a new initiative to enhance transparency in media, including developing an editorial policy that ensures source protection and achieves balance and neutrality in news presentation, thereby strengthening trust between the public and the media.

أَطْلَقَتْ رابِطَةُ الصَّحَفِيِّينَ حَمْلَةً تَوْعِيَةٍ ضِدَّ الصَّحافَةِ الصَّفْراءِ وَالإِثارَةِ المُتَعَمَّدَةِ، داعِيَةً إِلَى الالْتِزامِ بِأَخْلاقِيّاتِ الصَّحافَةِ وَمَعايِيرِها المِهْنِيَّةِ. تَسْتَهْدِفُ الحَمْلَةُ تَعْزِيزَ مِيثاقِ شَرَفِ الصَّحافَةِ وَضَمانَ تَقْدِيمَ مُحْتَوًى إِعْلامِيٍّ يَخْدِمُ الحَقِيقَةَ.

The Journalists' Association launched an awareness campaign against yellow journalism and deliberate sensationalism, calling for adherence to journalistic ethics and professional standards. The campaign aims to promote a code of honor in journalism and ensure the delivery of media content that serves the truth.

الأخْبارُ الزّائِفَةُ: تَحَدِّياتُ العَصْرِ الرَّقمِيِّ

في عَصْرِنا الرَّقْمِيِّ، أَصْبَحَتِ الأَخْبارُ الزّائِفَةُ ظاهِرَةً مُقْلِقَةً تُواجِهُ الإِعْلامَ والمُجْتَمَعَ. تَتَمَثَّلُ هَذِهِ الأَخْبارُ في مَعلوماتٍ مُضَلِّلَةٍ أَوْ مُزَوَّرَةٍ تُنْشَرُ عَبْرَ وَسائِلِ التَّواصُلِ الاجْتِماعِيِّ والمِنَصّاتِ الإِلِكْترونِيَّةِ بِقَصْدِ الإِثارَةِ المُتَعَمَّدَةِ أَوْ تَحْقيقِ أَهْدافٍ مُعَيَّنَةٍ، مِمّا يَسْتَدْعي مُعالَجَةً جادَّةً وَمَسْؤولَةً لِهَذِهِ القَضِيَّةِ.

التَّأْثيرُ وَالأَضْرارُ:

لَيْسَتِ الأَخْبارُ الزّائِفَةُ مُجَرَّدَ إِزْعاجٍ بَسيطٍ؛ فَهِيَ تَنْطَوي عَلى تَأْثيراتٍ خَطيرَةٍ تَشْمَلُ تَحَيُّزَ الرَّأْيِ العامِّ، وَتَقْويضَ النَّزاهَةِ الإِعْلامِيَّةِ، وَحَتّى التَّأْثيرَ عَلى العَمَلِيّاتِ الدِّيمُقْراطِيَّةِ والسِّياسِيَّةِ. يُمْكِنُ أَنْ تُؤَدّيَ إِلى تَشْويهِ سُمْعَةِ الأَفْرادِ أَوِ الكِياناتِ وَتَغْذِيَةِ الانْقِساماتِ الاجْتِماعِيَّةِ والسِّياسِيَّةِ.

المُواجَهَةُ وَالحُلولُ:

لِمُواجَهَةِ تَحَدِّياتِ الأَخْبارِ الزّائِفَةِ، يَجِبُ اعْتِمادُ مَجموعَةٍ مِنَ الاسْتِراتيجِيّاتِ الَّتي تَشْمَلُ التَّحَقُّقَ مِنْ صِحَّةِ المَعْلوماتِ وَنَشْرَ الوَعْيِ بَيْنَ الجُمْهورِ. يَلْعَبُ الصَّحَفِيّونَ وَمُنَظَّماتُ الإِعْلامِ دَوْرًا حَيَوِيًّا في هَذا المَجالِ عَبْرَ تَعْزيزِ مَعاييرِ التَّحْريرِ الأَخْلاقِيَّةِ، وَالتَّحَقُّقِ مِنَ المَصادِرِ، وَضَمانِ نَشْرِ الأَخْبارِ بِمَسْؤولِيَّةٍ وَشَفافِيَّةٍ.

كَما يَجِبُ عَلى وَسائِلِ الإِعْلامِ حِمايَةُ حُرِّيَّةِ الصَّحافَةِ وَفي الوَقْتِ نَفْسِهِ الالْتِزامُ بِحِيادِيَّةٍ وَنَزاهَةِ التَّغْطِيَةِ الإِخْبارِيَّةِ. إِنَّ التَّعاوُنَ بَيْنَ المُؤَسَّساتِ الإِعْلامِيَّةِ والكِياناتِ التَّعْليمِيَّةِ والحُكوماتِ أَمْرٌ ضَروريٌّ لِتَطْويرِ بَرامِجَ تَعْليمِيَّةٍ تُرَكِّزُ عَلى الأَمانِ الرَّقْمِيِّ وَمَحْوِ الأُمِّيَّةِ الإِعْلامِيَّةِ.

خاتِمَةٌ:

تُشَكِّلُ الأَخْبارُ الزّائِفَةُ تَحَدِّيًا جَوْهَرِيًّا في الحِفاظِ عَلى مُجْتَمَعٍ مُسْتَنيرٍ وَديمُقْراطِيٍّ. يَجِبُ أَنْ تَكونَ مُكافَحَتُها جُهْدًا مُشْتَرَكًا يَضُمُّ جَميعَ الأَطْرافِ المَعْنِيَّةِ في المُجْتَمَعِ لِضَمانِ تَدَفُّقِ مَعلوماتٍ دَقيقَةٍ وَمَوْثوقَةٍ، مِمّا يُساهِمُ في بِناءِ بيئَةٍ إِعْلامِيَّةٍ أَكْثَرَ صِحَّةً وَنَزاهَةً.

Fake News: Challenges of the Digital Age

In our digital era, fake news has become a concerning phenomenon facing both the media and society. This news consists of misleading or fabricated information published on social media and digital platforms, intended for deliberate sensationalism or to achieve specific goals, necessitating a serious and responsible approach to this issue.

Impact and Harm:

Fake news is not just a minor annoyance; it carries serious implications, including biasing public opinion, undermining media integrity, and even affecting democratic and political processes. It can lead to damaging the reputation of individuals or entities and fuel social and political divisions.

Confrontation and Solutions:

To address the challenges of fake news, a range of strategies must be adopted, including verifying information and raising public awareness. Journalists and media organizations play a crucial role in this area by promoting ethical editorial standards, checking sources, and ensuring responsible and transparent news dissemination.

Media must protect press freedom while also committing to the neutrality and integrity of news coverage. Cooperation between media institutions, educational bodies, and governments is essential to develop educational programs focused on digital safety and media literacy.

Conclusion:

Fake news poses a fundamental challenge in maintaining an enlightened and democratic society. Combating it should be a collective effort involving all stakeholders in society to ensure the flow of accurate and reliable information, contributing to a healthier and more honest media environment.

11.2.1.3 Essay: Plagiarism and Fabrication in Journalism

Track **38**

السَّرِقَةُ الأَدَبِيَّةُ وَالتَّزْويرُ: أَزْمَةُ النَّزاهَةِ في الصَّحافَةِ

تُعْتَبَرُ السَّرِقَةُ الأَدَبِيَّةُ وَالتَّزْويرُ مِنْ بَيْنِ أَخْطَرِ التَّحَدِّياتِ الَّتي تُواجِهُ الصَّحافَةَ اليَوْمَ. هَذِهِ الأَفْعالُ لا تُعَدُّ مُجَرَّدَ انْتِهاكاتٍ لِلْمَعايِيرِ المِهْنِيَّةِ، بَلْ تُمَثِّلُ أَيْضًا تَهْدِيدًا جَسيمًا لِمِصْداقِيَّةِ وَسائِلِ الإِعْلامِ وَالثِّقَةِ الَّتي يَمْنَحُها الجُمْهورُ لِلْمُحْتَوى الإِخْبارِيِّ.

تَأْثيراتُ السَّرِقَةِ الأَدَبِيَّةِ وَالتَّزْويرِ:

تُقَوِّضُ السَّرِقَةُ الأَدَبِيَّةُ، أَو اسْتِخْدامُ عَمَلِ شَخْصٍ آخَرَ دونَ الإِشارَةِ إِلَيْهِ، النَّزاهَةَ الأَساسِيَّةَ لِلْمُمارَساتِ الصَّحَفِيَّةِ. مِنْ ناحِيَةٍ أُخْرى، يُشيرُ التَّزْويرُ إِلى اخْتِلاقِ أَخْبارٍ أَو مَعْلوماتٍ كاذِبَةٍ، وَهُوَ يَخْلُقُ بيئَةً إِعْلامِيَّةً مُلَوَّثَةً يَصْعُبُ مَعَها تَمْييزُ الحَقائِقِ عَنِ الخَيالِ.

مُواجَهَةُ المُشْكِلَةِ:

لِمُعالَجَةِ هَذِهِ القَضايا، يَجِبُ عَلى وَسائِلِ الإعْلامِ تَبَنّي سِياساتٍ تَحْريرٍ صارِمَةٍ تَضْمَنُ التَّثَبُّتَ مِنَ الحَقائِقِ وَأَصالَةَ المُحْتَوى. يَنْبَغي تَدْريبُ الصَّحَفِيّينَ عَلى أَخْلاقِيّاتِ المِهْنَةِ وَتَعْزيزِ قِيَمِ الشَّفافِيَّةِ وَالحِيادِيَّةِ.

تَلْعَبُ المُساءَلَةُ دَوْرًا رَئيسِيًّا في هَذا السِّياقِ؛ فَمِنَ الضَّروريِّ أَنْ توجَدَ آلِيّاتٌ تَسْمَحُ بِتَقْييمِ الصَّحَفِيّينَ وَمُحاسَبَتِهِمْ عَلى عَمَلِهِمْ. كَما يَجِبُ عَلى الجُمْهورِ أَنْ يَكونَ نَشِطًا في البَحْثِ عَنِ المَصادِرِ المَوْثوقَةِ وَالتَّشْكيكِ في المُحْتَوى الّذي يَسْتَهْلِكُهُ.

خاتِمَةٌ:

في عالَمٍ تَتَزايَدُ فيهِ المَعْلوماتُ وَتَتَسارَعُ وَتيرَةُ تَدَفُّقِها، تَبْرُزُ الحاجَةُ الماسَّةُ لِلْحِفاظِ عَلى مَعاييرِ النَّزاهَةِ في الصِّحافَةِ. السَّرِقَةُ الأَدَبِيَّةُ وَالتَّزْويرُ لَيْسَتا مُجَرَّدَ مُشْكِلَتَيْنِ قانونِيَّتَيْنِ بَلْ هُما تَهْديدانِ لِلثَّقافَةِ الإعْلامِيَّةِ الشَّفّافَةِ وَالمَوْثوقَةِ. وَمِن خِلالِ تَعْزيزِ مَعاييرَ مِهْنِيَّةٍ قَوِيَّةٍ وَالالْتِزامِ بِها، يُمْكِنُ لِوَسائِلِ الإعْلامِ الحِفاظُ عَلى ثِقَةِ الجُمْهورِ وَتَعْزيزُ مَكانَتِها كَرَكائِزَ لِلدّيمُقْراطِيَّةِ.

Plagiarism and Forgery: The Integrity Crisis in Journalism

Plagiarism and forgery are among the most serious challenges facing journalism today. These acts are not only violations of professional standards but also pose a severe threat to the credibility of media and the trust that the public places in news content.

Impacts of Plagiarism and Forgery:

Plagiarism, or using someone else's work without proper credit, undermines the fundamental integrity of journalistic practices. Forgery, on the other hand, refers to the fabrication of false news or information, creating a media environment where it is difficult to distinguish facts from fiction.

Addressing the Problem:

To tackle these issues, media organizations must adopt strict editorial policies that ensure fact-checking and content authenticity. Journalists should be trained in professional ethics and the values of transparency and impartiality.

Accountability plays a key role in this context; it is essential to have mechanisms for evaluating and holding journalists accountable for their work. The public should also be active in seeking reliable sources and questioning the content they consume.

Conclusion:

In a world where information is abundant and its flow is rapid, there is a pressing need to maintain integrity standards in journalism. Plagiarism and forgery are not just legal problems but threats to a transparent and trustworthy media culture. By strengthening and adhering to robust professional standards, the media can maintain public trust and reinforce its role as a pillar of democracy.

11.2.1.4 Definition: Yellow Journalism

Track **39**

ما هِيَ الصِّحافَةُ الصَّفْراءُ؟

الصِّحافَةُ الصَّفْراءُ، المَعْروفَةُ أَيْضًا بِصِحافَةِ الإثارَةِ، هِيَ نَوْعٌ مِنَ الإعْلامِ يُعْطي الأوْلَوِيَّةَ لِلإثارَةِ وَالجَدَلِ عَلى حِسابِ الدِّقَّةِ وَالمَوْضوعِيَّةِ. تَتَمَيَّزُ بِعَناوينِها المُثيرَةِ، وَالقِصَصِ المُبالَغِ فيها، وَاسْتِخْدامِ الأخْبارِ المُضَلِّلَةِ أَوْ غَيْرِ المُؤَكَّدَةِ لِجَذْبِ اهْتِمامِ القُرّاءِ. تَهْدُفُ هَذِهِ المُمارَساتُ إلى زِيادَةِ مَبيعاتِ الصُّحُفِ وَنِسَبِ المُشاهَدَةِ دونَ الاعْتِبارِ لِلتَّأْثيرِ السَّلْبِيِّ عَلى جَوْدَةِ الإعْلامِ وَثِقَةِ الجُمْهورِ. الصِّحافَةُ الصَّفْراءُ تَخْلُقُ غالِبًا صورَةً مُشَوَّهَةً لِلْواقِعِ، وَتُسْهِمُ في تَرْويجِ الشّائِعاتِ وَنَشْرِ الفِتْنَةِ، مِمّا يَجْعَلُها تَحَدِّيًا كَبيرًا لِلنَّزاهَةِ وَالمِصْداقِيَّةِ في العَمَلِ الصَّحَفِيِّ.

What is Yellow Journalism?

Yellow journalism, also known as sensationalism, is a type of media that prioritizes excitement and controversy over accuracy and objectivity. It is characterized by sensational headlines, exaggerated stories, and the use of misleading or unverified news to attract readers' attention. These practices aim to increase newspaper sales and viewership ratings regardless of their negative impact on media quality and public trust. Yellow journalism often creates a distorted picture of reality, contributing to the spread of rumors and discord, posing a significant challenge to integrity and credibility in journalistic work.

11.2.2 Story Structure and News Writing

Track **40**

editing

تَحْريرٌ

تَتَطَلَّبُ عَمَلِيَّةُ التَّحْريرِ فَحْصَ النَّصِّ بِعِنايَةٍ لِضَمانِ دِقَّتِهِ وَوُضوحِهِ قَبْلَ النَّشْرِ.

The editing process requires careful examination of the text to ensure its accuracy and clarity before publishing.

investigative report

تَقْريرٌ تَحْقيقِيٌّ

كَشَفَ تَقْريرٌ تَحْقيقِيٌّ عَنْ تَجاوُزاتٍ في مُمارَساتِ الشَّرِكَةِ المالِيَّةِ.

An investigative report uncovered irregularities in the company's financial practices.

تَحْلِيلٌ

analysis

يُقَدِّمُ التَّحْلِيلُ الصَّحَفِيُّ رُؤْيَةً أَعْمَقَ لِلْأَحْدَاثِ، مُوَضِّحًا الأَسْبَابَ وَالتَّداعِياتِ.

Journalistic analysis provides deeper insight into events, explaining causes and consequences.

تَدْوِينٌ

blogging

يَسْتَخْدِمُ الصَّحَفِيّونَ التَّدْوِينَ لِمُشارَكَةِ تَجارِبِهِمِ الشَّخْصِيَّةِ وَآرائِهِمْ حَوْلَ مَوْضوعاتٍ مُخْتَلِفَةٍ.

Journalists use blogging to share their personal experiences and opinions on various topics.

تَعْلِيقٌ

commentary

يُمْكِنُ لِتَعْلِيقٍ في المَقالَةِ أَوِ الخَبَرِ أَنْ يُوَفِّرَ تَفْسِيراتٍ أَوْ وُجْهاتِ نَظَرٍ مُخْتَلِفَةً حَوْلَ الحَدَثِ.

A comment in an article or news piece can provide explanations or different perspectives on the event.

تَغْطِيَةٌ

coverage

تَتَضَمَّنُ تَغْطِيَةُ الأَخْبارِ مُتابَعَةَ الأَحْداثِ الجارِيَةِ وَتَقْدِيمَ تَقارِيرَ مُفَصَّلَةٍ لِلْجُمْهورِ.

News coverage involves following current events and providing detailed reports to the audience.

تَقْرِيرٌ • تَقارِيرُ

report

يُقَدِّمُ التَّقْرِيرُ الصَّحَفِيُّ مَعْلوماتٍ مُفَصَّلَةً حَوْلَ مَوْضوعٍ مُعَيَّنٍ، مُسْتَنِدًا إلى بَحْثٍ وَتَحْلِيلٍ شامِلٍ.

The journalistic report provides detailed information on a specific topic based on comprehensive research and analysis.

حَرَّرَ • تَحْرِيرٌ

to edit

حَرَّرَ المُحَرِّرُ النَّصَّ بِعِنايَةٍ لِضَمانِ سَلاسَتِهِ وَخُلُوِّهِ مِنَ الأَخْطاءِ اللُّغَوِيَّةِ.

The editor carefully edited the text to ensure its fluency and freedom from linguistic errors.

exclusive — حَصْرِيٌّ

تَسْعى الوَسائِلُ الإِعْلامِيَّةُ لِلْحُصولِ عَلى أَخْبارٍ حَصْرِيَّةٍ لِجَذْبِ انْتِباهِ أَكْبَرِ عَدَدٍ مِنَ القُرّاءِ أَوِ المُشاهِدينَ.

Media outlets strive to obtain exclusive news to attract the attention of as many readers or viewers as possible.

journalistic neutrality — حِيادٌ صَحَفِيٌّ

يُعْتَبَرُ الحِيادُ الصَّحَفِيُّ مَبْدَأً أَساسِيًّا لِتَقْديمِ الأَخْبارِ بِمَوْضوعِيَّةٍ وَدونَ تَحَيُّزٍ.

Journalistic neutrality is a fundamental principle for presenting news objectively and without bias.

headline news — خَبَرٌ رَئيسِيٌّ • أَخْبارٌ

يَتَصَدَّرُ الخَبَرُ الرَّئيسِيُّ الصَّفَحاتِ الأولى لِلصُّحُفِ وَالبَوّاباتِ الإِخْبارِيَّةِ بِسَبَبِ أَهَمِّيَّتِهِ البالِغَةِ.

The headline news dominates the front pages of newspapers and news portals due to its great importance.

controversial news — خَبَرٌ مُثيرٌ لِلْجَدَلِ

قَدْ تُؤَدّي تَغْطِيَةُ الأَخْبارِ المُثيرَةِ لِلْجَدَلِ في الإِعْلامِ إلى نِقاشاتٍ واسِعَةٍ وَآراءٍ مُتَبايِنَةٍ.

Covering controversial news in the media can lead to extensive discussions and divergent opinions.

accurate — دَقيقٌ

مِنَ المُهِمِّ أَنْ تَكونَ المَعْلوماتُ دَقيقَةً لِتَجَنُّبِ نَشْرِ الأَخْبارِ الزّائِفَةِ وَالمُضَلِّلَةِ.

It is important for information to be accurate to avoid spreading fake and misleading news.

citizen journalism — صِحافَةُ المُواطِنِ

تُسْهِمُ صِحافَةُ المُواطِنِ في تَعْزيزِ التَّغْطِيَةِ الإِخْبارِيَّةِ مِنْ خِلالِ مُشارَكَةِ الأَفْرادِ في نَقْلِ الأَحْداثِ.

Citizen journalism enhances news coverage by involving individuals in reporting events.

free press — صِحافَةٌ حُرَّةٌ

تُعْتَبَرُ الصِّحافَةُ الحُرَّةُ حَجَرَ الزّاوِيَةِ في المُجْتَمَعِ الدّيمُقْراطِيِّ، حَيْثُ تَسْمَحُ بِالْمُساءَلَةِ وَالشَّفافِيَّةِ.

Free press is considered the cornerstone of a democratic society, as it allows for accountability and transparency.

Free press is considered a cornerstone in a democratic society, allowing for accountability and transparency.

to comment

تَعْليقٌ •

عَلَّقَ

عَلَّقَ القُرَّاءُ عَلَى المَقالِ، مُعَبِّرِينَ عَنْ آرائِهِمْ وَتَحْليلاتِهِمْ.

Readers commented on the article, expressing their opinions and analyses.

news headline

عَناوينُ •

عُنْوانُ خَبَرٍ

يَجِبُ أَنْ يَكونَ عُنْوانُ الخَبَرِ جَذّابًا وَواضِحًا لِجَذْبِ انْتِباهِ القارِئِ.

The news headline should be catchy and clear to attract the reader's attention.

to cover

تَغْطِيَةٌ •

غَطّى

غَطّى الصَّحَفِيُّ الحَدَثَ الرِّياضِيَّ، مُقَدِّمًا تَقاريرَ مُفَصَّلَةً عَنِ المُبارَياتِ.

The journalist covered the sports event, providing detailed reports on the matches.

paragraph

فِقْرَةٌ

كُلُّ فِقْرَةٍ في المَقالِ يَجِبُ أَنْ تَحْتَوِيَ عَلَى فِكْرَةٍ مَرْكَزِيَّةٍ تُساهِمُ في تَطْويرِ القِصَّةِ.

Each paragraph in the article should contain a central idea that contributes to developing the story.

opening paragraph

فِقْرَةٌ افْتِتاحِيَّةٌ

تُقَدِّمُ الفِقْرَةُ الِافْتِتاحِيَّةُ لِلْمَقالِ نَظْرَةً عامَّةً عَلَى المَوْضوعِ وَتُحَدِّدُ نَبْرَةَ النَّصِّ.

The opening paragraph of an article provides an overview of the topic and sets the tone of the text.

author, writer

مُؤَلِّفٌ

يَعْمَلُ المُؤَلِّفُ عَلَى تَطْويرِ الأَفْكارِ وَصِياغَتِها في نَصٍّ مُتَّسِقٍ يَجْذِبُ القُرّاءَ.

The author works on developing ideas and articulating them in a coherent text that attracts readers.

follow-up

مُتابَعَةٌ

تُعْتَبَرُ المُتابَعَةُ جُزْءًا أَساسِيًّا مِنَ العَمَلِ الصَّحَفِيِّ لِتَوْفِيرِ أَحْدَثِ المَعْلُوماتِ حَوْلَ الأَحْداثِ الجارِيَةِ.

Following up is an essential part of journalistic work to provide the latest information on ongoing events.

interesting

مُثِيرٌ لِلِاهْتِمام

يَجِبُ أَنْ يَكونَ المُحْتَوى مُثِيرًا لِلِإهْتِمامِ لِجَذْبِ القُرَّاءِ وَتَشْجِيعِهِمْ عَلى الِاسْتِمْرارِ فِي القِراءَةِ.

The content should be interesting to attract readers and encourage them to continue reading.

controversial

مُثِيرٌ لِلْجَدَل

المَوْضوعاتُ المُثِيرَةُ لِلْجَدَلِ غالِبًا ما تُحَفِّزُ نِقاشاتٍ حادَّةً وَتَفاعُلاتٍ قَوِيَّةً بَيْنَ الجُمْهورِ.

Controversial topics often stimulate sharp debates and strong interactions among the audience.

media content

مُحْتَوًى إِعْلامِيٌّ

يَجِبُ أَنْ يَكونَ المُحْتَوى الإِعْلامِيُّ مَعْلوماتِيًّا وَمُفِيدًا لِلْجُمْهورِ.

The media content should be informative and useful to the audience.

editor

مُحَرِّرٌ

المُحَرِّرُ مَسْؤولٌ عَنْ تَنْقِيحِ المَقالاتِ وَضَمانِ جَوْدَتِها قَبْلَ النَّشْرِ.

The editor is responsible for revising articles and ensuring their quality before publication.

fake

مُزَيَّفٌ

يَجِبُ عَلى الصَّحَفِيِّينَ التَّحَقُّقُ مِنَ المَعْلوماتِ لِتَجَنُّبِ نَشْرِ أَخْبارٍ مُزَيَّفَةٍ.

Journalists must verify information to avoid publishing fake news.

source

مَصْدَرٌ • مَصادِرُ

يَعْتَمِدُ الصَّحَفِيّونَ عَلى مَصادِرَ مَوْثوقَةٍ لِجَمْعِ البَياناتِ وَالأَخْبارِ.

Journalists rely on reliable sources to gather data and news.

مُقابَلَةٌ

interview

تُوَفِّرُ المُقابَلَةُ فُرْصَةً لِلْحُصولِ عَلى تَصْريحاتٍ مُباشِرَةٍ وَآراءٍ مِنَ الأَشْخاصِ المَعْنِيّينَ.

An interview provides an opportunity to obtain direct statements and opinions from the concerned individuals.

مَقالٌ = مَقالَةٌ

article

كَتَبَ الصَّحَفِيُّ مَقالًا تَحْليلِيًّا يَسْتَعْرِضُ فيه تَأْثيرَ السِّياساتِ الجَديدَةِ.

The journalist wrote an analytical article reviewing the impact of new policies.

مَقالَةُ رَأْي

opinion article

نَشَرَتِ الصَّحيفَةُ مَقالَةَ رَأْيٍ تُناقِشُ مُسْتَقْبَلَ التَّكْنولوجْيا في التَّعْليمِ.

The newspaper published an opinion article discussing the future of technology in education.

مِلَفٌّ

file, in-depth report

يَحْتَوي المِلَفُّ عَلى مَجْموعَةٍ مِنَ المُسْتَنَداتِ وَالمَعْلوماتِ حَوْلَ مَوْضوعٍ مُحَدَّدٍ.

The dossier contains a collection of documents and information on a specific topic.

نَشَرَ • نَشْرٌ

to publish

نَشَرَتِ المَجَلَّةُ مَقالًا يَسْتَكْشِفُ التَّطَوُّراتِ في مَجالِ الذَّكاءِ الاصْطِناعِيِّ.

The magazine published an article exploring developments in the field of artificial intelligence.

هامٌّ

important

يُعْطى الخَبَرُ الهامُّ أَوْلَوِيَّةً في التَّغْطِيَةِ الإعْلامِيَّةِ نَظَرًا لِتَأْثيرِهِ الكَبيرِ.

Important news is given priority in media coverage due to its significant impact.

مُقابَلَةٌ مَعَ صَحَفِيٍّ حَوْلَ بِناءِ القِصَّةِ وَكِتابَةِ الأَخْبارِ

المُحاوِرُ: مَرْحَبًا، نَحْنُ اليَوْمَ مَعَ الصَّحَفِيِّ المُخَضْرَمِ أَحْمَد سامي لِنَتَحَدَّثَ عَنْ بِناءِ القِصَّةِ وَكِتابَةِ الأَخْبارِ في الصَّحافَةِ الحَديثَةِ. ما هوَ عُنْصُرُ الأَخْبارِ الَّذي تَعْتَبِرُهُ الأَهَمَّ في بِناءِ قِصَّةٍ إِخْبارِيَّةٍ؟

الصَّحَفِيُّ: شُكْرًا عَلى اسْتِضافَتي. أَعْتَقِدُ أَنَّ عُنْوانَ الخَبَرِ يُعَدُّ عُنْصُرًا حاسِمًا، فَهُوَ يَجْذِبُ انْتِباهَ القُرَّاءِ وَيُعْطي فِكْرَةً عَنْ مَضْمونِ القِصَّةِ. يَجِبُ أَنْ يَكونَ دَقيقًا وَمُثيرًا لِلاهْتِمامِ دونَ أَنْ يَكونَ مُثيرًا بِشَكْلٍ مُضَلِّلٍ.

المُحاوِرُ: في ضَوْءِ الجَدَلِ الدائِرِ حَوْلَ الأَخْبارِ المُزَيَّفَةِ، كَيْفَ يُمْكِنُ لِلصَّحَفيّينَ ضَمانُ دِقَّةِ تَقاريرِهِمْ؟

الصَّحَفِيُّ: تَبْدَأُ الدِّقَّةُ بِالتَّحَقُّقِ مِنَ المَصادِرِ وَتَحْليلِ المُحْتَوى الإِعْلامِيِّ بِعِنايَةٍ. مِنَ المُهِمِّ أَيْضًا مُتابَعَةُ القِصَّةِ بِشَكْلٍ حَصْرِيٍّ وَحِيادِيٍّ، وَذَلِكَ يَتَطَلَّبُ التَّحْريرَ وَالتَّعْليقَ الصَّحَفِيَّ المَدْروسَ لِضَمانِ عَدَمِ انْحِيازِ الخَبَرِ.

المُحاوِرُ: كَيْفَ تَرى دَوْرَ صِحافَةِ المُواطِنِ في هَذا السِّياقِ؟

الصَّحَفِيُّ: صِحافَةُ المُواطِنِ لَها دَوْرٌ كَبيرٌ في تَغْطِيَةِ الأَحْداثِ مِنْ مَنْظورِ شاهِدِ العِيانِ، لَكِنْ يَجِبُ تَدْقيقُ المُحْتَوى الَّذي يُنْتِجونَهُ. إِنَّها تُمَثِّلُ تَحَدِّيًا وَفُرْصَةً لِلصِّحافَةِ الحُرَّةِ لِتَوْسيعِ نِطاقِ التَّغْطِيَةِ وَتَعْميقِ التَّحْليلِ.

المُحاوِرُ: ما هِيَ الفِقْرَةُ الافْتِتاحِيَّةُ المِثالِيَّةُ في نَظَرِكَ؟

الصَّحَفِيُّ: الفِقْرَةُ الافْتِتاحِيَّةُ يَجِبُ أَنْ تَكونَ مُخْتَصَرَةً وَمُحْكَمَةً ، وَأَنْ تُقَدِّمَ جَوْهَرَ الخَبَرِ بِطَريقَةٍ تَجْذِبُ القارِئَ لِمُواصَلَةِ القِراءَةِ. يَجِبُ أَنْ تَعْكِسَ الخَبَرَ الرَّئيسِيَّ وَتُلَخِّصَ القِصَّةَ بِطَريقَةٍ جَذَّابَةٍ.

المُحاوِرُ: في خِتامِ هَذِهِ المُقابَلَةِ، هَلْ لَدَيْكَ نَصيحَةٌ لِلصَّحَفيّينَ الشَّبابِ؟

الصَّحَفِيُّ: نَصيحَتي هِيَ التَّمَسُّكُ بِمَبادِئِ الصِّحافَةِ الأَخْلاقِيَّةِ، وَالتَّحَقُّقُ دائِمًا مِنَ الحَقائِقِ، وَعَدَمُ التَّسَرُّعِ في نَشْرِ الأَخْبارِ دونَ مُتابَعَةٍ شامِلَةٍ. الصِّحافَةُ لَيْسَتْ مُجَرَّدَ نَقْلٍ لِلْأَخْبارِ، بَلْ هِيَ مَسْؤوليَّةٌ تُجاهَ المُجْتَمَعِ لِإيصالِ الحَقيقَةِ بِشَكْلٍ بارِزٍ وَمَوْثوقٍ.

Interview with a Journalist on Structuring a Story and Writing News

Interviewer: Hello. Today, we are with the veteran journalist Ahmed Samy to discuss story structuring and news writing in modern journalism. What news element do you consider most important in constructing a news story?

Journalist: Thank you for having me. I believe the headline is a crucial element, as it captures the readers' attention and gives an idea of the story's content. It should be accurate and interesting without being misleadingly sensational.

Interviewer: In light of the ongoing debate about fake news, how can journalists ensure the accuracy of their reports?

Journalist: Accuracy begins with verifying sources and carefully analyzing the media content. It's also important to follow the story in an exclusive and unbiased manner, which requires thoughtful editorial and journalistic commentary to ensure the news is not biased.

Interviewer: How do you see the role of citizen journalism in this context?

Journalist: Citizen journalism plays a significant role in covering events from the perspective of an eyewitness, but the content they produce must be scrutinized. It represents both a challenge and an opportunity for a free press to expand coverage and deepen analysis.

Interviewer: What is the ideal opening paragraph, in your opinion?

Journalist: The opening paragraph should be concise and well-crafted, presenting the essence of the news in a way that draws the reader to continue reading. It should reflect the main news and summarize the story in an engaging way.

Interviewer: To conclude this interview, do you have any advice for young journalists?

| Journalist: | My advice is to adhere to the principles of ethical journalism, always fact-check, and not rush to publish news without comprehensive follow-up. Journalism is not just about transferring news; it's a responsibility towards society to deliver the truth in a significant and reliable manner. |

11.2.3 Opinion Writing and Editorializing

Track **42**

to support

• تَأْيِيد   أَيَّدَ

أَيَّدَ الكاتِبُ القَراراتِ الحُكوميَّةَ في مَقالِهِ، مُقَدِّمًا أَسْبابًا مُفَصَّلَةً لِدَعْمِهِ.

The writer endorsed the government decisions in his article, providing detailed reasons for his support.

to criticize

• اِنْتِقاد   اِنْتَقَدَ

اِنْتَقَدَ العَمودُ الصَّحَفيُّ الإجْراءاتِ الحُكوميَّةَ، مُعْتَبِرًا أَنَّها غَيْرُ كافِيَةٍ لِمواجَهَةِ الأَزْمَةِ.

The newspaper column criticized the government measures, considering them insufficient to address the crisis.

editorial

تَحْريريٌّ

تَناوَلَ القِسْمُ التَّحْريريُّ في الصَّحيفَةِ قَضايا مُعَقَّدَةً بِمَقالاتٍ تَحْريريَّةٍ تَعْكِسُ وُجْهَةَ نَظَرِ النّاشِرِ.

The editorial section in the newspaper addresses complex issues with editorials that reflect the publisher's viewpoint.

analysis

تَحْليلٌ

يُقَدِّمُ الكاتِبُ تَحْليلًا عَميقًا لِلأَحْداثِ الجارِيَةِ، مُسْتَخْدِمًا بَياناتٍ وَإِحْصاءاتٍ لِدَعْمِ آرائِهِ.

The writer provides an in-depth analysis of current events, using data and statistics to support his opinions.

commentary

تَعْليقٌ

يَشْتَهِرُ العَمودُ الصَّحَفيُّ بِتَعْليقاتِهِ السّاخِرَةِ الَّتي تُلْقي الضَّوْءَ عَلى المُشْكِلاتِ الاِجْتِماعِيَّةِ.

The newspaper column is known for its satirical comments that highlight social issues.

تَعْليقُ رَأْي

opinion comment

نَشَرَتِ الصَّحيفَةُ تَعْليقَ رَأْيٍ يَنْتَقِدُ السِّياساتِ الحُكوميَّةَ الأَخيرَةَ.

The newspaper published an opinion comment criticizing recent government policies.

حُرٌّ

free

يُعْتَبَرُ النِّقاشُ الحُرُّ وَتَبادُلُ الآراءِ جُزْءًا أَساسيًّا مِنَ الدِّيمُقْراطيَّةِ.

Free debate and exchange of opinions are essential parts of democracy.

حَلَّلَ • تَحْليلٌ

to analyze

حَلَّلَ الخَبيرُ الاِقْتِصاديُّ البَياناتِ الماليَّةَ لِتَقْديمِ تَوَقُّعاتٍ عَنِ السّوقِ.

The economic expert analyzed the financial data to provide market forecasts.

رَأْيٌ • آراءٌ

opinion

تُعْرَفُ مَقالاتُ الرَّأْيِ بِطَرْحِها وُجْهاتِ نَظَرٍ شَخْصيَّةً حَوْلَ مَوْضوعاتٍ مُتَنَوِّعَةٍ.

Opinion articles are known for presenting personal viewpoints on various topics.

راجَعَ • مُراجَعَةٌ

to review

راجَعَ النّاقِدُ الأَدَبيُّ الرِّوايَةَ بِعنايَةٍ، مُوَضِّحًا نِقاطَ القُوَّةِ وَالضَّعْفِ فيها.

The literary critic carefully reviewed the novel, highlighting its strengths and weaknesses.

عَلَّقَ عَلَى • تَعْليقٌ

to comment on

عَلَّقَ السِّياسيُّ عَلَى التَّطَوُّراتِ الأَخيرَةِ، مُشيرًا إلى تَأْثيرِها عَلَى المُجْتَمَعِ.

The politician commented on recent developments, pointing out their impact on society.

كاتِبُ رَأْي • كُتّابٌ

opinion writer, opinion columnist

يُعْتَبَرُ كاتِبُ الرَّأْيِ مُؤَثِّرًا بِفَضْلِ تَحْليلاتِهِ الثّاقِبَةِ وَطَرْحِهِ المَوْضوعيِّ.

The opinion writer is influential due to his insightful analyses and objective presentation.

to write a report   كِتابَةٌ •   كَتَبَ تَقْرِيرًا

كَتَبَ الصَّحَفِيُّ تَقْرِيرًا شامِلًا عَنْ تَأْثيرِ التَّغَيُّرِ المُناخِيِّ عَلى الِاقْتِصادِ العالَمِيِّ.

The journalist wrote a comprehensive report on the impact of climate change on the global economy.

supportive   مُؤَيِّدٌ

يَجِبُ عَلى الكاتِبِ تَقْديمُ أَدِلَّةٍ وَحُجَجٍ مُؤَيَّدَةٍ لِتَعْزيزِ مَوْقِفِهِ في مَقالِ الرَّأْيِ.

The writer must provide supporting evidence and arguments to strengthen his position in the opinion article.

editor   مُحَرِّرٌ

يَعْمَلُ المُحَرِّرُ عَلى تَنْسيقِ مَقالاتِ الرَّأْيِ وَضَمانِ التَّنَوُّعِ في المَوْضوعاتِ وَوُجْهاتِ النَّظَرِ المُقَدَّمَةِ.

The editor works on organizing opinion articles and ensuring diversity in the topics and viewpoints presented.

opinion editor   مُحَرِّرُ رَأْي

يَخْتَصُّ مُحَرِّرُ الرَّأْي بِإِدارَةِ قِسْمِ الرَّأْي في الصَّحيفَةِ، مُخْتارًا المَقالاتِ الَّتي تُعَبِّرُ عَنْ آراءٍ مُتَنَوِّعَةٍ.

The opinion editor specializes in managing the opinion section of the newspaper, selecting articles that express diverse opinions.

editor-in-chief   مُديرُ تَحْريرٍ

يُشْرِفُ مُديرُ التَّحْريرِ عَلى العَمَلِيَّةِ التَّحْريرِيَّةِ بِأَكْمَلِها، ضامِنًا جَوْدَةَ المُحْتَوى الصَّحَفِيِّ.

The managing editor oversees the entire editorial process, ensuring the quality of the journalistic content.

editorial review   مُراجَعَةٌ تَحْريرِيَّةٌ

تَتَضَمَّنُ المُراجَعَةُ التَّحْريرِيَّةُ تَقْييمَ المُحْتَوى وَتَحْسينَهُ لِلتَّأَكُّدِ مِنْ دِقَّتِهِ وَفَعالِيَّتِهِ قَبْلَ النَّشْرِ.

The editorial review involves evaluating and enhancing content to ensure its accuracy and effectiveness before publication.

مُسْتَقِلٌّ

independent

يَحْرِصُ الصَّحَفِيُّ المُسْتَقِلُّ عَلى تَقْدِيمَ تَقارِيرَ مَوْضوعِيَّةٍ دونَ تَأْثِيرٍ مِنْ أَيَّةِ جِهاتٍ خارِجِيَّةٍ.

The independent journalist ensures objective reporting without influence from any external parties.

مَقالٌ تَحْلِيلِيٌّ

analytical article

يُقَدِّمُ المَقالُ التَّحْلِيلِيُّ رُؤىً مُعَمَّقَةً حَوْلَ قَضِيَّةٍ مُعَيَّنَةٍ، مُسْتَنِدًا إِلى بَياناتٍ وَأَدِلَّةٍ مُوَثَّقَةٍ.

The analytical article provides in-depth insights on a specific issue based on data and documented evidence.

مَقالٌ تَعْلِيقِيٌّ

commentary article

يَطْرَحُ المَقالُ التَّعْلِيقِيُّ وُجْهاتِ نَظَرٍ شَخْصِيَّةً وَتَفْسِيراتٍ حَوْلَ الأَحْداثِ الجارِيَةِ.

The commentary article presents personal viewpoints and interpretations of current events.

نَقْدِيٌّ

critical

تَفْحَصُ وَسائِلُ الإِعْلامِ الجَوانِبَ النَّقْدِيَّةَ لِسِياساتِ الحُكومَةِ الاِقْتِصادِيَّةِ.

The media examines the critical aspects of the government's economic policies.

11.2.3.1 Informative Article: Opinions in Journalism

Track **43**

مَقالاتُ الرَّأْيِ وَالتَّعْلِيقاتُ التَّحْرِيرِيَّةُ: فَنُّ النِّقاشِ العامِّ

مَقالاتُ الرَّأْيِ، أَوِ التَّعْلِيقاتُ التَّحْرِيرِيَّةُ، هِيَ نَوْعٌ مِنَ الكِتابَةِ الصَّحَفِيَّةِ الَّتي تُوَفِّرُ تَحْلِيلاتٍ وَآراءَ حَوْلَ مَوْضوعاتٍ مُخْتَلِفَةٍ، تَعْكِسُ وُجْهاتِ نَظَرٍ شَخْصِيَّةً، وَلَكِنْ بِأُسْلوبٍ مَدْروسٍ وَمُعْتَمِدٍ عَلى الحُجَّةِ. كاتِبُ الرَّأْيِ، سَواءً كانَ مُحَرِّرًا أَوْ كاتِبًا مُسْتَقِلًّا، يَسْتَكْشِفُ المَوْضوعاتِ الجارِيَةَ وَيُعَلِّقُ عَلَيْها، مُقَدِّمًا رُؤْيَةً ناقِدَةً أَوْ مُؤَيَّدَةً لِفِكْرَةٍ مُعَيَّنَةٍ.

يَلْعَبُ كُتّابُ الرَّأْيِ وَالمُحَرِّرونَ دَوْرًا حاسِمًا في تَشْكِيلِ النِّقاشِ العامِّ. مِنْ خِلالِ التَّحْلِيلِ وَتَعْلِيقاتِ الرَّأْيِ، يُساهِمونَ في تَوْسِيعِ أُفُقِ التَّفْكِيرِ وَتَحْفِيزِ النِّقاشِ بَيْنَ القُرّاءِ. يَجِبُ أَنْ يَتَّسِمَ الكُتّابُ بِالحُرِّيَّةِ في التَّعْبِيرِ عَنْ آرائِهِمْ، مَعَ الحِفاظِ عَلى الأَمانَةِ الفِكْرِيَّةِ وَالاِسْتِقْلالِيَّةِ، لِتَقْدِيمِ مَقالاتٍ تَحْلِيلِيَّةٍ وَتَعْلِيقِيَّةٍ ذاتِ مَعْنىً.

في الخِتامِ، فَإِنَّ مَقالَ الرَّأْيِ هُوَ رُكْنٌ أَساسِيٌّ في الصَّحافَةِ يُساعِدُ في تَنْوِيرِ الجُمْهورِ وَتَشْجِيعِ المُناقَشَةِ الصِّحِّيَّةِ حَوْلَ القَضايا المُهِمَّةِ، مِمّا يَجْعَلُهُ عُنْصُرًا لا يُمْكِنُ الاِسْتِغْناءُ عَنْهُ في الحِوارِ الدّيمُقْراطِيِّ.

Opinion articles, or editorial commentaries, are a type of journalistic writing that provide analyses and viewpoints on various topics, reflecting personal perspectives but with a reasoned and argumentative style. An opinion writer, whether an editor or a freelance author, explores current topics and comments on them, offering critical or supportive insights on a particular idea.

Opinion writers and editors play a crucial role in shaping public debate. Through their analyses and opinion commentaries, they contribute to broadening the thinking horizon and stimulating discussion among readers. Writers must have the freedom to express their views while maintaining intellectual honesty and independence to deliver meaningful analytical and commentary articles.

In conclusion, opinion articles are a fundamental pillar in journalism, helping to enlighten the public and encouraging healthy discussion on important issues, making them an indispensable element in democratic dialogue.

11.2.3.2 Article: Censorship in the Arab World

Track **44**

تَحَدِّياتُ الصِّحافَةِ في العالَمِ العَرَبيِّ: بَيْنَ الحُرِّيَّةِ والرِّقابَةِ

في العالَمِ العَرَبيِّ، تُواجِهُ الصِّحافَةُ تَحَدِّياتٍ كَبيرةً تَتَعَلَّقُ بِالحُرِّيَّةِ والرِّقابَةِ. كَثيرًا ما يُعَلِّقُ المُحَرِّرونَ وكُتّابُ الرَّأْيِ على الأَحْداثِ اليَوْميَّةِ بِطَريقَةٍ تَحْريريَّةٍ تُظْهِرُ تَأْييدًا لِلْحُكوماتِ، دونَ تَقْديمِ تَحْليلٍ نَقْديٍّ أو انْتِقادٍ لِلسِّياساتِ القائِمَةِ. هذا يَعودُ جُزْئيًّا إلى الضُّغوطِ الّتي تَفْرِضُها الأَنْظِمَةُ الحاكِمَةُ، مِمّا يَحِدُّ مِنَ الحُرِّيَّةِ التَّحْريريَّةِ ويَجْعَلُ مِنَ الصَّعْبِ إجْراءَ مُراجَعاتٍ تَحْريريَّةٍ حَقيقيَّةٍ.

في هذا السِّياقِ، يَبْرُزُ دَوْرُ المُحَرِّرينَ ومُديري التَّحْريرِ الّذينَ يُراجِعونَ المُحْتَوى بِعِنايَةٍ لِضَمانِ تَوافُقِهِ مَعَ الخُطوطِ العَريضَةِ لِلسِّياسَةِ الإعْلاميَّةِ المُعْتَمَدَةِ. يَكْتُبُ المُراسِلونَ تَقاريرَهُمْ مُرَكِّزينَ أَكْثَرَ على الأَخْبارِ الّتي تُعَزِّزُ صورَةَ الدَّوْلَةِ بِشَكْلٍ إيجابيٍّ، ويَتَجَنَّبونَ الغَوْصَ في قَضايا قَدْ تُثيرُ الجَدَلَ أو تُعَرِّضُهُمْ لِلْمُساءَلَةِ.

على الرَّغْمِ مِنْ ذَلِكَ، هُناكَ مُحاوَلاتٌ مِنْ قِبَلِ بَعْضِ الصَّحَفيّينَ المُسْتَقِلّينَ لِتَقْديمِ تَحْليلاتٍ وتَعْليقاتٍ تَنْتَقِدُ الواقِعَ وتُسَلِّطُ الضَّوْءَ على القَضايا الإشْكاليَّةِ. هؤُلاءِ الكُتّابُ يَسْعَوْنَ إلى تَحْريرِ الرَّأْيِ وإيجادِ مِساحَةٍ لِلْحِوارِ الحُرِّ، مُتَحَدِّينَ القُيودَ المَفْروضَةَ على حُرِّيَّةِ الصِّحافَةِ.

في خِضَمِّ هَذِهِ الأَجْواءِ، يَظَلُّ التَّوازُنُ بَيْنَ تَقْديمِ مُحْتَوى مُوافِقٍ لِلْأَنْظِمَةِ وبَيْنَ السَّعْيِ لِتَحْقيقِ الاسْتِقْلاليَّةِ التَّحْريريَّةِ أَمْرًا صَعْبَ المَنالِ. ومَعَ ذَلِكَ، يُعَدُّ الدَّوْرُ الّذي يَلْعَبُهُ الصَّحَفيّونَ في تَحْليلِ الأَحْداثِ وتَقْديمِ تَعْليقاتٍ تُساهِمُ في تَشْكيلِ الرَّأْيِ العامِّ أَمْرًا بالِغَ الأَهَمّيَّةِ. يَبْقى السُّؤالُ: إلى أَيِّ مَدى يُمْكِنُ أَنْ تُصْبِحَ الصِّحافَةُ في العالَمِ العَرَبيِّ حُرَّةً ومُسْتَقِلَّةً بِما يَكْفي لِتَقْديمِ تَحْليلٍ نَقْديٍّ حَقيقيٍّ؟

Challenges of Journalism in the Arab World: Between Freedom and Censorship

In the Arab world, journalism faces significant challenges related to freedom and censorship. Editors and opinion writers often comment on daily events in an editorial manner that shows support for governments without providing critical analysis or criticism of existing policies. This is partly due to the pressures imposed by ruling regimes, which limit editorial freedom and make it difficult to conduct genuine editorial reviews.

In this context, the role of editors and managing editors who carefully review content to ensure its compliance with the adopted media policy guidelines becomes prominent. Reporters write their reports focusing more on news that positively enhances the state's image, avoiding delving into issues that might provoke controversy or expose them to accountability.

Despite this, there are attempts by some independent journalists to provide analyses and commentaries that critique reality and highlight problematic issues. These writers strive for opinion freedom and seek to create a space for free dialogue, challenging the restrictions on press freedom.

Amidst these circumstances, the balance between presenting content that conforms to the regimes and striving for editorial independence is difficult to achieve. Nonetheless, the role played by journalists in analyzing events and providing commentaries that contribute to shaping public opinion is of great importance. The question remains: To what extent can journalism in the Arab world become free and independent enough to offer genuine critical analysis?

11.2.4 Investigative Journalism

Track **45**

أَجْرى مُقابَلَةً • إِجْراءٌ

to conduct an interview

أَجْرى الصَّحَفِيُّ مُقابَلَةً مَعَ شُهودٍ رَئيسِيينَ لِجَمْعِ مَعْلوماتٍ حَوْلَ القَضِيَّةِ.

The journalist conducted interviews with key witnesses to gather information about the case.

إِثْباتٌ

proof

يَهْدُفُ الصَّحَفِيُّ الاِسْتِقْصائِيُّ إلى إِثْباتِ الوَقائِعِ بِالأَدِلَّةِ وَالشَّهاداتِ.

The investigative journalist aims to substantiate facts with evidence and testimonies.

إِفْشاءٌ

disclosure

يُمْكِنُ أَنْ يُؤَدِّيَ إِفْشاءُ مَعْلوماتٍ حَسّاسَةٍ إلى تَحَوُّلاتٍ كَبيرَةٍ في الرَّأْيِ العامِّ وَالسِّياسَةِ.

The disclosure of sensitive information can lead to significant shifts in public opinion and policy.

اسْتِقْصاءٌ   investigation

يَتَطَلَّبُ الِاسْتِقْصاءُ مَهاراتٍ خاصَّةً في البَحْثِ وَالتَّحْليلِ لِكَشْفِ الحَقائِقِ.

Investigating requires special skills in research and analysis to uncover the facts.

تَحَقَّقَ • **تَحَقَّقَ**   to verify, fact-check

قامَ الصَّحَفِيُّ بِالتَّحَقُّقِ مِنَ الحَقائِقِ بِدِقَّةٍ قَبْلَ نَشْرِ القِصَّةِ لِتَجَنُّبِ نَقْلِ مَعْلوماتٍ خاطِئَةٍ.

The journalist carefully fact-checked before publishing the story to avoid disseminating incorrect information.

تَحَقُّقٌ مِنْ حَقائِقَ   fact-checking

يُعَدُّ التَّحَقُّقُ مِنَ الحَقائِقِ خُطْوَةً أَساسِيَّةً في الصَّحافَةِ الِاسْتِقْصائِيَّةِ لِضَمانِ الدِّقَّةِ وَمَنْعِ انْتِشارِ المَعْلوماتِ المُضَلِّلَةِ.

Fact-checking is a fundamental step in investigative journalism to ensure accuracy and prevent the spread of misinformation.

تَحْقيقٌ   inquiry, investigation

يَعْمَلُ الصَّحَفِيُّ عَلى تَحْقيقٍ يَكْشِفُ عَنْ مُمارَساتٍ غَيْرِ قانونِيَّةٍ في شَرِكَةٍ كَبيرَةٍ.

The journalist is working on an investigation that reveals illegal practices in a large company.

تَسْريبٌ   leak

أَدّى تَسْريبُ الوَثائِقِ إِلى كَشْفِ فَضائِحَ سِياسِيَّةٍ كُبْرى.

The leaking of documents led to the exposure of major political scandals.

تَسْريبُ مَعْلوماتٍ   information leak

كانَ تَسْريبُ المَعْلوماتِ حاسِمًا في تَوْجيهِ الِانْتِباهِ العامِّ إِلى قَضايا الفَسادِ.

The information leak was crucial in drawing public attention to corruption issues.

تَفْتيشٌ   inspection

نَفَّذَ الصَّحَفِيّونَ عَمَلِيّاتِ تَفْتيشٍ لِلْحُصولِ عَلى الوَثائِقِ الَّتي تَدْعَمُ اسْتِقْصاءَهُمْ.

Journalists carried out inspections to obtain documents that support their investigation.

investigative report

تَقْرِيرٌ اسْتِقْصَائِيٌّ • تَقَارِير

نَشَرَتِ الصَّحيفَةُ تَقْريرًا اسْتِقْصائِيًّا حَوْلَ الفَسادِ في الإدارَةِ المَحَلِّيَّةِ.

The newspaper published an investigative report on corruption in local administration.

document organization

تَنْظيمُ وَثائِق

تَطَلَّبَ التَّحْقيقُ تَنْظيمَ وَثائِقَ مُتَعَدِّدَةٍ لِإِنْشاءِ خَطٍّ زَمَنِيٍّ واضِحٍ لِلْأَحْداثِ.

The investigation required organizing multiple documents to create a clear timeline of events.

investigative newspaper

جَريدَةٌ اسْتِقْصائِيَّةٌ

كَشَفَتْ جَريدَةٌ اسْتِقْصائِيَّةٌ عَنْ وُجودِ شَبَكَةِ فَسادٍ واسِعَةٍ داخِلَ الحُكومَةِ مِنْ خِلالِ مُراجَعَةِ وَثائِقَ مُسَرَّبَةٍ.

An investigative newspaper uncovered a widespread corruption network within the government through a review of leaked documents.

freedom of the press

حُرِّيَّةُ صِحافَةٍ

تُعْتَبَرُ حُرِّيَّةُ الصِّحافَةِ حَجَرَ الأَساسِ لِلصِّحافَةِ الاسْتِقْصائِيَّةِ، مِمّا يُمَكِّنُها مِنْ تَناوُلِ القَضايا بِجُرْأَةٍ.

Press freedom is the cornerstone of investigative journalism, enabling it to address issues boldly.

to obtain information

حَصَلَ عَلى مَعْلوماتٍ • حُصولٌ

حَصَلَ مُراسِلٌ عَلى مَعْلوماتٍ سِرِّيَّةٍ تُفيدُ بِتَوَرُّطِ شَرِكَةٍ كُبْرى في التَّهَرُّبِ الضَّريبِيِّ.

A reporter obtained confidential information indicating a major company's involvement in tax evasion.

right to access information

حَقُّ وُصولٍ إلى مَعْلوماتٍ • حُقوقٌ

يَجِبُ ضَمانُ حَقِّ وُصولِ الصَّحَفِيّينَ إلى المَعْلوماتِ لِتَعْزيزِ الشَّفافِيَّةِ والمُساءَلَةِ.

Journalists' right of access to information must be ensured to enhance transparency and accountability.

to investigate

حَقَّقَ • تَحْقيقٌ

حَقَّقَ فَريقٌ مِنَ الصَّحَفِيّينَ في تَأْثيرِ التَّغَيُّرِ المُناخِيِّ عَلى الزِّراعَةِ صَغيرَةِ النِّطاقِ.

A team of journalists investigated the impact of climate change on small-scale agriculture.

evidence

دَليلٌ • أَدِلَّةٌ

يَجْمَعُ الصَّحَفِيّونَ الاسْتِقْصائِيّونَ أَدِلَّةً دامِغَةً لِدَعْمِ تَقاريرِهِمْ وَكَشْفِ الحَقائِقِ.

Investigative journalists gather compelling evidence to support their reports and uncover the truth.

to leak

سَرَّبَ • تَسْريبٌ

سَرَّبَ مَصْدَرٌ مَجْهولٌ وَثائِقَ تَكْشِفُ عَنِ انْتِهاكاتٍ لِحُقوقِ الإِنْسانِ في مِنْطَقَةِ النِّزاعِ.

An anonymous source leaked documents revealing human rights violations in a conflict zone.

confidential

سِرِّيٌّ

يَتَعامَلُ الصَّحَفِيّونَ الاسْتِقْصائِيّونَ مَعَ المَعْلوماتِ السِّرِّيَّةِ بِحِرْصٍ شَديدٍ لِحِمايَةِ مَصادِرِهِمْ.

Investigative journalists handle confidential information with extreme care to protect their sources.

eyewitness testimony

شَهادَةُ عِيانٍ

تُعَدُّ شَهادَةُ العِيانِ مُكَوِّنًا قَيِّمًا في الصَّحافَةِ الاسْتِقْصائِيَّةِ لِتَقْديمِ مَنْظورٍ شَخْصِيٍّ لِلْحَدَثِ.

Eyewitness testimony is a valuable component in investigative journalism for providing a personal perspective on the event.

shocking

صادِمٌ

قَدْ يَكونُ المُحْتَوى الاسْتِقْصائِيُّ صادِمًا عِنْدَما يَكْشِفُ عَنْ مَعْلوماتٍ تَتَعارَضُ مَعَ المُعْتَقَداتِ الشّائِعَةِ.

Investigative content can be shocking when it reveals information that contradicts common beliefs.

investigative journalism

صِحافَةٌ اسْتِقْصائِيَّةٌ = صِحافَةُ اسْتِقْصاءٍ

تَلْعَبُ الصَّحافَةُ الاسْتِقْصائِيَّةُ دَوْرًا حاسِمًا في كَشْفِ الحَقائِقِ وَتَعْزيزِ الدّيمُقْراطِيَّةِ.

Investigative journalism plays a crucial role in uncovering facts and promoting democracy.

صَحَفِيٌّ اسْتِقْصائِيٌّ

investigative journalist

يَتَمَيَّزُ الصَّحَفِيُّ الاسْتِقْصائِيُّ بِقُدْرَتِهِ عَلَى التَّعَمُّقِ في القِصَصِ وَكَشْفِ الجَوانِبِ المَخْفِيَّةِ.

The investigative journalist is characterized by the ability to delve into stories and uncover hidden aspects.

فاسِدٌ

corrupt

يُرَكِّزُ التَّحْقيقُ الاسْتِقْصائِيُّ عَلَى كَشْفِ الأَفْعالِ الفاسِدَةِ وَمُحاسَبَةِ المَسْؤولينَ.

Investigative inquiry focuses on exposing corrupt actions and holding those responsible accountable.

فَضَحَ • فَضْحٌ

to reveal

فَضَحَتْ صَحيفَةٌ مَحَلِّيَّةٌ شَبَكَةَ فَسادٍ داخِلَ البَلَدِيَّةِ.

A local newspaper exposed a network of corruption within the municipality.

فَضيحَةٌ صَحَفِيَّةٌ • فَضائِحُ

journalistic scandal

أَدَّتْ فَضيحَةٌ صَحَفِيَّةٌ إلى اسْتِقالَةِ عِدَّةِ مَسْؤولينَ بَعْدَ كَشْفِ تَوَرُّطِهِمْ في قَضايا رَشْوَةٍ.

A journalistic scandal led to the resignation of several officials after their involvement in bribery cases was exposed.

قِصَّةٌ اسْتِقْصائِيَّةٌ • قِصَصٌ

investigative story

نَشَرَتِ الجَريدَةُ قِصَّةً اسْتِقْصائِيَّةً كَشَفَتْ عَنْ تَضارُبِ مَصالِحَ كَبيرٍ في الإِدارَةِ العُلْيا.

The newspaper published an investigative story that revealed significant conflicts of interest in the upper management.

كَشَفَ • كَشْفٌ

to uncover, expose

كَشَفَتْ تَحْقيقاتٌ صَحَفِيَّةٌ عَنِ اسْتِغْلالِ العُمّالِ في مَصانِعِ الإِنْتاجِ الواسِعِ.

Journalistic investigations revealed the exploitation of workers in mass-production factories.

interesting

مُثِيرٌ لِلِاهْتِمام

يُعْتَبَرُ التَّحْقِيقُ الَّذِي يَكْشِفُ عَنْ مَشاكِلَ مُجْتَمَعِيَّةٍ كَبِيرَةٍ مُثِيرًا لِلِاهْتِمام وَيَجْذِبُ انْتِباهَ الجُمْهور.

An investigation that reveals significant social problems is interesting and captures public attention.

controversial

مُثِيرٌ لِلْجَدَل

كانَتِ المقالَةُ الَّتِي نُشِرَتْ مُثِيرَةً لِلْجَدَلِ في وسائِلِ الإِعْلام.

The published article was controversial in the media.

document review

مُراجَعَةُ وَثائِقَ

يَعْتَمِدُ الصَّحَفِيّونَ الِاسْتِقْصائِيّونَ عَلَى مُراجَعَةِ الوَثائِقِ لِفَهْمِ السِّياقِ وَجَمْعِ الأَدِلَّةِ.

Investigative journalists rely on document review to understand the context and gather evidence.

confidential source

• مَصادِرُ   مَصْدَرٌ سِرِّيٌّ

قَدْ يَحْصُلُ الصَّحَفِيّونَ الِاسْتِقْصائِيّونَ عَلَى مَعْلوماتٍ حَيَوِيَّةٍ مِنْ مَصادِرَ سِرِّيَّةٍ لِكَشْفِ قَضايا مُهِمَّةٍ.

Investigative journalists may obtain vital information from confidential sources to expose significant issues.

reliable source

مَصْدَرٌ مَوْثوقٌ بِهِ

يُشَكِّلُ الحُصولُ عَلَى مَعْلوماتٍ مِنْ مَصْدَرٍ مَوْثوقٍ بِهِ جُزْءًا أَساسِيًّا مِنَ الصَّحافَةِ الِاسْتِقْصائِيَّةِ.

Getting information from a reliable source is a fundamental part of investigative journalism.

misleading

مُضَلِّلٌ

قَدَّمَ المَقالُ مَنْظورًا مُضَلِّلًا حَوْلَ الوَضْعِ الِاقْتِصادِيِّ الحالِيِّ، مِمّا أَدّى إلى الِارْتِباكِ بَيْنَ القُرّاءِ.

The article presented a misleading perspective on the current economic situation, causing confusion among readers.

exclusive information

مَعْلومَةٌ حَضرِيَّةٌ

حَصَلَ الصَّحَفِيُّ عَلَى مَعْلوماتٍ حَصرِيَّةٍ بِشَأْنِ إِطْلاقِ الْمُنْتَجِ القادِمِ لِلشَّرِكَةِ.

The journalist obtained exclusive information regarding the company's upcoming product launch.

to publish • نَشَرَ   نَشَرَ

نَشَرَ مَوْقِعٌ إِخْبارِيٌّ قِصَّةً اسْتِقْصائِيَّةً عَنْ تَلَوُّثِ البِيئَةِ بِسَبَبِ النُّفاياتِ الصِّناعِيَّةِ.

A news website published an investigative story about environmental pollution due to industrial waste.

spread of fake news   نَشْرُ أَخْبارٍ زائِفَةٍ

يَجِبُ عَلَى الصَّحَفِيّينَ الاسْتِقْصائِيّينَ تَجَنُّبُ نَشْرِ أَخْبارٍ زائِفَةٍ عَنْ طَرِيقِ التَّحَقُّقِ المُسْتَمِرِّ مِنْ صِحَّةِ المَعْلُوماتِ.

Investigative journalists must avoid publishing fake news by continuously verifying the accuracy of information.

to document • تَوْثيقٌ   وَثَّقَ

يُوَثِّقُ الصَّحَفِيّونَ مَصادِرَهُمْ وَمَعْلوماتِهِمْ بِعِنايَةٍ لِضَمانِ دِقَّةِ التَّقارِيرِ الاسْتِقْصائِيَّةِ.

Journalists carefully document their sources and information to ensure the accuracy of investigative reports.

confidential document   وَثيقَةٌ سِرِّيَّةٌ

قَدْ يَعْتَمِدُ التَّحْقيقُ الاسْتِقْصائِيُّ عَلَى وَثائِقَ سِرِّيَّةٍ تَكْشِفُ عَنْ مُمارَساتٍ غَيْرِ قانونِيَّةٍ أَوْ غَيْرِ أَخْلاقِيَّةٍ.

Investigative research may rely on confidential documents that reveal illegal or unethical practices.

11.2.4.1 Mini-Articles

Track **46**

نَشَرَتْ جَرِيدَةٌ تَحْقِيقاتٍ مَحَلِّيَّةٌ تَقْرِيرًا اسْتِقْصائِيًّا مُثِيرًا لِلْجَدَلِ يَكْشِفُ عَنْ شَبَكَةِ فَسادٍ واسِعَةِ النِّطاقِ داخِلَ إِدارَةِ المَدِينَةِ. أَجْرَى الصَّحَفِيّونَ الاسْتِقْصائِيّونَ مُقابَلاتٍ مَعَ شُهودِ عِيانٍ وَحَصَلوا عَلَى وَثائِقَ سِرِّيَّةٍ تُثْبِتُ تَوَرُّطَ مَسْؤولينَ كِبارٍ في تَحْقيقِ مَنافِعَ شَخْصِيَّةٍ مِنْ مَشارِيعَ عامَّةٍ، مِمّا أَثارَ رُدودَ فِعْلٍ غاضِبَةً مِنَ الجُمْهورِ.

A local investigative newspaper published a controversial investigative report revealing a widespread corruption network within the city administration. Investigative journalists conducted interviews with eyewitnesses and obtained secret documents proving the involvement of high-ranking officials in gaining personal benefits from public projects, sparking angry public reactions.

كَشَفَ تَقْرِيرٌ اسْتِقْصَائِيٌّ فِي مَجَلَّةٍ مَعْرُوفَةٍ عَنْ تَسْرِيبِ مَعْلُوماتٍ حَسَّاسَةٍ مِنْ إِحْدَى كُبْرَياتِ شَرِكاتِ التِّكْنُولُوجْيا. تَوَصَّلَ الصَّحَفِيّونَ إِلَى أَنَّ بَياناتٍ خاصَّةً بِالْمُسْتَخْدِمِينَ تَمَّ بَيْعُها بِشَكْلٍ غَيْرِ قانونِيٍّ لِأَطْرافٍ ثالِثَةٍ. اسْتَنَدَ الْكَشْفُ إِلَى مَصادِرَ سِرِّيَّةٍ وَمُراجَعَةٍ دَقِيقَةٍ لِلْوَثائِقِ، مِمّا أَدَّى إِلَى كَشْفِ هَذِهِ الْمُمارَساتِ الْمُضَلِّلَةِ.

An investigative report published in a well-known magazine uncovered the leak of sensitive information from one of the largest technology companies. Journalists discovered that users' private data were illegally sold to third parties. The revelation was based on confidential sources and a meticulous review of documents, exposing these deceptive practices.

تَحْقِيقٌ اسْتِقْصائِيٌّ أَجْرَتْهُ شَبَكَةٌ إِخْبارِيَّةٌ رَصَدَ وَفَضَحَ كَيْفَ تَمَّ نَشْرُ أَخْبارٍ زائِفَةٍ لِلتَّأْثِيرِ عَلَى الرَّأْي العامِّ قَبْلَ الانْتِخاباتِ الوَطَنِيَّةِ. كَشَفَ صَحَفِيّونَ اسْتِقْصائِيّونَ الشَّبَكاتِ وَراءَ هَذِهِ الحَمَلاتِ، مُوَضِّحِينَ التِّقْنِيّاتِ الْمُسْتَخْدَمَةَ لِتَصْمِيمِ وَتَوْزِيعِ الْمُحْتَوَى الْمُضَلِّلِ عَلَى وَسائِلِ التَّواصُلِ الاِجْتِماعِيِّ.

An investigative report by a news network monitored and exposed how fake news was published to influence public opinion before the national elections. Investigative journalists uncovered the networks behind these campaigns, illustrating the techniques used to design and distribute misleading content on social media.

نَشَرَتْ صَحِيفَةٌ اسْتِقْصائِيَّةٌ قِصَّةً مُفَصَّلَةً حَوْلَ اسْتِغْلالِ العُمّالِ فِي مَصانِعِ النَّسِيجِ بِإِحْدَى الْمَناطِقِ الصِّناعِيَّةِ. كَشَفَ التَّحْقِيقُ عَنْ ظُروفِ عَمَلٍ غَيْرِ إِنْسانِيَّةٍ وانْتِهاكاتٍ لِحُقوقِ العُمّالِ، واسْتَنَدَ إِلَى شَهاداتٍ مُوَثَّقَةٍ مِنَ العُمّالِ وَتَفْتِيشِ المَواقِعِ، مِمّا أَثارَ دَعَواتٍ لِإِصْلاحِ القِطاعِ.

An investigative newspaper published a detailed story about the exploitation of workers in textile factories in an industrial area. The investigation revealed inhumane working conditions and violations of workers' rights, based on documented testimonies from workers and site inspections, leading to calls for sector reform.

قامَ مُراسِلونَ مِنْ قَناةٍ تِلْفِزْيونِيَّةٍ بِتَحْقِيقٍ مُوَسَّعٍ حَوْلَ كَيْفِيَّةِ تَأْثِيرِ الشَّرِكاتِ الكُبْرَى عَلَى السِّياساتِ البِيئِيَّةِ. اسْتَخْدَمَ الصَّحَفِيّونَ مَصادِرَ مَوْثوقَةً وَأَدِلَّةً مَلْموسَةً لِإِثْباتِ كَيْفَ تَمَّ تَجاهُلُ الْمَعايِيرِ البِيئِيَّةِ لِصالِحِ مَصالِحَ تِجارِيَّةٍ، مِمّا أَدَّى إِلَى تَبِعاتٍ سَلْبِيَّةٍ عَلَى البِيئَةِ والْمُجْتَمَعاتِ الْمَحَلِّيَّةِ.

Reporters from a television channel conducted an extensive investigation into how major companies influence environmental policies. Journalists used reliable sources and tangible evidence to demonstrate how environmental standards were overlooked in favor of business interests, leading to negative consequences for the environment and local communities.

11.2.5 Feature Writing and Long-Form Journalism

أَسْبابٌ وَنَتائِجُ
causes and consequences   *pl.*

يُرَكِّزُ تَحْليلُ الأَسْبابِ وَالنَّتائِجِ عَلَى تَقَصّي أَسْبابِ الأَحْداثِ وَتَبِعاتِها، مِمّا يُساعِدُ في فَهْمِ السِّياقِ الأَكْبَرِ.

Analyzing causes and consequences focuses on investigating the reasons for events and their aftermath, aiding in understanding the broader context.

اِنْتَقَدَ
to criticize   • اِنْتِقادٌ

في الصَّحافَةِ التَّحْليلِيَّةِ، يُمْكِنُ لِلْكاتِبِ اِنْتِقادُ السِّياساتِ العامَّةِ، مُقَدِّمًا بَدائِلَ بَنّاءَةً.

In analytical journalism, the writer can critique public policies, offering constructive alternatives.

بَحَثَ
to research   • بَحْثٌ

تَشْمَلُ كِتابَةُ المَقالاتِ الخاصَّةِ بَحْثًا مُعَمَّقًا لِلتَّعَمُّقِ في المَوْضوعِ وَفَهْمِ جَوانِبِهِ المُخْتَلِفَةِ.

Feature writing involves in-depth research to delve into the subject and understand its various aspects.

تَحْليلِيٌّ
analytical

يُقَدِّمُ المَقالُ التَّحْليلِيُّ تَفْسيراتٍ مُعَمَّقَةً لِلْقَضايا، مُسْتَخْدِمًا التَّحْليلَ النَّقْدِيَّ لِرَبْطِ الأَفْكارِ بِالأَدِلَّةِ.

The analytical article provides in-depth interpretations of issues, using critical analysis to connect ideas with evidence.

تَقْريرٌ طَويلٌ
long report   • تَقاريرُ

يَتَضَمَّنُ التَّقْريرُ الطَّويلُ عَرْضًا مُفَصَّلًا لِلْمَوْضوعِ، مَعَ اسْتِكْشافِ السِّياقاتِ، وَالأَبْعادِ، وَالتَّأْثيراتِ بِعُمْقٍ.

The long report includes a detailed presentation of the topic, exploring the contexts, dimensions, and impacts in depth.

حَلَّلَ
to analyze   • تَحْليلٌ

يُحَلِّلُ الصَّحَفِيّونَ البَياناتِ وَالشَّهاداتِ لِتَقْديمِ تَقْريرٍ يُفَسِّرُ الأَحْداثَ وَيُوَضِّحُ العَلاقاتِ وَالأَنْماطَ.

Journalists analyze data and testimonies to produce a report that explains events and clarifies relationships and patterns.

monitoring events

رَصْدُ أَحْداثٍ

يَشْمَلُ رَصْدُ الأَحْداثِ تَتَبُّعَ التَّطَوُّراتِ عَلى مَدى فَتْرَةٍ زَمَنِيَّةٍ لِتَقْديمِ تَحْليلٍ دَقيقٍ.

Monitoring events involves tracking developments over time to provide accurate analysis.

thorough, well-researched

رَصينٌ

يَجِبُ أَنْ يَكونَ التَّقْريرُ الطَّويلُ رَصينًا، مُعْتَمِدًا عَلى مَصادِرَ مَوْثوقَةٍ وَتَحْليلٍ مُعَمَّقٍ.

The long-form report should be thorough, relying on reliable sources and in-depth analysis.

reporting team

فَريقٌ صَحَفِيٌّ • فِرَقٌ

يَتَطَلَّبُ إِنْتاجُ التَّقاريرِ الطَّويلَةِ فَريقًا صَحَفِيًّا يَعْمَلُ مَعًا لِلْبَحْثِ، وَالتَّحْليلِ، وَالكِتابَةِ.

Producing long-form reports requires a journalistic team working together to research, analyze, and write.

active, effective

فَعّالٌ

أَلْقَتِ التَّغْطِيَةُ الصَّحَفِيَّةُ الفَعّالَةُ لِلصَّحَفِيِّ الضَّوءَ عَلى تَعْقيداتِ الوَضْعِ السِّياسِيِّ.

The journalist's effective reporting shed light on the complexities of the political situation.

meticulous

مُتَأَنٍّ

يَتَطَلَّبُ العَمَلُ الصَّحَفِيُّ المُتَأَنّي وَقْتًا لِلتَّأَكُّدِ مِنْ دِقَّةِ المَعْلوماتِ وَشُموليَّتِها.

Thorough journalism requires time to ensure the accuracy and comprehensiveness of information.

in-depth

مُعَمَّقٌ

يُشيرُ التَّحْليلُ المُعَمَّقُ إِلى اسْتِكْشافِ جَوانِبِ القِصَّةِ بِتَفْصيلٍ كَبيرٍ، مِمّا يَسْمَحُ بِفَهْمٍ أَعْمَقَ لِلْمَوْضوعِ.

In-depth analysis refers to exploring the aspects of the story in great detail, allowing for a deeper understanding of the subject.

مَقَالَةٌ اسْتِقْصَائِيَّةٌ

investigative article

تَكْشِفُ المَقَالَةُ الاسْتِقْصَائِيَّةُ عَنِ الحَقَائِقِ مِنْ خِلالِ تَحْقِيقٍ مَيْدَانِيٍّ وَبَحْثٍ مُكَثَّفٍ.

The investigative article uncovers facts through field investigation and extensive research.

مَقَالَةٌ تَحْلِيلِيَّةٌ

analytical article

تُقَدِّمُ المَقَالَةُ التَّحْلِيلِيَّةُ تَفْسِيرَاتٍ وَتَحْلِيلَاتٍ مُفَصَّلَةً لِلْأَحْدَاثِ، مُعْتَمِدَةً عَلَى البَيَانَاتِ وَالسِّيَاقَاتِ.

The analytical article provides detailed interpretations and analyses of events based on data and contexts.

مَقَالَةٌ تَفْصِيلِيَّةٌ

in-depth article

تَهْدُفُ المَقَالَةُ التَّفْصِيلِيَّةُ إِلَى تَوْسِيعِ فَهْمِ القَارِئِ لِمَوْضُوعٍ مُعَيَّنٍ مِنْ خِلالِ شَرْحٍ مُفَصَّلٍ وَمَعْلُومَاتٍ وَافِيَةٍ.

The in-depth article aims to broaden the reader's understanding of a specific topic through detailed explanations and extensive information.

مَقَالَةٌ خَاصَّةٌ

feature article

تَبْرُزُ المَقَالَةُ الخَاصَّةُ بِسَبَبِ جَوْدَتِها العَالِيَةِ، وأَصَالَتِها، وأُسْلُوبِها الجَذَّابِ.

The feature article stands out due to its high quality, originality, and engaging style.

مَلَفٌّ

file, dossier

يَتَنَاوَلُ المَلَفُّ قَضِيَّةً بِالتَّفْصِيلِ، مُقَدِّمًا تَحْلِيلًا شَامِلًا وَمُتَعَدِّدَ الأَبْعَادِ.

The dossier addresses an issue in detail, providing a comprehensive and multidimensional analysis.

مَوْضُوعِيٌّ

objective

يَجِبُ أَنْ يَكُونَ الصَّحَفِيُّ مَوْضُوعِيًّا، مُقَدِّمًا المَعْلُومَاتِ بِدُونِ تَحَيُّزٍ أَوْ تَأْثِيرَاتٍ شَخْصِيَّةٍ.

The journalist should be objective, presenting information without bias or personal influence.

وَثَّقَ • تَوْثِيقٌ

to document

يَعْنِي التَّوْثِيقُ جَمْعَ وَتَسْجِيلَ الأَدِلَّةِ وَالمَعْلُومَاتِ بِطَرِيقَةٍ مُنَظَّمَةٍ لِدَعْمِ الرِّوَايَةِ الصَّحَفِيَّةِ.

Documentation means collecting and recording evidence and information in an organized manner to support the journalistic narrative.

11.2.5.1 Essay: In-Depth Journalism

كِتابَةُ المَقالاتِ الخاصَّةِ والكِتاباتِ الصَّحَفِيَّةِ الطَّويلَةِ: رُؤًى وَتَحَدِّياتٌ

في عَصْرٍ يَتَّسِمُ بِسُرْعَةِ تَدَفُّقِ المَعْلوماتِ وَهَيْمَنَةِ وَسائِلِ الإعْلامِ السَّريعَةِ، تَبْرُزُ كِتابَةُ المَقالاتِ الخاصَّةِ والكِتاباتُ الصَّحَفِيَّةُ الطَّويلَةُ كَمَناراتٍ لِلتَّحْليلِ العَميقِ والفَهْمِ المُتَأَنّي لِلأحْداثِ. هذا النَّوْعُ مِنَ الصَّحافَةِ، الَّذي يَتَضَمَّنُ مَقالاتٍ تَحْقيقِيَّةً ومُتَعَمِّقَةً، يَدْعو إلى التَّفْكيرِ المُعَمَّقِ والفَحْصِ الشامِلِ لِلأسْبابِ والنَّتائِجِ المُتَعَلِّقَةِ بِالقَضايا المُخْتَلِفَةِ.

تَتَطَلَّبُ كِتابَةُ المَقالاتِ الخاصَّةِ بَحْثًا دَقيقًا وَرَصْدًا مُتَأَنِّيًا لِلأحْداثِ، حَيْثُ يَقومُ الصَّحَفِيّونَ بِجَمْعِ المَعْلوماتِ مِنْ مَصادِرَ مُتَعَدِّدَةٍ، وَتَوْثيقِ التَّجارِبِ والشَّهاداتِ لِإعْطاءِ صورَةٍ مُتَكامِلَةٍ عَنِ المَوْضوعِ. يَغْلِبُ الطّابَعُ التَّحْليلِيُّ عَلى هَذِهِ المَقالاتِ، حَيْثُ يَسْتَكْشِفُ الصَّحَفِيّونَ الأبْعادَ المُخْتَلِفَةَ لِلقِصَّةِ، مُعْتَمِدينَ عَلى مَهاراتِ النَّقْدِ والتَّحْليلِ.

تَلْعَبُ المَقالاتُ الخاصَّةُ والتَّقاريرُ الطَّويلَةُ دَوْرًا فَعّالًا في إثْراءِ الحِوارِ العامِّ وَتَعْزيزِ فَهْمِ المُجْتَمَعِ لِلقَضايا المُعَقَّدَةِ. إنَّها تُساهِمُ في تَشْكيلِ الرَّأْيِ العامِّ بِطَريقَةٍ مَوْضوعِيَّةٍ وَرَصينَةٍ، مُقَدِّمَةً تَحْليلاتٍ مُعَمَّقَةً تَتَناوَلُ الأسْبابَ والنَّتائِجَ بِأُسْلوبٍ شامِلٍ.

أَحَدُ التَّحَدِّياتِ الرَّئيسِيَّةِ في هَذا النَّوْعِ مِنَ الصَّحافَةِ هُوَ الحاجَةُ إلى الوَقْتِ والمَوارِدِ. فَالتَّقاريرُ الطَّويلَةُ تَتَطَلَّبُ فَريقًا صَحَفِيًّا مُخْتَصًّا وَمَوارِدَ مالِيَّةً كافِيَةً لِإجْراءِ البُحوثِ والتَّحْقيقاتِ اللازِمَةِ. بِالإضافَةِ إلى ذَلِكَ، في عالَمٍ يُهَيْمِنُ عَلَيْهِ اسْتِهْلاكُ الأخْبارِ السَّريعِ، قَدْ يَكونُ مِنَ الصَّعْبِ جَذْبُ اهْتِمامِ القُرّاءِ بِمُحْتَوًى طَويلٍ.

رَغْمَ التَّحَدِّياتِ، يَبْقى الطَّلَبُ عَلى الصَّحافَةِ المُعَمَّقَةِ قَوِيًّا، خاصَّةً في ظِلِّ التَّطَوُّراتِ العالَمِيَّةِ المُتَسارِعَةِ والحاجَةِ إلى فَهْمٍ أَعْمَقَ لِلقَضايا المُعَقَّدَةِ. التَّطَوُّراتُ التَّكْنولوجِيَّةُ تُوَفِّرُ أَيْضًا فُرَصًا جَديدَةً لِتَقْديمِ هَذا النَّوْعِ مِنَ الصَّحافَةِ بِطُرُقٍ مُبْتَكَرَةٍ، كَاسْتِخْدامِ الوَسائِطِ المُتَعَدِّدَةِ والتَّفاعُلِيَّةِ لِجَذْبِ القُرّاءِ.

تَبْقى كِتابَةُ المَقالاتِ الخاصَّةِ والكِتاباتُ الصَّحَفِيَّةُ الطَّويلَةُ رُكْنًا أَساسِيًّا في عالَمِ الإعْلامِ، مُوَفِّرَةً لِلقُرّاءِ تَحْليلاتٍ مُعَمَّقَةً وَنَظْرَةً شامِلَةً عَلى الأحْداثِ الَّتي تُشَكِّلُ عالَمَنا.

Feature Writing and Long-Form Journalism: Insights and Challenges

In an era characterized by the rapid flow of information and the dominance of quick media, feature writing and long-form journalism stand out as beacons of deep analysis and careful understanding of events. This type of journalism, which includes investigative and in-depth articles, calls for profound thinking and comprehensive examination of the causes and consequences related to various issues.

Feature writing requires meticulous research and careful monitoring of events, where journalists gather information from multiple sources and document experiences and testimonies to provide a complete picture of the subject. These articles are analytical in nature, with journalists exploring the different dimensions of the story, relying on their skills in criticism and analysis.

Feature articles and long reports play an effective role in enriching public dialogue and enhancing society's understanding of complex issues. They contribute to shaping public opinion in an objective and serious manner, offering in-depth analyses that address the causes and consequences comprehensively.

One of the main challenges in this type of journalism is the need for time and resources. Long reports require a specialized journalistic team and sufficient financial resources to conduct the necessary research and investigations. Moreover, in a world dominated by quick news consumption, it may be difficult to attract readers' interest in long-form content.

Despite the challenges, the demand for in-depth journalism remains strong, especially in light of rapid global developments and the need for a deeper understanding of complex issues. Technological advancements also provide new opportunities to present this type of journalism innovatively, such as using multimedia and interactive elements to engage readers.

Feature writing and long-form journalism continue to be a fundamental pillar in the media world, providing readers with profound analyses and a comprehensive view of the events shaping our world.

Unit 12
Accidents and Incidents

Accidents and incidents are unexpected events that can have significant impacts on individuals and communities. This unit provides a detailed vocabulary set to discuss various types of accidents and incidents in Arabic, enhancing your ability to understand and communicate about these critical situations.

We begin with **Transportation Accidents**, where you will explore vocabulary related to different modes of transportation. **Road and Highway Accidents** covers terminology for traffic collisions, vehicle crashes, and related road safety issues. **Airline and Aviation Incidents** introduces the language used to describe events such as plane crashes, emergency landings, and other aviation-related mishaps. **Maritime and Shipping Mishaps** focuses on accidents involving boats, ships, and other maritime vessels. This section also includes **Infrastructure**, addressing terminology related to the impact of accidents on public works and structures.

Next, we cover Industrial and **Workplace Accidents**, a crucial area for understanding safety in various work environments. **Manufacturing, Factory, and Construction Site Incidents** introduces terms related to accidents that occur in industrial settings, including equipment malfunctions and structural collapses. **Mining and Extraction Accidents** delves into the language used to describe incidents in mining operations and resource extraction sites. **Public Venue Incidents** addresses accidents that can occur in places where people gather, such as stadiums, theaters, and event spaces.

Finally, we explore **Medical Emergencies**, providing you with vocabulary to discuss health-related crises. **Medical Conditions** covers terminology for various acute medical issues, such as heart attacks, strokes, and allergic reactions. **Trauma and Injuries** focuses on the language used to describe physical injuries resulting from accidents, including fractures, burns, and lacerations.

Understanding the vocabulary in this unit is essential not only for comprehending news reports but also for discussing and analyzing the causes, responses, and implications of various accidents and incidents. This knowledge is crucial for anyone looking to engage with Arabic media on topics related to public safety and emergency response, offering a comprehensive perspective on how such events are reported and discussed in the Arab world and beyond.

12.1 Transportation Accidents

12.1.1 Road and Highway Accidents

آمِنٌ

safe

بَعْدَ تَطْبِيقِ الإِجْراءاتِ الجَديدَةِ، أَصْبَحَ الطَّريقُ آمِنًا لِجَميعِ المُسْتَخْدِمينَ.

After implementing the new procedures, the road became safe for all users.

أَبْطَأَ • إِبْطاءٌ

to slow down

أَبْطَأَ السّائِقُ سُرْعَتَهُ عِنْدَما رَأى أَطْفالًا يَعْبُرونَ الشّارِعَ.

The driver slowed down when he saw children crossing the street.

أَبْلَغَ عَنْ حادِثَةٍ • إِبْلاغٌ

to report an accident

أَبْلَغَ الشُّهودُ الشُّرْطَةَ عَنْ حادِثَةٍ وَقَعَتْ عَلى ناصِيَةِ الشّارِعِ.

The witnesses reported an accident that occurred at the street corner to the police.

أَسْرَعَ • إِسْراعٌ

to speed, hurry

أَسْرَعَتْ سَيّاراتُ الإِسْعافِ لِنَقْلِ المُصابينَ إلى المُسْتَشْفى بَعْدَ الحادِثِ.

Ambulances hurried to transport the injured to the hospital after the accident.

أُصيبَ • إِصابَةٌ

to be injured

أُصيبَ ثَلاثَةُ أَشْخاصٍ في الحادِثِ، وَنُقِلوا عَلى الفَوْرِ إلى المُسْتَشْفى.

Three people were injured in the accident and were immediately taken to the hospital.

> أُصيبَ is the passive form of the hollow measure-IV verb أَصابَ (to injure). The passive construction indicates that the subject is receiving the action rather than performing it.

أَغْلَقَ طَريقًا • إِغْلاقٌ

to close a road

أَغْلَقَتِ الشُّرْطَةُ الطَّريقَ المُؤَدّيَ إلى مَوْقِعِ الحادِثِ لِتَسْهيلِ عَمَلِيَّةِ التَّحْقيقِ.

The police closed the road leading to the accident site to facilitate the investigation process.

to rescue — إِنْقاذٌ • أَنْقَذَ

أَنْقَذَ العُمّالُ طِفْلَةً عالِقَةً تَحْتَ الأَنْقاضِ بَعْدَ انْهِيارِ جِسْرٍ.

The workers rescued a girl trapped under the rubble after a bridge collapse.

debris removal — إِزالَةُ حُطامٍ

تَمَّتْ إِزالَةُ الحُطامِ بِسُرْعَةٍ لِإِعادَةِ فَتْحِ الطَّريقِ أَمامَ حَرَكَةِ المُرورِ.

The debris was quickly removed to reopen the road to traffic.

traffic signal — إِشارَةُ مُرورٍ

خَرَقَ السّائِقُ إِشارَةَ المُرورِ الحَمْراءَ مِمّا تَسَبَّبَ في وُقوعِ حادِثٍ خَطيرٍ.

The driver breached the red traffic signal, causing a serious accident.

serious injury — إِصابَةٌ بالِغَةٌ

تَعَرَّضَ السّائِقُ لِإِصاباتٍ بالِغَةٍ بَعْدَ أَنِ انْقَلَبَتْ سَيّارَتُهُ عَلى الطَّريقِ السَّريعِ.

The driver sustained severe injuries after his car flipped on the highway.

to obey traffic rules — اِحْتِرامٌ • اِحْتَرَمَ قَواعِدَ المُرورِ

مِنَ الضَّروريِّ احْتِرامُ قَواعِدِ المُرورِ لِتَجَنُّبِ الحَوادِثِ والحِفاظِ عَلى الأَمانِ.

It is essential to respect traffic rules to avoid accidents and maintain safety.

collision — اِصْطِدامٌ

نَتَجَ عَنِ الاِصْطِدامِ تَحَطُّمُ زُجاجِ السَّيّارَةِ الأَمامِيِّ وَتَضَرُّرُ البابِ الجانِبِيِّ.

The collision resulted in the car's windshield being shattered and the side door damaged.

to collide — اِصْطِدامٌ • اِصْطَدَمَ

اِصْطَدَمَتِ الشّاحِنَةُ بِعَمودِ الإِنارَةِ مِمّا أَدّى إلى انْقِطاعِ الكَهْرَباءِ في المِنْطَقَةِ.

The truck collided with the streetlight, leading to a power outage in the area.

الْتَزَم

• الْتِزامٌ

to comply, adhere

الْتَزَمَ السّائِقونَ بِالسُّرْعَةِ الْمُحَدَّدَةِ لِتَجَنُّبِ الْمَخاطِرِ.

The drivers adhered to the speed limit to avoid dangers.

انْتَبَه

• انْتِباهٌ

to heed, pay attention

انْتَبِهْ لِلْإِشاراتِ وَالْعَلاماتِ الْمُرورِيَّةِ أَثْناءَ الْقِيادَةِ في اللَّيْلِ.

Pay attention to traffic signs and signals while driving at night.

انْتِهاكُ قاعِدَةِ مُرورٍ

violation of a traffic rule

يُعَدُّ تَجاهُلُ إِشاراتِ الْمُرورِ انْتِهاكًا خَطيرًا لِقَواعِدِ الْمُرورِ.

Ignoring traffic lights is a serious violation of traffic rules.

انْخِفاضُ رُؤْيَةٍ

reduced visibility

أَدّى انْخِفاضُ الرُّؤْيَةِ بِسَبَبِ الضَّبابِ إلى تَباطُؤِ حَرَكَةِ الْمُرورِ عَلى الطَّريقِ.

Reduced visibility due to fog led to slow traffic on the road.

انْزَلَق

• انْزِلاقٌ

to skid

انْزَلَقَتِ السَّيّارَةُ عَلى الطَّريقِ الْمُبْتَلِّ وَكادَتْ أَنْ تَصْطَدِمَ بِالْحاجِزِ.

The car skidded on the wet road and nearly collided with the barrier.

انْفِجارُ إِطارٍ

tire burst

حَدَثَ انْفِجارُ إِطارٍ مُفاجِئٌ مِمّا أَدّى إلى فُقْدانِ السّائِقِ السَّيْطَرَةَ عَلى السَّيّارَةِ.

A sudden tire burst caused the driver to lose control of the car.

انْقَلَب

• انْقِلابٌ

to overturn, rollover

انْقَلَبَتِ السَّيّارَةُ عِدَّةَ مَرّاتٍ بَعْدَ أَنِ اصْطَدَمَتْ بِالْحاجِزِ الْجانِبِيِّ.

The car overturned several times after it hit the side barrier.

بالِغٌ

severe

تُعْتَبَرُ الإصاباتُ البالِغَةُ مِنَ الأمورِ الشّائِعَةِ في حَوادِثِ الطُّرُقِ الخَطيرَةِ.

Severe injuries are common in serious road accidents.

تَجاوَزَ • تَجاوُزٌ

to overtake, pass

تَجاوَزَ السّائِقُ الشّاحِنَةَ بِحَذَرٍ عَلى الطَّريقِ السَّريعِ.

The driver cautiously overtook the truck on the highway.

تَجاوُزٌ غَيْرُ قانونيٍّ

illegal overtaking

يُعاقَبُ عَلى التَّجاوُزِ غَيْرِ القانونيِّ بِغَراماتٍ ماليَّةٍ كَبيرَةٍ.

Illegal overtaking is punished with hefty fines.

تَجَنَّبَ • تَجَنُّبٌ

to avoid

تَجَنَّبَ السّائِقُ الحادِثَ بِالْكادِ بَعْدَ أَنْ فَرْمَلَتِ السَّيّارَةُ المُقابِلَةُ فَجْأَةً.

The driver barely avoided an accident after the opposite car braked suddenly.

تَحْقيقٌ في حادِثَةٍ

accident investigation

بَدَأَتِ السُّلُطاتُ تَحْقيقًا في حادِثَةِ الاصْطِدامِ الَّتي أَدَّتْ إلى إغْلاقِ الطَّريقِ الرَّئيسيِّ.

The authorities began an investigation into the collision incident that led to the closure of the main road.

تَحَكَّمَ • تَحَكُّمٌ

to control

يَجِبُ عَلى السّائِقينَ التَّحَكُّمُ في مَرْكَباتِهِمْ بِشَكْلٍ صَحيحٍ لِتَجَنُّبِ الحَوادِثِ.

Drivers must control their vehicles properly to avoid accidents.

تَسَبَّبَ • تَسَبُّبٌ

to cause

يَتَسَبَّبُ الإرْهاقُ وَقِلَّةُ الِانْتِباهِ في حَوادِثَ خَطيرَةٍ عَلى الطُّرُقِ.

Fatigue and lack of attention cause serious accidents on the roads.

تَشَتُّتٌ أَثْناءَ القِيادَةِ

distracted driving

يُعَدُّ التَّشَتُّتُ أَثْناءَ القِيادَةِ سَبَبًا رَئيسِيًّا لِوُقوعِ الحَوادِثِ.

Distracted driving is a major cause of accidents.

تَصادُمٌ جانِبِيٌّ

side impact

وَقَعَ تَصادُمٌ جانِبِيٌّ عِنْدَ التَّقاطُعِ بِسَبَبِ عَدَمِ احْتِرامِ إِشاراتِ المُرورِ.

A side collision occurred at the intersection due to disregard for traffic signals.

تَصادُمٌ خَلْفِيٌّ

rear-end collision

نَجَمَ التَّصادُمُ الخَلْفِيُّ عَنْ عَدَمِ الِانْتِباهِ وَالتَّوَقُّفِ المُفاجِئِ.

The rear-end collision resulted from inattention and sudden stopping.

تَقْريرُ شُرْطَةٍ • تَقاريرُ

police report

قَدَّمَ الضّابِطُ تَقْريرَ شُرْطَةٍ مُفَصَّلًا عَنِ الحادِثِ.

The officer submitted a detailed police report about the accident.

تَلَفُ مَرْكَبَةٍ

vehicle damage

تَسَبَّبَ الحادِثُ في تَلَفِ مَرْكَبَةِ العائِلَةِ بِشَكْلٍ كَبيرٍ.

The accident caused significant damage to the family's vehicle.

حادِثَةُ طَريقٍ • حَوادِثُ

road accident

وَقَعَتْ حادِثَةُ طَريقٍ مُرَوِّعَةٌ عَلى الطَّريقِ السَّريعِ اللَّيْلَةَ الماضِيَةَ.

A horrific road accident occurred on the highway last night.

حافَظَ عَلى مَسافَةٍ آمِنَةٍ • حِفاظٌ

to maintain a safe distance

حافِظْ عَلى مَسافَةٍ آمِنَةٍ مِنَ السَّيّاراتِ الأُخْرى لِتَجَنُّبِ الِاصْطِدامِ.

Maintain a safe distance from other cars to avoid collision.

to warn حَذَّرَ • تَحْذِيرٌ

حَذَّرَتِ الشُّرْطَةُ السَّائِقِينَ مِنَ الظُّروفِ الجَوِّيَّةِ السَّيِّئَةِ الَّتي قَدْ تَزِيدُ مِنْ خَطَرِ وُقوعِ حَوادِثَ.

The police warned drivers about the bad weather conditions that could increase the risk of accidents.

to investigate حَقَّقَ • تَحْقِيقٌ

حَقَّقَ المُحَقِّقونَ في أَسْبابِ الحادِثِ لِمَنْعِ تَكْرارِهِ.

The investigators looked into the causes of the accident to prevent its recurrence.

> Keep in mind that many verbs have multiple meanings, which can usually be determined from the context. For instance, حَقَّقَ can mean 'to achieve' and, in this context, it is a transitive verb that takes a direct object. However, when it means 'to investigate,' it requires the preposition في before its object.

emergency service خِدْمَةُ طَوارِئَ

اِسْتَدْعَتِ الحادِثَةُ اِسْتِجابَةً فَوْرِيَّةً مِنْ قِبَلِ خِدْمَةِ الطَّوارِئِ.

The incident prompted an immediate response from the emergency service.

dangerous خَطِيرٌ

تُعْتَبَرُ حالَةُ الطُّرُقِ خَطِيرَةً جِدًّا في ظِلِّ تَساقُطِ الثُّلوجِ الكَثيفِ.

The road condition is considered very dangerous under heavy snowfall.

speeding, excessive speed سُرْعَةٌ زائِدَةٌ

تَسَبَّبَتِ السُّرْعَةُ الزّائِدَةُ في فِقْدانِ السَّائِقِ السَّيْطَرَةَ عَلى السَّيّارَةِ.

Excessive speed caused the driver to lose control of the car.

to maintain صانَ • صِيانَةٌ

صانَ النِّظامُ الجَديدُ سَلامَةَ السَّائِقِينَ عَلى الطُّرُقاتِ.

The new system preserved the safety of drivers on the roads.

ضبابٌ

fog

أَدّى الضَّبابُ الكَثيفُ إِلى تَقْليلِ الرُّؤْيَةِ عَلى الطَّريقِ السَّريعِ.

The dense fog led to reduced visibility on the highway.

طَفيفٌ

minor

كانَتِ الإِصاباتُ طَفيفَةً بِالرَّغْمِ مِنْ شِدَّةِ الحادِثِ.

The injuries were minor despite the severity of the accident.

غَيْرُ مُتَوَقَّع

unexpected

وَقَعَ الحادِثُ بِشَكْلٍ غَيْرِ مُتَوَقَّعٍ عَلى طَريقٍ سالِكٍ.

The accident occurred unexpectedly on a clear road.

فَقَدَ السَّيْطَرَة   • فِقْدانٌ / فَقْدٌ / فُقْدانٌ

to lose control

فَقَدَ السّائِقُ السَّيْطَرَةَ عَلى المَرْكَبَةِ بَعْدَ انْفِجارِ الإِطارِ.

The driver lost control of the vehicle after the tire exploded.

قِيادَةٌ تَحْتَ تَأْثيرِ الكُحول

driving under the influence of alcohol

تَمَّ القَبْضُ عَلى السّائِقِ بِتُهْمَةِ القِيادَةِ تَحْتَ تَأْثيرِ الكُحولِ.

The driver was arrested for driving under the influence of alcohol.

قَيَّمَ أَضرارًا   • تَقْييمٌ

to assess damages

قَيَّمَتْ شَرِكَةُ التَّأْمينِ الأَضْرارَ النّاتِجَةَ عَنِ الحادِثِ.

The insurance company assessed the damages resulting from the accident.

مُبَلَّلٌ

wet

أَصْبَحَتِ الطُّرُقُ مُبَلَّلَةً وَزَلِقَةً بَعْدَ هُطولِ الأَمْطارِ الغَزيرَةِ.

The roads became wet and slippery after heavy rain.

reckless

مُتَهَوِّرٌ

وُصِفَتْ تَصَرُّفَاتُ السَّائِقِ بِأَنَّها مُتَهَوِّرَةٌ وَغَيْرُ مَسْؤولَةٍ.

The driver's actions were described as reckless and irresponsible.

traffic violation

مُخالَفَةُ مُرورٍ

تَلَقَّى السَّائِقُ مُخالَفَةَ مُرورٍ لِعَدَمِ الْتِزامِهِ بِالْإِشاراتِ.

The driver received a traffic violation for not adhering to the signals.

visible

مَرْئِيٌّ

كانَ العَمودُ الكَهْرَبائِيُّ مَرْئِيًّا بِالْكادِ بِسَبَبِ العاصِفَةِ.

The electric pole was barely visible due to the storm.

pedestrians

مُشاةٌ *pl.*

يَجِبُ عَلى السَّائِقينَ تَوَخّي الحَذَرِ عِنْدَ المُرورِ بِالْقُرْبِ مِنَ المُشاةِ.

Drivers should be cautious when passing near pedestrians.

insurance information

مَعْلوماتُ تَأْمينٍ *pl.*

بَعْدَ الحادِثِ، تَبادَلَ السَّائِقونَ مَعْلوماتِ التَّأْمينِ لِتَسْهيلِ عَمَلِيَّةِ التَّعْويضِ.

After the accident, the drivers exchanged insurance information to facilitate the compensation process.

fatal

مُميتٌ

تَحَوَّلَ الحادِثُ المُميتُ إلى مَوْضوعِ تَحْقيقٍ شامِلٍ مِنْ قِبَلِ الشُّرْطَةِ.

The fatal accident turned into a subject of comprehensive investigation by the police.

to survive

نَجا • نَجاةٌ

نَجا الرُّكّابُ بِأُعْجوبَةٍ مِنَ الحادِثِ دونَ أَيِّ إِصاباتٍ خَطيرَةٍ.

The passengers miraculously survived the accident without any serious injuries.

نُقْطَةٌ عَمْياءُ   • نِقاطٌ / نُقْطاتٌ / نُقَطٌ

blind spot

لَمْ يُلاحِظِ السّائِقُ السَّيّارَةَ الأُخْرى بِسَبَبِ وُجودِها في نُقْطَةٍ عَمْياءَ.

The driver did not notice the other car due to it being in a blind spot.

وَفَياتٌ   *pl.*

fatalities

أَدّى الحادِثُ المُرَوِّعُ إلى وَفَياتٍ وَعِدَّةِ إصاباتٍ خَطيرَةٍ.

The horrific accident led to fatalities and several serious injuries.

12.1.1.1 Mini-Articles

Track **50**

وَقَعَ حادِثُ طَريقٍ مُميتٌ عَلى الطَّريقِ السَّريعِ أَمْسِ، نَتيجَةَ انْفِجارِ إطارِ سَيّارَةٍ أَدّى إلى انْقِلابِها. الحادِثُ، الَّذي أَسْفَرَ عَنْ وَفاةِ شَخْصَيْنِ وَإصابَةِ آخَرينَ بِإصاباتٍ بالِغَةٍ، تَسَبَّبَ في إغْلاقِ الطَّريقِ لِساعاتٍ بَيْنَما كانَتْ فِرَقُ الإنْقاذِ تَعْمَلُ عَلى إزالَةِ الحُطامِ. أَبْلَغَ شُهودُ عِيانٍ أَنَّ السَّيّارَةَ كانَتْ تَسيرُ بِسُرْعَةٍ زائِدَةٍ قَبْلَ أَنْ تَفْقِدَ السَّيْطَرَةَ.

A deadly road accident occurred on the highway yesterday due to a tire explosion that led to the vehicle overturning. The accident, which resulted in the death of two people and serious injuries to others, caused the road to be closed for hours while rescue teams worked to clear the debris. Eyewitnesses reported that the car was speeding before losing control.

أُصيبَ عِدَّةُ أَشْخاصٍ في تَصادُمٍ خَلْفيٍّ بَيْنَ ثَلاثِ سَيّاراتٍ عَلى طَريقٍ مُبَلِّلٍ بالقُرْبِ مِنَ المَدينَةِ. يُشيرُ التَّحْقيقُ الأَوَّليُّ إلى أَنَّ انْتِهاكَ قَواعِدِ المُرورِ وَالتَّشَتُّتَ أَثْناءَ القِيادَةِ كانا السَّبَبَ وَراءَ الحادِثِ. أَصْدَرَتِ الشُّرْطَةُ تَقْريرًا يُنَبِّهُ السّائِقينَ إلى أَهَمِّيَّةِ اتِّباعِ قَواعِدِ المُرورِ وَالحِفاظِ عَلى مَسافَةٍ آمِنَةٍ خاصَّةً في ظُروفِ الطَّقْسِ السَّيِّئَةِ.

Several people were injured in a rear-end collision involving three cars on a wet road near the city. The initial investigation suggests that a traffic rule violation and distracted driving were the causes of the accident. The police issued a report warning drivers of the importance of obeying traffic rules and maintaining a safe distance, especially in bad weather conditions.

في حادِثَةٍ غَيْرِ مُتَوَقَّعَةٍ، اصْطَدَمَتْ سَيّارَةٌ بِحاجِزٍ عَلى جِسْرٍ مُرْتَفِعٍ، مِمّا أَدّى إلى تَعَلُّقِها عَلى حافَّةِ الجِسْرِ. سارَعَتْ خِدْماتُ الطَّوارِئِ وَالمُشاةُ الَّذينَ شَهِدوا الحادِثَ لِإنْقاذِ السّائِقِ الَّذي أُصيبَ إصابَةً طَفيفَةً. يُذْكَرُ أَنَّ السّائِقَ فَقَدَ السَّيْطَرَةَ بِسَبَبِ انْزِلاقِ السَّيّارَةِ عَلى الطَّريقِ المُبَلَّلِ. وَقَدْ أَثارَتِ الحادِثَةُ دَعَواتٍ لِزِيادَةِ التَّحَكُّمِ وَالأَمانِ عَلى الجُسورِ، خاصَّةً خِلالَ الأَحْوالِ الجَوِّيَّةِ السَّيِّئَةِ.

In an unexpected incident, a car collided with a barrier on an elevated bridge, leaving it hanging over the edge. Emergency services and pedestrians who witnessed the incident rushed to rescue the slightly injured driver. It is noted that the driver lost control due to the car sliding on the wet road. The incident sparked calls for increased control and safety on bridges, especially during bad weather.

وَقَعَتْ حادِثَةٌ خَطِيرَةٌ صَباحَ اليَوْمِ عَلَى الطَّرِيقِ السَّرِيعِ بِسَبَبِ انْخِفاضِ الرُّؤْيَةِ نَتِيجَةَ الضَّبابِ الكَثِيفِ، مِمَّا أَدَّى إلى تَصادُمٍ جانِبِيٍّ بَيْنَ شاحِنَةٍ وَعِدَّةِ مَرْكَباتٍ. أَسْفَرَ الحادِثُ عَنْ وَفاةِ شَخْصٍ وَإصابَةِ العَدِيدِ بِجُرُوحٍ مُتَفاوِتَةٍ. أَغْلَقَتْ قُوَّاتُ الأَمْنِ الطَّرِيقَ بِشَكْلٍ مُؤَقَّتٍ لِلسَّماحِ بِأَعْمالِ الإنْقاذِ وَتَحْقِيقِ الشُّرْطَةِ في أَسْبابِ الحادِثِ.

A dangerous road accident occurred this morning on the highway due to reduced visibility from dense fog, leading to a side collision between a truck and several vehicles. The accident resulted in one death and many injuries of varying severity. Security forces temporarily closed the road to allow for rescue operations and police investigation into the cause of the accident.

وَقَعَ حادِثُ اصْطِدامٍ مُرَوِّعٌ بَيْنَ حافِلَةٍ مَدْرَسِيَّةٍ وَسَيَّارَةٍ خاصَّةٍ عِنْدَ إشارَةِ مُرُورٍ في مِنْطَقَةٍ مُزْدَحِمَةٍ بِالْمَدِينَةِ. الحافِلَةُ، الَّتي كانَتْ تُقِلُّ طُلَّابًا إلى المَدْرَسَةِ، انْقَلَبَتْ بَعْدَ الاصْطِدامِ، مِمَّا تَطَلَّبَ جُهُودًا بُطُولِيَّةً مِنَ المارَّةِ وَخِدْماتِ الطَّوارِئِ لِإنْقاذِ الأَطْفالِ وَالسّائِقَيْنِ. أَنْقَذَتِ الاسْتِجابَةُ السَّرِيعَةُ جَمِيعَ الرُّكَّابِ وَالسّائِقَيْنِ، لَكِنْ بَعْضَهُمْ أُصِيبَ إصاباتٍ بالِغَةٍ. تَمَّ التَّأْكِيدُ عَلَى أَهَمِّيَّةِ اليَقَظَةِ وَالحَذَرِ أَثْناءَ القِيادَةِ بِالْقُرْبِ مِنَ المَدارِسِ وَالمَناطِقِ الحَيَوِيَّةِ.

A horrific collision between a school bus and a private car at a traffic light in a busy area of the city occurred. The bus, carrying students to school, overturned after the collision, requiring heroic efforts from passersby and emergency services to rescue the children and drivers. The rapid response saved all passengers and drivers, but some sustained serious injuries. The importance of vigilance and caution while driving near schools and vital areas was emphasized.

12.1.1.2 Fictional Article: Traffic Accident in Cairo

Track **51**

حادِثَةٌ مُرَوِّعَةٌ عَلَى كُوبْرِي أُكْتُوبَرَ في القاهِرَةِ

في حادِثَةٍ مُؤْسِفَةٍ وَقَعَتْ صَباحَ اليَوْمِ، شَهِدَ كُوبْرِي أُكْتُوبَرَ بِالْقاهِرَةِ حادِثَ سَيْرٍ خَطِيرًا أَدَّى إلى ازْدِحامٍ مُرُورِيٍّ هائِلٍ وَأَسْفَرَ عَنْ عِدَّةِ إصاباتٍ بالِغَةٍ. وَفْقًا لِلتَّقارِيرِ الأَوَّلِيَّةِ، تَسَبَّبَ انْفِجارُ إطارِ شاحِنَةٍ كَبِيرَةٍ في فِقْدانِ السّائِقِ السَّيْطَرَةَ، مِمَّا أَدَّى إلى اصْطِدامِهِ بِأَرْبَعِ سَيَّاراتٍ كانَتْ تَسِيرُ بِجانِبِهِ.

أَبْلَغَ شُهُودُ العِيانِ عَنْ مُشاهَدَتِهِمْ لِلشّاحِنَةِ وَهِيَ تَنْزَلِقُ بِشَكْلٍ مُفاجِئٍ قَبْلَ أَنْ تَرْتَطِمَ بِالْحَواجِزِ الجانِبِيَّةِ وَتَصْطَدِمَ بِالسَّيَّاراتِ المُجاوِرَةِ. أَدَّى الاصْطِدامُ العَنِيفُ إلى تَصادُمٍ جانِبِيٍّ لِسَيَّارَتَيْنِ، بَيْنَما انْقَلَبَتْ سَيَّارَةٌ ثالِثَةٌ نَتِيجَةً لِلتَّأْثِيرِ الشَّدِيدِ.

هُرِعَتْ قُوَّاتُ الإِنْقَاذِ وَخِدْمَاتُ الطَّوارِئِ إِلَى مَكَانِ الحَادِثِ فَوْرَ تَلَقِّيهَا لِلْبَلَاغِ، حَيْثُ قَامَ رِجَالُ الإِسْعَافِ بِتَقْدِيمِ الإِسْعَافَاتِ الأَوَّلِيَّةِ لِلْمُصَابِينَ وَنَقْلِهِمْ إِلَى المُسْتَشْفَيَاتِ القَرِيبَةِ. تَمَّ تَسْجِيلُ عِدَّةِ إِصَابَاتٍ بَالِغَةٍ وَتَلَقَّتِ الحَالَاتُ الحَرِجَةُ العِنَايَةَ الفَوْرِيَّةَ.

كَانَتِ الأَضْرَارُ المَادِّيَّةُ بَالِغَةً أَيْضًا، حَيْثُ تَعَرَّضَتِ السَّيَّارَاتُ المُتَوَرِّطَةُ فِي الحَادِثِ لِتَلَفٍ كَبِيرٍ، وَأُغْلِقَ الطَّرِيقُ لِعِدَّةِ سَاعَاتٍ لِإِزَالَةِ حُطَامِ الحَادِثِ وَتَسْهِيلِ تَحْقِيقِ الشُّرْطَةِ. أَبْدَتِ السُّلُطَاتُ المَحَلِّيَّةُ تَأْكِيدَها عَلَى ضَرُورَةِ التَّحْقِيقِ فِي أَسْبَابِ الحَادِثِ، مُشَدِّدَةً عَلَى أَهَمِّيَّةِ احْتِرَامِ قَوَاعِدِ المُرُورِ وَالِانْتِبَاهِ أَثْنَاءَ القِيَادَةِ لِتَجَنُّبِ مِثْلِ هَذِهِ الحَوَادِثِ المَأْسَاوِيَّةِ فِي المُسْتَقْبَلِ.

وَقَدْ أَثَارَ الحَادِثُ مَوْجَةً مِنَ النِّقَاشِ عَلَى مَوَاقِعِ التَّوَاصُلِ الِاجْتِمَاعِيِّ حَوْلَ ضَرُورَةِ تَعْزِيزِ تَدَابِيرِ السَّلَامَةِ عَلَى الطُّرُقِ، خَاصَّةً عَلَى الجُسُورِ وَالطُّرُقِ السَّرِيعَةِ فِي مِصْرَ. طَالَبَ المُوَاطِنُونَ بِإِجْرَاءَاتٍ أَكْثَرَ صَرَامَةً لِلْحَدِّ مِنَ السُّرْعَةِ الزَّائِدَةِ وَتَحْسِينِ ظُرُوفِ الطُّرُقِ لِضَمَانِ سَلَامَةِ الجَمِيعِ.

A Horrific Accident on the October Bridge in Cairo

In a regrettable event that occurred this morning, the October Bridge in Cairo witnessed a serious traffic accident that led to massive congestion and resulted in several severe injuries. According to initial reports, a tire explosion in a large truck caused the driver to lose control, leading to a collision with four other vehicles beside it.

Eyewitnesses reported seeing the truck suddenly slide before hitting the side barriers and colliding with the adjacent cars. The violent collision caused a side crash of two cars, while a third car overturned due to the severe impact.

Rescue forces and emergency services rushed to the scene as soon as they received the report, where paramedics provided first aid to the injured and transported them to nearby hospitals. Several severe injuries were recorded, and the critical cases received immediate care.

The material damage was also significant, with the vehicles involved in the accident sustaining major damage, and the road was closed for several hours to clear the debris and facilitate the police investigation. The local authorities emphasized the necessity of investigating the cause of the accident, stressing the importance of obeying traffic rules and being attentive while driving to prevent such tragic accidents in the future.

The incident sparked a wave of discussion on social media about the need to enhance safety measures on the roads, especially on bridges and highways in Egypt. Citizens demanded stricter measures to curb speeding and improve road conditions to ensure everyone's safety.

تَحَدِّياتُ السَّلامَةِ عَلى طُرُقِ لُبنانَ: مُعَدَّلاتُ الحَوادِثِ وَالسُّلوكِيّاتُ المُرورِيَّةُ

يُواجِهُ لُبنانُ تَحَدِّيًا كَبيرًا في مَجالِ السَّلامَةِ المُرورِيَّةِ، حَيثُ كَشَفَت دِراسَةٌ حَديثَةٌ أَنَّهُ يَحتَلُّ المَرتَبَةَ الأولى عالَمِيًّا مِنْ حَيثُ خُطورَةِ القِيادَةِ، مَعَ مُعَدَّلٍ وَفَياتٍ يَصِلُ إلى 22 لِكُلِّ 100,000 نَسَمَةٍ. يَرجِعُ هذا الواقِعُ المُؤسِفُ إلى عَوامِلَ عِدَّةٍ، مِنْها سوءُ حالَةِ الطُّرُقِ وَالسُّلوكِيّاتُ الخَطِرَةُ في القِيادَةِ.

وَفقًا لِتَقريرٍ حَديثٍ، يُعاني لُبنانُ مِنْ أَحَدِ أَسوَأِ الطُّرُقِ جَودَةً عالَمِيًّا، مِمّا يُعَرِّضُ السّائِقينَ وَالمُشاةَ لِمَخاطِرَ دائِمَةٍ. تُظهِرُ الإحصائِيّاتُ المُرورِيَّةُ ارتِفاعًا في عَدَدِ الحَوادِثِ، حَيثُ تَمَّ تَسجيلُ 1099 حادِثًا مُرورِيًّا في الأشهُرِ السِّتَّةِ الأولى مِنْ عامِ 2023، ما يَدُلُّ عَلى زِيادَةٍ عِندَ المُقارَنَةِ بِالفَترَةِ ذاتِها مِنَ العامِ السّابِقِ.

تُعزى الحَوادِثُ المُرورِيَّةُ لِأَسبابٍ عَديدَةٍ، تَشمَلُ القِيادَةَ المُتَهَوِّرَةَ وَعَدَمَ احتِرامِ قَواعِدِ المُرورِ، كالسُّرعَةِ الزّائِدَةِ وَالتَّجاوُزاتِ غَيرِ القانونِيَّةِ. كَما أَنَّ الظُّروفَ الجَوِّيَّةَ، مِثلَ انخِفاضِ الرُّؤيَةِ بِسَبَبِ الضَّبابِ أَوِ الطُّرُقِ المُبَلَّلَةِ، تَزيدُ مِنْ مَخاطِرِ الحَوادِثِ.

رَغمَ جُهودِ السُّلُطاتِ اللُّبنانِيَّةِ، الَّتي شَمَلَت تَركيبَ راداراتٍ مُرورِيَّةٍ لِرَصدِ السُّرعَةِ الزّائِدَةِ، لا تَزالُ الغَراماتُ المَفروضَةُ عَلى المُخالَفاتِ المُرورِيَّةِ مُنخَفِضَةً، مِمّا يُقَلِّلُ مِنْ فاعِلِيَّةِ هَذِهِ الإجراءاتِ في تَحسينِ السَّلامَةِ عَلى الطُّرُقِ. يَعكِسُ هذا الحالُ حاجَةً ماسَّةً لِإعادَةِ النَّظَرِ في السِّياساتِ المُرورِيَّةِ وَتَشديدِ العُقوباتِ لِضَمانِ التِزامٍ أَفضَلَ بِالقَوانينِ.

يُعَدُّ تَحسينُ جودَةِ الطُّرُقِ وَرَفعُ وَعيِ السّائِقينَ بِأَهَمِّيَّةِ القِيادَةِ الآمِنَةِ مِنَ الخُطواتِ الأساسِيَّةِ لِلحَدِّ مِنْ حَوادِثِ الطُّرُقِ في لُبنانَ. مِنَ الضَّروريِّ التَّركيزُ عَلى تَعزيزِ التَّوعِيَةِ المُرورِيَّةِ وَتَحفيزِ السّائِقينَ عَلى اتِّباعِ مُمارَساتِ القِيادَةِ الآمِنَةِ لِتَقليلِ مُعَدَّلاتِ الحَوادِثِ المُرورِيَّةِ وَالارتِقاءِ بِمُستَوى السَّلامَةِ عَلى الطُّرُقِ في لُبنانَ.

Safety Challenges on Lebanese Roads: Accident Rates and Traffic Behaviors

Lebanon faces a significant challenge in traffic safety, as a recent study revealed that it ranks first globally in terms of driving danger, with a death rate of 22 per 100,000 inhabitants. This unfortunate reality is attributed to several factors, including poor road conditions and dangerous driving behaviors.

According to a recent report, Lebanon suffers from one of the worst road qualities globally, posing constant risks to drivers and pedestrians. Traffic statistics show an increase in the number of accidents, with 1,099 traffic incidents recorded in the first six months of 2023, indicating an increase compared to the same period the previous year.

Traffic accidents are attributed to various reasons, including reckless driving and non-compliance with traffic rules, such as speeding and illegal overtaking. Additionally, weather conditions like reduced visibility due to fog or wet roads increase the risks of accidents.

Despite the Lebanese authorities' efforts, which included the installation of traffic radars to monitor speeding, the fines imposed for traffic violations remain low, reducing the effectiveness of these measures in improving road safety. This situation reflects an urgent need to review traffic policies and tighten penalties to ensure better compliance with laws.

Improving road quality and raising drivers' awareness of the importance of safe driving are fundamental steps to reduce road accidents in Lebanon. It is crucial to focus on enhancing traffic awareness and motivating drivers to adopt safe driving practices to decrease traffic accident rates and improve road safety in Lebanon.

12.1.2 Airline and Aviation Incidents

أَجْلى

to evacuate • إِجْلاءٌ

تَمَّ إِجْلاءُ الطّاقِمِ بِأمانٍ بَعْدَ الإبْلاغِ عَنْ دُخانٍ في مَقْصورَةِ الطّائِرَةِ.

the cabin crew was safely evacuated after smoke was reported in the aircraft cabin.

أَصابَتْهُ صاعِقَةٌ

to be struck by lightning • إِصابَةٌ

أَصابَتْ صاعِقَةٌ طائِرَةَ الرُّكّابِ أثْناءَ الرِّحْلَةِ، مِمّا تَسَبَّبَ في أضْرارٍ بِالْجَناحِ.

Lightning struck the passenger plane during the flight, causing damage to the wing.

أَعْلَنَ حالَةَ طَوارِئَ

to declare an emergency • إِعْلانٌ

أَعْلَنَ الطَّيّارُ حالَةَ الطَّوارِئِ بَعْدَ فَشَلِ أَحَدِ المُحَرِّكاتِ.

The pilot declared an emergency after one of the engines failed.

إِجراءُ سَلامَةٍ

safety procedure

تَمَّ تَنْفيذُ إِجْراءِ السَّلامَةِ بِدِقَّةٍ عِنْدَ اكْتِشافِ تَسَرُّبِ الوَقودِ.

The safety procedure was executed precisely when a fuel leak was detected.

to disappear
إِخْتَفَى • اِخْتِفَاءٌ

اِخْتَفَتِ الطَّائِرَةُ عَنِ الرّادارِ في ظُروفٍ غامِضَةٍ.

The aircraft disappeared from radar under mysterious circumstances.

to catch fire
اِشْتَعَلَتْ نيرانٌ في • اِشْتِعالٌ

اِشْتَعَلَتِ النّيرانُ في الطّائِرَةِ بَعْدَ تَعَرُّضِ مُحَرِّكِها لِعُطْلٍ فَنّيٍّ خِلالَ الرِّحْلَةِ.

The plane caught fire after its engine experienced a technical failure during the flight.

bird strike
اِصْطِدامٌ بِطائِرٍ

تَسَبَّبَ اصْطِدامٌ بِالطُّيورِ في تَلَفِ المُحَرِّكِ وَلَكِنَّ الطَّائِرَةَ هَبَطَتْ بِسَلامٍ.

A bird strike caused engine damage, but the plane landed safely.

turbulence
اِضْطِرابٌ جَوِّيٌّ

تَعَرَّضَتِ الرِّحْلَةُ لِاضْطِرابٍ جَوِّيٍّ شَديدٍ مِمّا أثارَ الهَلَعَ بَيْنَ الرُّكّابِ.

The flight experienced severe turbulence, causing panic among the passengers.

to deviate from its course
إِنْحَرَفَ عَنْ مَسارِهِ • اِنْحِرافٌ

اِنْحَرَفَتِ الطّائِرَةُ عَنْ مَسارِها بِسَبَبِ الظُّروفِ الجَوِّيَّةِ السَّيِّئَةِ.

The aircraft deviated from its course due to bad weather conditions.

to slide off the runway
إِنْزَلَقَ عَلَى المَدْرَجِ • اِنْزِلاقٌ

اِنْزَلَقَتِ الطّائِرَةُ عَلَى المَدْرَجِ بِسَبَبِ الجَليدِ لَكِنْ لَمْ يُصَبْ أَحَدٌ بِأَذًى.

The aircraft slid on the runway due to ice, but no one was injured.

emergency exit
بابُ طَوارِئَ • أَبْوابٌ

اِسْتَخْدَمَ الرُّكّابُ بابَ الطَّوارِئِ لِلْخُروجِ بِسُرْعَةٍ بَعْدَ الهُبوطِ.

The passengers used the emergency exit to quickly leave after landing.

تجاوَزَ مَدْرَجَ الهُبوطِ

• تَجاوَزٌ

to overshoot the runway

تَجاوَزَتِ الطّائِرَةُ مَدْرَجَ الهُبوطِ بِسَبَبِ السُّرْعَةِ الزّائِدَةِ.

The plane overshot the landing runway due to excessive speed.

تَحَطَّمَ

• تَحَطُّمٌ

to crash

تَحَطَّمَتِ الطّائِرَةُ في الجِبالِ بِسَبَبِ الظُّروفِ الجَوِّيَّةِ السَّيِّئَةِ.

The plane crashed in the mountains due to bad weather conditions.

تَحْليلُ حُطامٍ

debris analysis

أَجْرى المُحَقِّقونَ تَحْليلًا لِحُطامِ الطّائِرَةِ لِتَحْديدِ سَبَبِ الحادِثِ.

Investigators conducted an analysis of the plane wreckage to determine the cause of the crash.

تَسْجيلُ رِحْلَةٍ

flight recording

كَشَفَ تَسْجيلُ الرِّحْلَةِ عَنِ اللَّحَظاتِ الأَخيرَةِ قَبْلَ الحادِثِ.

The flight recording revealed the last moments before the crash.

تَسَرُّبُ وَقودٍ

fuel leak

تَسَبَّبَ تَسَرُّبُ وَقودٍ في الطّائِرَةِ في حالَةِ طَوارِئَ أَثْناءَ الرِّحْلَةِ.

A fuel leak in the plane caused an emergency during the flight.

تَعْليماتُ طَوارِئَ

pl.

emergency instructions

اِتَّبَعَ الرُّكّابُ تَعْليماتِ الطَّوارِئِ بِدِقَّةٍ لِضَمانِ سَلامَتِهِم.

The passengers followed the emergency instructions carefully to ensure their safety.

خَطَأٌ بَشَرِيٌّ

• أَخْطاءٌ

human error

أَشارَ التَّحْقيقُ إلى الخَطَأِ البَشَرِيِّ كَسَبَبٍ رَئيسِيٍّ لِلْحادِثِ.

The investigation pointed to human error as a major cause of the accident.

life vest   سُتَرٌ •   سُتْرَةُ نَجاةٍ

في حَوادِثِ الطَّيَرَانِ، يُعَدُّ اسْتِخْدامُ سُتْرَةِ النَّجاةِ أَمْرًا حَيَوِيًّا لِبَقاءِ الرُّكّابِ في حالاتِ الهُبوطِ الطّارِئِ في الماءِ.

In aviation accidents, a life vest is crucial for passengers' survival in emergency water landings.

black box   صَناديقُ •   صُنْدوقٌ أَسْوَدُ

عُثِرَ عَلى الصُّنْدوقِ الأَسْوَدِ لِلطّائِرَةِ مِمّا ساعَدَ في تَحْديدِ أَسْبابِ الحادِثِ.

The plane's black box was found, which helped determine the causes of the crash.

cabin pressure   ضَغْطُ كابينَةٍ

انْخَفَضَ ضَغْطُ الكابينَةِ فَجْأَةً، مِمّا أَدّى إلى إِصابَةِ بَعْضِ الرُّكّابِ.

The cabin pressure dropped suddenly, causing some passengers to be injured.

bad weather   طَقْسٌ سَيِّئٌ

أُجْبِرَتِ الرِّحْلَةُ عَلى تَحْويلِ مَسارِها بِسَبَبِ الطَّقْسِ السَّيِّئِ المُفاجِئِ.

The flight was forced to divert due to sudden bad weather.

engine failure   عُطْلُ مُحَرِّكٍ

عَلى الرَّغْمِ مِنَ العِنايَةِ وَالصِّيانَةِ، عانَتِ الطّائِرَةُ مِنْ عُطْلِ مُحَرِّكٍ غَيْرِ مُتَوَقَّعٍ.

Despite care and maintenance, the aircraft suffered from an unexpected engine failure.

mechanical failure   أَعْطالٌ •   عُطْلٌ ميكانيكِيٌّ

لَمْ تُكْمِلِ الطّائِرَةُ رِحْلَتَها كَما كانَ مُخَطَّطًا بَعْدَ أَنْ عانَتْ مِنْ عُطْلٍ ميكانيكِيٍّ.

The aircraft did not complete its journey as planned after it suffered from a mechanical failure.

to lose communication   فَقْدٌ / فُقْدانٌ / فِقْدانٌ •   فَقَدَ الاتِّصالَ

بَعْدَ فُقْدانِ الاتِّصالِ، بَدَأَ بُرْجُ المُراقَبَةِ عَمَلِيّاتِ البَحْثِ وَالإِنْقاذِ.

After losing contact, the control tower initiated search and rescue operations.

to lose control

فَقَدَ السَّيْطَرَةَ

فَقَدَ الطَّيَّارُ السَّيْطَرَةَ عَلَى الطَّائِرَةِ لِلَحَظَاتٍ بِسَبَبِ الِاضْطِرَابِ الجَوِّيِّ الشَّدِيدِ.

The pilot lost control of the aircraft for moments due to severe air turbulence.

decompression

فِقْدَانُ الضَّغْطِ

لَمْ يُؤَدِّ فِقْدَانُ الضَّغْطِ فِي الكَابِينَةِ إِلَى حَالَةِ هَلَعٍ بِفَضْلِ تَدْرِيبِ الطَّاقِمِ.

The loss of cabin pressure did not lead to panic, thanks to the crew's training.

oxygen masks

أَقْنِعَةٌ • قِنَاعُ أُكْسُجِينٍ

لَمْ يَجِدِ الرُّكَّابُ أَقْنِعَةَ الأُكْسُجِينِ سَرِيعًا بِسَبَبِ الفَوْضَى النَّاجِمَةِ عَنْ فِقْدَانِ الضَّغْطِ.

The passengers did not immediately find the oxygen masks due to the chaos resulting from the pressure loss.

investigation committee

لِجَانٌ • لَجْنَةُ تَحْقِيقٍ

شُكِّلَتْ لَجْنَةُ تَحْقِيقٍ لِفَحْصِ الأَسْبَابِ وَرَاءَ الحَادِثِ الجَوِّيِّ.

An investigation committee was formed to examine the causes behind the air incident.

emergency exit

مَخَارِجُ • مَخْرَجُ طَوَارِئَ

لَمْ يَتَمَكَّنِ الرُّكَّابُ مِنْ فَتْحِ مَخْرَجِ الطَّوَارِئِ بِسُرْعَةٍ بِسَبَبِ الدُّخَانِ الكَثِيفِ.

The passengers were unable to open the emergency exit quickly due to heavy smoke.

emergency chutes

مَزَالِقُ • مَزْلَقَةُ طَوَارِئَ

بِسَبَبِ العُطْلِ، لَمْ تُفْتَحْ مَزْلَقَةُ الطَّوَارِئِ كَمَا كَانَ مُتَوَقَّعًا.

Due to the malfunction, the emergency slide did not deploy as expected.

navigation problem

مَشَاكِلُ • مُشْكِلَةُ تَوْجِيهٍ

نَتِيجَةً لِمُشْكِلَةِ تَوْجِيهٍ، أُضْطُرَّ الطَّيَّارُ لِاسْتِخْدَامِ الأَنْظِمَةِ اليَدَوِيَّةِ.

Due to a steering problem, the pilot had to use manual systems.

navigation system

نِظامُ مِلاحَةٍ

عِنْدَما تَعَطَّلَ نِظامُ المِلاحَةِ، اعْتَمَدَ الطَّيّارونَ عَلى الخَرائِطِ وَالمُعَدّاتِ الِاحْتِياطِيَّةِ.

When the navigation system failed, the pilots relied on maps and backup equipment.

hydraulic system

نِظامٌ هَيْدروليكِيٌّ • أَنْظِمَةٌ / نُظُمٌ

لَمْ يَكُنْ فَشَلُ النِّظامِ الهَيْدروليكِيِّ مُتَوَقَّعًا، مِمّا أَدّى إلى صُعوباتٍ في التَّحَكُّمِ.

The failure of the hydraulic system was not anticipated, leading to control difficulties.

emergency landing

هُبوطٌ اضْطِرارِيٌّ

نَفَّذَتِ الطّائِرَةُ هُبوطًا اضْطِرارِيًّا في حَقْلٍ مُجاوِرٍ بَعْدَ انْقِطاعِ الوَقودِ.

The aircraft made an emergency landing in a nearby field after running out of fuel.

to plunge from the sky

هَوى مِنَ السَّماءِ • هُوِيٌّ

لَمْ تَهْوِ الطّائِرَةُ مِنَ السَّماءِ كَما ادَّعَتِ التَّقاريرُ الأَوَّلِيَّةُ.

The plane did not plummet from the sky as initial reports claimed.

12.1.2.1 Mini-Articles

Track **54**

في حادِثَةٍ نادِرَةٍ، اصْطَدَمَتْ طائِرَةٌ تِجارِيَّةٌ بِطائِرٍ أَثْناءَ إقْلاعِها مِنْ مَطارِ بَيْروتَ، مِمّا أَدّى إلى أَضْرارٍ بِالمُحَرِّكِ الأَيْمَنِ وَإجْبارِ الطَّيّارِ عَلى إعْلانِ حالَةِ الطَّوارِئِ. تَمَّ إجْلاءُ الرُّكّابِ بِسَلامَةٍ عَبْرَ مَزْلَقَةِ الطَّوارِئِ، وَلَمْ تُسَجَّلْ إصاباتٌ خَطيرَةٌ.

In a rare incident, a commercial aircraft collided with a bird during its takeoff from Beirut airport, causing damage to the right engine and forcing the pilot to declare an emergency. Passengers were safely evacuated via the emergency slide, and no serious injuries were reported.

تَحَطَّمَتْ طائِرَةُ رُكّابٍ بَعْدَ فِقْدانِ ضَغْطِ الكابينَةِ عَلى ارْتِفاعٍ شاهِقٍ، ما أَدّى إلى هُبوطٍ اضْطِرارِيٍّ مَأْساوِيٍّ. الحادِثُ، الَّذي وَقَعَ في ظُروفِ طَقْسٍ سَيِّئَةٍ، أَسْفَرَ عَنْ فِقْدانِ عِدَّةِ أَرْواحٍ وَإصابَةِ البَعْضِ بِجُروحٍ بالِغَةٍ. وَصَلَتْ فِرَقُ الإنْقاذِ بِسُرْعَةٍ، وَبَدَأَتْ لَجْنَةُ تَحْقيقٍ عَمَلَها لِتَحْليلِ الحُطامِ وَالصُّنْدوقِ الأَسْوَدِ.

A passenger plane crashed after losing cabin pressure at a high altitude, leading to a tragic forced landing. The accident, which occurred in bad weather conditions, resulted in the loss of several lives and serious injuries to others. Rescue teams arrived quickly, and an investigative committee began its work to analyze the wreckage and the black box.

انْزَلَقَتْ طائِرَةُ رُكّابٍ عَلَى المَدْرَجِ بَعْدَ هُبوطِها في مَطارِ الكُوَيْتِ بِسَبَبِ عُطْلٍ ميكانيكِيٍّ في نِظامِ الهَيْدروليك. تَسَبَّبَ الحادِثُ في تَلَفٍ كَبيرٍ لِجِسْمِ الطّائِرَةِ، لَكِنْ بِفَضْلِ مَهارَةِ الطَّيّارِ وَتَجاوُبِ طاقِمِ الطّائِرَةِ مَعَ تَعْليماتِ الطَّوارِئِ، تَمَّ إِجْلاءُ جَميعِ الرُّكّابِ دونَ إِصاباتٍ خَطيرَةٍ.

A passenger plane skidded on the runway after landing at Kuwait airport due to a mechanical fault in the hydraulic system. The incident caused significant damage to the aircraft, but thanks to the pilot's skill and the crew's response to emergency instructions, all passengers were evacuated without serious injuries.

أُضْطُرَّتْ طائِرَةٌ مُتَوَجِّهَةٌ مِنَ الدَّمّامِ إلى القاهِرَةِ لِلْهُبوطِ الاِضْطِرارِيِّ في الأُرْدُنَّ بَعْدَ تَعَرُّضِها لِاِضْطِراباتٍ جَوِّيَّةٍ شَديدَةٍ أَثَّرَتْ عَلَى نِظامِ المِلاحَةِ. حافَظَ الطّاقِمُ عَلَى الهُدوءِ وَأَعْلَنَ حالَةَ الطَّوارِئِ، مِمّا مَكَّنَ مِنْ هُبوطِ الطّائِرَةِ بِسَلامٍ دونَ وُقوعِ أَيَّةِ إِصاباتٍ.

A plane flying from Dammam to Cairo was forced to make an emergency landing in Jordan after encountering severe atmospheric disturbances that affected the navigation system. The crew maintained calm and declared an emergency, allowing the plane to land safely without any injuries.

تَحَطَّمَتْ طائِرَةُ شَحْنٍ في صَحْراءِ السُّعودِيَّةِ بَعْدَ فِقْدانِها الاِتِّصالَ بِبُرْجِ المُراقَبَةِ. أَدَّتِ الحادِثَةُ إلى تَحْليلِ حُطامٍ واسِعٍ وَبَحْثٍ مُكَثَّفٍ عَنِ الصُّنْدوقِ الأَسْوَدِ لِتَحْديدِ أَسْبابِ الحادِثِ، حَيْثُ تُشيرُ التَّحْقيقاتُ الأَوَّلِيَّةُ إلى مُشْكِلَةِ تَوْجيهٍ وَعُطْلٍ في نِظامِ التَّحَكُّمِ.

A cargo plane crashed in the Saudi desert after losing contact with the control tower. The incident led to extensive debris analysis and an intensive search for the black box to determine the causes of the accident, where preliminary investigations point to a steering problem and a fault in the control system.

12.1.2.2 Historical Account: The Disappearance of Flight 370

Track **55**

الغُموضُ يَكْتَنِفُ اخْتِفاءَ الرِّحْلَةِ الجَوِّيَّةِ 370 لِلْخُطوطِ الجَوِّيَّةِ الماليزِيَّةِ

في مارِسَ 2014، شَهِدَ العالَمُ واحِدًا مِنْ أَكْبَرِ الأَلْغازِ في تاريخِ الطَّيَرانِ: اخْتِفاءَ الرِّحْلَةِ الجَوِّيَّةِ 370 التّابِعَةِ لِلْخُطوطِ الجَوِّيَّةِ الماليزِيَّةِ. الطّائِرَةُ، الَّتي كانَتْ في رِحْلَةٍ مِنْ كُوالالَمْبورْ إلى بِكينْ، فَقَدَتِ الاِتِّصالَ مَعَ بُرْجِ المُراقَبَةِ الجَوِّيَّةِ بَعْدَ ساعَةٍ تَقْريبًا مِنْ إِقْلاعِها، وَأَصْبَحَ مَصيرُها لُغْزًا إلى اليَوْمِ.

بَعْدَ اختِفائِها مِنْ عَلى شاشاتِ الرّادارِ، أُطلِقَتْ عَمَلِيّاتُ بَحْثٍ واسِعَةُ النِّطاقِ في مُحاوَلَةٍ لِتَحْديدِ مَوْقِعِ الطّائِرَةِ وَال 239 شَخْصًا عَلى مَتْنِها. أشارَتِ التَّحْقيقاتُ وَتَحْليلُ البَياناتِ مِنَ الأقْمارِ الصِّناعِيَّةِ إلى أنَّ الطّائِرَةَ قَدِ انْحَرَفَتْ بِشَكْلٍ كَبيرٍ عَنْ مَسارِها المُحَدَّدِ وَرُبَّما أنْهَتْ رِحْلَتَها في جَنوبِ المُحيطِ الهِنْدِيِّ.

عَلى الرَّغْمِ مِنَ الجُهودِ الدَّوْلِيَّةِ المُكَثَّفَةِ، لَمْ يُعْثَرْ سِوى عَلى بِضْعِ قِطَعٍ مِنْ حُطامِ الطّائِرَةِ طافِيَةً عَلى سَواحِلِ إفْريقيا، مِمّا أدّى إلى تَكَهُّناتٍ حَوْلَ سَبَبِ الحادِثِ. تَشْمَلُ النَّظَريّاتُ المُتَعَلِّقَةُ باخْتِفاءِ الرِّحْلَةِ MH370 فِقْدانَ الضَّغْطِ في الكابينَةِ، وَالعُطَلَ الميكانيكِيَّ، وَالخَطَأَ البَشَرِيَّ، وَحَتّى احْتِمالاتِ التَّدَخُّلِ الإجْرامِيِّ.

أدَّتِ التَّحْقيقاتُ المُسْتَمِرَّةُ وَعَمَلِيّاتُ البَحْثِ إلى تَحْسيناتٍ في إجْراءاتِ السَّلامَةِ وَتَتَبُّعِ الطّائِراتِ عَلى مُسْتَوى العالَمِ، شَمِلَ ذَلِكَ تَحْديثَ مُتَطَلَّباتِ نِظامِ التَّتَبُّعِ الجَوِّيِّ لِضَمانِ عَدَمِ تَكْرارِ مِثْلِ هَذِهِ الحَوادِثِ الغامِضَةِ. حَتّى اليَوْمَ، تَظَلُّ الرِّحْلَةُ MH370 مَحْفورَةً في ذاكِرَةِ الطَّيَرانِ العالَمِيِّ كَواحِدَةٍ مِنْ أكْثَرِ الحَوادِثِ إثارَةً لِلْجَدَلِ وَالحُزْنِ.

Mystery shrouds the disappearance of Malaysia Airlines Flight 370

In March 2014, the world witnessed one of the greatest mysteries in aviation history: the disappearance of Malaysia Airlines Flight 370. The plane, which was on a flight from Kuala Lumpur to Beijing, lost contact with air traffic control about an hour after takeoff, and its fate remains a mystery to this day.

After vanishing from radar screens, extensive search operations were launched in an attempt to locate the aircraft and the 239 people on board. Investigations and analysis of satellite data suggested that the plane had significantly deviated from its planned route and might have ended its journey in the southern Indian Ocean.

Despite intense international efforts, only a few floating debris pieces were found off the coasts of Africa, leading to speculation about the cause of the incident. Theories about the disappearance of Flight MH370 include cabin pressure loss, mechanical failure, human error, and even possibilities of criminal interference.

Ongoing investigations and search efforts have led to improvements in global aviation safety procedures and aircraft tracking, including updating the air tracking system requirements to ensure such mysterious incidents do not recur. To this day, Flight MH370 remains etched in the memory of global aviation as one of the most controversial and sorrowful events.

تَحَدِّياتُ السَّلامَةِ الجَوِّيَّةِ في العالَمِ العَرَبِيِّ: أَبْرَزُ حَوادِثِ الطَّيَرانِ

شَهِدَ العالَمُ العَرَبِيُّ عِدَّةَ حَوادِثِ طَيَرانٍ مَأْساوِيَّةٍ، مِمّا يَسْتَدْعي تَسْليطَ الضَّوْءِ عَلى مَسائِلِ السَّلامَةِ الجَوِّيَّةِ. مِنْ فِقْدانِ الاتِّصالِ إلى الأَعْطالِ الميكانيكِيَّةِ وَالخَطَأِ البَشَرِيِّ، تَكْشِفُ كُلُّ حادِثَةٍ عَنْ تَحَدِّياتٍ مُخْتَلِفَةٍ في قِطاعِ الطَّيَرانِ.

رِحْلَةُ مِصْرَ للطَّيَرانِ MS804 (2016)

تَحَطَّمَتْ هَذِهِ الرِّحْلَةُ مِنْ باريسَ إلى القاهِرَةِ فَوْقَ البَحْرِ الأَبْيَضِ المُتَوَسِّطِ في مايو 2016، مِمّا أَدّى إلى وَفاةِ جَميعِ الأَشْخاصِ الـ 66 عَلى مَتْنِها. تُشيرُ التَّحْقيقاتُ إلى أَنَّ حَريقًا بِقُمْرَةِ القِيادَةِ قَدْ يَكونُ سَبَبَ الكارِثَةِ، مَعَ التَّرْكيزِ عَلى تَحْليلِ الصُّنْدوقِ الأَسْوَدِ لِفَهْمِ الأَحْداثِ الأَخيرَةِ.

رِحْلَةُ الخُطوطِ الجَوِّيَّةِ الجَزائِرِيَّةِ AH5017 (2014)

اِخْتَفَتِ الطّائِرَةُ في يوليو 2014 خِلالَ رِحْلَتِها مِنْ واغادوغو إلى الجَزائِرِ العاصِمَةِ وَتَحَطَّمَتْ في شَمالِ مالي، ما أَسْفَرَ عَنْ وَفاةِ 116 شَخْصًا. تَناوَلَتْ تَحْقيقاتُ لَجْنَةِ السَّلامَةِ فَرْضِيّاتٍ عِدَّةً مِنْها الاِضْطِراباتُ الجَوِّيَّةُ وَالعُطْلُ الميكانيكِيُّ كَأَسْبابٍ مُحْتَمَلَةٍ.

تَحَطُّمُ الطّائِرَةِ الإماراتِيَّةِ في روسيا (2016)

في مارِسَ 2016، تَحَطَّمَتْ طائِرَةٌ تابِعَةٌ للخُطوطِ الجَوِّيَّةِ الإماراتِيَّةِ أَثْناءَ مُحاوَلَتِها الهُبوطَ في مَطارِ روستوف - أون - دون، مِمّا أَدّى إلى وَفاةِ 62 شَخْصًا. أَرْجَعَتْ لِجانُ التَّحْقيقِ السَّبَبَ إلى خَطَأٍ بَشَرِيٍّ تَحْتَ تَأْثيرِ الطَّقْسِ السَّيِّئِ، مِمّا أَدّى إلى فِقْدانِ السَّيْطَرَةِ وَتَحَطُّمِ الطّائِرَةِ.

حادِثُ طَيَرانِ الخَليجِ في البَحْرَيْنِ (2000)

تَحَطَّمَتْ طائِرَةٌ تابِعَةٌ لِطَيَرانِ الخَليجِ قُرْبَ البَحْرَيْنِ في أُغُسْطُسَ 2000، مِمّا أَسْفَرَ عَنْ وَفاةِ 143 شَخْصًا. أَشارَ التَّحْقيقُ إلى خَطَأٍ بَشَرِيٍّ في التَّعامُلِ مَعَ الظُّروفِ الجَوِّيَّةِ الصَّعْبَةِ، مَعَ التَّرْكيزِ عَلى قَضايا التَّدْريبِ وَإجراءاتِ السَّلامَةِ.

رِحْلَةُ الخُطوطِ الجَوِّيَّةِ اليَمَنِيَّةِ IY626 (2009)

في يونيو 2009، سَقَطَتْ طائِرَةٌ تابِعَةٌ للخُطوطِ الجَوِّيَّةِ اليَمَنِيَّةِ في المُحيطِ الهِنْدِيِّ أَثْناءَ رِحْلَتِها مِنْ صَنْعاءَ إلى موروني، جُزُرِ القُمُرِ، مِمّا أَدّى إلى وَفاةِ 152 شَخْصًا. الحادِثُ، الَّذي شَهِدَ نَجاةَ طِفْلٍ واحِدٍ فَقَطْ، تَمَّ تَحْليلُهُ

بِعُمْقٍ لِفَهْمِ أَسْبابِ فَقْدِ السَّيْطَرَةِ عَلَى الطَّائِرَةِ. كَشَفَتِ التَّحْقِيقاتُ عَنْ مُشْكِلاتٍ فِي نِظامِ الْمِلاحَةِ وَإِجْراءاتِ الطَّوارِئِ الَّتِي لَمْ تُدَرْ بِالشَّكْلِ الأَمْثَلِ.

تُظْهِرُ هَذِهِ الْحَوادِثُ الْجَوِّيَّةُ الْمَأْساوِيَّةُ فِي الْعالَمِ الْعَرَبِيِّ أَهَمِّيَّةَ الصِّيانَةِ الدَّقِيقَةِ، وَالتَّدْرِيبِ الْمُتَخَصِّصِ لِلطَّواقِمِ، وَتَحْدِيثِ الأَنْظِمَةِ التَّقْنِيَّةِ وَالْمِلاحِيَّةِ لِضَمانِ أَعْلَى مُسْتَوَياتِ الأَمانِ. كُلُّ حادِثٍ يُعَدُّ دَرْسًا يَجِبُ الاسْتِفادَةُ مِنْهُ لِتَعْزِيزِ سَلامَةِ الطَّيَرانِ وَحِمايَةِ أَرْواحِ النّاسِ.

Challenges of Air Safety in the Arab World: Major Aviation Accidents

The Arab world has witnessed several tragic aviation incidents, highlighting the need for attention to air safety. From loss of communication to mechanical failures and human error, each incident reveals different challenges in the aviation sector.

EgyptAir Flight MS804 (2016)

This flight from Paris to Cairo crashed over the Mediterranean Sea in May 2016, killing all 66 people on board. Investigations suggest that a cockpit fire may have caused the disaster, with a focus on analyzing the black box to understand the final moments.

Air Algérie Flight AH5017 (2014)

The plane disappeared in July 2014 during its flight from Ouagadougou to Algiers and crashed in northern Mali, killing 116 people. The safety committee's investigations explored several hypotheses, including atmospheric disturbances and mechanical failure as possible causes.

Emirates Plane Crash in Russia (2016)

In March 2016, an Emirates airline plane crashed while attempting to land at Rostov-on-Don airport, killing 62 people. Investigative committees attributed the cause to human error under bad weather conditions, leading to loss of control and the crash.

Gulf Air Accident in Bahrain (2000)

A Gulf Air plane crashed near Bahrain in August 2000, resulting in 143 deaths. The investigation pointed to human error in handling difficult weather conditions, focusing on training issues and safety procedures.

Yemenia Flight IY626 (2009)

In June 2009, a Yemenia airline plane crashed into the Indian Ocean on its flight from Sanaa to Moroni, Comoros, killing 152 people. The incident, which had only one child survivor, was thoroughly analyzed to understand the causes of the plane's loss of control. Investigations revealed problems with the navigation system and emergency procedures that were not optimally managed.

These tragic air incidents in the Arab world underscore the importance of meticulous maintenance, specialized crew training, and updating technical and navigational systems to ensure the highest safety levels. Each accident serves as a lesson to enhance aviation safety and protect human lives.

12.1.3 Maritime and Shipping Mishaps

أَنْقَذَ

to rescue, save   • إِنْقاذٌ

قامَتْ فِرَقُ الإِنْقاذِ بِإِنْقاذِ رُكّابِ الْيَخْتِ الْغارِقِ في وَقْتٍ قِياسِيٍّ.

Rescue teams saved the passengers of the sinking yacht in record time.

إِجْلاءُ الطّاقِمِ وَالرُّكّابِ

crew and passenger evacuation

تَمَّ إِجْلاءُ الطّاقِمِ وَالرُّكّابِ بِأمانٍ بَعْدَ تَعَطُّلِ مُحَرِّكِ السَّفينَةِ.

The crew and passengers were safely evacuated after the ship's engine failed.

إِنْحَرَفَ عَنْ مَسارِهِ

to deviate from its course   • إِنْحِرافٌ

إِنْحَرَفَتِ السَّفينَةُ عَنْ مَسارِها بِسَبَبِ عاصِفَةٍ قَوِيَّةٍ.

The ship deviated from its course due to a strong storm.

إِنْقَلَبَ

to capsize   • إِنْقِلابٌ

تَسَبَّبَتِ الأَمْواجُ الْعاتِيَةُ في انْقِلابِ سَفينَةٍ قُرْبَ السّاحِلِ.

The violent waves caused a ship to capsize near the coast.

تَسَرُّبٌ زَيْتِيٌّ

oil leak

تَمَّ اكْتِشافُ تَسَرُّبٍ زَيْتِيٍّ مِنَ النّاقِلَةِ، مِمّا تَسَبَّبَ في مَخاوِفَ بيئِيَّةٍ.

An oil leak was detected from the tanker, causing environmental concerns.

تَصادَمَ

to collide   • تَصادُمٌ

تَصادَمَتِ السَّفينَتانِ في الضَّبابِ الْكَثيفِ أَثْناءَ مُحاوَلَتِهِما الدُّخولَ إلى الْميناءِ.

The two ships collided in heavy fog while trying to enter the harbor.

harbor collision

تَصادُمٌ في ميناءٍ

تَسَبَّبَتِ الأَخْطاءُ في التَّوْجيهِ في تَصادُمٍ في الميناءِ، مِمّا أَلْحَقَ أَضرارًا بِالرَّصيفِ.

Errors in steering caused a collision in the port, damaging the dock.

hull breach

ثَغْرَةٌ في الهَيْكَلِ

حَدَّدَ الغَوّاصونَ ثَغْرَةً في هَيْكَلِ السَّفينَةِ، مِمّا اسْتَدْعى إِصْلاحاتٍ فَوْرِيَّةً.

Divers identified a leak in the ship's hull, necessitating immediate repairs.

to run aground

جَنَحَ • جُنوحٌ

جَنَحَتِ السَّفينَةُ التِّجارِيَّةُ عَلى الشِّعابِ المَرْجانِيَّةِ أَثْناءَ مُحاوَلَتِها تَجَنُّبَ عاصِفَةٍ.

The cargo ship ran aground on the coral reefs while trying to avoid a storm.

onboard fire

حَريقٌ عَلى مَتْنٍ (سَفينَةٍ) • حَرائِقُ

اِنْدَلَعَ حَريقٌ عَلى مَتْنِ السَّفينَةِ، مِمّا اسْتَدْعى تَدَخُّلَ فِرَقِ الإِطْفاءِ البَحْرِيَّةِ.

A fire broke out on board the ship, requiring the intervention of marine firefighting teams.

lifeboat

زَوْرَقُ نَجاةٍ • زَوارِقُ

اِسْتَخْدَمَ الرُّكّابُ زَوارِقَ النَّجاةِ بَعْدَ تَعَرُّضِ السَّفينَةِ لِعُطْلٍ فَنِّيٍّ كَبيرٍ.

The passengers used the lifeboats after the ship experienced a major technical malfunction.

ship

سَفينَةٌ • سُفُنٌ

تَمَكَّنَتِ السَّفينَةُ مِنْ تَجَنُّبِ الاِصْطِدامِ في اللَّحْظَةِ الأَخيرَةِ بِفَضْلِ التَّنْبيهاتِ الفَوْرِيَّةِ مِنْ نِظامِ المِلاحَةِ.

The ship managed to avoid collision at the last moment thanks to immediate alerts from the navigation system.

harsh weather condition

ظَرْفٌ جَوِّيٌّ قاسٍ • ظُروفٌ

غادَرَتِ السَّفينَةُ الميناءَ عَلى الرَّغْمِ مِنَ التَّحْذيراتِ مِنَ الظُّروفِ الجَوِّيَّةِ القاسِيَةِ.

The ship left the port despite warnings of harsh weather conditions.

search and rescue operation

عَمَلِيَّةُ بَحْثٍ وَإِنْقاذٍ

بَدَأَتْ عَمَلِيَّةُ بَحْثٍ وَإِنْقاذٍ فَوْرَ الإِبْلاغِ عَنِ اخْتِفاءِ قارِبِ صَيْدٍ صَغيرٍ.

A search and rescue operation began immediately after a small fishing boat was reported missing.

cleanup operation

عَمَلِيَّةُ تَنْظيفٍ

قادَتِ الشَّرِكَةُ عَمَلِيَّةَ تَنْظيفٍ لِلتَّعامُلِ مَعَ التَّسَرُّبِ النِّفْطِيِّ النّاتِجِ عَنِ الحادِثِ.

The company led a cleanup operation to deal with the oil spill resulting from the accident.

to sink

غَرِقَ • غَرَقٌ

غَرِقَتِ السَّفينَةُ بِسُرْعَةٍ بَعْدَ اصْطِدامِها بِجِسْمٍ غامِضٍ تَحْتَ الماءِ.

The ship sank quickly after it collided with an unidentified underwater object.

to lose contact

فَقَدَ الاتِّصالَ • فَقْدٌ / فُقْدانٌ / فِقْدانٌ

فَقَدَتِ السَّفينَةُ الاتِّصالَ بِبُرْجِ المُراقَبَةِ خِلالَ العاصِفَةِ الشَّديدَةِ.

The ship lost contact with the control tower during the severe storm.

cargo loss

فِقْدانُ بَضائِعَ

نَتَجَ عَنِ الحادِثِ فِقْدانُ بَضائِعَ قَيِّمَةٍ كانَتْ عَلى مَتْنِ السَّفينَةِ.

The incident resulted in the loss of valuable goods that were on board the ship.

navigational issues

مُشْكِلَةٌ في المِلاحَةِ • مَشاكِلُ

تَسَبَّبَتْ مَشاكِلُ في المِلاحَةِ في جُنوحِ السَّفينَةِ عَلى الشّاطِئِ.

Navigational issues caused the ship to run aground on the beach.

غَرِقَتْ سَفِينَةُ شَحْنٍ تَحْمِلُ بَضَائِعَ ثَمِينَةً فِي البَحْرِ الأَحْمَرِ بَعْدَ تَسَرُّبٍ مُفَاجِئٍ فِي الهَيْكَلِ. فُقِدَ الِاتِّصَالُ بِالسَّفِينَةِ بَعْدَ سَاعَاتٍ مِنْ إِرْسَالِ نِدَاءِ اسْتِغَاثَةٍ. أُجْرِيَتْ عَمَلِيَّةُ بَحْثٍ وَإِنْقَاذٍ وَاسِعَةُ النِّطَاقِ، وَتَمَّ إِنْقَاذُ الطَّاقِمِ بِأَكْمَلِهِ بِوَاسِطَةِ زَوَارِقِ النَّجَاةِ، بَيْنَما شَرَعَتْ فِرَقٌ مُتَخَصِّصَةٌ فِي عَمَلِيَّةِ تَنْظِيفٍ لِلْحَدِّ مِنَ الأَضْرَارِ البِيئِيَّةِ.

A cargo ship carrying valuable goods sank in the Red Sea after a sudden hull breach. The ship lost contact hours after sending a distress call. An extensive search and rescue operation was conducted, and the entire crew was saved using lifeboats, while specialized teams initiated a cleanup operation to minimize environmental damage.

وَقَعَ تَصَادُمٌ بَيْنَ سَفِينَتَيْنِ فِي مِيناءِ جِدَّةَ، مِمَّا أَدَّى إِلَى انْدِلَاعِ حَرِيقٍ هَائِلٍ عَلَى مَتْنِ إِحْدَاهُما. تَمَّ إِجْلَاءُ الطَّاقِمِ وَالرُّكَّابِ فِي الوَقْتِ المُنَاسِبِ، وَتَدَخَّلَتْ فِرَقُ الإِطْفَاءِ لِلسَّيْطَرَةِ عَلَى الحَرِيقِ. أَثَّرَ الحَادِثُ سَلْبًا عَلَى عَمَلِيَّاتِ المِيناءِ وَتَسَبَّبَ فِي تَأْخِيرِ الشَّحْنِ وَفِقْدَانِ بَعْضِ البَضَائِعِ.

A collision between two ships in Jeddah port led to a massive fire on one of them. The crew and passengers were evacuated in time, and firefighting teams intervened to control the fire. The incident negatively affected port operations, causing shipment delays and loss of some cargo.

انْحَرَفَتْ سَفِينَةُ رُكَّابٍ عَنْ مَسَارِها بِسَبَبِ الظُّرُوفِ الجَوِّيَّةِ القَاسِيَةِ فِي بَحْرِ عُمانَ. وَاجَهَتِ السَّفِينَةُ أَمْوَاجًا عَاتِيَةً مِمَّا أَدَّى إِلَى مَشَاكِلَ فِي التَّوْجِيهِ. وَبِفَضْلِ الِاسْتِجَابَةِ السَّرِيعَةِ لِفِرَقِ الإِنْقَاذِ، تَمَّ إِنْقَاذُ الرُّكَّابِ وَالطَّاقِمِ بِأَمَانٍ.

A passenger ship veered off course due to harsh weather conditions in the Sea of Oman. The ship encountered high waves, causing steering problems. Thanks to the quick response of rescue teams, passengers and crew were safely rescued.

تَعَرَّضَتْ سَفِينَةُ شَحْنٍ لِتَسَرُّبٍ زَيْتِيٍّ كَبِيرٍ أَثْنَاءَ رِحْلَتِها فِي الخَلِيجِ العَرَبِيِّ. التَّسَرُّبُ، الَّذِي بَدَأَ مِنْ مُحَرِّكِ السَّفِينَةِ، تَسَبَّبَ فِي تَلَوُّثٍ مَائِيٍّ وَاسِعٍ. انْطَلَقَتْ عَمَلِيَّاتُ تَنْظِيفٍ مُكَثَّفَةٍ لِمُوَاجَهَةِ الكَارِثَةِ البِيئِيَّةِ، وَأُجْرِيَ تَحْقِيقٌ لِتَحْدِيدِ أَسْبَابِ التَّسَرُّبِ.

A cargo ship experienced a significant oil leak during its journey in the Arabian Gulf. The leak, originating from the ship's engine, caused widespread water pollution. Intensive cleaning operations were launched to address the environmental disaster, and an investigation was initiated to determine the causes of the leak.

انْقَلَبَتْ سَفِينَةُ صَيْدٍ فِي البَحْرِ المُتَوَسِّطِ بِسَبَبِ الأَمْوَاجِ العَالِيَةِ، مِمَّا أَدَّى إِلَى سُقُوطِ طَاقِمِها فِي المَاءِ. تَمَّ تَنْفِيذُ عَمَلِيَّةِ بَحْثٍ وَإِنْقَاذٍ فَوْرِيَّةٍ نَجَحَتْ فِي إِنْقَاذِ جَمِيعِ أَفْرَادِ الطَّاقِمِ، الَّذِينَ تَمَكَّنُوا مِنَ الصُّمُودِ بِاسْتِخْدَامِ زَوَارِقِ النَّجَاةِ حَتَّى وُصُولِ المُسَاعَدَةِ.

A fishing vessel capsized in the Mediterranean Sea due to high waves, throwing its crew into the water. An immediate search and rescue operation was successful in saving all crew members, who managed to survive using lifeboats until help arrived.

12.1.4 Infrastructure

Track **59**

to repair

• إِصْلاحٌ
أَصْلَحَ

أَصْلَحَتِ الفِرَقُ التِّقَنِيَّةُ الجِسْرَ المُتَضَرِّرَ في زَمَنٍ قِياسِيٍّ.

The technical teams repaired the damaged bridge in record time.

to rebuild

• إِعادَةٌ
أَعادَ بِناءَ

أَعادَتِ السُّلُطاتُ بِناءَ المَبْنى التّاريخِيِّ بَعْدَ الزِّلْزالِ المُدَمِّرِ.

The authorities rebuilt the historical building after the devastating earthquake.

> أَعادَ + verbal noun (masdar) is analogous to the English prefix 're-' on a verb, used to indicate the repetition or renewal of an action.

to reroute traffic

• إِعادَةٌ
أَعادَ تَوْجيهَ المُرورِ

تَمَّتْ إِعادَةُ تَوْجيهِ المُرورِ بِسَبَبِ أَعْمالِ البِناءِ في الشّارِعِ الرَّئيسِيِّ.

Traffic was redirected due to construction work on the main street.

repair

إِصْلاحٌ

بَدَأَتْ عَمَلِيّاتُ إِصْلاحِ الطَّريقِ بَعْدَ الانْهِيارِ الأَرْضِيِّ.

Road repair operations began after the landslide.

reconstruction

إِعادَةُ إِعْمارٍ

تُشارِكُ عِدَّةُ مُنَظَّماتٍ في إِعادَةِ إِعْمارِ المَناطِقِ المُتَضَرِّرَةِ مِنَ الفَيَضاناتِ.

Several organizations are involved in the reconstruction of areas affected by the floods.

to respond • اِسْتِجابَةٌ اِسْتَجابَ

اِسْتَجابَتْ فِرَقُ الإطْفاءِ بِسُرْعَةٍ لِلْبَلاغاتِ عَنْ حَريقٍ في المَصْنَعِ.

Firefighting teams responded quickly to reports of a fire in the factory.

emergency response اِسْتِجابَةُ طَوارِئَ

نَفَّذَتِ السُّلُطاتُ اسْتِجابَةَ طَوارِئَ لِمُواجَهَةِ الفَيَضاناتِ الشَّديدَةِ.

The authorities implemented an emergency response to deal with the severe floods.

sewage blockage اِنْسِدادُ الصَّرْفِ الصِّحِّيِّ

تَسَبَّبَ اِنْسِدادُ الصَّرْفِ الصِّحِّيِّ في تَراكُمِ المِياهِ في الشَّوارِعِ.

Sewage blockage caused water to accumulate in the streets.

to to be cut off • اِنْعِزالٌ اِنْعَزَلَ

اِنْعَزَلَ الحَيُّ بِالْكامِلِ عَنْ شَبَكَةِ المِياهِ بِسَبَبِ تَلَفِ الأنابيبِ.

The entire neighborhood was isolated from the water network due to pipe damage.

pipe burst اِنْفِجارُ أُنْبوبَةٍ

أَدّى اِنْفِجارُ أُنْبوبَةٍ إلى تَسَرُّبِ مِياهٍ كَبيرٍ في المِنْطَقَةِ.

The explosion of a pipe led to a significant water leak in the area.

power outage اِنْقِطاعُ تَيّارٍ كَهْرَبائِيٍّ

سَبَّبَ انْقِطاعُ تَيّارٍ كَهْرَبائِيٍّ فَوْضى في أَنْظِمَةِ الإشاراتِ المُرورِيَّةِ.

A power outage caused chaos in traffic signal systems.

to collapse • اِنْهِيارٌ اِنْهارَ

اِنْهارَ جِسْرُ الوادي بِسَبَبِ الفَيَضاناتِ العارِمَةِ اللَّيْلَةَ الماضِيَةَ.

The valley bridge collapsed due to last night's torrential floods.

collapse

انْهِيارٌ

يُظْهِرُ التَّحْقيقُ أَنَّ انْهِيارَ المَبْنى كانَ نَتيجَةً لِإهْمالِ الصِّيانَةِ.

The investigation shows that the building's collapse was due to maintenance negligence.

infrastructure

بِنْيَةٌ تَحْتِيَّةٌ • بِنًى

تُعْتَبَرُ البِنْيَةُ التَّحْتِيَّةُ القَوِيَّةُ أَساسِيَّةً لِتَحْسينِ جَوْدَةِ الحَياةِ في المُدُنِ.

Strong infrastructure is essential for improving quality of life in cities.

to leak

تَسَرَّبَ • تَسَرُّبٌ

تَسَرَّبَتِ المِياهُ مِنَ السَّدِّ المُتَصَدِّعِ، مِمّا أَثارَ مَخاوِفَ مِنْ فَيَضانٍ وَشيكٍ.

Water leaked from the cracked dam, raising fears of an imminent flood.

to malfunction, to break down

تَعَطَّلَ • تَعَطُّلٌ

تَعَطَّلَتِ الإشاراتُ المُرورِيَّةُ، مِمّا أَدّى إلى ازْدِحامٍ شَديدٍ خِلالَ ساعَةِ الذُّرْوَةِ.

The traffic lights malfunctioned, leading to severe congestion during rush hour.

to deteriorate

تَلَفَ • تَلَفٌ

تَلَفَتِ الأَرْصِفَةُ بِسُرْعَةٍ نَتيجَةَ غِيابِ الصِّيانَةِ المُنْتَظَمَةِ.

Sidewalks deteriorated quickly due to lack of regular maintenance.

maintenance

صِيانَةٌ

تَشْمَلُ الصِّيانَةُ الدَّوْرِيَّةُ التَّحَقُّقَ مِنْ جَميعِ الأَنْظِمَةِ الحَيَوِيَّةِ لِمَنْعِ الأَعْطالِ.

Routine maintenance includes checking all vital systems to prevent malfunctions.

damage

ضَرَرٌ • أَضْرارٌ

بَدَأَتِ السُّلُطاتُ في تَقْييمِ أَضْرارِ العاصِفَةِ عَلى الطُّرُقِ وَالجُسورِ.

The authorities began assessing the storm damage to roads and bridges.

to flood, be inundated

غَرَق • غَرِقَ

غَرِقَ الشّارِعُ الرّئيسِيُّ بَعْدَ الأَمْطارِ الغَزيرَةِ المُفاجِئَةِ.

The main street flooded following sudden heavy rains.

street flooding

غَرَقُ شارِعٍ

تَسَبَّبَتِ الأَمْطارُ الغَزيرَةُ في غَرَقِ شَوارِعِ المَدينَةِ وَعَرْقَلَةِ حَرَكَةِ المُرورِ.

The heavy rain caused city streets to flood and disrupt traffic.

structural failure

فَشَلٌ هَيْكَلِيٌّ

أَشارَ التَّقْريرُ إلى فَشَلٍ هَيْكَلِيٍّ في السَّدِّ.

The report indicated a structural failure in the dam.

to assess, to evaluate

قَيَّمَ • تَقْييمٌ

قَيَّمَ المُهَنْدِسونَ حالَةَ الجِسْرِ لِتَحْديدِ الحاجَةِ لإصْلاحاتٍ عاجِلَةٍ.

Engineers assessed the condition of the bridge to determine the need for urgent repairs.

12.1.4.1 Mini-Articles

Track **60**

اِنْهارَ جِسْرٌ مُروريٌّ رَئيسيٌّ في القاهِرَةِ بِسَبَبِ فَشَلٍ هَيْكَلِيٍّ، مِمّا أَدّى إلى اِنْعِزالِ مِنْطَقَةٍ سَكَنِيَّةٍ وَتَعَطُّلِ حَرَكَةِ المُرورِ. اِسْتَجابَتْ فِرَقُ الإنْقاذِ سَريعًا، وَبَدَأَتْ عَمَلِيّاتِ إعادَةِ بِناءِ الجِسْرِ، مَعَ إعادَةِ تَوْجيهِ المُرورِ لِتَقْليلِ الاِزْدِحامِ.

A major traffic bridge in Cairo collapsed due to structural failure, isolating a residential area and disrupting traffic flow. Rescue teams responded quickly, initiating bridge reconstruction efforts and rerouting traffic to alleviate congestion.

وَقَعَ اِنْفِجارٌ كَبيرٌ في مِنْطَقَةٍ سَكَنِيَّةٍ بِدُبَيِّ بِسَبَبِ تَسَرُّبٍ لِلْغازِ، مِمّا أَدّى إلى تَلَفٍ كَبيرٍ في البِنْيَةِ التَّحْتِيَّةِ. نَفَّذَتِ السُّلُطاتُ اِسْتِجابَةَ طَوارِئَ سَريعَةً، شَمِلَتْ إصْلاحَ التَّسَرُّبِ وَإجْراءَ تَقْييمٍ شامِلٍ لِلأَضْرارِ.

A large explosion occurred in a residential area in Dubai due to a gas leak, causing significant infrastructure damage. Authorities implemented a rapid emergency response, fixing the leak and conducting a comprehensive damage assessment.

شَهِدَتْ مَدِينَةُ جِدَّةَ انْقِطَاعًا شَامِلًا لِلتَّيَّارِ الكَهْرَبائِيِّ بَعْدَ تَعَطُّلِ مَحَطَّةِ الطَّاقَةِ الرَّئِيسِيَّةِ، مِمَّا أَثَّرَ عَلَى الخِدْمَاتِ وَالأَعْمَالِ. اسْتَجَابَتْ وَزَارَةُ الطَّاقَةِ بِسُرْعَةٍ، حَيْثُ عَزَّزَتْ أَعْمَالَ الصِّيَانَةِ وَأَعَادَتِ الخِدْمَةَ فِي أَقْرَبِ وَقْتٍ مُمْكِنٍ.

Jeddah experienced a widespread power outage after the main power station malfunctioned, affecting services and businesses. The Ministry of Energy responded promptly, enhancing maintenance work and restoring service as soon as possible.

تَسَبَّبَتِ الأَمْطَارُ الغَزِيرَةُ فِي بَيْرُوتَ فِي غَرَقِ عِدَّةِ شَوَارِعَ، بَعْدَ انْسِدادٍ مُفَاجِئٍ فِي الصَّرْفِ الصِّحِّيِّ. عَمِلَتْ فِرَقُ الطَّوَارِئِ عَلَى إِزَالَةِ الِانْسِدادِ وَإِجْرَاءِ تَنْظِيفٍ وَاسِعِ النِّطَاقِ لِلْمَنَاطِقِ المُتَضَرِّرَةِ.

Heavy rains in Beirut flooded several streets, following a sudden blockage in the sewage system. Emergency teams worked on removing the blockage and conducting extensive cleaning of the affected areas.

تَعَرَّضَتْ مِنْطَقَةُ المَارِينَا فِي الإِسْكَنْدَرِيَّةِ لِغَرَقٍ جُزْئِيٍّ بِسَبَبِ فَشَلٍ هَيْكَلِيٍّ فِي المِصَدَّاتِ البَحْرِيَّةِ، مِمَّا أَلْحَقَ ضَرَرًا بِالْمُمْتَلَكَاتِ وَالبِنْيَةِ التَّحْتِيَّةِ. أَعْلَنَتِ الحُكُومَةُ خُطَطًا لِإِعَادَةِ إِعْمَارِ المِنْطَقَةِ وَتَحْسِينِ مَعَايِيرِ السَّلَامَةِ لِتَجَنُّبِ مِثْلِ هَذِهِ الحَوَادِثِ فِي المُسْتَقْبَلِ.

The Marina area in Alexandria partially flooded due to structural failure in the sea barriers, damaging properties and infrastructure. The government announced plans to reconstruct the area and improve safety standards to prevent such incidents in the future.

12.2 Industrial and Workplace Accidents

12.2.1 Manufacturing, Factory, and Construction Site Incidents
Track **61**

to evacuate

• إِخْلَاءٌ

أَخْلَى

بَعْدَ وُقُوعِ الحَادِثِ، أَخْلَتِ السُّلُطَاتُ المَصْنَعَ وَأَجْلَتِ العُمَّالَ لِضَمَانِ سَلَامَتِهِمْ.

After the incident, the authorities evacuated the factory and removed the workers to ensure their safety.

to extinguish

• إِخْمَادٌ

أَخْمَدَ

أَخْمَدَ رِجَالُ الإِطْفَاءِ الحَرِيقَ فِي مَوْقِعِ البِنَاءِ قَبْلَ أَنْ يَتَسَبَّبَ فِي المَزِيدِ مِنَ الأَضْرَارِ.

Firefighters extinguished the fire at the construction site before it could cause more damage.

to injure	• إِصابَةٌ	أَصابَ

أَصابَ انْفِجارٌ مُفاجِئٌ عِدَّةَ عُمّالٍ في مَصْنَعِ الكيماويّاتِ الأُسْبوعَ الماضِيَ.

A sudden explosion injured several workers at the chemical plant last week.

to repair, to fix	• إِصْلاحٌ	أَصْلَحَ

بَعْدَ الحادِثِ، أَصْلَحَتِ الشَّرِكَةُ الآلاتِ التّالِفَةَ لِاسْتِئْنافِ الإِنْتاجِ.

After the incident, the company repaired the damaged machinery in order to resume production.

to be harmed, to be injured	• إِصابَةٌ	أُصيبَ

أُصيبَ العامِلُ بِجُروحٍ طَفيفَةٍ بَعْدَ سُقوطِهِ مِنَ السَّقّالَةِ وَنُقِلَ إلى المُسْتَشْفى.

The worker was injured with minor wounds after falling from the scaffolding and was transported to the hospital.

to close, to shut down	• إِغْلاقٌ	أَغْلَقَ

أَغْلَقَتِ السُّلُطاتُ المَصْنَعَ مُؤَقَّتًا لِلتَّحْقيقِ في مَعاييرِ السَّلامَةِ بَعْدَ الحادِثِ.

Authorities temporarily closed the factory to investigate safety standards following the incident.

to rescue	• إِنْقاذٌ	أَنْقَذَ

أَنْقَذَ الزُّمَلاءُ العامِلَ الَّذي عَلِقَ تَحْتَ الأَنْقاضِ بَعْدَ انْهِيارِ جُزْءٍ مِنَ المَوْقِعِ.

Colleagues rescued the worker who was trapped under the debris after part of the site collapsed.

safety procedure	إِجْراءُ سَلامَةٍ

يَقومُ المُشْرِفونَ بِإِجْراءاتِ السَّلامَةِ بِانْتِظامٍ لِضَمانِ بيئَةِ عَمَلٍ آمِنَةٍ.

Supervisors regularly conduct safety procedures to ensure a safe working environment.

heat stress	إِجْهادٌ حَرارِيٌّ

يُعاني العُمّالُ في الخارِجِ مِنْ إِجْهادٍ حَرارِيٍّ خِلالَ مَوْجاتِ الحَرِّ الشَّديدِ.

Workers outside suffer from heat stress during severe heatwaves.

immediate evacuation

إِخْلاءٌ فَوْرِيٌّ

تَمَّ الإِخْلاءُ الفَوْرِيُّ لِلْمَصْنَعِ بَعْدَ اكْتِشافِ تَسَرُّبِ غازٍ خَطِيرٍ.

The factory was immediately evacuated after detecting a dangerous gas leak.

fatigue

إِرْهاقٌ

يُؤَدِّي إِرْهاقُ العُمّالِ إِلى زِيادَةِ خَطَرِ وُقوعِ حَوادِثَ.

Worker fatigue leads to an increased risk of accidents.

first aid

إِسْعافاتٌ أَوَّلِيَّةٌ

pl.

تُقَدِّمُ مَحَطَّةُ العَمَلِ إِسْعافاتٍ أَوَّلِيَّةً لِأَيِّ مُوَظَّفٍ يُعاني مِنْ إِصاباتٍ طَفيفَةٍ.

The workstation provides first aid to any employee suffering from minor injuries.

injury

إِصابَةٌ

تَحْدُثُ إِصابَةٌ في كُلِّ دَقيقَةٍ داخِلَ المُنْشَآتِ الصِّناعِيَّةِ حَوْلَ العالَمِ.

An injury occurs every minute within industrial facilities worldwide.

physical injury

إِصابَةٌ جَسَدِيَّةٌ

تَعَرَّضَ العامِلُ لِإِصابَةٍ جَسَدِيَّةٍ بِسَبَبِ سُقوطِ مُعَدّاتٍ ثَقيلَةٍ.

The worker sustained a physical injury due to the fall of heavy equipment.

work-related injury

إِصابَةُ عَمَلٍ

كانَتْ إِصابَةُ العَمَلِ ناتِجَةً عَنْ عَدَمِ اسْتِخْدامِ مُعَدّاتِ الحِمايَةِ الشَّخْصِيَّةِ.

The work injury resulted from not using personal protective equipment.

noise-induced injury

إِصابَةٌ ناتِجَةٌ عَنِ الضَّوْضاءِ

يُعاني بَعْضُ العُمّالِ مِنْ إِصاباتٍ ناتِجَةٍ عَنِ الضَّوْضاءِ بِسَبَبِ العَمَلِ المُسْتَمِرِّ بِجانِبِ الآلاتِ الصّاخِبَةِ.

Some workers suffer from noise-induced injuries due to continuous work next to loud machines.

spontaneous combustion

اِحْتِراقٌ ذاتِيٌّ

حَدَثَ الِاحْتِراقُ الذّاتِيُّ لِلْمَوادِّ الكيمْيائِيَّةِ بِسَبَبِ التَّخْزينِ غَيْرِ السَّليمِ.

The spontaneous combustion of chemicals occurred due to improper storage.

to burn (down)

اِحْتَرَقَ • اِحْتِراقٌ

اِحْتَرَقَ المُسْتَوْدَعُ بِالْكامِلِ نَتيجَةً لِلشَّرارَةِ الكَهْرَبائِيَّةِ.

The warehouse burned completely down due to an electrical spark.

> The verb اِحْتَرَقَ means 'to burn' intransitively, indicating that the subject is burning. The transitive form of this verb is أَحْرَقَ, which means 'to burn' something, requiring a direct object.

to suffocate, choke

اِخْتَنَقَ • اِخْتِناقٌ

اِخْتَنَقَ العُمّالُ بِالدُّخانِ بَعْدَ أَنِ اشْتَعَلَتِ النّيرانُ في قِسْمِ الطِّلاءِ.

The workers choked on smoke after a fire broke out in the painting section.

to respond

اِسْتَجابَ • اِسْتِجابَةٌ

اِسْتَجابَتْ فِرَقُ الطَّوارِئِ عَلى الفَوْرِ لِلْإِبْلاغِ عَنْ تَسَرُّبِ الغازِ في المَصْنَعِ.

Emergency teams responded immediately to reports of a gas leak in the factory.

to strike, to collide

اِصْطَدَمَ • اِصْطِدامٌ

اِصْطَدَمَتِ الرّافِعَةُ بِالْجِدارِ بِسَبَبِ خَطَأٍ في التَّوْجيهِ، مِمّا أَدّى إِلى تَلَفٍ كَبيرٍ.

The crane collided with the wall due to a steering error, causing significant damage.

to comply, to adhere

اِلْتَزَمَ • اِلْتِزامٌ

اِلْتَزَمَتِ الشَّرِكَةُ بِأَعْلى مَعاييرِ الأَمانِ لِحِمايَةِ عُمّالِها.

The company adhered to the highest safety standards to protect its workers.

to slip

اِنْزَلَقَ • اِنْزِلاقٌ

اِنْزَلَقَ العامِلُ عَلى الأَرْضِيَّةِ المُبَلَّلَةِ وَأُصيبَ بِكُسورٍ.

The worker slipped on the wet floor and suffered fractures.

انْفِجارٌ

explosion

وَقَعَ انْفِجارٌ في القِسْمِ الشَّماليِّ مِنَ المَصْنَعِ، مِمّا تَسَبَّبَ في إصاباتٍ مُتَعَدِّدَةٍ.

An explosion occurred in the northern section of the factory, causing multiple injuries.

انْفِجارٌ كيمْيائيٌّ

chemical explosion

تَسَبَّبَ الانْفِجارُ الكيمْيائيُّ في الوَرْشَةِ في إجْلاءِ العُمّالِ.

The chemical explosion in the workshop led to the evacuation of workers.

انْفَجَرَ • انْفِجارٌ

to explode

انْفَجَرَتِ الإسْطوانَةُ بِسَبَبِ الضَّغْطِ الزّائِدِ، مِمّا أَدّى إلى تَحَطُّمِ النَّوافِذِ.

The cylinder exploded due to excessive pressure, shattering the windows.

انْهارَ • انْهِيارٌ

to collapse

انْهارَ جُزْءٌ مِنَ المَبْنى بَعْدَ إزالَةِ دِعاماتِ الدَّعْمِ بِشَكْلٍ غَيْرِ صَحيحٍ.

Part of the building collapsed after the support beams were incorrectly removed.

انْهِيارٌ جُزْئيٌّ

partial collapse

حَدَثَ انْهِيارٌ جُزْئيٌّ في المُسْتَوْدَعِ بِسَبَبِ تَخْزينِ البَضائِعِ بِشَكْلٍ غَيْرِ مُتَوازِنٍ.

A partial collapse occurred in the warehouse due to unbalanced storage of goods.

انْهِيارُ سَقْفِ مَصْنَعٍ

factory roof collapse

بَعْدَ انْهِيارِ سَقْفِ المَصْنَعِ، اسْتَجابَتْ فِرَقُ الطَّوارِئِ بِسُرْعَةٍ لِضَمانِ سَلامَةِ العُمّالِ.

After the factory roof collapse, emergency teams responded quickly to ensure worker safety.

تَأْهيلٌ

rehabilitation

بَدَأَتِ الشَّرِكَةُ في تَأْهيلِ المَوْقِعِ بَعْدَ الحادِثِ لِاسْتِئْنافِ العَمَلِ.

The company began rehabilitating the site after the incident to resume work.

to avoid • تَجَنَّبْ — تَجَنَّبَ

تَجَنَّبَ العُمَّالُ الإِصاباتِ الخَطيرَةَ بِفَضْلِ التَّدريبِ المُسْتَمِرِّ عَلى السَّلامَةِ.

The workers avoided serious injuries thanks to ongoing safety training.

warning — تَحْذيرٌ

أَصْدَرَتِ الإِدارَةُ تَحْذيرًا لِجَميعِ العامِلينَ بَعْدَ اكْتِشافِ مَخاطِرِ الأَمانِ.

The management issued a warning to all employees after discovering safety hazards.

accident investigation — تَحْقيقٌ في حادِثَةٍ

بَدَأَتِ الإِدارَةُ تَحْقيقًا في حادِثَةِ الاِنْهِيارِ لِمَعْرِفَةِ الأَسْبابِ وَتَحْديدِ المَسْؤوليّاتِ.

The management started an investigation into the collapse incident to determine the causes and responsibilities.

hazard control — تَحَكُّمٌ في المَخاطِرِ

يَتَطَلَّبُ التَّحَكُّمُ في المَخاطِرِ تَحْديثَ البُروتوكولاتِ وَتَحْسينَ إِجْراءاتِ السَّلامَةِ.

Risk control requires updating protocols and improving safety procedures.

safety training — تَدْريبٌ عَلى السَّلامَة

يَجِبُ أَنْ يَخْضَعَ جَميعُ العُمَّالِ لِلتَّدريبِ عَلى السَّلامَةِ قَبْلَ بَدْءِ العَمَلِ في المَوْقِعِ.

All workers must undergo safety training before starting work at the site.

to cause • تَسَبَّبْ — تَسَبَّبَ في

تَسَبَّبَ الإِهْمالُ في صِيانَةِ المُعَدَّاتِ في وُقوعِ عِدَّةِ حَوادِثَ في المَصْنَعِ.

Neglect in equipment maintenance caused several accidents at the factory.

to leak • تَسَرَّبْ — تَسَرَّبَ

تَسَرَّبَ الغازُ السّامُّ مِنَ الخَزّانِ في المَصْنَعِ، مِمّا تَسَبَّبَ في إِخْلاءٍ عاجِلٍ.

Toxic gas leaked from the tank in the factory, causing an urgent evacuation.

gas leak

تَسَرُّبُ غازٍ

تَسَبَّبَ تَسَرُّبُ غازِ الأُمونْيا في إِخْلاءِ الطّابَقِ السُّفْليِّ مِنَ المَصْنَعِ.

An ammonia gas leak caused the evacuation of the factory's lower floor.

poisoning

تَسَمُّمٌ

أَدّى تَسَمُّمٌ غِذائيٌّ في كافِتيرِيا المَصْنَعِ إلى مَرَضِ عَشَراتِ العُمّالِ.

Food poisoning in the factory cafeteria led to the illness of dozens of workers.

work permit

تَصْريحُ عَمَلٍ • تَصْريحاتٌ / تَصاريحُ

لا يُسْمَحُ بِبَدْءِ الأَعْمالِ الخَطِرَة دونَ تَصْريحِ عَمَلٍ مُعْتَمَدٍ.

No dangerous work is allowed to start without an approved work permit.

to trip

تَعَثَّرَ • تَعَثُّرٌ

تَعَثَّرَ أَحَدُ العُمّالِ عَلى الأَرْضِيَّةِ غَيْرِ المُسْتَوِيةِ وَأُصيبَ بِكَسْرٍ في السّاقِ.

One of the workers tripped on the uneven floor and suffered a leg fracture.

to be subjected to; be exposed to

تَعَرَّضَ لِـ • تَعَرُّضٌ

تَعَرَّضَ المَوْقِعُ لِفَحْصٍ شامِلٍ بَعْدَ الإِبْلاغِ عَنْ مُخالَفاتِ الأَمانِ.

The site was subjected to a thorough inspection after reports of safety violations.

to be exposed to radiation

تَعَرَّضَ لِإِشْعاعٍ • تَعَرُّضٌ

تَعَرَّضَ العالِمُ لِإِشْعاعٍ بِسَبَبِ تَسَرُّبٍ مِنَ المُعَدّاتِ الطِّبِّيَّةِ في المُخْتَبَرِ.

The scientist was exposed to radiation due to a leak from medical equipment in the laboratory.

toxic exposure

تَعَرُّضٌ لِسُمومٍ

نُقِلَ العُمّالُ إلى المُسْتَشْفى بِسَبَبِ التَّعَرُّضِ المُحْتَمَلِ لِسُمومٍ بَعْدَ الحادِثِ في المُخْتَبَرِ.

Workers were transported to the hospital due to potential toxic exposure following the incident in the laboratory.

تَعَطَّلَ · تَعَطُّلٌ

to break down, to malfunction

تَعَطَّلَ النِّظامُ الهَيْدروليكيُّ أَثْناءَ الوَرْدِيَّةِ اللَّيْلِيَّةِ، مِمّا أَدّى إلى تَأْخيرِ الإِنْتاجِ.

The hydraulic system malfunctioned during the night shift, leading to production delays.

تَقْريرُ حادِثٍ · تَقاريرُ

accident report

أَعَدَّ المُشْرِفُ تَقْريرَ حادِثٍ مُفَصَّلًا بَعْدَ وُقوعِ الحادِثِ في المُسْتَوْدَعِ.

The supervisor prepared a detailed accident report following the incident in the warehouse.

تَقْييمُ مَخاطِرَ

risk assessment

يَجِبُ أَنْ يَشْمَلَ تَقْييمُ المَخاطِرِ الخاصُّ بِالمَصْنَعِ جَميعَ الآلاتِ والمَوادِّ الكيمْيائِيَّةِ المُسْتَخْدَمَةِ.

The factory's risk assessment must include all machinery and chemicals used.

تَهْوِيَةٌ

ventilation

تَمَّ تَحْسينُ تَهْوِيَةِ المَصْنَعِ لِتَقْليلِ خَطَرِ التَّعَرُّضِ لِلْمَوادِّ الضّارَّةِ.

The factory's ventilation was improved to reduce the risk of exposure to harmful substances.

جُرِحَ · جُرْحٌ

to be injured

جُرِحَ العامِلُ في يَدِهِ أَثْناءَ تَشْغيلِ الماكينَةِ بِدونِ حِمايَةٍ كافِيَةٍ.

The worker was injured in his hand while operating the machine without adequate protection.

جُرْحٌ قَطْعِيٌّ

laceration

أَسْفَرَ الحادِثُ عَنْ جُرْحٍ قَطْعِيٍّ عَميقٍ في ذِراعِ العامِلِ.

The incident resulted in a deep laceration in the worker's arm.

جِسْمٌ ساقِطٌ · أَجْسامٌ

falling object

تَسَبَّبَ جِسْمٌ ساقِطٌ مِنَ الرّافِعَةِ في إِصابَةِ اثْنَيْنِ مِنَ العُمّالِ.

A falling object from the crane injured two workers.

حادِثٌ تَشْغيليٌّ

operational accident • حَوادِثُ

وَقَعَ حادِثٌ تَشْغيليٌّ عِنْدَما فَشِلَ نِظامُ الأمانِ في إيقافِ الماكينَةِ.

An operational accident occurred when the safety system failed to stop the machine.

> The word حادِثٌ refers to an 'incident, occurance, happening' and can be either good or bad. However, حادِثَةٌ specifically denotes a bad incident or an accident. Therefore, while every حادِثَةٌ is a حادِثٌ, not every حادِثٌ is a حادِثَةٌ. When referring to a bad incident or an accident, these terms can be used interchangeably.

حادِثَةُ آلاتٍ

machinery accident

أَدَّتْ حادِثَةُ الآلاتِ تِلْكَ إلى تَوَقُّفِ الإنتاجِ لِعِدَّةِ ساعاتٍ.

That machinery incident led to several hours of production downtime.

حَذَّرَ

to warn • تَحْذيرٌ

حَذَّرَ مُفَتِّشُ السَّلامَةِ العُمّالَ مِنْ مَخاطِرِ اسْتِخْدامِ المُعَدّاتِ دونَ حِمايَةٍ كافِيَةٍ.

The safety inspector warned the workers of the risks of using equipment without adequate protection.

حَريقٌ

fire • حَرائِقُ

انْدَلَعَ حَريقٌ في القِسْمِ الكَهْرَبائيِّ وَتَمَّتِ السَّيْطَرَةُ عَلَيْهِ بِسُرْعَةٍ.

A fire broke out in the electrical section and was quickly controlled.

حَريقُ مَصْنَعٍ

factory fire

تَسَبَّبَ حَريقُ مَصْنَعِ النَّسيجِ في خَسائِرَ مادِّيَّةٍ هائِلَةٍ وَتَوَقُّفِ العَمَلِ لِأسابيعَ.

The textile factory fire caused massive material losses and work stoppage for weeks.

حَقَّقَ

to investigate, look into • تَحْقيقٌ

حَقَّقَ المُحَقِّقونَ في أسْبابِ حَريقِ المَصْنَعِ لِتَحْديدِ ما إذا كانَ هُناكَ إهْمالٌ.

Investigators looked into the causes of the factory fire to determine if there was any negligence.

to protect	حِمايَةٌ •	حَمى

يَحْمي النِّظامُ الأوتوماتيكيُّ العُمّالَ مِنَ الإصاباتِ بِفَصْلِ الآلَةِ تِلْقائِيًّا عِنْدَ اسْتِشْعارِ الخَطَرِ.

The automatic system protects workers from injuries by automatically shutting down the machine when danger is detected.

to monitor, to observe	رَصْدٌ •	رَصَدَ

رَصَدَ مُديرُ السَّلامَةِ مُسْتَوَياتِ الغازِ في المَصْنَعِ باسْتِمْرارٍ لِتَجَنُّبِ الحَوادِثِ.

The safety manager continuously monitored gas levels in the factory to avoid accidents.

to fall	سُقوطٌ •	سَقَطَ

سَقَطَ صُنْدوقُ أَدَواتٍ مِنَ الرَّفِّ مِمّا تَسَبَّبَ في إصاباتٍ طَفيفَةٍ.

A toolbox fell from the shelf, causing minor injuries.

to fall from a height	سُقوطٌ •	سَقَطَ مِنَ ارْتِفاعٍ

سَقَطَ العامِلُ مِنَ ارْتِفاعِ عَشَرَةِ أَمْتارٍ أَثْناءَ تَرْكيبِ الهَيْكَلِ الخارِجِيِّ لِلْمَبْنى.

The worker fell from a height of ten meters while installing the building's exterior structure.

to control, to manage	سَيْطَرَةٌ •	سَيْطَرَ

سَيْطَرَتْ فِرَقُ الإطْفاءِ عَلى حَريقِ المَصْنَعِ قَبْلَ انْتِشارِهِ إلى المَناطِقِ المُجاوِرَةِ.

The firefighting teams controlled the factory fire before it spread to adjacent areas.

to isolate, to quarantine	عَزْلٌ •	عَزَلَ

عَزَلَ الفَنِّيّونَ المِنْطَقَةَ المُتَضَرِّرَةَ لِمَنْعِ انْتِشارِ التَّلَوُّثِ الكيمْيائِيِّ.

Technicians isolated the affected area to prevent the spread of chemical contamination.

to inspect, to examine	فَحْصٌ •	فَحَصَ

فَحَصَ الفَريقُ الفَنِّيُّ المُعَدّاتِ بَعْدَ تَلَقّي تَقاريرَ عَنْ أَعْطالٍ مُحْتَمَلَةٍ.

The technical team inspected the equipment after receiving reports of potential malfunctions.

فَحْصٌ دَوْرِيٌّ • فُحوصٌ

regular inspection

يُجْرى الفَحْصُ الدَّوْرِيُّ لِضَمانِ عَدَمِ وُجودِ تَسَرُّبِ غازٍ أَوْ مَوادَّ خَطِرَةٍ.

Periodic inspections are conducted to ensure there are no gas leaks or hazardous materials.

فِقْدانُ سَمْعٍ

hearing loss

عانى بَعْضُ العُمّالِ مِنْ فِقْدانِ السَّمْعِ بِسَبَبِ التَّعَرُّضِ المُسْتَمِرِّ لِمُسْتَوى عالٍ مِنَ الضَّوْضاءِ.

Some workers suffered from hearing loss due to continuous exposure to high noise levels.

قاعِدَةُ سَلامَةٍ • قَواعِدُ

safety rule

إنَّ قاعِدَةَ السَّلامَةِ الخاصَّةَ بِارْتِداءِ الخَوْذاتِ داخِلَ المَصْنَعِ غَيْرُ قابِلَةٍ لِلتَّفاوُضِ.

The safety rule of wearing helmets inside the factory is non-negotiable.

قَيَّمَ • تَقْييمٌ

to assess, to evaluate

قَيَّمَتِ اللَّجْنَةُ الأَضْرارَ بَعْدَ الحَريقِ لِتَحْديدِ تَكْلِفَةِ الإِصْلاحاتِ.

The committee assessed the damage after the fire to determine the cost of repairs.

مُعَدّاتُ حِمايَةٍ شَخْصِيَّةٍ pl.

personal protective equipment (PPE)

يُطْلَبُ مِنْ جَميعِ العُمّالِ ارْتِداءُ مُعَدّاتِ حِمايَةٍ شَخْصِيَّةٍ أَثْناءَ العَمَلِ.

All workers are required to wear personal protective equipment while working.

نَبَّهَ • تَنْبيهٌ

to alert, to notify

نَبَّهَ المُوَظَّفونَ الإِدارَةَ عَلى الفَوْرِ بَعْدَ اكْتِشافِ خَلَلٍ في نِظامِ الأَمانِ.

The employees immediately alerted the management after discovering a fault in the safety system.

وِقايَةٌ مِنَ الحَريقِ

fire prevention

يَجِبُ تَنْفيذُ تَدابيرِ الوِقايَةِ مِنَ الحَريقِ في جَميعِ أَنْحاءِ المُنْشَأَةِ.

Fire prevention measures must be implemented throughout the facility.

وُقوعُ حادِثٍ

أَدّى وُقوعُ حادِثٍ في قِسْمِ الطِّلاءِ إلى إيقافِ العَمَلِ لِعِدَّةِ ساعاتٍ.

An accident in the painting department led to work being stopped for several hours.

12.2.1.1 Mini-Articles

Track **62**

أَخْلَتِ السُّلُطاتُ مَصْنَعًا في الجَزائِرِ بَعْدَ وُقوعِ انْفِجارٍ كيميائيٍّ مُدَوٍّ. أُصيبَ عِدَّةُ عُمّالٍ بِإصاباتٍ جَسَدِيَّةٍ نَتيجَةَ الحادِثَةِ، وَسارَعَتْ فِرَقُ الإسْعافِ بِتَقْديمِ الإسْعافاتِ الأَوَّليَّةِ وَإخْمادِ الحَريقِ. أُغْلِقَ المَصْنَعُ لِإجْراءِ تَحْقيقاتٍ شامِلَةٍ وَتَقْييمِ المَخاطِرِ.

Authorities evacuated a factory in Algeria after a loud chemical explosion occurred. Several workers were injured in the incident, and emergency response teams quickly provided first aid and extinguished the fire. The factory was closed for comprehensive investigations and risk assessment.

سَقَطَ عامِلٌ مِنَ ارْتِفاعٍ في مَوْقِعِ بِناءٍ بِدُبَيَّ، مِمّا تَسَبَّبَ في إصاباتٍ جَسَدِيَّةٍ خَطيرَةٍ. تَمَّ إجْراءُ إخْلاءٍ فَوْريٍّ لِلْمَوْقِعِ واسْتِدْعاءُ فِرَقِ الإسْعافِ لِتَقْديمِ العِلاجِ اللّازِمِ. هَذا وَتُحَقِّقُ السُّلُطاتُ في إجْراءاتِ السَّلامَةِ المُتَّبَعَةِ والتِزامِ الشَّرِكَةِ بِقَواعِدِ العَمَلِ.

A worker fell from a height at a construction site in Dubai, resulting in serious physical injuries. An immediate evacuation of the site was conducted, and ambulance crews were called to provide necessary treatment. Authorities are investigating the safety procedures followed and the company's compliance with work regulations.

احْتَرَقَ مَصْنَعٌ في القاهِرَةِ بِسَبَبِ تَسَرُّبِ غازٍ، مِمّا اسْتَدْعى عَمَلِيَّةَ إجْلاءٍ لِلْعُمّالِ وَإغْلاقَ المَصْنَعِ. تَحَكَّمَتْ فِرَقُ الإطْفاءِ في الحَريقِ وَأَخْمَدَتِ النّيرانَ بِفَعاليَّةٍ. أُنْقِذَ العُمّالُ وَلَمْ تَقَعْ إصاباتٌ خَطيرَةٌ.

A factory in Cairo caught fire due to a gas leak, prompting an evacuation of the workers and closure of the factory. Firefighting teams controlled and effectively extinguished the fire. The workers were rescued, and no serious injuries occurred.

انْهارَ سَقْفُ مَصْنَعٍ في المَغْرِبِ، مِمّا أَدّى إلى إصاباتٍ بَيْنَ العُمّالِ وَتَعَطُّلِ العَمَليّاتِ. فَحَصَتِ السُّلُطاتُ الهَيْكَلَ المُنْهارَ وَكَشَفَتْ عَنْ فَشَلٍ هَيْكَليٍّ، مِمّا أَدّى إلى تَحْذيراتٍ بِشَأْنِ البُنى التَّحْتيَّةِ المُماثِلَةِ.

A factory roof in Morocco collapsed, causing injuries among the workers and disrupting operations. Authorities examined the collapsed structure and revealed a structural failure, leading to warnings about similar infrastructures.

تَصَادَمَتْ آلَاتٌ فِي مَصْنَعٍ لِتَصْنِيعِ السَّيَّارَاتِ بِالسُّعُودِيَّةِ، مِمَّا تَسَبَّبَ فِي حَادِثٍ تَشْغِيلِيٍّ خَطِيرٍ. أَصْلَحَ الفَنِّيُّونَ الأَضْرَارَ وَأُعِيدَ تَدْرِيبُ العُمَّالِ عَلَى إِجْرَاءَاتِ السَّلَامَةِ لِتَجَنُّبِ حَوَادِثَ مُمَاثِلَةٍ.

Machinery collided in a car manufacturing plant in Saudi Arabia, causing a serious operational accident. Technicians repaired the damage, and workers were retrained on safety procedures to prevent similar accidents.

أُصِيبَ عِدَّةُ عُمَّالٍ بِإِجْهَادٍ حَرَارِيٍّ فِي مَوْقِعِ بِنَاءٍ بِقَطَرَ بِسَبَبِ الظُّرُوفِ الجَوِّيَّةِ القَاسِيَةِ. اِسْتَجَابَتْ فِرَقُ الإِسْعَافِ بِتَقْدِيمِ العِلَاجِ اللَّازِمِ وَنَبَّهَتْ إِلَى أَهَمِّيَّةِ تَوْفِيرِ تَهْوِيَةٍ كَافِيَةٍ وَمُعَدَّاتِ وِقَايَةٍ لِلْعُمَّالِ.

Several workers suffered from heat stress at a construction site in Qatar due to harsh weather conditions. Emergency teams responded by providing necessary treatment and emphasized the importance of adequate ventilation and protective equipment for the workers.

12.2.1.2 Fictional Article: Factory Explosion in Saudi Arabia

Track **63**

اِنْفِجَارٌ كِيمْيَائِيٌّ مُدَمِّرٌ فِي مَصْنَعٍ بِالْمَمْلَكَةِ العَرَبِيَّةِ السُّعُودِيَّةِ

فِي حَادِثٍ مَأْسَاوِيٍّ شَهِدَهُ مَصْنَعُ كِيمَاوِيَّاتٍ بِالْقُرْبِ مِنَ الرِّيَاضِ، أَسْفَرَ انْفِجَارٌ كِيمْيَائِيٌّ عَنْ إِصَابَاتٍ بَالِغَةٍ وَأَضْرَارٍ جَسِيمَةٍ بِالْمُنْشَأَةِ. الحَادِثُ، الَّذِي وَقَعَ صَبَاحَ الأَرْبِعَاءِ، أَدَّى إِلَى الإِجْلَاءِ الفَوْرِيِّ لِلْعُمَّالِ وَإِغْلَاقِ المِنْطَقَةِ المُحِيطَةِ.

صَرَّحَ عَبْدُ اللهِ النَّجَّارُ، الخَبِيرُ فِي السَّلَامَةِ الصِّنَاعِيَّةِ قَائِلًا: "نَجَمَ الانْفِجَارُ عَنْ تَسَرُّبٍ غَازِيٍّ تَفَاعَلَ مَعَ مَوَادَّ كِيمْيَائِيَّةٍ مُتَوَاجِدَةٍ بِالْمَصْنَعِ، مِمَّا أَدَّى إِلَى تَفَاعُلٍ سَرِيعٍ وَخَطِيرٍ." وَأَضَافَ أَنَّ "التَّحْقِيقَاتِ الأَوَّلِيَّةَ تُشِيرُ إِلَى احْتِمَالِ وُجُودِ تَقْصِيرٍ فِي تَطْبِيقِ إِجْرَاءَاتِ السَّلَامَةِ."

تَمَّ اسْتِدْعَاءُ فِرَقِ الإِسْعَافَاتِ الأَوَّلِيَّةِ لِمُعَالَجَةِ الجَرْحَى عَلَى الفَوْرِ، حَيْثُ أُصِيبَ عِدَّةُ عُمَّالٍ بِحَالَاتِ اخْتِنَاقٍ نَتِيجَةَ التَّعَرُّضِ لِلدُّخَانِ الكَثِيفِ. سَيْطَرَتْ فِرَقُ الإِطْفَاءِ عَلَى الحَرِيقِ الَّذِي نَشِبَ بَعْدَ الانْفِجَارِ، مُسْتَخْدِمَةً مُعَدَّاتِ حِمَايَةٍ شَخْصِيَّةٍ لِتَجَنُّبِ التَّعَرُّضِ لِلسُّمُومِ.

د. سَلْمَى حُسَيْن، الأَخِصَّائِيَّةُ فِي السُّمُومِ الصِّنَاعِيَّةِ، نَبَّهَتْ إِلَى أَنَّ "العُمَّالَ المُتَوَاجِدِينَ فِي وَقْتِ الحَادِثِ قَدْ يُعَانُونَ مِنْ تَأْثِيرَاتٍ صِحِّيَّةٍ طَوِيلَةِ الأَمَدِ، بِمَا فِي ذَلِكَ فِقْدَانُ السَّمْعِ وَالتَّسَمُّمُ بِسَبَبِ اسْتِنْشَاقِ الغَازَاتِ السَّامَّةِ."

فَتَحَتِ السُّلْطَاتُ تَحْقِيقًا شَامِلًا فِي مُلَابَسَاتِ الحَادِثِ، مَعَ التَّرْكِيزِ عَلَى تَقْيِيمِ مَخَاطِرِ المَوَادِّ الكِيمْيَائِيَّةِ المُسْتَخْدَمَةِ وَتَحْدِيدِ مَدَى الْتِزَامِ المَصْنَعِ بِقَوَاعِدِ السَّلَامَةِ وَالتَّهْوِيَةِ الكَافِيَةِ لِمَنْعِ تَكْرَارِ مِثْلِ هَذِهِ الحَوَادِثِ.

A devastating chemical explosion at a factory in Saudi Arabia

In a tragic incident at a chemical plant near Riyadh, a chemical explosion resulted in severe injuries and extensive damage to the facility. The accident, which occurred on Wednesday morning, led to the immediate evacuation of workers and the closure of the surrounding area.

Abdullah Al-Najjar, an expert in industrial safety, stated, "The explosion was caused by a gas leak that interacted with chemicals present in the factory, leading to a rapid and dangerous reaction." He added that "preliminary investigations indicate a possible negligence in applying safety procedures."

First aid teams were called to treat the injured immediately, with several workers suffering from suffocation due to exposure to dense smoke. Firefighting teams controlled the fire that erupted following the explosion, using personal protective equipment to avoid exposure to toxins.

Dr. Salma Hussein, a specialist in industrial toxins, warned that "workers present at the time of the incident may suffer from long-term health effects, including hearing loss and poisoning due to inhaling toxic gases."

Authorities have launched a comprehensive investigation into the circumstances of the incident, focusing on assessing the risks of the chemicals used and determining the factory's compliance with safety and adequate ventilation rules to prevent such incidents from recurring.

12.2.2 Mining and Extraction Accidents

Track **64**

heat stress

إِجْهادٌ حَرارِيٌّ

تَسَبَّبَ الإِجْهادُ الحَرارِيُّ في انْهِيارِ عِدَّةِ عُمّالٍ خِلالَ الوَرْدِيَّةِ الصَّيْفِيَّةِ في المَنْجَمِ.

Heat stress caused several miners to collapse during the summer shift in the mine.

mine rescue

إِنْقاذٌ في مَنْجَمٍ

نَجَحَتْ عَمَلِيَّةُ الإِنْقاذِ في المَنْجَمِ في اسْتِخْراجِ العُمّالِ المُحاصَرينَ بَعْدَ الإِنْهِيارِ.

The mine rescue operation successfully extracted trapped workers after the collapse.

suffocation

اِخْتِناقٌ

تَسَبَّبَ اخْتِناقٌ داخِلَ المَنْجَمِ في وَفاةِ عامِلٍ بِسَبَبِ نَقْصٍ في الأُكْسُجينِ.

Choking inside the mine led to a worker's death due to a lack of oxygen.

gas explosion

انْفِجارُ غازٍ

وَقَعَ انْفِجارُ غازٍ مُدَمِّرٌ مِمّا أَدّى إلى تَوَقُّفِ الإنْتاجِ وَإجْلاءِ العُمّالِ.

A devastating gas explosion occurred, leading to production halt and workers' evacuation.

coal dust explosion

انْفِجارُ غُبارٍ فَحْمِيٍّ

تَسَبَّبَ انْفِجارُ غُبارٍ فَحْمِيٍّ في تَدْميرٍ كَبيرٍ في جُزْءٍ مِنَ المَنْجَمِ.

A coal dust explosion caused significant destruction in part of the mine.

ventilation cutoff

انْقِطاعُ تَهْوِيَةٍ

أَدّى انْقِطاعُ التَّهْوِيَةِ داخِلَ المَنْجَمِ إلى تَدَهْوُرٍ سَريعٍ لِجَوْدَةِ الهَواءِ.

The interruption of ventilation inside the mine led to a rapid deterioration in air quality.

landslide

انْهِيارٌ أَرْضِيٌّ

حَدَثَ انْهِيارٌ أَرْضِيٌّ قُرْبَ المَنْجَمِ، مِمّا أَثَّرَ عَلى طُرُقِ الوُصولِ والإمْدادِ.

A landslide occurred near the mine, affecting access and supply routes.

rockfall

انْهِيارُ صُخورٍ

تَسَبَّبَ انْهِيارُ صُخورٍ في إصاباتٍ خَطيرَةٍ بَيْنَ عُمّالِ المَنْجَمِ.

A rockfall caused serious injuries among the miners.

mine collapse

انْهِيارُ مَنْجَمٍ

شَهِدَ المَنْجَمُ انْهِيارًا مُرَوِّعًا أَدّى إلى عَمَلِيّاتِ بَحْثٍ وَإنْقاذٍ مُكَثَّفَةٍ.

The mine experienced a horrific collapse, leading to extensive search and rescue operations.

underground

تَحْتَ الأَرْضِ

يُواجِهُ العُمّالُ تَحَدِّياتٍ خَطيرَةً عِنْدَ العَمَلِ تَحْتَ الأَرْضِ بِسَبَبِ ظُروفِ العَمَلِ الصَّعْبَةِ.

Workers face serious challenges when working underground due to difficult working conditions.

tunnel water leakage

تَسَرُّبُ مِياهِ نَفَقٍ

تَسَبَّبَ تَسَرُّبُ مِياهٍ في النَّفَقِ بِتَعْطيلِ العَمَلِيّاتِ اليَوْمِيَّةِ لِلْمَنْجَمِ.

Water leakage in the tunnel disrupted the daily operations of the mine.

metal poisoning

تَسَمُّمٌ بِالْمَعادِنِ

عانى بَعْضُ العُمّالِ مِنْ تَسَمُّمٍ بِالْمَعادِنِ نَتيجَةَ التَّعَرُّضِ المُسْتَمِرِّ لِلْمَوادِّ الخَطِرَةِ.

Some workers suffered from metal poisoning due to continuous exposure to hazardous materials.

radiation exposure

تَعَرُّضٌ لِإِشْعاعٍ

تَعَرَّضَ العُمّالُ لِلْإِشْعاعِ بِسَبَبِ عَدَمِ كِفايَةِ التَّدابيرِ الوِقائِيَّةِ في المَنْجَمِ.

Workers were exposed to radiation due to inadequate protective measures in the mine.

dust exposure

تَعَرُّضٌ لِغُبارٍ

تَعَرُّضُ العُمّالِ لِلْغُبارِ بِشَكْلٍ مُسْتَمِرٍّ يَزيدُ مِنْ خَطَرِ الإِصابَةِ بِأَمْراضٍ تَنَفُّسِيَّةٍ.

Workers constantly exposed to dust are at an increased risk of respiratory diseases.

underground fire

حَريقٌ تَحْتَ الأَرْضِ • حَرائِقُ

اِنْدَلَعَ حَريقٌ تَحْتَ الأَرْضِ، مِمّا تَسَبَّبَ في إِخْلاءٍ عاجِلٍ لِلْمَنْجَمِ.

An underground fire broke out, causing an urgent evacuation of the mine.

psychological trauma

صَدْمَةٌ نَفْسِيَّةٌ

يُعاني العَديدُ مِنَ العُمّالِ مِنْ صَدْمَةٍ نَفْسِيَّةٍ بَعْدَ النَّجاةِ مِنَ انْهِيارِ مَنْجَمٍ.

Many workers suffer from psychological shock after surviving a mine collapse.

trapped

عالِقٌ

بَقِيَ عُمّالُ الإِنْقاذِ في سِباقٍ مَعَ الزَّمَنِ لِتَحْريرِ العُمّالِ العالِقينَ بَعْدَ الاِنْهِيارِ.

Rescue workers raced against time to free workers trapped after the collapse.

عامِلٌ مَفْقودٌ • عُمَّالٌ

missing worker

بَدَأَتْ عَمَلِيَّةُ البَحْثِ عَنِ العامِلِ المَفْقودِ فَوْرًا بَعْدَ الإبْلاغِ عَنْ فِقْدانِهِ تَحْتَ الأَرْضِ.

The search for the missing worker began immediately after he was reported lost underground.

غَرَقُ مَنْجَمٍ

mine flooding

تَسَبَّبَ انْهِيارٌ داخِلِيٌّ في غَرَقِ مَنْجَمٍ، وَأَدّى إلى فِقْدانِ مُعَدّاتٍ ثَمينَةٍ.

An internal collapse caused a mine to flood, resulting in the loss of valuable equipment.

فِقْدانُ سَمْعٍ

hearing loss

يُواجِهُ عُمّالُ المَناجِمِ خَطَرَ فِقْدانِ السَّمْعِ بِسَبَبِ الضَّوْضاءِ المُسْتَمِرَّةِ.

Mine workers face the risk of hearing loss due to constant noise.

فَيَضانٌ تَحْتَ الأَرْضِ

underground flooding

حَدَثَ فَيَضانٌ تَحْتَ الأَرْضِ بَعْدَ اخْتِراقِ المِياهِ لِلْجُدْرانِ الحاجِزَةِ لِلْمَنْجَمِ.

An underground flood occurred after water breached the mine's barrier walls.

مَرَضُ الرِّئَةِ السَّوْداءِ • أَمْراضٌ

black lung disease

يَرْتَبِطُ مَرَضُ الرِّئَةِ السَّوْداءِ بِشَكْلٍ مُباشِرٍ بِالْعَمَلِ طَويلِ الأَمَدِ في مَناجِمِ الفَحْمِ.

Black lung disease is directly associated with long-term work in coal mines.

مَرَضٌ رِئَوِيٌّ • أَمْراضٌ

pulmonary disease

يَزْدادُ خَطَرُ الإصابَةِ بِالْمَرَضِ الرِّئَوِيِّ بَيْنَ العُمّالِ نَتيجَةً لِتَعَرُّضِهِمْ لِلْغُبارِ وَالمَوادِّ الكيميائِيَّةِ.

The risk of pulmonary disease increases among workers due to exposure to dust and chemicals.

مَنْجَمٌ • مَناجِمُ

mine

تَمَّ افْتِتاحُ المَنْجَمِ الجَديدِ بِالرَّغْمِ مِنَ المَخاوِفِ المُتَعَلِّقَةِ بِالسَّلامَةِ وَالبيئَةِ.

The new mine was opened despite concerns related to safety and the environment.

وَقَعَ انْفِجارُ غازٍ قَوِيٌّ في مَنْجَمِ فَحْمٍ بِجَنوبِ المَغْرِبِ، مِمّا أَدّى إلى انْهِيارٍ جُزْئِيٍّ لِلْمَنْجَمِ واحْتِجازِ عِدَّةِ عُمّالٍ تَحْتَ الأَرْضِ. اسْتَجابَتْ فِرَقُ الإنْقاذِ سَريعًا، وَنُقِلَ العُمّالُ المُصابونَ إلى المُسْتَشْفى لِعِلاجِ إصاباتِهِمُ النّاتِجَةِ عَنِ الإنْفِجارِ وَالاخْتِناقِ.

A powerful gas explosion occurred in a coal mine in southern Morocco, resulting in a partial collapse of the mine and trapping several workers underground. Rescue teams responded quickly, and the injured workers were transported to the hospital for treatment of their injuries from the explosion and suffocation.

تَسَبَّبَ فَيَضانٌ مُفاجِئٌ في إغْلاقِ مَنْجَمِ ذَهَبٍ كَبيرٍ في السّودانِ. المِياهُ الغَزيرَةُ الَّتي تَسَرَّبَتْ إلى الأَنْفاقِ أَدَّتْ إلى غَرَقِ المَنْجَمِ وَفِقْدانِ عامِلٍ، مِمّا أَثارَ عَمَلِيَّةَ إنْقاذٍ مُكَثَّفَةٍ. قالَ خَبيرٌ في التَّعْدينِ: "الحاجَةُ ماسَّةٌ لِتَحْسينِ تَدابيرِ السَّلامَةِ في المَناجِمِ لِمُواجَهَةِ هَذِهِ الكَوارِثِ."

A sudden flood closed a large gold mine in Sudan. The floodwaters that leaked into the tunnels caused the mine to flood and a worker to go missing, triggering an intensive rescue operation. A mining expert stated, "There is an urgent need to improve safety measures in mines to address these disasters."

تَعَرَّضَ مَنْجَمٌ لِلنُّحاسِ في عُمانَ لانْهِيارٍ أَرْضِيٍّ كَبيرٍ، مِمّا تَسَبَّبَ في تَوَقُّفِ الإنْتاجِ وَإصابَةِ العَديدِ مِنَ العُمّالِ. أَغْلَقَتِ السُّلُطاتُ المَنْجَمَ مُؤَقَّتًا لِإجْراءِ تَقْييمِ مَخاطِرَ وَتَأْكيدِ سَلامَةِ البِنْيَةِ التَّحْتِيَّةِ.

A copper mine in Oman experienced a significant landslide, causing production to halt and injuring several workers. Authorities temporarily closed the mine to conduct a risk assessment and ensure the safety of the infrastructure.

أُصيبَ العَديدُ مِنْ عُمّالِ مَناجِمِ الفوسْفاتِ في الأُرْدُنِّ بِتَسَمُّمٍ بِالمَعادِنِ نَتيجَةَ تَعَرُّضِهِمُ المُسْتَمِرِّ لِلْغُبارِ وَالمَوادِّ الكيميائِيَّةِ. وَأَشارَتِ التَّقاريرُ الطِّبِّيَّةُ إلى ظُهورِ أَعْراضِ الأَمْراضِ الرِّئَوِيَّةِ بَيْنَ العُمّالِ، مِمّا دَعا السُّلُطاتِ لِمُراجَعَةِ إجْراءاتِ السَّلامَةِ وَالصِّحَّةِ المِهْنِيَّةِ.

Several workers in Jordan's phosphate mines suffered from metal poisoning due to continuous exposure to dust and chemicals. Medical reports indicated the emergence of pulmonary disease symptoms among the workers, prompting authorities to review safety and occupational health procedures.

انْدَلَعَ حَريقٌ تَحْتَ الأَرْضِ في مَنْجَمٍ بِالجَزائِرِ، مِمّا تَسَبَّبَ في انْقِطاعِ التَّهْوِيَةِ وَصُعوبَةٍ في التَّنَفُّسِ لِلْعُمّالِ. تَمَّ إخْلاءُ المَنْجَمِ فَوْرًا، وَأَخْمَدَ رِجالُ الإطْفاءِ الحَريقَ بَعْدَ ساعاتٍ مِنَ الجُهودِ المُضْنِيَةِ. "تَتَطَلَّبُ عَمَلِيّاتُ الإنْقاذِ في المَناجِمِ تَدْريبًا مُتَخَصِّصًا وَمُعَدّاتٍ حَديثَةً لِتَجَنُّبِ مِثْلِ هَذِهِ الحَوادِثِ"، كَما أَفادَ خَبيرٌ في السَّلامَةِ المِهْنِيَّةِ.

An underground fire broke out in a mine in Algeria, causing ventilation to cut off and making it difficult for workers to breathe. The mine was immediately evacuated, and firefighters extinguished the fire after hours of strenuous efforts. "Rescue operations in mines require specialized training and modern equipment to avoid such incidents," stated a safety expert.

12.2.3 Public Venue Incidents

أَخْلَى • إِخْلَاءٌ

to evacuate, clear

أَخْلَى الأَمْنُ القَاعَةَ فَوْرَ تَلَقِّي تَحْذِيرٍ بِوُجُودِ تَهْدِيدٍ أَمْنِيٍّ.

Security evacuated the hall immediately upon receiving a security threat warning.

أُصِيبَ • إِصَابَةٌ

to get injured, be affected

أُصِيبَ عِدَّةُ أَشْخَاصٍ خِلَالَ الِازْدِحَامِ في المَهْرَجَانِ الموسيقيِّ.

Several people were injured during the congestion at the music festival.

أَغْلَقَ مِنْطَقَةً خَطِرَةً • إِغْلَاقٌ

to close off a dangerous area

أَغْلَقَتِ السُّلُطَاتُ المِنْطَقَةَ الخَطِرَةَ بَعْدَ الِاكْتِشَافِ المُفَاجِئِ لِلتَّسَرُّبِ الكِيميائِيِّ.

The authorities closed off the dangerous area following the sudden discovery of a chemical leak.

أَنْقَذَ • إِنْقَاذٌ

to rescue, save

أَنْقَذَ رِجَالُ الإِطْفَاءِ الزُّوَّارَ العَالِقِينَ في المَبْنى المُحْتَرِقِ.

Firefighters rescued visitors trapped in the burning building.

إِشَارَةٌ إِرْشَادِيَّةٌ

signage

نُصِبَتْ إِشَارَاتٌ إِرْشَادِيَّةٌ لِتَوْجِيهِ الحُشُودِ بَعِيدًا عَنْ مَوْقِعِ الحادِثِ.

Guidance signs were erected to direct crowds away from the accident site.

إِصَابَةٌ جَسَدِيَّةٌ

physical injury

تَعَرَّضَتِ امْرَأَةٌ لِإِصَابَةٍ جَسَدِيَّةٍ نَتِيجَةَ الدَّفْعِ وَالشَّدِّ في المَدْخَلِ.

A woman suffered a physical injury due to pushing and shoving at the entrance.

to burn, catch fire   اِحْتِراقٌ •   اِحْتَرَقَ

اِحْتَرَقَ المَسْرَحُ أَثْناءَ العَرْضِ الموسيقيِّ، مِمّا أَدّى إلى إِجْلاءِ الجُمْهورِ عَلى الفَوْرِ.

The theater caught fire during the musical performance, leading to the immediate evacuation of the audience.

to suffocate, choke   اِخْتِناقٌ •   اِخْتَنَقَ

اِخْتَنَقَ الشّابُّ حَتّى المَوْتِ بِسَبَبِ الدُّخانِ الكَثيفِ خِلالَ حَريقٍ في النّادي اللَّيْليِّ.

The young man suffocated to death due to heavy smoke during a fire in the nightclub.

overcrowding   اِزْدِحامٌ

تَسَبَّبَ ازْدِحامُ الزُّوّارِ في تَأْخيرِ بَدْءِ العَرْضِ.

The congestion of visitors caused a delay in the start of the show.

severe overcrowding   اِزْدِحامٌ شَديدٌ

واجَهَ الحَدَثُ ازْدِحامًا شَديدًا مِمّا أَدّى إلى مَشاكِلَ في التَّنْظيمِ.

The event faced severe overcrowding, leading to organizational problems.

to collapse, break down   اِنْهِيارٌ •   اِنْهارَ

اِنْهارَ السَّقْفُ جُزْئِيًّا بِسَبَبِ الوَزْنِ الزّائِدِ لِلْمُعَدّاتِ.

The roof partially collapsed due to the excess weight of equipment.

structural collapse   اِنْهِيارٌ هَيْكَليٌّ

شَهِدَ المَبْنى انْهِيارًا هَيْكَليًّا بَعْدَ سَنَواتٍ مِنَ الإِهْمالِ.

The building experienced a structural collapse after years of neglect.

to gather, assemble   تَجَمُّعٌ •   تَجَمَّعَ

تَجَمَّعَ الآلافُ في السّاحَةِ العامَّةِ لِلاِحْتِجاجِ ضِدَّ القَراراتِ الحُكوميَّةِ.

Thousands gathered in the public square to protest against government decisions.

crowd control

تَحَكُّمٌ بِالْحُشودِ

نَفَّذَتِ السُّلُطاتُ التَّحَكُّمَ بِالْحُشودِ لِمَنْعِ الِازْدِحامِ خِلالَ الِاحْتِفالاتِ.

The authorities executed crowd control to prevent overcrowding during the celebrations.

riot control measures   *pl.*

تَدابيرُ مُكافَحَةِ شَغَبٍ

وَضَعَتِ الشُّرْطَةُ تَدابيرَ مُكافَحَةِ شَغَبٍ لِلتَّعامُلِ مَعَ المُتَظاهِرينَ العُنُفِ.

The police put in place riot control measures to deal with violent protesters.

to stampede   تَدافَعَ •

تَدافَعَ

تَدافَعَ الحُضورُ بِشَكْلٍ مُفاجِئٍ عِنْدَ سَماعِ صَوْتِ الِانْفِجارِ، مِمّا تَسَبَّبَ في عِدَّةِ إِصاباتٍ.

The audience stampeded suddenly upon hearing the explosion sound, causing several injuries.

stampede

تَدافُعٌ

وَقَعَ تَدافُعٌ خَطيرٌ عِنْدَ مَدْخَلِ الحَفْلِ، مِمّا أَدّى إِلى عِدَّةِ إِصاباتٍ.

A serious stampede occurred at the entrance of the concert, leading to several injuries.

to crowd together, jostle   تَزاحَمَ •

تَزاحَمَ

تَزاحَمَ الزُّوّارُ في المَعْرِضِ الفَنِّيِّ، مِمّا أَعاقَ الحَرَكَةَ وَالتَّنَقُّلَ بِسُهولَةٍ.

Visitors crowded together at the art exhibition, hindering easy movement and access.

food poisoning

تَسَمُّمٌ غِذائيٌّ

أُصيبَ العَديدُ مِنَ الحُضورِ بِتَسَمُّمٍ غِذائيٍّ بَعْدَ تَناوُلِ الطَّعامِ مِنَ الباعَةِ المُتَجَوِّلينَ.

Many attendees suffered from food poisoning after eating food from street vendors.

to trip, stumble   تَعَثَّرَ •

تَعَثَّرَ

في الفَوْضى الَّتي تَلَتِ الحَفْلَ، تَعَثَّرَ أَحَدُ حُضورِ الحَفْلِ عَلى السُّلَّمِ، ما أَدّى إِلى إِثارَةِ حالَةٍ وَجيزَةٍ مِنَ الذُّعْرِ بَيْنَ الجُمْهورِ.

In the chaotic aftermath of the concert, a concert-goer stumbled on the stairs, triggering a brief panic among the crowd.

exposure to sun and heat

تَعَرُّضٌ للشَّمْسِ وَالحَرَارَة

تَعَرَّضَ العَديدُ مِنَ الزُّوّارِ للشَّمْسِ وَالحَرَارَةِ خِلالَ الجَوْلَةِ الخارِجِيَّةِ.

Many visitors were exposed to the sun and heat during the outdoor tour.

security barrier

حاجِزٌ أَمْنِيٌّ ● حَواجِزٌ

تَمَّ إِنْشاءُ حاجِزٍ أَمْنِيٍّ لِفَصْلِ المُتَظاهِرينَ عَنِ الشُّرْطَة.

A security barrier was established to separate the protesters from the police.

fireworks-related accident

حادِثٌ ناجِمٌ عَنْ أَلْعاب ناريَّةٍ ● حَوادِثٌ

وَقَعَ حادِثٌ ناجِمٌ عَنِ الأَلْعابِ النّاريَّةِ، مِمّا أَدّى إلى إِلْغاءِ الاِحْتِفالِ.

An accident caused by fireworks occurred, leading to the cancellation of the celebration.

to occur, happen

حَدَثَ ● حُدوثٌ

حَدَثَ انْقِطاعٌ لِلتَّيّارِ الكَهْرَبائيِّ خِلالَ الحَفْلِ، مِمّا تَسَبَّبَ في الاِرْتِباكِ وَالفَوْضى.

A power outage happened during the concert, causing confusion and chaos.

to monitor, supervise

راقَبَ ● مُراقَبَةٌ

راقَبَ المَسْؤولونَ الجَماهيرَ لِضَمانِ الْتِزامِهِمْ بِالقَواعِدِ.

The officials monitored the crowds to ensure their compliance with the rules.

to control, manage

سَيْطَرَ ● سَيْطَرَةٌ

سَيْطَرَتِ الشُّرْطَةُ عَلى الوَضْعِ بَعْدَ انْدِلاعِ مُشاجَرَةٍ بَيْنَ مَجموعَتَيْنِ.

The police controlled the situation after a fight broke out between two groups.

to scream, shout, yell

صَرَخَ ● صُراخٌ / صَريخٌ

صَرَخَ المُتَحَدِّثُ بِقُوَّةٍ لِلَفْتِ انْتِباهِ الجُمْهورِ حينَ انْدَلَعَ الشِّجارُ.

The speaker screamed loudly to attract the audience's attention when the fight broke out.

طِفْلٌ مَفْقُودٌ • أَطْفالٌ

lost child

بَدَأَتْ عَمَلِيَّةُ بَحْثٍ واسِعَةُ النِّطاقِ بَعْدَ الإِبْلاغِ عَنْ طِفْلٍ مَفْقُودٍ في المَهْرَجانِ.

A widespread search operation began after a child was reported missing at the festival.

فَقَدَ • فَقْدٌ / فِقْدانٌ / فُقْدانٌ

to lose

فَقَدَ الرَّجُلُ وَعْيَهُ بِسَبَبِ الحَرارَةِ الشَّديدَةِ وَالِازْدِحامِ خِلالَ المَهْرَجانِ.

The man lost consciousness due to the extreme heat and overcrowding at the festival.

نُقْطَةُ تَفْتيشٍ • نِقاطٌ / نُقَطٌ

checkpoint

وُضِعَتْ نِقاطُ التَّفْتيشِ لِزِيادَةِ الأَمانِ خِلالَ الحَدَثِ الكَبيرِ.

Checkpoints were set up to enhance security during the major event.

هَلَعٌ

panic

اِنْتَشَرَ الهَلَعُ بَيْنَ الحُضورِ بَعْدَ سَماعِ صَوْتِ انْفِجارٍ.

Panic spread among the attendees after the sound of an explosion was heard.

وَجَّهَ جَماهيرَ • تَوْجيهٌ

to direct a crowd

وَجَّهَ المُنَظِّمونَ الجَماهيرَ بِكَفاءَةٍ إلى مَخارِجِ الطَّوارِئِ.

The organizers efficiently directed the crowds to the emergency exits.

12.2.3.1 Mini-Articles

أَثْناءَ فَعالِيّاتِ مَهْرَجانٍ مَحَلِّيٍّ حاشِدٍ، اِنْهارَ هَيْكَلُ مَسْرَحٍ مِمّا أَدّى إلى إِصابَةِ عَدَدٍ مِنَ الحُضورِ بِإِصاباتٍ جَسَدِيَّةٍ مُتَفاوِتَةٍ. سارَعَتْ فِرَقُ الإِنْقاذِ لِإِخْلاءِ المِنْطَقَةِ وَتَقْديمِ الإِسْعافاتِ الأَوَّلِيَّةِ لِلْمُصابينَ، بَيْنَما تَمَّ التَّحَكُّمُ بِالحُشودِ لِمَنْعِ المَزيدِ مِنَ الإِصاباتِ. أُغْلِقَتِ المِنْطَقَةُ المُحيطَةُ تَحَسُّبًا لِأَيِّ انْهِياراتٍ إِضافِيَّةٍ.

During the events of a crowded local festival, the structure of a stage collapsed, resulting in various physical injuries among attendees. Rescue teams quickly evacuated the area and provided first aid to the injured, while the crowds were controlled to prevent further injuries. The surrounding area was closed off in anticipation of any additional collapses.

خِلالَ احْتِفالِ زِفافٍ في قاعَةٍ كَبيرَةٍ، تَسَبَّبَ اسْتِخْدامُ الأَلْعابِ النّارِيَّةِ في حادِثٍ مَأْساوِيٍّ. الأَلْعابُ النّارِيَّةُ الَّتي لَمْ تُسْتَخْدَمْ بِطَريقَةٍ آمِنَةٍ أَدَّتْ إلى اشْتِعالِ النّارِ، مِمّا أثارَ حالَةً مِنَ الهَلَعِ بَيْنَ الحُضورِ. تَمَكَّنَتْ فِرَقُ الطَّوارِئِ مِنَ السَّيْطَرَةِ عَلى الحَريقِ وَإنْقاذِ الضُّيوفِ.

At a wedding celebration in a large hall, the use of fireworks led to a tragic accident. The fireworks, not used safely, ignited a fire, causing panic among the attendees. Emergency teams managed to control the fire and rescue the guests.

في مَرْكَزٍ تِجارِيٍّ مُزْدَحِمٍ، وَقَعَ تَدافُعٌ شَديدٌ بِسَبَبِ الإعْلانِ عَنْ تَخْفيضاتٍ كَبيرَةٍ، ما أَسْفَرَ عَنْ عِدَّةِ إصاباتٍ بَيْنَ المُتَسَوِّقينَ. تَمَّ اسْتِدْعاءُ السُّلُطاتِ لِتَقومَ بِالتَّحَكُّمِ في الحُشودِ وَإعادَةِ النِّظامِ، وَتَمَّ نَقْلُ المُصابينَ إلى المُسْتَشْفَياتِ القَريبَةِ.

In a busy shopping center, a severe stampede occurred due to announcements of significant discounts, resulting in several injuries among shoppers. Authorities were called in to control the crowds and restore order, and the injured were transported to nearby hospitals.

تَعَرَّضَ مَطْعَمٌ مَشْهورٌ لِحادِثِ تَسَمُّمٍ غِذائِيٍّ أَثَّرَ عَلى العَديدِ مِنَ الزَّبائِنِ. تَجَمَّعَ المُصابونَ بِالتَّسَمُّمِ في المَراكِزِ الصِّحِّيَّةِ المَحَلِّيَّةِ بَحْثًا عَنْ عِلاجٍ، مِمّا أَدّى إلى ازْدِحامٍ شَديدٍ وَتَحَدِّياتٍ في تَقْديمِ الرِّعايَةِ الطِّبِّيَّةِ اللّازِمَةِ.

A popular restaurant experienced a food poisoning incident affecting many customers. Those affected by the poisoning gathered at local health centers seeking treatment, leading to severe congestion and challenges in providing the necessary medical care.

خِلالَ مَهْرَجانٍ موسيقِيٍّ كَبيرٍ، أُبْلِغَ عَنْ فِقْدانِ طِفْلٍ مِمّا أثارَ قَلَقًا كَبيرًا. نَشَرَ الأَمْنُ وَالمُتَطَوِّعونَ نِقاطَ تَفْتيشٍ وَبَدَأوا عَمَلِيّاتِ بَحْثٍ مُكَثَّفَةٍ. اسْتُخْدِمَتِ الإشاراتُ الإرْشادِيَّةُ وَالنِّداءاتُ عَبْرَ مُكَبِّراتِ الصَّوْتِ لِتَوْجيهِ الجَماهيرِ وَالمُساعَدَةِ في العُثورِ عَلى الطِّفْلِ المَفْقودِ.

During a large music festival, a child was reported missing, causing significant concern. Security and volunteers set up checkpoints and started extensive search operations. Directional signs and announcements over loudspeakers were used to guide the crowds and help find the missing child.

كارِثَةُ مِنى: تَدافُعٌ مَأْساوِيٌّ يُخَلِّفُ مِئاتِ الضَّحايا خِلالَ الحَجِّ

في حادِثَةٍ مُرَوِّعَةٍ هَزَّتِ العالَمَ الإسْلامِيَّ، وَقَعَ تَدافُعٌ مُمِيتٌ في مِنى، بِالقُرْبِ مِنْ مَكَّةَ المُكَرَّمَةِ، خِلالَ مَوْسِمِ الحَجِّ عامَ 2015. الكارِثَةُ الَّتي حَدَثَتْ في 24 سِبْتَمْبَرَ، تَسَبَّبَتْ في وَفاةِ أَكْثَرَ مِنْ 700 حاجٍّ، وَفْقًا لِلتَّقارِيرِ الرَّسْمِيَّةِ، بَيْنَما أَشارَتْ تَقْديراتٌ أُخْرى إلى أَنَّ العَدَدَ تَجاوَزَ الأَلْفَيْنِ.

نَجَمَ التَّدافُعُ عَنِ ازْدِحامٍ شَديدٍ في مَوْقِعِ رَمْيِ الجَمَراتِ، وَهُوَ جُزْءٌ مِنْ مَناسِكِ الحَجِّ، حَيْثُ يَقومُ الحُجّاجُ بِرَمْيِ الحَصى عَلى الأَعْمِدَةِ الَّتي تَرْمُزُ لِلشَّيْطانِ. تَسَبَّبَ الازْدِحامُ وَانْخِفاضُ الرُّؤْيَةِ في صُعوبَةِ التَّحَكُّمِ بِالحُشودِ، مِمّا أَدّى إلى فِقْدانِ السَّيْطَرَةِ.

أَثْناءَ الفَوْضى، واجَهَ العَديدُ مِنَ الحُجّاجِ صُعوباتٍ جَمَّةً، حَيْثُ تَعَرَّضوا لِإصاباتٍ جَسَدِيَّةٍ مُتَعَدِّدَةٍ، وَسَطَ مُحاوَلاتٍ يائِسَةٍ لِلنَّجاةِ. هُرِعَتْ فِرَقُ الإنْقاذِ وَالخِدْماتِ الطِّبِّيَّةِ إلى المَكانِ، وَتَمَّ إغْلاقُ المَناطِقِ الخَطِرَةِ لِتَسْهيلِ عَمَلِيّاتِ الإنْقاذِ وَإجْلاءِ المُصابينَ.

أَثارَتِ الحادِثَةُ تَساؤُلاتٍ حَوْلَ تَدابيرِ مُكافَحَةِ الشَّغَبِ وَإدارَةِ الأَمْنِ في تَجَمُّعاتٍ دينِيَّةٍ كَبيرَةٍ مِثلَ الحَجِّ. في أَعْقابِ المَأْساةِ، سَعَتِ السُّلُطاتُ السُّعودِيَّةُ لِمُراجَعَةِ وَتَحْسينِ إجْراءاتِ التَّحَكُّمِ بِالحُشودِ وَأَمْنِ الحُجّاجِ، لِضَمانِ عَدَمِ تَكْرارِ مِثلِ هَذِهِ الأَحْداثِ المَأْساوِيَّةِ.

هَذِهِ الكارِثَةُ، الَّتي تُعَدُّ واحِدَةً مِنْ أَسْوَأِ الحَوادِثِ في تاريخِ الحَجِّ، تَظَلُّ تَذْكيرًا قَوِيًّا بِأَهَمِّيَّةِ الأَمْنِ وَالسَّلامَةِ في الفَعالِيّاتِ الدينِيَّةِ الضَّخْمَةِ، وَضَرورَةِ اتِّخاذِ كافَّةِ التَّدابيرِ اللّازِمَةِ لِحِمايَةِ الحُجّاجِ.

Mina disaster: A tragic stampede leaves hundreds of victims during Hajj

In a horrific incident that shook the Islamic world, a deadly stampede occurred in Mina, near Mecca, during the Hajj season in 2015. The disaster on September 24 resulted in the death of over 700 pilgrims, according to official reports, while other estimates suggested the number exceeded two thousand.

The stampede was caused by severe congestion at the site of the stoning of the devil, a part of the Hajj rituals where pilgrims throw stones at pillars symbolizing Satan. The overcrowding and reduced visibility led to difficulties in crowd control, resulting in loss of control.

During the chaos, many pilgrims faced extreme difficulties, with numerous physical injuries, amidst desperate attempts to survive. Rescue teams and medical services rushed to the scene, and hazardous areas were closed to facilitate rescue operations and the evacuation of the injured.

The incident raised questions about anti-riot measures and security management in large religious gatherings like the Hajj. Following the tragedy, Saudi authorities sought to review and improve crowd control procedures and the safety of pilgrims to ensure that such tragic events do not recur.

This catastrophe, one of the worst in the history of the Hajj, remains a powerful reminder of the importance of security and safety in large religious events and the necessity of taking all necessary measures to protect the pilgrims.

12.3 Medical Emergencies

Track **69**

أُصيبَ • إصابَةٌ

to be afflicted, get affected

أُصيبَ عَدَدٌ مِنَ الرُّكّابِ بِجُروحٍ خَطيرَةٍ بَعْدَ تَعَرُّضِ الحافِلَةِ لِحادِثٍ.

Several passengers were injured after the bus was involved in an accident.

أَلَمٌ في الصَّدْرِ • آلامٌ

chest pain

شَكا المَريضُ مِنْ أَلَمٍ حادٍّ في الصَّدْرِ قَبْلَ أَنْ يُنْقَلَ إلى المُسْتَشْفى.

The patient complained of severe chest pain before being taken to the hospital.

إنْعاشٌ قَلْبِيٌّ رِئَوِيٌّ

cardiopulmonary resuscitation (CPR)

أُجْرِيَتْ عَمَلِيَّةُ إنْعاشٍ قَلْبِيٍّ رِئَوِيٍّ لِسَيِّدَةٍ عَجوزٍ تَوَقَّفَ قَلْبُها في مَرْكَزِ التَّسَوُّقِ.

CPR was performed on an elderly woman whose heart stopped at the shopping center.

اِسْتَجابَ • اِسْتِجابَةٌ

to respond

اِسْتَجابَ الأَطِبّاءُ بِسُرْعَةٍ لِحالَةِ الطَّوارِئِ بَعْدَ وُصولِ الضَّحايا إلى قِسْمِ الطَّوارِئِ.

The doctors responded quickly to the emergency after the victims arrived at the emergency department.

اِسْتِجابَةٌ فَوْرِيَّةٌ

immediate response

جَرَت اِسْتِجابَةٌ فَوْرِيَّةٌ لِلْحادِثِ، وَنُقِلَ المُصابونَ إلى المُسْتَشْفى بِسُرْعَةٍ.

There was an immediate response to the accident, and the injured were quickly transported to the hospital.

خِدْمَةُ طَوارِئَ

emergency service

تَمَّ الاِتِّصالُ بِخِدْماتِ الطَّوارِئِ فَوْرَ مُلاحَظَةِ انْهِيارِ رَجُلٍ في السّوقِ العامِّ.

Emergency services were contacted immediately after a man collapsed in the public market.

طَلَبُ مُساعَدَةٍ طِبِّيَّةٍ • طَلَبٌ

to seek medical help

طَلَبَ رَجُلٌ مُسِنٌّ مُساعَدَةً طِبِّيَّةً بَعْدَ شُعورِهِ بِالدُّوارِ وَالضَّعْفِ.

An elderly man sought medical help after feeling dizzy and weak.

عالَجَ • مُعالَجَةٌ / عِلاج

to treat

عالَجَ الأَطِبّاءُ في المَوْقِعِ رِياضِيًّا شابًّا أُصيبَ خِلالَ المُباراةِ.

Doctors on site treated a young athlete who was injured during the game.

عانى • مُعاناةٌ

to suffer

عانى الطِّفْلُ مِنْ رَدِّ فِعْلٍ تَحَسُّسِي شَديدٍ بَعْدَ تَناوُلِ طَعامًا مُعَيَّنًا.

The child suffered from a severe allergic reaction after eating a certain food.

فَقَدَ الوَعْيَ • فَقْدٌ / فِقْدانٌ / فُقْدانٌ

to faint

فَقَدَ اللّاعِبُ الوَعْيَ بَعْدَ التَّعَرُّضِ لِضَرْبَةٍ قَوِيَّةٍ عَلى الرَّأْسِ خِلالَ مُباراةٍ لِكُرَةِ القَدَمِ.

The player lost consciousness after suffering a heavy blow to the head during a soccer match.

12.3.1 Medical Conditions

Track **70**

إِنْسولين

insulin

تَمَّ إِعْطاءُ الإِنْسولين لِلْمَريضِ بَعْدَ اكْتِشافِ ارْتِفاعِ مُسْتَوَياتِ السُّكَّرِ في الدَّمِ بِشَكْلٍ خَطيرٍ.

Insulin was administered to the patient after dangerously high blood sugar levels were detected.

to choke

إِخْتَنَقَ • اِخْتِناقٌ

اِخْتَنَقَ الغَوّاصُ بِسَبَبِ خَلَلٍ في مُعَدّاتِ الغَوْصِ تَحْتَ الماءِ.

The diver choked due to a malfunction in the underwater diving equipment.

high blood sugar, hyperglycemia

اِرْتِفاعُ السُّكَّرِ في الدَّمِ

تَمَّ نَقْلُ المَريضِ إلى المُسْتَشْفى بِسَبَبِ ارْتِفاعٍ خَطيرٍ في مُسْتَوياتِ السُّكَّرِ في الدَّمِ.

The patient was taken to the hospital due to a dangerous rise in blood sugar levels.

low blood sugar, hypogylcemia

اِنْخِفاضُ السُّكَّرِ في الدَّمِ

تَمَّ عِلاجُ المَريضِ في الوَقْتِ المُناسِبِ بَعْدَ أَنْ عانى مِنَ انْخِفاضِ السُّكَّرِ في الدَّمِ.

The patient was treated in time after suffering from a drop in blood sugar.

low body temperature

اِنْخِفاضٌ في حَرارَةِ الجِسْمِ

يُعاني الرَّجُلُ مِنَ انْخِفاضٍ حادٍّ في حَرارَةِ الجِسْمِ بَعْدَ قَضاءِ ساعاتٍ في البَرْدِ.

The man is suffering from a severe drop in body temperature after spending hours in the cold.

drug poisoning

تَسَمُّمٌ دَوائِيٌّ

تَمَّ نَقْلُ عِدَّةِ أشْخاصٍ إلى المُسْتَشْفى بَعْدَ تَسَمُّمٍ دَوائِيٍّ ناتِجٍ عَنْ جُرْعَةٍ زائِدَةٍ.

Several people were hospitalized after drug poisoning due to an overdose.

food poisoning

تَسَمُّمٌ غذائِيٌّ

أُصيبَ العَديدُ مِنَ الأشْخاصِ بِتَسَمُّمٍ غذائِيٍّ بَعْدَ تَناوُلِ الطَّعامِ في الحَفْلِ.

Many people were afflicted with food poisoning after eating at the party.

chemical poisoning

تَسَمُّمٌ كيميائِيٌّ

تَعَرَّضَ العُمّالُ لِتَسَمُّمٍ كيميائِيٍّ بَعْدَ حادِثٍ في المَصْنَعِ.

The workers were exposed to chemical poisoning after an accident at the factory.

تَشَنَّجَ • تَشَنُّج

to convulse

تَشَنَّجَ الطَّالِبُ أَثْناءَ الفَصْلِ الدِّراسِيِّ بِشَكْلٍ مُفاجِئٍ، مِمّا أَثارَ نِقاشًا حَوْلَ أَهَمِّيَّةِ تَدْريبِ المُعَلِّمينَ عَلَى الإِسْعافاتِ الأَوَّلِيَّةِ.

The student convulsed suddenly during class, sparking a discussion on the importance of training teachers in first aid.

تَشَنُّج

convulsion

تَعَرَّضَتِ الفَتاةُ لِتَشَنُّجاتٍ بَعْدَ ارْتِفاعٍ شَديدٍ في دَرَجَةِ حَرارَتِها.

The girl experienced convulsions after a severe increase in her temperature.

تَشَوُّشُ وَعْي

confusion

شَهِدَتِ المُسْتَشْفى حالاتِ تَشَوُّشٍ لِلْوَعْيِ بَيْنَ مَرْضى الحَرارَةِ الشَّديدَةِ.

The hospital witnessed cases of altered consciousness among patients with severe heat.

تَعَرُّضٌ مُباشِرٌ لِأَشِعَّةِ الشَّمْسِ

direct sun exposure

تَسَبَّبَ التَّعَرُّضُ المُباشِرُ لِأَشِعَّةِ الشَّمْسِ في إِصابَةِ عِدَّةِ سُيّاحٍ بِضَرْبَةِ شَمْسٍ.

Direct exposure to the sun caused several tourists to suffer from heatstroke.

تَعَرَّقَ • تَعَرُّقٌ

to sweat

بَدَأَ المَريضُ يَتَعَرَّقُ بِشَكْلٍ شَديدٍ قَبْلَ أَنْ يَفْقِدَ الوَعْيَ، مِمّا كانَ مُؤَشِّرًا عَلى نَوْبَةٍ قَلْبِيَّةٍ وَشيكَةٍ.

The patient began to sweat heavily before losing consciousness, which was an indicator of an imminent heart attack.

تَنَفَّسَ بِصُعوبَةٍ • تَنَفُّسٌ

to breathe with difficulty

أُبْلِغَ عَنْ حالاتِ تَنَفُّسٍ بِصُعوبَةٍ في المُخَيَّمِ الصَّيْفِيِّ بِسَبَبِ الغُبارِ.

Cases of breathing difficulty were reported in the summer camp due to dust.

to swell

تَوَرَّمَ • تَوَرُّم

تَوَرَّمَ ذِراعُ العامِلِ بَعْدَ لَدْغَةٍ مِنْ حَشَرَةٍ مَجْهولَةٍ خِلالَ رِحْلَةِ تَخْييمٍ، مِمّا أَثارَ الاِهْتِمامَ بِأَهَمِّيَّةِ التَّعَرُّفِ عَلى الحَشَراتِ السّامَّةِ.

A worker's arm swelled after being bitten by an unknown insect during a camping trip, raising awareness about the importance of recognizing poisonous insects.

swelling

تَوَرُّم

تَسَبَّبَتْ لَدْغَةُ حَشَرَةٍ في تَوَرُّمِ يَدِ طِفْلٍ أَثْناءَ الرِّحْلَةِ الخارِجِيَّةِ.

An insect bite caused swelling in a child's hand during the outdoor trip.

epinephrine injector

حُقْنَةُ إِبينِفْرين • حُقَنْ

اِسْتَخْدَمَ الطّالِبُ حُقْنَةَ الإِبينِفْرين بَعْدَ تَعَرُّضِهِ لِرَدِّ فِعْلٍ تَحَسُّسِيٍّ شَديدٍ.

The student used an epinephrine injector after experiencing a severe allergic reaction.

high body temperature

دَرَجَةُ حَرارَةِ جِسْمٍ مُرْتَفِعَةٌ

أُدْخِلَ المُتَسابِقُ إِلى المُسْتَشْفى بِدَرَجَةِ حَرارَةِ جِسْمٍ مُرْتَفِعَةٍ بَعْدَ السِّباقِ.

The racer was admitted to the hospital with a high body temperature after the race.

low body temperature

دَرَجَةُ حَرارَةِ جِسْمٍ مُنْخَفِضَةٌ

وُجِدَ المُتَنَزِّهُ في حالَةٍ خَطيرَةٍ بِدَرَجَةِ حَرارَةِ جِسْمٍ مُنْخَفِضَةٍ بَعْدَ فَتْرَةٍ طَويلَةٍ في الثَّلْجِ.

The hiker was found in critical condition with a low body temperature after a long time in the snow.

psychological support

دَعْمٌ نَفْسِيٌّ

قَدَّمَتِ المَجْموعَةُ دَعْمًا نَفْسِيًّا لِلنّاجينَ مِنَ الحادِثِ المُرَوِّعِ.

The group provided psychological support to the survivors of the horrific accident.

dizziness

دُوارٌ

شَعَرَ الرَّجُلُ بِدُوارٍ شَديدٍ وَتَمَّ نَقْلُهُ فَوْرًا إِلى غُرْفَةِ الطَّوارِئِ.

The man felt severe dizziness and was immediately transported to the emergency room.

allergic reaction   • رُدودٌ   رَدُّ فِعْلٍ تَحَسُّسِيٌّ

يُظْهِرُ الطِّفْلُ رَدَّ فِعْلٍ تَحَسُّسِيًّا شَديدًا بَعْدَ تَناوُلِ الفولِ السّودانيِّ.

The child shows a severe allergic reaction after eating peanuts.

trembling, shivering   رَعْشَةٌ

بَدَأَتْ رَعْشَةٌ شَديدَةٌ في المَريضِ بِسَبَبِ الإنْفِلْوَنْزا وَالحُمّى.

Severe shivering began in the patient due to the flu and fever.

coughing   سُعالٌ

أَدّى السُّعالُ المُسْتَمِرُّ إلى تَشْخيصِ الرَّجُلِ بِالْتِهابٍ رِئَوِيٍّ حادٍّ.

Persistent coughing led to the man being diagnosed with severe pneumonia.

to cough   • سُعالٌ   سَعَلَ

سَعَلَ السِّياسِيُّ بِشَكْلٍ مُتَكَرِّرٍ خِلالَ الخِطابِ، مِمّا أَثارَ قَلَقَ الحُضورِ بِشَأْنِ حالَتِهِ الصِّحِّيَّةِ.

The politician coughed repeatedly during the speech, raising concerns among the audience about his health condition.

headache   صُداعٌ

اِشْتَكى الرَّجُلُ مِنْ صُداعٍ مُسْتَمِرٍّ أَدّى إلى زِيارَةِ الطَّوارِئِ.

The man complained of persistent headaches leading to an emergency room visit.

anaphylactic shock   صَدْمَةٌ تَحَسُّسِيَّةٌ

دَخَلَتِ المَريضَةُ في صَدْمَةٍ تَحَسُّسِيَّةٍ بَعْدَ التَّعَرُّضِ لِلَدْغَةِ نَحْلَةٍ.

The patient went into anaphylactic shock after being stung by a bee.

speech difficulty   صُعوبَةٌ في الكَلامِ

نُقِلَ رَجُلٌ إلى المُسْتَشْفى بَعْدَ مُعاناتِهِ مِنْ صُعوبَةٍ في الكَلامِ وَالحَرَكَةِ.

A man was transported to the hospital after suffering from difficulty in speaking and movement.

arm weakness

ضَعْفٌ فِي الذِّراعِ

أَبْلَغَتِ امْرَأَةٌ عَنْ ضَعْفٍ وَخِدْرٍ فِي الذِّراعِ، مِمّا أَثارَ مَخاوِفَ مِنَ السَّكْتَةِ الدِّماغِيَّةِ.

A woman reported arm weakness and numbness, raising concerns of a stroke.

shortness of breath

ضيقُ تَنَفُّسٍ

أُدْخِلَ الطِّفْلُ إِلى قِسْمِ الطَّوارِئِ بِسَبَبِ ضيقِ التَّنَفُّسِ وَالحُمّى.

The child was admitted to the emergency department due to shortness of breath and fever.

skin rash

طَفْحٌ جِلْدِيٌّ

ظَهَرَ طَفْحٌ جِلْدِيٌّ عَلى جِلْدِ عِدَّةِ طُلّابٍ بَعْدَ التَّعَرُّضِ لِمادَّةٍ غَيْرِ مَعْروفَةٍ.

A skin rash appeared on the skin of several students after exposure to an unknown substance.

nausea

غَثَيانٌ

تَمَّ الإِبْلاغُ عَنْ حالاتِ غَثَيانٍ وَتَقَيُّؤٍ فِي مَدْرَسَةٍ مَحَلِّيَّةٍ بَعْدَ تَناوُلِ طَعامٍ مُلَوَّثٍ.

Cases of nausea and vomiting were reported at a local school after contaminated food was consumed.

stomach pumping

غَسيلُ مَعِدَةٍ

أُجْرِيَ غَسيلُ مَعِدَةٍ لِلشّابِّ بَعْدَ تَناوُلِهِ مَوادَّ سامَّةً عَنْ طَريقِ الخَطَأِ.

Gastric lavage was performed on the young man after he accidentally ingested toxic substances.

activated charcoal

فَحْمٌ نَشِطٌ

تَمَّ تَقْديمُ الفَحْمِ النَّشِطِ لِلْمَريضِ بَعْدَ حادِثَةِ تَسَمُّمٍ غِذائِيٍّ.

Activated charcoal was administered to the patient after a food poisoning incident.

vomiting

قَيْءٌ

أُصيبَتِ الطّالِبَةُ بِقَيْءٍ مُتَكَرِّرٍ بَعْدَ تَناوُلِ وَجْبَةٍ فاسِدَةٍ.

The student experienced repeated vomiting after eating a spoiled meal.

مَرَضُ السُّكَّرِيّ
diabetes

• أَمْراضٌ

تُوُفِّيَ مَريضٌ بِمَرَضِ السُّكَّرِيّ بَعْدَ عَدَمِ تَلَقِّي الإِنْسولينِ اللَّازِمِ في الوَقْتِ المُحَدَّدِ.

A patient with diabetes died after failing to receive the necessary insulin on time.

مَرْكَزُ مُكافَحَةِ السُّمومِ
poison control center

• مَراكِزُ

أَطْلَقَ مَرْكَزُ مُكافَحَةِ السُّمومِ حَمْلَةَ تَوْعِيَةٍ حَوْلَ مَخاطِرِ التَّسَمُّمِ المَنْزِلِيّ وَكَيْفِيَّةِ الوِقايَةِ مِنْها، بَعْدَ ارْتِفاعٍ في حالاتِ التَّسَمُّمِ بِمَوادِّ التَّنْظيفِ.

The Poison Control Center launched an awareness campaign about the dangers of household poisoning and how to prevent it, following an increase in poisoning cases with cleaning substances.

مُزيلُ الرَّجَفانِ
defibrillator

اسْتَخْدَمَتِ المُمَرِّضَةُ مُزيلَ الرَّجَفانِ لإِنْقاذِ مَريضٍ تَعَرَّضَ لِنَوْبَةٍ قَلْبِيَّةٍ.

The nurse used a defibrillator to save a patient who had a cardiac arrest.

مُسَبِّبُ حَساسِيَّةٍ
allergen

حَدَثَتْ رُدودُ فِعْلٍ تَحَسُّسِيَّةٌ بَيْنَ الحُضورِ في الحَفْلِ بَعْدَ التَّعَرُّضِ لِمُسَبِّبِ حَساسِيَّةٍ غَيْرِ مَعْلومٍ.

Allergic reactions occurred among attendees at the concert after exposure to an undisclosed allergen.

مُسْتَوى السُّكَّرِ في الدَّمِ
blood sugar level

تَمَّتْ مُراقَبَةُ مُسْتَوى السُّكَّرِ في الدَّمِ لِلْمَريضِ لِلتَّأَكُّدِ مِنَ اسْتِقْرارِ حالَتِه.

The patient's blood sugar level was monitored to ensure his condition was stable.

مُشْكِلَةٌ تَنَفُّسِيَّةٌ
breathing problem

• مَشاكِلُ

انْتَشَرَتْ مُشْكِلَةٌ تَنَفُّسِيَّةٌ في القَرْيَةِ بِسَبَبِ تَلَوُّثِ الهَواءِ الشَّديدِ.

A respiratory problem spread in the village due to severe air pollution.

oxygen deficiency نَقْصُ أُكْسُجِينٍ

أَشَارَتِ الدِّرَاسَاتُ إِلَى أَنَّ نَقْصَ الأُكْسُجِينِ فِي الدِّمَاغِ يُمْكِنُ أَنْ يُؤَدِّيَ إِلَى ضَرَرٍ دَائِمٍ.

Studies have indicated that oxygen deficiency in the brain can lead to permanent damage.

seizure نَوْبَةٌ

تَعَرَّضَ المَرِيضُ لِنَوْبَةِ صَرَعٍ فِي المَكْتَبَةِ مِمَّا أَثَارَ الهَلَعَ بَيْنَ الزُّوَّارِ.

The patient had a seizure in the library, causing panic among the visitors.

asthma attack نَوْبَةُ رَبْوٍ

أُصِيبَ الطِّفْلُ بِنَوْبَةِ رَبْوٍ بَعْدَ اللَّعِبِ فِي الحَدِيقَةِ المَلِيئَةِ بِالأَزْهَارِ.

The child had an asthma attack after playing in the flower-filled garden.

seizure نَوْبَةُ صَرَعٍ

تَعَرَّضَتِ الفَتَاةُ لِنَوْبَةِ صَرَعٍ فِي المَدْرَسَةِ مِمَّا اسْتَدْعَى التَّدَخُّلَ الطِّبِّيَّ الفَوْرِيَّ.

The girl had a seizure at school, requiring immediate medical intervention.

12.3.1.1 Mini-Articles

Track **71**

أُصِيبَ رَجُلٌ فِي الخَمْسِينَ مِنْ عُمْرِهِ بِأَلَمٍ حَادٍّ فِي الصَّدْرِ أَثْنَاءَ التَّسَوُّقِ فِي مَرْكَزٍ تِجَارِيٍّ. اسْتَجَابَتْ خِدْمَاتُ الطَّوَارِئِ فَوْرِيًّا، حَيْثُ قَامَ المُسْعِفُونَ بِإِجْرَاءِ إِنْعَاشٍ قَلْبِيٍّ رِئَوِيٍّ لِلْمُصَابِ الَّذِي فَقَدَ وَعْيَهُ. بِفَضْلِ اسْتِجَابَتِهِمِ السَّرِيعَةِ، تَمَكَّنُوا مِنْ إِنْقَاذِ حَيَاتِهِ وَنَقْلِهِ إِلَى المُسْتَشْفَى لِتَلَقِّي العِلَاجِ المُنَاسِبِ.

A man in his fifties experienced severe chest pain while shopping in a mall. Emergency services responded immediately, with paramedics performing cardiopulmonary resuscitation on the unconscious victim. Thanks to their rapid response, they were able to save his life and transport him to the hospital for appropriate treatment.

عَانَتْ عَائِلَةٌ مِنْ تَسَمُّمٍ غِذَائِيٍّ بَعْدَ تَنَاوُلِ وَجْبَةٍ فِي مَطْعَمٍ مَحَلِّيٍّ، حَيْثُ ظَهَرَتْ عَلَيْهِمْ أَعْرَاضُ الغَثَيَانِ وَالقَيْءِ وَارْتِفَاعِ دَرَجَةِ الحَرَارَةِ. طُلِبَتِ المُسَاعَدَةُ الطِّبِّيَّةُ فَوْرًا، وَتَمَّ نَقْلُهُمْ إِلَى أَقْرَبِ مُسْتَشْفًى حَيْثُ تَلَقَّوْا غَسِيلَ المَعِدَةِ وَالعِلَاجَ لِتَقْلِيلِ الأَعْرَاضِ وَمَنْعِ المَزِيدِ مِنَ المُضَاعَفَاتِ.

A family suffered from food poisoning after eating at a local restaurant, exhibiting symptoms of nausea, vomiting, and high body temperature. Immediate medical assistance was requested, and they were transported to the nearest hospital where they received stomach washing and treatment to reduce symptoms and prevent further complications.

تَعَرَّضَ طِفْلٌ يَبْلُغُ مِنَ العُمْرِ 8 سَنَواتٍ لِنَوْبَةٍ رَبْوٍ حادَّةٍ أَثْناءَ اللَّعِبِ في الحَديقَةِ. وَالِدُهُ، الَّذي كانَ بِجانِبِهِ، اِسْتَجابَ فَوْرًا وَطَلَبَ المُساعَدَةَ الطِّبِّيَّةَ بَيْنَما حاوَلَ تَهْدِئَةَ تَنَفُّسِ اِبْنِهِ بِاسْتِخْدامِ جِهازِ الِاسْتِنْشاقِ الخاصِّ بِهِ. وَصَلَتْ خِدْمَةُ الطَّوارِئِ سَريعًا وَقَدَّمَتِ الدَّعْمَ اللّازِمَ لِلطِّفْلِ، مِمّا أَدّى إلى اسْتِقْرارِ حالَتِهِ.

An 8-year-old child had a severe asthma attack while playing in the park. His father, who was with him, responded immediately and called for medical help while trying to calm his son's breathing using his inhaler. Emergency services arrived quickly and provided the necessary support for the child, stabilizing his condition.

في يَوْمٍ صَيْفِيٍّ حارٍّ، تَعَرَّضَ رَجُلٌ لِلشَّمْسِ وَالحَرارَةِ لِفَتَراتٍ طَويلَةٍ مِمّا أَدّى إلى تَشَنُّجاتٍ وَارْتِفاعِ دَرَجَةِ حَرارَةِ جِسْمِهِ. أَبْلَغَ شُهودُ العِيانِ عَنِ الحادِثَةِ، واسْتَجابَتْ خِدْمَةُ الطَّوارِئِ بِسُرْعَةٍ، مُقَدِّمَةً الإِسْعافاتِ الأَوَّلِيَّةِ لِخَفْضِ دَرَجَةِ حَرارَتِهِ وَنَقْلِهِ إلى المُسْتَشْفى لِتَلَقّي العِلاجِ.

On a hot summer day, a man was exposed to the sun and heat for extended periods, leading to cramps and elevated body temperature. Witnesses reported the incident, and emergency services responded quickly, providing first aid to lower his temperature and transporting him to the hospital for treatment.

عانَتْ فَتاةٌ في المَدْرَسَةِ مِنْ رَدِّ فِعْلٍ تَحَسُّسِيٍّ شَديدٍ، مِمّا تَسَبَّبَ في صُعوبَةٍ في التَّنَفُّسِ وَتَوَرُّمٍ. اِسْتَجابَتِ المَدْرَسَةُ بِسُرْعَةٍ، حَيْثُ قَدَّمَ المُسْعِفونَ حُقْنَةَ إِبينِفْرين وَتَمَّ طَلَبُ المُساعَدَةِ الطِّبِّيَّةِ العاجِلَةِ. نُقِلَتْ إلى المُسْتَشْفى لِتَلَقّي المَزيدِ مِنَ العِلاجِ وَالمُراقَبَةِ لِضَمانِ اسْتِقْرارِ حالَتِها.

A girl at school suffered from a severe allergic reaction, causing difficulty in breathing and swelling. The school swiftly responded, with paramedics administering an epinephrine injection and urgent medical assistance was called. She was taken to the hospital for further treatment and monitoring to ensure her condition stabilized.

التَّعامُلُ مَعَ الطَّوارِئِ الطِّبِّيَّةِ: نَصائِحُ مِنْ خَبيرٍ

مُقَدِّمَةُ البَرْنامَج: مَساءُ الخَيْرِ، مُشاهِدينا الكِرامَ. نُرَحِّبُ بِكُمْ في بَرْنامَجِنا الطِّبِّيِّ، حَيْثُ نُناقِشُ اليَوْمَ مَوضوعَ الطَّوارِئِ الطِّبِّيَّةِ وَكَيْفِيَّةَ التَّعامُلِ مَعَها. نَسْتَضيفُ الدُّكتورَ عَلي حَسَن، الخَبيرَ في طِبِّ الطَّوارِئِ، لِيُعْطينا نَظْرَةً عَميقَةً حَوْلَ هَذا المَوْضوعِ الهامِّ. المُقَدِّمَةُ: دُكتورُ عَليّ، مَرْحَبًا بِكَ. لِنَبْدَأْ بِالسُّؤالِ الأَوَّلِ: ما هِيَ أَهَمِّيَّةُ خِدْماتِ الطَّوارِئِ في مُجْتَمَعِنا؟

دُكتورُ عَليّ: شُكْرًا لَكِ. تُمَثِّلُ خِدْماتُ الطَّوارِئِ الخَطَّ الأَوَّلَ لِلدِّفاعِ في الحالاتِ الطِّبِّيَّةِ الحَرِجَةِ، كَنَوْباتِ القَلْبِ، وَالسَّكَتاتِ الدِّماغِيَّةِ، وَالحالاتِ الَّتي يَفْقِدُ فيها الشَّخْصُ الوَعْيَ. حَيْثُ يُمْكِنُ لِاسْتِجابَتِها الفَوْرِيَّةِ وَقُدْرَتِها عَلى التَّعامُلِ مَعَ مِثلِ هَذِهِ الحالاتِ أَنْ تُنْقِذَ حَياةَ النّاسِ.

المُقَدِّمَةُ: وَماذا عَنِ الحالاتِ الَّتي يُعاني فيها الأَشْخاصُ مِنْ أَلَمٍ في الصَّدْرِ أَوْ صُعوبَةٍ في التَّنَفُّسِ؟

دُكتورُ عَليّ: قَدْ يَكونُ أَلَمُ الصَّدْرِ مُؤَشِّرًا لِنَوْبَةٍ قَلْبِيَّةٍ، وَيَتَطَلَّبُ تَدَخُّلًا طِبِّيًا سَريعًا. الاسْتِجابَةُ السَّريعَةُ وَطَلَبُ المُساعَدَةِ الطِّبِّيَّةِ يُمْكِنُ أَنْ يَكونا حاسِمَيْنِ. كَذَلِكَ، فَإِنَّ الأَشْخاصَ الَّذينَ يُعانونَ مِنْ صُعوبَةٍ في التَّنَفُّسِ قَدْ يُواجِهونَ حالَةً طارِئَةً تَنَفُّسِيَّةً، كَنَوْبَةِ الرَّبْوِ، وَيَحْتاجونَ إلى تَدَخُّلٍ فَوْرِيٍّ لِضَمانِ تَوْفيرِ الأُكْسِجينِ الكافي.

المُقَدِّمَةُ: في حالاتِ الحَساسِيَّةِ الشَّديدَةِ وَالتَّعَرُّضِ لِمُسَبِّباتِ الحَساسِيَّةِ، ما هِيَ الخُطُواتُ الَّتي يَجِبُ اتِّخاذُها؟

دُكتورُ عَليّ: في حالاتِ رُدودِ الفِعْلِ التَّحَسُّسِيَّةِ أَوْ صَدْمَةِ الحَساسِيَّةِ، مِنَ الضَّروريِّ إعْطاءُ حُقْنَةِ إبينفرين فَوْرًا لِلْمُساعَدَةِ في مُواجَهَةِ الأَعْراضِ الخَطيرَةِ كَتَوَرُّمِ الحَلْقِ وَصُعوبَةِ التَّنَفُّسِ. يَجِبُ أَيْضًا طَلَبُ المُساعَدَةِ الطِّبِّيَّةِ العاجِلَةِ لِلتَّعامُلِ مَعَ الحالَةِ بِشَكْلٍ كامِلٍ.

المُقَدِّمَةُ: كَيْفَ يُمْكِنُ التَّعَرُّفُ عَلى عَلاماتِ الجَلْطَةِ الدِّماغِيَّةِ وَما هِيَ خُطُواتُ الإِسْعافِ الأَوَّليِّ؟

دُكتورُ عَليّ: عَلاماتُ الجَلْطَةِ الدِّماغِيَّةِ تَشْمَلُ تَشَوُّشَ الكَلامِ، ضَعْفًا في الذِّراعِ أَوِ الوَجْهِ، وَفِقْدانَ القُدْرَةِ عَلى الكَلامِ. مِنَ المُهِمِّ اسْتِدْعاءُ خِدْمَةِ الطَّوارِئِ فَوْرًا عِنْدَ مُلاحَظَةِ هَذِهِ الأَعْراضِ. السُّرْعَةُ في التَّعامُلِ مَعَ الجَلْطَةِ الدِّماغِيَّةِ حاسِمَةٌ لِلْحَدِّ مِنَ الأَضْرارِ وَزِيادَةِ فُرَصِ الشِّفاءِ.

المُقَدِّمَةُ: كَثِيرًا ما نَسْمَعُ عَنْ مَرْضى السُّكَّرِيِّ وَمَشاكِلِ التَّعَرُّضِ المُباشِرِ لِأَشِعَّةِ الشَّمْسِ، خاصَّةً في بِلادِنا الحارَّةِ. ما نَصِيحَتُكَ لِهَؤُلاءِ المَرْضى؟

دُكْتُورُ عَلِيّ: يَحْتاجُ مَرْضى السُّكَّرِيِّ إلى مُراقَبَةِ مُسْتَوى السُّكَّرِ في الدَّمِ بِانْتِظامٍ وَالتَّأَكُّدِ مِنْ حَمْلِ إِنْسُولِينَ إِضافِيٍّ أَوْ أَقْراصِ الجُلُوكُوزِ عِنْدَ الحاجَةِ. التَّعَرُّضُ المُباشِرُ لِأَشِعَّةِ الشَّمْسِ يُمْكِنُ أَنْ يُؤَدِّيَ إلى الجَفافِ وَارْتِفاعِ دَرَجَةِ حَرارَةِ الجِسْمِ، لِذَلِكَ يَجِبُ عَلَيْهِم ارْتِداءُ مَلابِسَ واقِيَةٍ، وَاسْتِخْدامُ الكِرِيماتِ الواقِيَةِ مِنَ الشَّمْسِ، وَشُرْبُ كَمِّياتٍ كافِيَةٍ مِنَ الماءِ.

المُقَدِّمَةُ: وَأَخِيرًا، ما هِيَ الرِّسالَةُ الَّتي تَوَدُّ تَوْجِيهَها لِلْجُمْهُورِ بِخُصُوصِ الاسْتِعْدادِ لِلطَّوارِئِ الطِّبِّيَّةِ؟

دُكْتُورُ عَلِيّ: رِسالَتي هِيَ أَنَّ كُلَّ شَخْصٍ يَجِبُ أَنْ يَكُونَ لَدَيْهِ مَعْرِفَةٌ أَساسِيَّةٌ بِالإِسْعافاتِ الأَوَّلِيَّةِ وَكَيْفِيَّةِ التَّعامُلِ مَعَ الحالاتِ الطّارِئَةِ. يُمْكِنُ أَنْ يَكُونَ الفَرْقُ بَيْنَ الحَياةِ وَالمَوْتِ في كَثيرٍ مِنَ الأَحْيانِ هُوَ اسْتِجابَةً سَرِيعَةً وَمُناسِبَةٌ. أَنْصَحُ الجَمِيعَ بِحُضُورِ دَوْراتِ الإِسْعافاتِ الأَوَّلِيَّةِ وَتَعَلُّمِ كَيْفِيَّةِ اسْتِخْدامِ مُزِيلِ الرَّجَفانِ وَإِجْراءِ الإِنْعاشِ القَلْبِيِّ الرِّئَوِيِّ.

المُقَدِّمَةُ: شُكْرًا جَزِيلًا لَكَ، دُكْتُورُ عَلِيّ، على هَذِهِ المَعْلُوماتِ القَيِّمَةِ وَنَصائِحِكَ الهامَّةِ. نَتَمَنّى لَكُمْ مُشاهِدِينا الكِرامَ دَوامَ الصِّحَّةِ وَالسَّلامَةِ.

Managing Medical Emergencies: Expert Tips

Program Host: Good evening, dear viewers. Welcome to our medical show, where today we discuss emergency medical situations and how to handle them. We host Dr. Ali Hassan, an expert in emergency medicine, to give us an in-depth look at this important topic. Dr. Ali, welcome. Let's start with the first question: What is the importance of emergency services in our community?

Dr. Ali: Thank you. Emergency services represent the first line of defense in critical medical situations, such as heart attacks, strokes, and cases where an individual loses consciousness. Their immediate response and ability to handle such situations can save lives.

Host: What about cases where individuals experience chest pain or difficulty breathing?

Dr. Ali: Chest pain can be an indicator of a heart attack and requires rapid medical intervention. Quick response and seeking medical help can be crucial. Likewise, individuals who suffer from difficulty breathing may be experiencing an emergency respiratory condition, like an asthma attack, and need immediate intervention to ensure sufficient oxygen supply.

Host: In cases of severe allergies and exposure to allergens, what steps should be taken?

Dr. Ali: In severe allergic reactions, like anaphylaxis, it's essential to administer an epinephrine injection immediately to counteract severe symptoms like throat swelling and breathing difficulties. Medical help should also be sought urgently to fully address the condition.

Host: How can we recognize the signs of a stroke and what are the first aid steps?

Dr. Ali: Stroke signs include speech confusion, weakness in the arm or face, and loss of speech ability. It's important to call emergency services immediately upon noticing these symptoms. Quick action in treating a stroke is critical to minimize damage and improve recovery chances.

Host: We often hear about diabetic patients and the direct exposure to sunlight, especially in our hot countries. What is your advice for these patients?

Dr. Ali: Diabetic patients need to monitor their blood sugar levels regularly and ensure they carry extra insulin or glucose tablets when needed. Direct sunlight exposure can lead to dehydration and increase body temperature, so they should wear protective clothing, use sunscreen, and drink adequate amounts of water.

Host: Finally, what message would you like to convey to the public regarding preparation for medical emergencies?

Dr. Ali: My message is that everyone should have basic knowledge of first aid and how to deal with emergency situations. Often, the difference between life and death can be a quick and appropriate response. I advise everyone to attend first aid courses and learn how to use a defibrillator and perform cardiopulmonary resuscitation.

Host: Thank you very much, Dr. Ali, for this valuable information and your important advice. We wish our viewers good health and safety.

12.3.2 Trauma and Injuries

إصابةُ دِماغٍ

brain injury

بَعْدَ الحادِثِ، أُدْخِلَ السّائِقُ إلى العِنايَةِ المُرَكَّزَةِ بِسَبَبِ إصابَةِ الدِّماغِ الخَطيرَةِ.

After the accident, the driver was admitted to the ICU due to a serious brain injury.

تَدَلّي الوَجْه

facial drooping

لاحَظَتِ الأُسْرَةُ تَدَلّي وَجْهِ الجَدَّةِ وَسارَعوا بِنَقْلِها إلى المُسْتَشْفى.

The family noticed the grandmother's facial droop and rushed her to the hospital.

تَشَوُّشُ الكَلامِ

slurred speech

لاحَظَ شاهِدُ العِيانِ تَشَوُّشَ كَلامِ الرَّجُلِ قَبْلَ أَنْ يَسْقُطَ مَغْشِيًّا عَلَيْهِ.

An eyewitness observed the man's slurred speech before he collapsed unconscious.

تَوَقُّفُ القَلْبِ

cardiac arrest

تَوَقَّفَ قَلْبُ الرّاكِبِ فَجْأَةً عَلى مَتْنِ الطّائِرَةِ، مِمّا اسْتَدْعى التَّدَخُّلَ الطِّبِّيَّ الفَوْرِيَّ.

The passenger's heart stopped suddenly on the plane, necessitating immediate medical intervention.

جَلْطَةٌ دِماغِيَّةٌ

ischemic (brain) stroke

نُقِلَتِ المَرْأَةُ إلى المُسْتَشْفى بَعْدَ الشَّكِّ في إصابَتِها بِجَلْطَةٍ دِماغِيَّةٍ خِلالَ حَفْلِ الزِّفافِ.

The woman was transported to the hospital after suspecting she had a stroke during the wedding party.

The term جَلْطَةٌ alone means 'blood clot.' However, both سَكْتَةٌ دِماغِيَّةٌ and جَلْطَةٌ دِماغِيَّةٌ translate to 'stroke.' Medically, a سَكْتَةٌ can occur due to two main reasons: a hemorrhage or a clot. Therefore, a جَلْطَةٌ is seen as one of the causes of a سَكْتَةٌ.

حالَةٌ طارِئَةٌ تَنَفُّسِيَّةٌ

respiratory emergency

تَمَّ الإعْلانُ عَنْ حالَةٍ طارِئَةٍ تَنَفُّسِيَّةٍ بَعْدَ انْتِشارِ الدُّخانِ في المَبْنى المُكْتَظِّ.

A respiratory emergency was declared after smoke filled the crowded building.

سَكْتَةٌ دماغِيَّةٌ   (cerebral) stroke

بَدَأَتِ السَّكْتَةُ الدِّماغِيَّةُ بِصُداعٍ شَديدٍ، مِمّا دَفَعَ الشّابَّ لِطَلَبِ المُساعَدَةِ عَلى الفَوْرِ.

The stroke began with severe headaches, prompting the young man to seek help immediately.

فَقَدَ القُدْرَةَ عَلى الكَلامِ   •   فَقْدٌ / فِقْدانٌ / فُقْدانٌ   to lose the ability to speak

فَقَدَ المُمَثِّلُ الشَّهيرُ القُدْرَةَ عَلى الكَلامِ بَعْدَ الحادِثِ، مِمّا أَثَّرَ عَلى مَسيرَتِهِ المِهْنِيَّةِ.

The famous actor lost the ability to speak after the accident, affecting his career.

نَوْبَةٌ قَلْبِيَّةٌ   heart attack

تَعَرَّضَ المُديرُ لِنَوْبَةٍ قَلْبِيَّةٍ أَثْناءَ الاِجْتِماعِ الهامِّ، مِمّا أَثارَ الذُّعْرَ بَيْنَ المُوَظَّفينَ.

The manager suffered a heart attack during the important meeting, causing panic among the employees.

12.3.2.1 Mini-Articles

Track **74**

أُصيبَ رَجُلٌ في الأَرْبَعيناتِ مِنْ عُمْرِهِ بِإصابَةٍ دماغِيَّةٍ بالِغَةٍ بَعْدَ تَعَرُّضِهِ لِحادِثِ سَيْرٍ مُرَوِّعٍ. اِسْتَجابَتْ خِدْمَةُ الطَّوارِئِ بِسُرْعَةٍ، وَتَمَّ طَلَبُ المُساعَدَةِ الطِّبِّيَّةِ العاجِلَةِ. قَدَّمَ فَريقُ الإِنْقاذِ الإِسْعافاتِ الأَوَّلِيَّةَ وَنَفَّذَ إِنْعاشًا قَلْبِيًّا رِئَوِيًّا قَبْلَ نَقْلِهِ إِلى المُسْتَشْفى لِعِلاجِ تَداعِياتِ الإِصابَةِ.

A man in his forties suffered a severe brain injury after being involved in a horrific car accident. Emergency services responded quickly, and urgent medical help was requested. The rescue team provided first aid and performed cardiopulmonary resuscitation before transferring him to the hospital for treatment of the injury's repercussions.

عانى مُوَظَّفٌ في الخَمْسيناتِ مِنْ عُمْرِهِ فَجْأَةً مِنْ سَكْتَةٍ دماغِيَّةٍ أَثْناءَ العَمَلِ، مِمّا تَسَبَّبَ في تَشَوُّشِ الكَلامِ. طَلَبَ زُمَلاؤُهُ المُساعَدَةَ الطِّبِّيَّةَ عَلى الفَوْرِ، حَيْثُ تَمَّ تَأْمينُ اسْتِجابَةٍ فَوْرِيَّةٍ مِنْ خِدْمَةِ الطَّوارِئِ الَّتي عالَجَتِ الحالَةَ بِسُرْعَةٍ وَنَفَّذَتِ الإِجْراءاتِ اللّازِمَةَ لِتَقْليلِ الضَّرَرِ الدِّماغِيِّ.

A worker in his fifties suddenly suffered a stroke at work, causing slurred speech. His colleagues immediately sought medical help, with emergency services providing a prompt response that quickly addressed the situation and carried out necessary procedures to minimize brain damage.

خِلالَ حَفْلِ زَواجٍ، أُصِيبَ أَحَدُ الضُّيوفِ بِنَوْبَةٍ قَلْبِيَّةٍ مُفاجِئَةٍ، مِمّا أَدّى إلى فِقْدانِ الوَعْي. تَمَّ إجْراءُ إنْعاشٍ قَلْبِي رِئَوِيٍّ فَوْرِيٍّ مِنْ قِبَلِ أَحَدِ الحاضِرِينَ حَتّى وَصَلَتْ خِدْمَةُ الطَّوارِئِ، الَّتي نَقَلَتْهُ بَعْدَ ذَلِكَ إلى المُسْتَشْفى لِتَلَقِّي العِلاجِ الطّارِئ.

During a wedding ceremony, one of the guests had a sudden heart attack, leading to unconsciousness. Immediate cardiopulmonary resuscitation was performed by one of the attendees until the emergency service arrived, who then transported him to the hospital for emergency treatment.

تَعَرَّضَتْ طِفْلَةٌ في المَدْرَسَةِ لِحالَةٍ تَنَفُّسِيَّةٍ طارِئَةٍ، مِمّا اسْتَدْعى التَّدَخُّلَ الفَوْرِيَّ. اِسْتَجابَ المُعَلِّمونَ بِسُرْعَةٍ وَطَلَبوا العَوْنَ الطِّبِّيَّ، حَيْثُ تَمَّ تَقْديمُ الأُكْسُجينِ وَالإسْعافاتِ الأَوَّلِيَّةِ قَبْلَ وُصولِ خِدْمَةِ الطَّوارِئِ الَّتي نَقَلَتْها لِلْمُسْتَشْفى لِمَزيدٍ مِنَ الفُحوصاتِ وَالعِلاج.

A girl at school experienced an emergency respiratory condition, necessitating immediate intervention. Teachers responded quickly and called for medical assistance, where oxygen and first aid were provided before the arrival of emergency services, which then transported her to the hospital for further examinations and treatment.

خِلالَ مُباراةِ كُرَةِ قَدَمٍ مَحَلِّيَّةٍ، تَعَرَّضَ أَحَدُ اللّاعِبينَ لِسَكْتَةٍ دِماغِيَّةٍ مُفاجِئَةٍ، مِمّا أَدّى إلى تَوَقُّفِ اللُّعْبَةِ عَلى الفَوْرِ. عانى اللّاعِبُ مِنْ تَهَدُّلِ الوَجْهِ وَفِقْدانِ القُدْرَةِ عَلى الكَلامِ، مِمّا اسْتَدْعى تَدَخُّلَ خِدْمَةِ الطَّوارِئِ الَّتي قامَتْ بِإجْراءاتِ الإنْقاذِ الحَيَوِيَّةِ وَنَقْلِهِ بِسُرْعَةٍ إلى المُسْتَشْفى لِتَلَقِّي العِنايَةِ الطِّبِّيَّةِ اللّازِمَة.

During a local soccer match, one of the players suffered a sudden stroke, immediately halting the game. The player experienced facial drooping and lost the ability to speak, prompting the emergency service to intervene, perform life-saving measures, and quickly transport him to the hospital for necessary medical care.

lingualism

Visit our website for information on current and upcoming titles and free language learning resources.

www.lingualism.com